LEARNING ON THEIR FEET

A Sourcebook for Kinesthetic Learning
Across the Curriculum K-8

by

Carol Glynn

DISCOVER
WRITING
PRESS

Discover Writing Press
PO Box 264
Shoreham, VT 05770
1-800-613-8055
Fax 802 -897-2084
www.discoverwriting.com

Illustrations by Chuck Jones and Carol Glynn
Cover and book design by Jim Burns

Every effort has been made to contact the students and copyright holders to reprint borrowed material. We regret any oversights that may have occurred and would be happy to rectify them in future printings of this work.

**For Dan and Marisa
and for Grandpap
(Charles Harris Smith 1908-2000)**

Many Thanks To:

The Connecticut Commission on the Arts, Colchester Intermediate
School (students and staff), Rogers Magnet School, students and
teachers throughout New England, Chuck Jones, Kim Hassenfeld,
Barbara Jones, Charles and Lois Jones, Terry and Eric Perkins,
Karen Loiselle, Amy Goldbas, Maureen Haaland, Michael Burke,
Mona Rogers, Jim Burns and Barry Lane.

Table of Contents

Ingredient Games

GAMES

Warm Ups

WARM UPS

Science

K-8 SCIENE

Math

K-8 MATH

Social Studies

K-8 SOC. STU.

Language Arts

K-8 LAN. ARTS

The Greatest Job in the World

When I was a kid, people were always telling me that when I grew up, I should consider training to do the job they had, to become what they were. In their eyes, I was born to be a teacher, a choral instructor, a camp director, a Brownie leader, a school counselor, a theater director, among others. At the time I didn't understand the compliment, yet something in their tone let me know they were offering me a special gift.

In high school, Miss H's meaning was clear, however, when she agreed to write me a college recommendation explaining that her Chem Study course had been more challenging than that at most universities—but only if I promised not to major in science. My guess is she never truly recovered from the seven broken test tubes on the first day of class.

Through all this unrequested job counseling, no one ever told me that I was meant for the job I have, until now. That's because no one knew it was a real job.

My career itself is tricky to describe. I tell a story that says, "This is the tale of a wife, mother, artist, teacher, writer, worker"—but even that doesn't exactly cut it. My husband has asked for two words to describe what I do, so he can explain it to people. I came up with Work Hard, which worked for years, until a friend recently recommended Have Fun, which I like better.

In reality, I travel around performing one-woman shows, for kids of all ages, as well as a mythology play I do with a friend. When I'm not performing, I'm teaching workshops and inservices in schools and community settings, connecting the arts of drama and writing into a wide variety of requested topics, and designing hundreds of dramatic games to use as teaching tools. I've created a multitude of original plays with students in all grades, on curriculum topics ranging from historical legends and earthquakes to prime numbers and trickster tales. I've written, directed, and toured original, educational, and social issue plays with middle school and high school students, and with socially, emotionally challenged teens.

Touring soup kitchen fund-raisers and local churches with a singing troupe of male prisoners was undeniably memorable, and using the arts as a communication tool between incarcerated mothers and their kids has touched my heart forever.

My job is the greatest job in the world, because every day I have an opportunity to work with dedicated teachers and administrators, many of whom have become lifelong friends, exchange ideas with bright, engaging students, create fun and exciting curriculum-based activities, and share my writing through stories and plays.

A curious side effect of this profession for me is an unexpected deep commitment to using the arts as an educational tool. I didn't know I'd feel this way when I began years ago, but I've seen too many firsthand examples of miraculous personal and educational growth, in people of all ages, through artistically based educational projects, to be anything but passionate about the results.

In this new adventure, which you are holding in your hand, I have the opportunity to share this passion with you. The drama ideas and activities you'll find in this book were designed over years of work with tens of thousands of students. They are time tested, and created through a process of joy, laughter, hard work, patience on my husband's part, and many, many miles on my car.

At this writing, it appears that I have indeed become something of a teacher, a choral instructor, a camp director, a Brownie leader, a school counselor, and a theater director, among others. I've even acted out science concepts as a teaching tool, and organized several environmental museums. But don't tell Miss H. She'll smash her test tubes.

The Normal Classroom

Somewhere out there, I can hear a teacher's voice saying, "Teaching with drama sounds intriguing, but it will never work with my class. I don't have a normal class this year."

I'll tell you a secret. There is no such thing as a "normal" classroom. A place where someone is teaching and someone is learning is about as normal as it gets. Everything else, including the walls, the space, the class size, the supplies, the equipment, the teaching styles, the salaries, the program funding, the special services, the innovative programs, the ages, the languages, the disorders, the attitudes, the socioeconomic breakdown, the maturity levels, the administrative policies, and the morale are variables within a normal classroom. Normal is where we start. Everything that's added makes us interesting.

How to Use This Book

My hope is that this book will serve you in two ways. The first is to provide you with an easy reference for hundreds of dramatic recipes, ideas, and activities to use across the curriculum from grades K through 8. The second is to provide you with the ingredients to make you so comfortable using drama as a teaching tool that you will continue to cook up just the right recipes to fit all the variables in your "normal" classroom.

The basic staple activities, or "Ingredient Games," are listed for you in Chapter Seven. Valuable in their own right, they are all easily adaptable across the curriculum. Throughout the activities by grade and subject, I will refer back to the basic structure of these games.

Across the United States, specific curriculum topics are studied at different grade levels. When you are seeking an activity for your grade and subject, please feel free to check the activities in the other levels. These ideas are easily adaptable to many levels. A main activity for K-2 may work beautifully as a warm-up in 3-4, or even 5-8. Often a multilevel activity is listed in K-2 because I don't want anyone to miss it, and K-2 is the beginning. As in learning the piano, even adults don't start out playing a Mozart concerto on the first day. With work, they will progress quickly, but they still have to learn how to play.

If you find an activity that suits you, but you think it would work better if you added spices, or cooked it longer, go for it. These recipes are designed to be adapted. I change them all the time.

As with any new cooking technique, don't feel you need to add twelve new recipes to your repertoire the first week. Try one out, see where it takes you. If you like that one, build it into your routine, share it with a friend, and then, a few days later, pick another one. When I'm excited about something, I leap wholeheartedly into it with wild abandon, but I'm only in one place for a short period of time. Gradual intravenous feeding may have a longer-term effect on your teaching style and techniques.

— CHAPTER ONE —

Why Drama?

D r. Harold Kranz began every history course he taught at Connecticut College by explaining the optical illusion of the rabbit and the duck. "If you want to learn about ancient civilizations," he stated, looking at each one of us, "you are going to have to look at the times the way the people did who lived within them. Thousands of years ago, people would look at trees and see more than leaves and branches. They believed the trees had gods in them. If you want to learn about the people, and understand the decisions they made, you're going to have to see the trees, too."

I took several courses with Professor Kranz, and each time, he would follow up his rabbit/duck demonstration by saying that in twenty years, we may remember nothing of his class, but we would probably remember the rabbit and the duck.

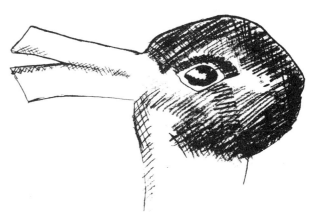

I share the rabbit/duck illusion in all my teacher workshops, because I believe that if we want students to learn, we need to learn to present the material in a way that they can see it. While we may be teaching duck, they may only be able to see rabbit. While we may be doing back handsprings to insert the information into the child's brain, we keep hitting the same wall. Seeing the way the student sees can open the window we need to get through.

I would love to find an illusion with eight different options, because it would be a clearer depiction of the variety of ways students learn. At the same time, I'm quite sure I wouldn't enjoy looking at it. All those illusions, at once, would probably give me a headache. Yet in every classroom we need that many windows to reach all of the students.

In seventeen years of teaching drama workshops, I have witnessed the "magic" windows that drama unlocks. I've seen kids smile, create, elaborate, share ideas, cooperate, gain self-esteem, take on responsibility, and assimilate curriculum topics, all while teachers are swearing that they've never done it before.

When Dr. Howard Gardner wrote *Frames of Mind: The Theory of Multiple Intelligences* in 1983, I could have kissed him. I knew all those intelligences were out there. I'd seen them. I just didn't know what they were called.

The Eight Multiple Intelligences

Linguistic Intelligence (Word Smart)
Musical Intelligence (Music Smart)
Logical-Mathematical Intelligence (Number Smart)
Visual-Spatial Intelligence (Picture Smart)
Interpersonal Intelligence (People Smart)
Intrapersonal Intelligence (Self Smart)
Kinesthetic Intelligence (Body Smart)
Natural Intelligence (Nature Smart)

Dr. Sue Teele, director of the Education Extension at the University of California at Riverside, has compiled data that supports the idea that students don't use the same intelligences at every level of their academic development. Verbal-linguistic intelligence (word smart) is at a higher level of intensity from kindergarten through the third grade. Logical-mathematical intelligence (number smart) shines its strongest light from first through fourth grade.

Kinesthetic (body smart) and visual-spatial (picture smart) are the strongest intelligences from pre-K through grade six. This supports my experience that having students actively learn on their feet is a highly effective means of reaching all students at the elementary level.

Often middle school students are taught through individual assignments, yet Dr. Teele's data again supports the theory that these students are drawn to using their visual-spatial, kinesthetic, musical, and interpersonal (people smart) intelligences. Again, her findings indicate that teaching the curriculum using drama would provide these students with the opportunity to capitalize on the intensity of their dominant multiple intelligences at this stage.

In nineteen years of teaching the curriculum through drama, I have joyfully observed successful benefits of teaching while supporting all the multiple intelligences. Using drama as a teaching tool will open a myriad of windows in your classroom. Your students will be integrating, assimilating, and cooperating—and all the while they'll be having a blast. The positive effects of using drama in your classroom may surprise you, but I know they'll delight you.

CHAPTER TWO

The Kinesthetic Learner

I've been sitting at this computer writing student plays for the last several hours. My brain has officially just shut down. As a kinesthetic learner, I felt my body start twitching about an hour ago. My legs then grew stiff with a somewhat painful energy deep within them just short of cramping, and my productivity rate slowed down dramatically, as I stretched, noticed a sense of hunger, felt a kink in my left ankle, and added a few daydreams about taking the dog for a walk in the cool autumn rain.

As a contrast to this increasingly overwhelming urge I still have to get up and leap around like a maniac, I was drawing near the conclusion of a pressure-causing project that has been sitting heavily on my mood for the last three days. I could almost taste the sense of accomplishment at finishing it.

At the prospect of having a reason to leap around the room joyfully, I pushed on. But, at the brink of the conclusion, just when the group of dancing, rapping Y2K bugs, in the fifth grade, play were about to be obliterated by the sheer ingenuity of the brave students in Mr. G's class, thereby saving students, classrooms, and yes, entire communities all over the world...my brain switch shut off, giving me nothing.

C. GLYNN

I have been working on a topic I controlled, initiated, and pursued in a creative way, and one that I enjoy. If I were attempting to absorb a subject involving any sort of struggle in a noncreative way, on someone else's timeline, my brain would have short-circuited in a matter of minutes.

I am now experiencing the blank-brain state I often refer to, in a most politically incorrect way, as "brain dead." This is not being helped one iota by my six-year-old daughter, the one I hired to fold the laundry/distract herself, for fifty cents, who is putting on a very loud sock puppet show for the dog and cat, complete with songs and dances about finding a long-lost mate, three feet from my chair.

In a moment, I will take a break, run around, do Tae Bo, give the dog a bath, watch the puppet show, add a song and dance of my own, and then my brain will be ready to function once more. Whether the six-year-old will allow me to resume my work is always another question.

As an adult, I am well acquainted with these sensations. I know that the mere act of sitting in one place is a major factor in my current lack of ability to function properly. As a student in school years ago, I had no idea what this was about.

In college, I remember the repeated scenario of having a paper due, finding a quiet place to spread out my books, ideas, notes, snacks, pens, and markers, working for just long enough to form a strategy—and wham, without warning, or so it seemed, my brain would shut down completely. So, after wasting time forcing myself to concentrate on topics I did not love so well as writing plays in which fifth graders save the world, I would pack everything up, walk across campus to jump-start my synapses, unpack all of my belongings again, and work for a while, until the whole process required repeating.

In life, being a kinesthetic learner hasn't hindered me. I believe it has helped guide and support me through my wildly active career choice. In elementary school, I don't remember that I was so active, but I recognize my old self in antsy students whom I meet every day. In my heart I always say a little prayer that these children aren't medicated. If we medicate all the antsy children today, where will we get the energy driven leaders of tomorrow?

As a child, I was so competitive with my sister that I would make sure I learned the material somehow, even if my brain shut down in class. I do remember listening to the teacher's lesson from the back of the room while decorating the bulletin boards. I was too young to determine whether they were giving me a tremendous movement opportunity or taking advantage of the creative child with too much energy. Possibly a little of both.

My daughter's first grade teacher, Mrs. Haaland, says that after about ten to fifteen minutes, her students cannot take in any more information, so she gives them a little break. It doesn't need to be long, maybe a minute. One day it's running in a circle around the room. Another day, it's something else, but then everyone goes right back to working, and they're able to continue learning. From day one, I've thought this woman was brilliant. Her methods are so much more productive than yelling at the students or willing them to sit still, focus, and listen. The students are so used to letting their ya-yas out on a regular basis, and following this release up with resuming productivity, that Mrs. Haaland rarely, if ever, has control problems.

I recently attended an informational meeting in my town, at which our middle school principal described the typical learning style of sixth through eighth graders. He said their attention span at that age is approximately eight to nine minutes. Based on all the hormones that are surging through their bodies, and the vise grip of social acceptance in which they try to function, this is just who they are. He said that because of this, the best possible learning program for them is one with hands-on, active activities. I agree wholeheartedly, and I hope this is truly what the school believes in, and not just slick, shiny, town meeting jargon.

My experience has demonstrated that while many younger students are believed to be kinesthetic learners, the assumption is common that this need to move and be active while learning somehow dissolves far earlier than it actually does. About every three months, the news reports another state, town, or district that considers recess a waste of time. I always imagine the meeting where this issue is discussed, and wonder how many times, if any, the decision makers remember that the commodity they are discussing, within the educational system, is children.

One simple fact in favor of the no-recess argument is that in most districts, the required curriculum dramatically exceeds the available teaching time. A friend of mine added up the actual teaching hours required to teach the stated curriculum in her town and found that the students would be in class every day until six P.M. through the end of July.

So how is a teacher expected to cover curriculum and allow for enough active breaks to keep the students' interest juices flowing? By using the arts as a teaching tool. Make moving activities an integral part of the teaching experience. You're not wasting time having the students move around if they're learning math at the same time, right? And like my daughter's first-grade class, the more you do it, the more the students will realize that these methods are part of their everyday experience, and the more drama and the arts will become a tool with a positive control influence, not a negative one.

I realize that I may be preaching to the choir, that if you're reading this book, you're most likely not resisting adding new active ideas into your classroom. It's simply that every time I become complacent, and start to believe that we're all teaching the same way, I encounter a new experience in a new town that sends me reeling back, staring at my deepest beliefs, bolstering them up with yet another reason to believe so strongly in active teaching.

Just the other day, I had a meeting with three teachers in a school I worked in years ago. All three teachers were professional, kind, and cooperative, yet within three minutes two out of the three let me know that there was a problem with this year's class, and that my methods of active teaching might not work. One of them went as far as to say that his students couldn't handle anything the least bit, the least bit...

"Stimulating," I put in, a bit sarcastically.

"Right. That's it," he agreed.

"I'm not scared," I responded, but I lied. It wasn't the students who frightened me. It was a complex set of circumstances, fed by semi-territorial teachers who have gone too long being unsupported in their quest to go out on a limb for their kids. I only dreaded going for a week. The project is working out just fine now.

Yesterday, while waiting outside my daughter's dance class, I sat, laptop poised, ready to tackle a class play on simple machines, when another mom/high school science teacher entered, planning book in hand, who was trying to generate creative teaching methods for her chemistry class with a group of juniors who were taking the course only because three science credits were required to graduate. Talking to herself, out loud, she joked with some exasperation, pointing to the chemical equations before her, "Now, how am I supposed to make this stuff interesting and active?"

Needless to say, my self-imposed simple machine deadline evaporated. She explained the chemical equations to me. I described my "become the molecule" theory to her. In one hour, with the help of another mom, a children's book author, who was equally enchanted by our discussion, my new friend had an active plan to share with her students. Commending her on her readiness to accept new ideas, I explained that some teachers are reluctant to attack new teaching methods until they can predict the exact outcome before it occurs. Her response was refreshing.

"Who cares?" she chuckled. "I have to be in there for eighty-eight minutes, and so do they. Standing there talking at them doesn't work. Why not try this?" My kinesthetic spirit rode happily on the tracks of her creative, positive attitude for days.

CHAPTER THREE

How to Use Drama as an Integral Teaching Tool

Teachers everywhere know the thrill of the moment when a student has crossed over the line of understanding. The student's face softens and the corners of her mouth slowly begin to smile. Her eyes beam with the light of recognition, and her desire to continue working grows exponentially. Her burst of enthusiasm is contagious. Suddenly, she wants more, more, more, and like a toddler who has just learned to walk, she's on a mission. She wants to try out this new knowledge all the time.

One of my favorite moments is when I experience this with teachers: when the idea of using drama as a regular teaching tool leaps from something that I do to something that they could do on a regular basis.

Ever more practical than a toddler, teachers don't dash around the room knocking things over (except in rare cases). Usually they start asking questions: What a wonderful way to learn! I never thought of doing it this way. When should I use these ideas? Every day? I shouldn't do this all the time, should I? It would be exhausting. You're not suggesting that I give up seat work altogether, are you? How do I fit this in with everything else I have to do?

No, I don't suggest you do this all day, every day. It can be exhausting. I know: I do it all day on many days. People are always commenting on how much energy I have. I usually respond by saying that it isn't a matter of how much energy I have, it's a matter of how much energy I use.

Even though this process helps focus extra energy, and serves as a catalyst to share your students' energy, you will need to find the best way to integrate drama into your regular day, for you and for your students. Knowing that they will have a chance to express themselves kinesthetically at some point will help focus them, and also the regular routine will help them use their drama time well and not waste it fooling around. Once the ideas are set up and running, the learning machine will run on their power, not just yours.

The following are suggestions. There is no right way or wrong way to integrate drama into your teaching style. Feel free to try all of these ideas, or combinations of them. Whatever works best for you and your kids. It's your classroom. You decide.

Drama as a Daily Routine:

Perhaps you'll choose to introduce drama as follows:

* as part of your morning routine, after lunch count and homework collecting, to warm the students up and bring them fully into the classroom from wherever and whatever they have just been, physically and emotionally

* before lunch, when their brains and their stomachs are one

* right after lunch, when their high-fructose snacks have truly kicked in

* at the end of the day, when they have nothing left to give, and the snacks have dropped their blood sugar to the center of the earth.

Whenever you do it, a daily routine of drama and kinesthetic activity works well.

How do you find time for drama? Remember, you're not taking time out to teach something new. You're using a different tool to teach what is already on your docket.

You could pick a favorite ingredient game for the week and play it every day, switching the curriculum link each day to include something you addressed the day before.

Play Swoosh every morning:

Monday:	go over the rules and play for fun.
Tuesday:	go over Greek gods and goddesses
Wednesday:	go over words that begin with the letter H
Thursday:	go over countries involved in World War I
Friday:	work on the 9 tables in multiplication.

Or play every day as a way to review or prepare for a new curriculum topic. Swoosh preparation for a math test on Friday:

Monday:	Swoosh with counting in multiples
Tuesday:	Swoosh the 4 tables
Wednesday:	Swoosh the 8 tables
Thursday:	Swoosh the 4, 8, and 6 tables
Friday:	Swoosh up to the 9 tables.

As you will discover, many of the activities not only address specific curriculum topics, but work well to bring a group together as a team. Starting off the day with a team-building exercise can set a positive learning atmosphere for the whole day.

A Few Times a Week, at a Scheduled Time (Maintenance)

If you see your students in forty-five-minute segments, an everyday drama activity would be next to impossible. You may want to consider doing a short activity every Tuesday and Friday, again using this time to review or set up a curriculum topic. If the game is familiar, jumping right into it won't be a problem, and playing for fifteen to twenty minutes, when it's expected, can help focus students for the rest of your class time.

TIP: This idea would work best with whole group or outline activities such as Swoosh, Pass the Object, Lean and Leave, or Statues, where minimal student personal anxiety is involved, especially at first. Improvisation and deeper character work, with personal investment, would involve a longer time period, maybe weekly, or biweekly with a warm-up and close-down. This could be a time to set up an outline idea for students to develop further, on their own time or on another day.

Spreading an Idea over a Week

If your chosen activity involves a whole group setup, with a smaller group or individual follow-up, giving a few minutes to it every day will spread the activity nicely over the course of your unit. Small groups can practice or work on writing skits for their morning work, as other morning details are ironed out with individual students.

As a Weekly Lesson

Have drama, once a week, for fifty minutes to an hour and a half. Take the time to:

WARM UP: With simple movement games and activities, give students the time to link their minds, their bodies, and their multiple intelligences to work together before following complex requests, especially in front of the whole class. For example, it is easier to move as a crustacean on the ocean floor in front of your peers after a short warm-up with them than it is to leap to it directly from a math test, where your brain is still deep in problem #12.

Sample warm-up activities are listed later in this book. They are valuable activities themselves, encouraging teamwork, self discipline, listening, and following directions.

TIP: When limited time is a factor, it may be tempting to forget the warm-up. I know how tempting. I've done it, and paid for it. This is also a chance to set rules—behavioral, supportive, and so forth. You may shorten the warm-up to a minute or two, but touching base to connect with each other and warming up physically will save backpedaling during the next step. How can you do shortened drama sessions without a warm-up? Easy. Shortened drama sessions are usually an adapted warm-up activity. You're not skipping the warm-up. You're skipping everything else.

INTRODUCE THE MAIN IDEA OR ACTIVITY: Read a story, or introduce research options. After a fun warm-up, students are ready to focus on what's next. This is a great opportunity to read a story, introduce a concept, or refer to research options around the room. Inform them that they will need this information to participate in the next drama activity. It's a fabulous motivation. Kids who ordinarily couldn't care less about a topic will absorb it quickly as part of a game.

CONNECT WITH THE MAIN ACTIVITY: Connect the main curriculum topic with drama. Working as a class or in small groups, students follow your directions and then brainstorm, design, construct, and build an impromptu presentation, based on the specific curriculum topic. Pay attention to their ideas; they work as fabulous examples in future workshops.

Preface any final presentations by saying something like this: "You've all had a short time to pull these ideas together, and you're here to learn from each other. Please look for the positive aspects of any performance first, and then take a moment to point out ways that the presentation could work even better, not only for this group but for following groups." I often thank a student who seems embarrassed at specific criticism, telling them I'm so glad they put their back to the audience, because I forgot to mention it beforehand, and now we all can learn. Soon, they'll be correcting their own backs to the audience, too-quiet voices, etc.

TIP: Don't give them too much time to work together. Give five minutes at first and then extend it with a compliment. "You're working so well, I'm going to give you three more minutes." Or " I love the detail you have in here, I'm going to give you more time, because I want to see all the details I can get!" If you give them twenty minutes, they'll argue for fifteen and pull the piece together in five minutes anyway.

Sometimes the main activity, particularly in grades K-2, will be a group activity guided by you. It may be too much for them to create their own activities in small groups—although, after they have a few months of regular drama and modeled lessons under their belt, try it for fun; they'll probably surprise you.

CLOSE THEM DOWN: Sitting down to a quiet activity immediately after a productive drama session is asking for trouble. Settle them down within the drama session, or your next activity will pay the price. This can be as simple as gathering back in a circle for a short stretch, deep breaths, and passing a look and a smile around in a circle. Sitting down for a short discussion if you have time also works well. What was your favorite part of drama today? If it's a larger project, discuss where they should go from here, how much of it will be completed in class, how much will have to be done at home. I try to remind myself to use a quiet voice and to speak slowly during a close-down. Quiet, calm, and slow are not natural states for me, so in my case a reminder is necessary. Several time-tested close-down activities are listed in the warm-up section.

Drama as an Introduction to a Unit: Igniting Curiosity

I'm constantly asked to cover a curriculum topic, completely, in one hour. Since this is impossible, I do as much research as possible and focus on the concept within the topic that I think will draw the students into the unit as quickly as possible. Many of the drama activities you will find in the subject sections of this book are results of this process.

When I leave the workshop, the students are anxious to buckle down in a unit. They have a taste of the exciting elements of it, and already have many questions they would like to investigate. They want to learn more about the Indiana bat, to use one example, because they've been one for forty-five minutes.

TOPIC: Environment—Endangered Species: Extinction

CONCEPT: Loss of habitat is the largest contributing factor in the endangerment of animals.

I begin with a warm-up of Lean and Leave (see directions in the Ingredient Games) to open a discussion on how interdependent our environment is.

Next, I tell them the concept, as stated above.

I talk about habitats—what they are, and how easy it is for us, as humans, to move to a new one. I talk about bald eagles, their huge nests which are large enough for three grown men to play cards in, and how cumbersome it would be for an eagle to build a new one. I talk about rain forest animals whose homes are being destroyed and how hard it is for them to move on.

Then we play the habitat game (complete directions and story model in Science 3-4) where, as a class, siting in a circle, we invent a new animal, name it, and decide on five elements of its environment that are crucial to its survival—in other words, its habitat. (These can be silly or serious. We just want them to get the concept.)

Then we match each element with a color, and pass out five colored squares to each student. Students lay the squares in front of them.

Next, we discuss what the animal looks like and how it moves. Three students volunteer to be this animal and stand, squat, or hang near a habitat.

After that, I improvise a story about the sad destruction of several elements within this animal's community. Some habitats are protected for a variety of reasons, and the three animals move from disturbed habitats to new ones. Eventually all the habitats are destroyed and the three animals have a dramatic dying scene in the center of the circle.

The results are palpable. This may be an animal who sipped pink lemonade out of Tweety Bird cups, and wore orange polka dotted sneakers, but nobody wants it to die. The students are invested in the life of an imaginary animal which they had an opportunity to know briefly.

I like to follow up by playing the song "Habitat" by B. Oliver, on a CD called Earth Revival, Songs for Nature Folk, by Tom Callinan and Ann Shapiro.

Habitat works well in grades three to eight. The depth of the discussion varies. Use this drama session as the beginning of an environment unit on endangered species and your students will begin the unit with an understanding of habitats, a desire to know the habitats of specific species and to learn why their habitats are being destroyed. If we're really lucky, they also want to know what they can do to prevent the destruction.

Drama as a Tool for Assessment: Tapping into Their Accumulated Knowledge

You're in the middle of a unit, and you want to get a handle on how much information your students are absorbing. You've been out with the Boola Boola flu and you're not sure what the sub has actually covered. Rather than hand them a pop quiz (heck, you have to grade those!), play a game in which specific unit information is required. A few rounds of Swoosh, or Pass the Object, or I Remember Ball or Math Ball and you'll know right away where they stand. If you've done your part, and it's clear that they've dropped the ball (pun intended), tell them about the quiz they'll be having on Friday.

Playing an information-required game, as a review, a day or so before a test, will also let them know where they stand. This information can be helpful if they thought they knew it all, and weren't planning to study.

Drama as a Final Project

Individuals and Small Groups

Using drama as a presentation tool is a perfect match with final unit projects. Have students present their final reports dramatically. Going one step further than the traditional oral report will liven up any topic. Students are still responsible for covering the required information, but in this case it may involve some dialogue, or a monologue or two. Here's an example:

REPORT TOPIC: Everyday Life in Colonial Times, by A. Student

As an individual project, A. Student could invent a character from colonial times and present a monologue from her character's point of view.

As an individual or group project, A. Student could read or describe the daily life of a child, a wife, a schoolteacher, a farmer, and a politician during colonial times, or she could write, direct, and star in four or five short scenes where she interviews the same characters within their own settings. A. Student could work with several others as part of a group project, or she could be in control of her own report, asking others to be in her project. They, in turn, could ask her to be in theirs. Using the games Pass the Object and Create a Place, found in the Ingredient Games, a student could involve many props, or none at all. The focus would be on the detailed content within the scenes. Guest actors and actresses would read their responses, keeping rehearsal time to a manageable time frame.

TIP: Remind all actors to keep the relationships true. It's very easy for A. Student's best friend Sally, who is playing a child, to want to be sassy or disrespectful to any classmate who is playing the teacher or the parent. But stepping out of character to giggle with a friend detracts from the true historical circumstances and conditions. Accepting the responsibility of being in a friend's report presentation requires respect for A. Student, the material, and the characters within.

Is this asking too much of your students? It isn't. At Lyme Consolidated School, in Lyme, Connecticut, the first graders put on a play every week. The first grade director of the week chooses a story, casts the play with five or six classmates, often starring himself, directs the play, chooses the costumes, makes or adapts any props, creates a program, a poster, and invitations, and on Friday the five-minute play, read from the book by a first-grade narrator, is performed for anyone who can find the time to come, including the kindergarten class, parents, beaming grandparents, the school nurse, and visiting resident artists. They're good! I've cried through many of them. Every student rises to the occasion.

After the play, the director answers any questions. Everyone signs his or her poster and the director's name is revealed for the following week. The teacher involvement is heavy during the first few weeks, but after that, he or she serves as a theatrical consultant.

There are a few discussions about being fair, and making sure everyone has a chance to be in a play, but teachers don't seem to have any trouble working this out. There are many plays, and students learn to involve everyone.

As an added bonus, the kindergartners, next year's first graders, have the opportunity to see twenty-four model plays and are primed for first grade, and for reading, writing, and performing.

Final Projects as a Class

As a visiting artist, I'm often hired to write, direct, and present a curriculum-related play with an entire class. The final production is usually presented to the entire school, or a few of the younger grades, depending on the performance space.

A production involving the entire class may indeed be the nightmare that teachers are afraid of when the word drama is mentioned in the first place. It is, however, manageable, in addition to exhilarating, motivating, and something the students will remember for the rest of their lives.

Any doctor will tell you that the general public has no problem telling them of their aches and pains. Once someone hears that I am a performer, I am treated to a detailed account of his or her last performance, dating all the way back to playing the turkey in a kindergarten Thanksgiving play. As a theater student, in college, this used to drive me crazy, because here I was pouring sweat and tears into whatever grand production I was involved in, insulted by the mere comparison. Now, I enjoy every minute of these stories, because these memories are always wrapped in joy. Imagine the students in your class, retelling tales of their special performance thirty and forty years from now. I hope the related curriculum topic lasts as long.

I laugh to think that I'm sending students off into the future, to reflect on their role as Benedict Arnold, who was always out of place, the talking back end of George Washington's horse, or the mantle layer of the earth's surface, living through an earthquake.

Drama as a Celebration: For Fun

The unit test is over. The reports are done. Or maybe they're not, but the superintendent just evaluated your class and you're all frazzled. The students have spent all morning taking mastery tests. They finally have read enough books to win the pizza party. Whatever the reason, reward yourselves. Play a game. Act out skits. Take this time to learn new basic games, or play an old favorite. Feel free to tie the activity into curriculum or not. Drama is a valuable teaching tool, because first and foremost, it's fun. Sometimes plain old fun is what is needed the most.

How to Use Drama to Include All Students

What If Your Students Have Handicaps?
Will Learning on Their Feet Work for Them?

Each one of these activities has been developed to meet a variety of needs, including curricular needs, class size, and age level. Each one has been adapted a thousand times to accommodate class personality, teacher comfort zone, available space, and allotted time. Each time a game is played, it is a little different, revealing the multiple intelligences of the group at hand. What if the students have handicaps? No big deal. The activities are adapted to allow them to do their very best with the many strengths they do have. Remember that while I'm giving you the structure, you're building these activities from scratch every time. There are no perfect puzzle pieces to squeeze into. If there were, no class would fit.

Back in the days when I spent time auditioning for other people's plays, I always tried to audition on the first day. If there was only one day of auditions, I did my best to arrive early enough to be seen at the beginning. Why? Because I am tall, with broad shoulders, and if the director was going to cast me, he or she had to keep my height in mind when casting those to play with me. If I showed up at the very end and gave the best audition of my life, it wouldn't matter, because by then the director often had a specific puzzle nearly completed, and my piece wouldn't fit.

Over the years, I have written and adapted dozens of plays on curriculum subjects, and each play has a lead role for every student in the class. One lead role may have words with fewer syllables. Another one may have more physical requirements and fewer lines. But they are all lead roles. I tell the students up front that no one part is more important than another part. We all have to work together, or there will be holes in our play. In the same way, we couldn't do an activity in a class that did not include everyone; then there would be holes in the class.

Process Versus Product

To me, process and product are equally important. This fact alone might separate me from other directors, because I'll cast the kid who needs the boost over the talented kid with the attitude, every time. Fortunately we don't have to worry about surviving the critics for a long run on Broadway. Usually, if you open the door to possibility for a kid, by giving him a chance he never had, he'll surprise everyone, especially himself. I have found that if I work this way, I'm building more than a product with perfect holes to squeeze into. We're building a great experience, with a step up they can stretch to, which kids can take or not. Obviously I don't tell them about stretching. It's all part of the process.

Drama has a way of cracking doors open. Teachers notice the specific changes in their kids more than I do, because by the time I know the kids, they've changed. I'm forever hearing comments like "I had no idea he could do that." I have actually become almost complacent about this statement. I almost expect to hear it—mostly because I have heard it at least once a week for fifteen years. Now, my daughter is in school, and I think of the possibility of that statement being said about her. So now, I'm the "enrichment mom," bringing in as much arts in education as I possibly can.

Mrs. Nichols' Trickster Tale

I've worked at Rogers Magnet School in Stamford, Connecticut, for years. Each year we create five or six original "trickster tales," based on stories the teachers have chosen to extend their Battle of the Wits unit. This year, one class had a girl who was severely hearing impaired. This in itself was not a problem, , but this child hovered over her desk, closing herself off from the rest of the class, barely speaking above a whisper.

One day I was holding loud auditions. The students know that no one part is better than the other, and it's fine to make mistakes but Mrs.Glynn likes it loud. This child could not be heard by anyone-at all. In other words, while the rest of us were bellowing across the room, a mouse sitting on her nose wouldn't have heard her. So, when it came to casting the play, I added several nonspeaking walk-on roles for her.

To my surprise, she was furious. She never confronted me directly, but went to her teacher, Mrs. Nichols, and insisted that she have a chance to speak in the play. I crumbled at the thought that she felt she was denied this chance because she was hearing impaired. In complete honesty, that had nothing to do with it. The reality was that when she said her lines, no one would know she was speaking.

When Mrs. Nichols told me how this child stood up and demanded a chance, when she had never stood up for anything before, I agreed immediately that we had to give her something to say. When the question came down to what was important, there was no question. The other students were already memorizing their lines, and had ownership over them, so we added a new line. We told her that she would make a comment about the bride at the end of the play if she promised to try her very best to use her biggest, loudest voice. She agreed, beaming.

Over the course of the next few weeks, I noticed her smiling more often, standing up straighter, and not secluding herself quite as much. Was this all because of one line in a play? No way. Perhaps this line was a seed we planted, or a chance that hit at just the right time for her, when all the other conditions were in place for a jump-start. When it came time for her line in the play, she stood tall, bellowing with everything she had, and I could hear her all the way from the front row. Being the mush-head that I am, I immediately burst into tears and missed the rest of the play. What did the three hundred people in the audience think about not hearing a line?

What audience?

Tom and the Refrigerator Door

Drama works especially well in a special-needs classroom. The structure of the challenge is different from the usual ones, which opens a big window for kids to climb through and shine.

Once, while working for the Penny Ante Theater, I was teaching a workshop in a special-needs classroom. Tom, the business manager, had tagged along to take photographs for publicity. At one point, when I was knee deep in a giant human refrigerator, the teacher leaned over to Tom and said, "That's odd, that child never participates in anything."

"Which one?" Tom inquired.

"The one playing the door," she responded.

Tom looked to see a child who was beaming, opening and closing, with a loud squeaky sound. "That child?" he said aghast. The teacher nodded.

As our new business manager, Tom had a tendency to give off airs about how important he was to the company. He had no clue what we really did, and not so secretly thought we were wasting precious company dollars by fooling around all day. After watching a refrigerator door spring to life, he let up on us, just a bit.

Emotional and Other Challenges

When writing a student play, I rarely give the characters names, unless it's an obvious historical figure or something of the sort. Most of the time I use numbers or letters to depict a part (Students A, B, and C; Narrators 1, 2, and 3). This plan helps tremendously in casting, because no one sees one number as more important than any other number. Yet, within the numbers, there are characters. Most of the wise guy lines are said by the same number kid, giving him a wise guy character. There is often a student who knows what is going on because he has done the homework, and one or two who need to ask questions, because they haven't. This way the students can educate the audience on the topic at hand, while moving the story along.

Recently, by luck of the draw, most of the funny lines, in a one-hundred-year school celebration play by fourth graders, went to a student with a high level of social and emotional challenges. I deliberately included the humorous character he was playing, because the historical timeline this class was covering included the Depression and World War II, and the whole thing was in need of a little levity.

This child said every line as if it were mumbled, depressing news. My ego, which wanted an entertaining product for the big night, cringed every time he said a word. (I didn't know about his challenges until later.) Several times, I considered switching his lines, but I didn't. We explained to him that he had the funny lines and that the audience needed to hear them as if he were excited about them. One day after several rehearsals, he said a line loudly and clearly, with a smile. The class broke into spontaneous applause. The next time, however, he mumbled the line to his feet. The night of the performance he started off slowly, but soon said one line just loud enough for the audience to hear. They roared. He glanced at me, crouched in the makeshift stage pit, and I nodded. He nodded back. The rest of the lines were just fine. His reactions were not huge, but we all knew he had had a little moment in the sun.

So, will teaching the curriculum through drama work for people with special challenges? The answer is yes, if you let it. Think of your students with special challenges as tall people showing up at the audition early, because they want the best part, and know that the rest may need to be filled in around them. Try building each activity keeping the special requirements in mind, not as an added question to tackle at the end, but as a unique opportunity to start with.

* If you're creating a giant digestive system and you have students in wheelchairs, figure out what part of the digestive system would be great seated. Begin with that part, and build the rest accordingly.

* If you have blind students, make sure you add sound to your activities. Special sound effects, either verbal or instrumental, will help all the musically intelligent people in your class.

* If your students are deaf or hearing impaired, don't worry. Drama is highly visual. Communication can only be enhanced by using visual gestures and emotions.

* If your students are emotionally challenged, drama works well because it has an identifiable structure in which everyone can be himself.

* Students diagnosed with ADHD do well with drama because it is kinesthetic, and moving their bodies helps reconnect their brains to the task.

The only handicap I know of that will not work with drama is a noncooperative or bad attitude. Students quickly realize that they need to cooperate if they are going to accomplish anything. In my mind, that is a valuable lesson in itself.

—————— CHAPTER FIVE ——————

Setting Up Rules: What's Your Comfort Zone?

What is a comfort zone? It's the range of order and control within which people are most comfortable working. For teachers, it is a personal gauge which helps them set the daily structure for twenty-four personalities, simultaneously. Surrounded by a fine, fragile line, a comfort zone area varies slightly from day to day. Once crossed, the boundary line dissolves, opening up the class to a sense of chaos and destruction.

I have an enormous comfort zone at work. At home, the edges of it swing back and forth like a pendulum, depending on how many nerves I have fried while not paying attention. My six-year-old daughter knows enough to ask, "Is it a good time to spin?", before she personifies a tornado, inches from my desk.

Over the years, I've seen a variety of comfort zones among teachers. I pay attention to them. A guest artist in a classroom is something like a guest in one's home. As much as possible, I play by the host's rules. If I'm frightened by the teacher's comfort zone, there is a good chance the teacher is frightened by me. As in any generalization, this is not always true, but it's a good place to start. If the comfort zone is very strict and small, it may be better to bump against it slowly, rather than swing open the barn door. Remember, the students are also used to the comfort zone. Swinging open barn doors too quickly may invite them to become animals.

If you would like to use drama as a teaching tool, it is important to identify and consider your comfort zone. Drama is livelier than silent reading, but it doesn't have to be chaotic. Once you have identified your comfort zone, you can set up the rules for any drama activity to fit within your zone. Over time, as you recognize the value of using drama as a teaching tool you may find that you have a broader comfort zone for drama than for other activities, but it is still important that the students know there is a behavioral limit. Being firm within that limit, and within the rules you set up will reinforce the idea for you and for them that even though drama is fun, it is still valuable and worthy of respect.

Different Teachers: Different Styles

As a guest artist, I return to many schools year after year. While the funding is never secure from one project to the next, returning so often does make me feel as if I am a part of the school community, a nice benefit for us nomad teacher types. I begin to remember birthdays, attend retirement parties, and participate in staff basketball challenges against other schools (until they discover the keen athletic ability that helped to guide me toward drama in the first place). One of my favorite schools even has a permanent mailbox with my name on it.

One surprising result of seeing the same teachers with different classes, year after year, is that I get a clear picture of their teaching styles and their comfort zones. The students may be dramatically different each year, but except in rare cases, the overall behavior and general habits of the class are remarkably similar.

This simple observation would probably shock most teachers, who are trying every new strategy they can muster to re-create the supportive learning environment they achieved by the last day of the previous school year. However, just as any Carol Glynn Production, no matter what the teaching environment or topic, can be noted a mile away for its combination of sophisticated wit and blatant goofiness, any one teacher's class bears his or her mark as well.

Patty

Patty, a dear friend of mine, grew up in a family with eight children and is very comfortable with a moderate amount of continuous sound in her classroom. It's all productive. Students are either concentrating quietly on their own work, helping others, or having completed the assigned task, are beginning to discuss a separate group project.

No matter what Patty is doing, the moment the sound steps not so quietly over the line from productivity into wasting time, she looks up, addresses it, and everyone settles back to what they were doing.

Kate

Another friend, Kate, has worked with gifted and talented students as a classroom grade level teacher, and is now a math resource teacher for individuals and small groups of students in grades 4-8. She is an excellent teacher, wherever she is, having received district teacher of the year awards and other commendations.

Kate has an unusually soft spot in her heart for the mischievous, impish streak in kids. Where with other teachers, these students may have practiced tucking this side of their personalities into their shoe, with Kate, they can let it all hang out. As in any relationship, the fewer sides of yourself you have to shield, the more comfortable you are to be yourself in other ways. Therefore, if you need extra help catching up or springing forward, on a limited-time basis, say, once or twice a week, a teacher with this particular style is perfect.

The two years I put on plays with Kate's regular grade level class were great fun.
While not behaviorally inappropriate, both classes sparkled with an impish vitality all their own. When I heard that Kate had accepted a position to work one-on-one in math, I was saddened for the future classrooms she would not lead, but now I appreciate that this decision, while fabulous for her current students, is also best for her. Impish vitality, taken to an extreme, on a class-wide level, can be overwhelmingly exhausting. She may live longer this way.

Three Hundred Years of Teaching Experience

Working much like a chameleon, I have slithered, happily, through hundreds of classes picking up colorful control tips along the way. One teacher would admonish the class for not paying attention as a group, but just at the moment they began to focus, she would become distracted by three separate individual problems and take time out to handle them. By the time she was ready to address the entire class, she had lost them again. This habit smacked me with self-recognition, and I have worked to address this issue in my own teaching. Neither one of us does this nearly as much as we used to.

I was recently complimented by a teacher who kept insisting I must have had my own classroom at some point, because I handled her class so well. She was shocked that drama could enrich her classroom so much, without an atmosphere of complete insanity. I considered telling her it was because I've benefited from three hundred years of teaching experience, but simply thanked her instead.

I know her compliment is high praise, because I've heard horror stories of artists, and guest parents, who insist on being the good guy to the extent of positioning the teacher to be the bad guy. One teacher told me of a parent who actually told her second graders that they didn't need to follow these silly rules like raising their hand when they had an idea. "Just call out when you have something to say," he told them. Within seven minutes he had lost entire control of the class, and was trying to make eye contact with the "bad guy teacher" who had sent him helpful tips on handling the class in the first place. The teacher, who was weeks away from retirement, just looked at him. I'm not going to rescue you, she thought. You did this to yourself.

Like many people, this parent confused simple class courtesy with restricting student initiative. He thought having fun meant having no rules. Many people consider drama to be a loose, casual activity, where there are no rules. I think this is why the idea of drama frightens some teachers, snapping the fragile line around their comfort zones. Any teacher recognizes that the concept of no rules means losing entire control of the class.

The Extremes

When paying attention to your comfort zone, it is important not to be judgmental. A comfort zone is neither good nor bad, unless you feel it is getting in your own way. Here are some examples of extreme comfort zones. In all three cases, control was a problem, but not always because there wasn't enough.

Miss B.

As a senior in high school, I was given the opportunity to play the role of Nurse Ratched, in Ken Kesey's *One*

Flew over the Cuckoo's Nest. For my evil role model, I chose Miss. B, one of my English teachers. She was afraid of her students, and therefore treated us all as if we were evil, so we would have no opportunity to take advantage of her. I don't remember much about what Miss B. taught. Her classes were not memorable, except for two examples.

The first had to do with two school rules. As eighteen-year-old seniors, we were considered adults, and permitted to sign our own late slips and absence notes. I'll tell you right now that this did not sound like a completely ludicrous idea when I was eighteen, but even then I saw some of the drawbacks.

As you might guess, this rule was being taken advantage of by some students, so the administration cracked down by declaring that more than twelve absences from required courses would prevent us from graduating. Miss B., who must have known her class was deadly slow, wanted to prevent students from intentionally missing as many days as possible during her nine weeks, so she divided the twelve days over the four marking periods, and declared that if any student missed more than three classes during her nine weeks, she would automatically fail us and prevent us from graduating. She also declared that it didn't matter if the note was signed by a parent or a doctor. She wouldn't believe it any more than our own signatures. Any absence would be an unexcused absence. I remember contesting her decision, because it wasn't fair, but that only made me suspect.

As luck would have it, I contracted strep throat during her nine weeks, but I didn't miss more than three days. I do remember being yelled at for not participating because my throat was too sore to talk for a long time. Her comfort zone was lined with steel.

The second Miss B. story is more humorous in nature, but at the time, all I could feel was compassion for her, which wiped her out as my evil role model.

My friend Myra was presenting a book report on *Johnny Got His Gun,* by Dalton Trumbo, an incredibly moving story about a young man awakening in a hospital only to discover that all of his limbs, and most of his face, had been blown off during battle. Myra wanted students who hadn't read the book to personalize the physical sensation of not having the use of any limbs, hearing, sight, or smell, which the reader truly recognizes through Johnny's thoughts.

Inviting a student volunteer by the name of Ben to join her in front of the class, Myra began to wind thick gauze around his head. Winding down around his eyes, and toward his nose, she explained the connection to the book, and how Johnny counted the changes in temperature from morning to night, in order to grasp a sense of passing days.

From the rear corner of the room, Miss B. stiffened. Suddenly aware of a strange sound she couldn't identify, she craned her neck from side to side, eyeing her students carefully. She cased the room, attempting to sniff out the perpetrators. More sounds. A creaking chair here and there. A small chuckle. Students were straightening in their chairs. Now deep, round laughter, as Myra slowly wound the gauze around Ben's wiggling, itchy nose. The class was waking up, paying attention, and enjoying themselves.

For Miss B. it must have seemed a reasonable transition, a well thought out realization, but to us, it happened in a flash. Bursting out of her chair, Miss B. lumbered heavily across the room. Tearing at Myra's hands and Ben's face, she ripped the gauze away from them, clutching it close to her chest, bellowing, "Stop! Stop! Stop! I won't have it! You're having fun! I won't have it! You're having fun! There will be no fun in this class!"

From then on, no one made a peep in Miss B.'s class. Everyone spoke in calm, slow voices, and only if it was absolutely necessary. She had pulled us all into her needle-head-sized comfort zone, achieving her goal in the process. We were all afraid of her, but not because she was powerful. We thought she was crazy.

The only book I remember reading in Miss B.'s class was *Johnny Got His Gun* by Dalton Trumbo.

Mr. O.: Controlling a Need to Control

Mr. O. was a second-grade teacher, a very calm, quiet, thin father of two, in his forties, with wire rim glasses. Unlike Miss B., he didn't appear to be afraid of anything. His smile was genuine and he looked me in the eye when he talked to me. He was extremely gracious.

I had been hired as an artist in residence to work with four second-grade classes in that school once a week for eight weeks. Mr. O. went out of his way to make sure I had everything I needed. He was somewhat concerned with the prospect of needing to move desks in his classroom, but wanted to make sure that I had enough room to work, so he made arrangements to use the computer room, which had a large open space in the middle. Many teachers don't like to move desks. Often the old desks are cumbersome or there is limited space in the room. My comfort zone radar didn't even beep. This was nothing out of the ordinary.

I ate lunch with the second-grade teachers, chatting away about the morning activities, chuckling over student responses. Throughout, Mr. O. sat , listening attentively, occasionally murmuring, "You did that this morning?" but never saying much more.

After recess, I met Mr. O.'s class as they were entering the computer room. I instructed them to form a standing circle and raise their hands above their heads for a warm-up.

Immediately, a redheaded boy standing two students from my left shrieked as if he had been stabbed, and ran out of the room. Mr. O. and the paraprofessional exchanged glances. Smiling, Mr. O calmly walked out in pursuit of the student. In eight weeks he never seemed anxious or out of control. Before they had returned, another boy, with dark brown hair, yelled "No! No! No!" and also ran out of the room. The aide took off after him. In contrast, she wasn't a bit calm.

So there I was, alone with eighteen second graders whose names I did not know, who had a scream and fly rate of about one every three minutes. What did I do? I kept going with the warm-up. Having worked in a variety of school populations, I was used to unexpected behavior. For five years I worked with a group of socially and emotionally challenged students, where seeing a fist fight break out in the middle of class was not uncommon. I was wide awake, but still within my comfort zone.

We were down to wiggling our toes when the brown-haired boy returned with the aide, whose name I never did learn, because I never saw her after that day. Loud moans could be heard from the red-haired boy across the hall. This was all too much for the rest of the students, who started popping like springs, one by one, into a variety of wiggle dances all over the room. The aide threw her hands up in the air as I started singing.

"Everybody freeze. Everybody freeze. Freeze your nose, your toes, your knees. Everybody sit. Everybody sit. Slowly sink to the floor and sit."

When Mr. O. reappeared with the red-haired boy, we were on the floor, in a circle, playing Pass the Object, which, with many verbal observations on my part, could be dragged out to fit any time period. Mr. O. lined them up through an intricate, time-consuming process which they seemed to be familiar with.

"I have a few questions," I murmured quietly.

"Me too," he responded. "We'll talk next week."

The following week, we talked a little, but not nearly enough. Mr. O. moved the desks in his room. Moving into the computer room had been too big a change for the students. I asked everyone to get into a circle, which caused several wild, emotional outbursts, but no one fled the room. Progress?

As this story unfolded, I came to understand that these students were not struggling with special challenges, that Mr. O. was not only their second-grade teacher, he had been their first-grade teacher, too, and every parent had requested that he teach their child again, because he seemed to have such fine control of the class.

I was used to unusual behavior, priding myself on not being thrown by the exceptional circumstances, yet every week I would drive home from this school banging my head on the steering wheel, completely at a loss. I'm sure Mr. O. did the same, only much more calmly. His students never acted this way when I wasn't there, he claimed. I was sure he thought the problem was something I was doing, but he was too polite to tell me what. I, in turn, redesigned my curriculum a thousand times a week, but it didn't seem to matter much what I did.

I dreaded going. My math drama ideas were working beautifully in the other classes, but it didn't make me feel any better. I had never felt like such a failure before. Fifteen years of experience down the tubes. It was time to pack it in and become a bank teller.

Finally, about the third week—by which time Mr. O.'s class was way behind all the others—he disclosed in the kindest possible manner that he had a very specific, orderly way of transitioning the students from one activity to another, and that these students, having had him the year before, had never experienced transitioning any other way. When I come in and give a completely outrageous request, like "stand in a circle," they have no idea how to do that by themselves. So they react by behaving badly. Even as he said it, it was clear to me that he was not blaming me; he behaved as if he were as puzzled by all of this as I was.

"Stand in a circle!" I responded entirely too loudly, in contrast to his soft, even tone. "That's just the beginning. Standing in a circle is the simplest thing I do. Everything else moves from there."

"That's the problem, then," he answered.

On the way home, I considered dropping his class. In thousands of classes, I had never ever dropped one, but this was a nightmare. Mr. O. was consistently calm, because he controlled his environment so carefully and completely that there was never any chance of conflict. His students never moved without a specific direction from him, so in their entire school career, they were never given the chance to take responsibility for their own physical actions. Here I was trying to teach in a way that involved student creativity and initiative. This was clearly an environment where teaching through the arts would not work, a first for me. I wanted to scream like crazy and run from the room.

The following week, to his credit, Mr. O. surprised the heck out of me. Turning to me as the other teachers left the lunch table, he said, "Your workshops have made me think a great deal about the way I have been teaching my students. I realized that the way I manage them doesn't give them much personal responsibility, and in the long run, I'm not sure that's good. So, I've been working all week to slowly ease up on the transition systems. Perhaps you'll notice a difference."

Tears sprang to my eyes. Goose bumps rose all over my arms, and I smiled calmly and said, "That's wonderful. I really appreciate your effort."

"It's really for them," he replied. "I think this will be better for them in the long run."

Over the next few weeks, we worked together closely. Mr. O. was encouraging his students to become more independent, and giving me tips to handle them while they grew. "Speak more slowly," he suggested. "If you give too many directions at once, they'll retreat." Considering his words, I realized he was right, and that slowing down my directions and waiting for the students to be completely settled was good advice in all my classes. Working as a team, we were pulling each other in, from the opposite ends of the earth. As often happens, my biggest nightmare was becoming a fabulous learning experience.

By the end of the eight weeks, we gathered two classes together at a time to present some of our most intriguing drama and math activities. Mr. O.'s class was no different from the rest.

You must be wondering, as I am, how these children ever managed to go to art, or gym, or have a substitute teacher. I have no idea. Perhaps people who live to avoid conflict never get sick. As for gym and art, I never asked. I wasn't sure how to approach it with Mr. O. without implying blame, and as a guest in his classroom, I never discussed it with anyone else.

When the PTO representative called me for comments, good and bad, about how the residency went from my point of view, I told her it was wonderful, that I had learned a great deal about drama and math, and that I had a few challenges with one of the teachers' teaching styles, but we put our heads together and worked together for the students.

Mr. O's comfort zone was created out of what he thought was best for his students. I continue to credit him for his ability to recognize when his personal style was blocking their growth, and for his rapid, aggressive willingness to do what it took to alleviate the problem. Occasionally I find myself banging my head on the steering wheel on the way home. Smiling, I remember him and his class, and wish today's problem could be so easily remedied.

The Penny Ante Theater

During the early eighties, I was single, living in New London, Connecticut, and working for a small theater called The Penny Ante Theater. I traveled New England with two other actors, Rob Richter and Kevin Kane, and our director and founder, Nancy Kerr, performing shows and teaching workshops to students and teachers that were similar to what I do now. It would be safe to say that I'm the spin-off series of the Penny Ante Theater, which I closed in 1986.

We juggled so many projects simultaneously that the local community often believed there were twenty-five of us, instead of four. In addition we all had second jobs in restaurants because The Penny Ante Theater only paid us $135 a week.

Having received a large grant from the Greater Hartford Arts Council to do teacher training workshops, classroom workshops, and performances in all twenty-four of the Hartford public schools, we drove our white station wagon, "Betsy," to Hartford four to five times a week.

One of the schools in our rotation was built adjacent to a subsidized housing community. In all the inner city schools I have worked in since then, I have never seen anything quite like it. The buildings occupied the same grounds, set apart only by playground equipment, which was shared by both communities.

I only remember one workshop at this school. It is safe to say, I blocked the rest out, but since the last one was clearly icing on the cake, the first three I taught that day must have been equally tasty.

For some reason, Rob and I were teaching this workshop together, in the cafeteria. Somebody thought it would be a good idea to double the number of kids and put them in a large open space for the last period on a Friday. It's just that kind of thinking that leads to building a school within a subsidized housing community in the first place.

Together, Rob and I could usually handle any crowd. The more extreme the circumstance, the faster we slid into performance personas, bellowing directions as cheerily as possible, in circus barker fashion. But this was different. All day long I had observed odd behavior from the students. Glassy eyed and immune to our stimuli, they operated wildly in a vacuum, as if the controlling energy deep within them wasn't their own. I didn't own a television at the time, but this was definitely The Twilight Zone. I truly didn't want to speculate about whether they were under the influence of drugs. They were so young.

This last workshop wasn't working at all. The third- and fourth-grade students would only respond if we dealt with them one on one, and there were sixty of them flying all over the room. At one end, I managed to have three or four students following me, and starting to get the point of the exercise. Spying Rob from across the room, I could see he was doing about as well.

In the back of the room stood three or four men wearing suit pants and vests, with their shirt sleeves rolled up. I'm not sure who they were—teachers, guards, aides? In any case, they weren't paying any attention to the chaos before them. They just stood there chatting away as if nothing at all was happening. Their comfort zones were colossal.

Just off center of this large oval space stood a slim African-American woman in her early fifties, of medium height, wearing a neat white blouse, a long slim navy skirt, and high heels. Her head was tilted slightly to the side, which managed to amplify her enormous eyes, which seemed both frightened and resolved. Her eyes looked directly into mine, half begging, half apologizing.

At twenty-three, I remember feeling that I was letting her down, that there was something about the program that was causing this mess and that there was some simple answer that would solve it, but I just didn't know what it was. Looking back now, I know I would handle the whole thing differently today. Age may or may not bring wisdom, but the perspective it does offer helps us stand up for reasonable conditions.

Immediately after the workshop, Rob and I met Kevin outside the side door and headed off to find "Betsy." Kevin had been waiting near the school door for all of two minutes when he was approached by a man from the playground who offered to sell him heroin.

None of us said a word during the fifty-minute ride home. I sat alone in the backseat, crouched down in horror. Halfway home I flipped through the newspaper lying on the seat to distract myself. The top story was about a woman in Hartford who was convicted and sent to jail for falsifying an address so her son could go to a school in the suburbs. Mentally, I told her to move over. I would be sitting right next to her.

In this story, the comfort zones had long since been eradicated. The students, with little or no structure, weren't comfortable. They were wacked out! The African-American woman was the only one who seemed to want something, but between her tense body posture and her woeful eyes, it was clear she wasn't getting it.

Sharing these last three tales of school environments that have long since changed, I've hoped to demonstrate vast ranges in comfort zones. Miss B.'s was pin-sized, and lined with steel. Mr. O.'s was constructed with intentional kindness, and altered with the same motivation, and the school in Hartford had destroyed any semblance of a comfortable working environment, and personal structure, long before I arrived.

In each story, the defining comfort zone was blocking creativity and productivity. Naturally, to me this is a disaster, because I believe the two go hand in hand, especially if the productivity you're looking for has anything to do with progress.

Adapting Drama Rules to Fit Your Comfort Zone

The only way to discover the limits
of the possible
is to go beyond them to the impossible.
Arthur C. Clarke

One of the differences between using drama as a teaching tool and handing out worksheets is that you won't always know the outcome before you begin. Each time you do an activity, your students will generate new ideas that you hadn't even thought of. (In all honesty, that's my favorite part.) You won't have all the answers every time, especially if you are developing a larger project. This fact alone can rattle the cages of your comfort zone, but relax. That's fine. You are allowed to make mistakes, and so are your students. Often re-creating an image, or a concept, in a completely dreadful way serves beautifully as a catalyst to help you and them define what you are really seeking. It's valuable for your students to recognize that creation is a process for you as much as it is for them.

You have to know what you want to get.
But when you know that, let it take you.
And if it seems to take you off the track,
don't hold back, because perhaps that is
instinctively where you want to be.
And if you hold back and try to be
always where you have been before,
you will go dry.
Gertrude Stein

But, as with any lesson you teach, especially if you yourself are trying something new, it's important to define the rules before you begin. By doing so, you can gently remind a student of an existing rule, without feeling that you are constantly telling them how not to do something, just as you are encouraging them to create their own solutions.

Consistent Rules

Every lesson I teach begins with the following rules:

* Your ideas must be appropriate.
* There will be no weapons or violence.
* We are all trying new experiences, so we must be positive and supportive of each other.
* I have no problems with mistakes, just make them loud mistakes.
* Please do not use the name of another classmate in your work without his or her permission.

I always get a groan at the request for no violence. Students are attracted to it, thinking that it is powerful, funny, and cool. I always respond the same way, by saying that drama is about solving problems in a creative way. Weapons and violence do not have anything to do with solutions. They only create more problems. So violence is not an acceptable choice.

Extra Rules

In addition to the consistent rules, I add a few that are appropriate for the next activity.

Example: In Lean and Leave, students pose as if they are leaning on another student, while they are actually supporting their own weight. My introduction to this lesson involves a humorous demonstration of the difference between leaning while supporting one's own weight and leaning with all of one's might.

"Supporting one's own weight is a special activity challenge which I am sure this class can handle. I can just tell," I declare boldly, blatantly bribing them with praise.

I then make it very clear that anyone who cannot support their own weight will be asked to leave. I may even ask them to raise their hands if they agree to support their own weight. If they're not sure, they may sit aside now, so we won't have any problems. No one ever sits out, but if anyone ever did, I would thank them for their honesty, and compliment them on knowing their limits.

Setting Goals

I also set a few goals we will be aiming for in addition to the main problem within the activity.

Example: Swoosh. "Remember that, even with all these curriculum connections, this game is still about energy, so I'm not looking for someone to pass the energy in a dull, flat, uninterested way. I'm looking for pizzazz!"

Reminding someone of the rules and goals may be as simple as gently shaking your head at them. At the other extreme, I have gone as far as saying, "Thank you for doing that. I neglected to mention that we need to try to remember to face the audience as much as possible during the skit. I'm so glad you reminded me. Now it's clear to everyone." Or, " Nice negative nonsupportive gesture, Phil. Did everyone catch that? We'll have to add that to the negative gestures we won't be doing in this class. Thanks!" Or, "Did I mention the words non-violent, appropriate? Yes. Oh, good. Just checking."

When adapting an idea that works with an older group to a younger group, it's important to seek out any points where the control needed to achieve the activity is beyond the maturity level of the younger age group, and adjust accordingly.

Example: Acting out a story, with kindergarten students. The story: *Where the Wild Things Are*, by Maurice Sendak.

Where the Wild Things Are is an excellent story to act out with younger grades or family groups. Students will have a fabulous time with the repetitive sequence of rolling their terrible eyes, and gnashing their terrible teeth, and showing their terrible claws, in addition to taking turns acting out the live characters, such as Max, his dog, his angry mother, and the monsters; and the setting, like the bed that turns into a forest, and the carpet that turns into green grass. It's great fun. Talk about living literature! My daughter still talks about being the glass of milk when she was five.

Do you remember the section where all the monsters crown Max king, and Max says, "Let the wild rumpus start"?

Planning ahead any wild rumpus sections with the students before you begin acting out the whole story will help ease everyone through any potential medical emergencies. There are several ways to handle this creatively and reasonably, so give your students the benefit of practicing this tricky part in advance. Then you'll be able to breeze through this section of the book without stopping to create new rules, and breaking the creative flow of the story.

Idea #1: Have the students create one giant frozen statue of monsters dancing wildly. Pretend to take their picture. Have them slowly move to another pose as you count to five. Take another imaginary picture.

Idea #2: Divide into several small groups in advance, and label them with numbers, letters, or monster names, then practice having each group dance briefly in place when you call their name, and freeze in place when a different group is called. Praise them highly for being able to stop all at the same time.

Idea #3: As the students are sitting on the floor in the beginning, practice having a wild dancing rumpus all at the same time, wiggling everything but their rear ends. Have a wild nose rumpus, a wild hands rumpus, a wild knees rumpus, a wild tongue rumpus, all from a seated position. Then add them all together.

In activities like this, a little group preparation can be a great help. So if you're reading a story, or planning an activity, and there is a "wild rumpus" type section in it, don't let the whole idea scare you off from doing it. Plan it out with your students in advance. Take their suggestions on how to handle it. Having solved the trickiest section first, you may then help ease any student comfort zones in the more direct sections.

CHAPTER SIX

Drama Supplies: Essentials and Extras

The activities in this book will not require many extra supplies. The extent to which you would like to collect props, costumes, and set pieces is clearly up to you. I have learned that this, too, is directly connected to one's personal style.

For years I traveled with minimal props, promoting pantomime, physicality, and visualization, until I taught a graduate arts in education course with Bobbie Nidzgorski, a gifted and talented teacher and a master puppeteer. Bobbie had more props, gadgets, and just plain stuff than anyone I had ever known. For years after that, I hauled more than I needed all over the state, completely cognizant of the fact that this was all her fault. She inspired me. I couldn't help myself.

Now I have reverted back to a happy medium, except when I'm working on a student production. The props involved for four to five classes, each with twenty-four lead roles, can pack any touring station wagon to the gills.

For the everyday drama session, I am a firm believer in minimal props. Students may want to create a few small items out of construction paper and add them to a skit. I never have a problem with that, unless the props become more important than the scene. Whenever using props, I always suggest that the entire scene be worked out before anyone spends time making or selecting props. If this isn't done, students may end up with beautiful decorations, but no scene.

CHUCK JONES

The List

Beach Balls

Many activities involve having a ball with numbers, letters, or transitional phrases written on it. Beach balls work well, and once deflated take up minimal storage space. **Tip:** Write on them with permanent marker, or the students will wear the topic home on their hands.

Colorful Cloth

An extra bonus for the visual-spatial learners, the presence of colorful cloth will stimulate their senses and keep them involved. An extremely useful tool, cloth can become anything—a river, a brook, a scarf, a belt, a

time machine door, oxygen, blood, anything. Use cloth to accent a particular focal point, and students will remember it longer. I went to a workshop recently where as a group we were acting out a living cell. The woman portraying the nucleus was draped in a green cloth. Each time I saw her over the next several days, I remembered her as the green nucleus woman. **Tip:** Do not under any circumstances let the children put the cloth over their heads—just as you would not encourage them to share hats. The only good aspect of lice is that they have no problems crossing racial, social, and economic boundaries.

Sound Effects

Sound effects make great accents for scenes and concepts. They are also a great tool for students who are not yet comfortable acting and speaking in front of the class. "The door creaked," "the window slammed," and "the wind howled" are all good opportunities to demonstrate the wonderful world of extra details.

A simple box of clackers and boingers is a wonderful addition to any classroom.

Homemade instruments created from recycled garbage work beautifully.

Paula Silvert, a family friend, directs a state orchestra of musicians with Down's syndrome and special needs in Maryland. The Merry Music Makers play concerts along with tapes of Mozart, Debussy, and other composers. Each person has an instrument, works hard, gets nervous, and hears the applause. Paula isn't a bit picky about the instruments themselves. There are kazoo sections and stick sections. She says that if it makes music, they have it.

Another musician friend of mine says knowing when not to play an instrument is the most difficult part of having it. I have used sound effects as a motivational and instructional tool to help students who need to reinforce the idea of appropriate times for appropriate behaviors. We start together, and stop together. They follow a script and play on cue. Sometimes they take turns directing each other. It works wonders.

Space

Space is the most important requirement for drama. Unless you have an unusually large classroom, moving some desks will be important. Some teachers have a regular desk-moving plan, where each student knows exactly what to do, and it takes about three minutes. If you are fortunate enough to have extra space outside the classroom in your school, your class could move there for drama, but drama within your classroom works just as well. Drama in a familiar environment also reinforces the idea that established classroom rules and manners apply to these activities as well.

A Judgment-Free Environment

It's not included in supply catalogs, but every classroom needs vast amounts of it. No one can think of a new idea, or even one they already know well, if they feel they will be arrested by the Stupid Idea Police. A drama session is the perfect place to exercise positive reinforcement. Coaching from the leader or teacher is essential. You will witness some outrageous ideas. Some of them might not be wonderful or even remotely doable, but there is something in every idea or presentation that is valuable. Make a rule that student critiques must begin with positive statements first, before they move on to positive suggestions.

No one grows or learns anything if everything is great. Suggestions for improvement can always be made. Centering on the idea that drama is always a work in progress will help encourage students to dig deeper for their best work.

CHAPTER SEVEN

The Ingredient Games

There's no food in this house," my husband complains. I open an overflowing cupboard and a box of couscous falls on my head.

"There's plenty of food in the house," I reply painfully.

"I know, but there's nothing I can eat. It's all...all..." He pauses in search of the word he wants.

"Ingredients," I fill in for him.

"Yeah, ingredients—nothing edible."

My husband has many talents. Puttering in the kitchen enough to combine a few simple ingredients is not one of them. He could if he would, but he has no interest in it. Not to mention the fact that the Glynn habit of waiting to eat until his blood sugar level is in his toe doesn't provide him with the extra patience to cook.

I, on the other hand, love ingredients. There's security in them. I buy most things in bulk, because I like knowing that what I need will be there, without dropping everything for a last-minute trip to the store. This is not to say that I actually cook anything special very often. My creative need to blend and mix ingredients to reach a variety of extraordinary results is often more than satisfied at work. Whenever there is an entirely home-cooked meal around my house, my husband is known to announce, "Wow, we're like a real family."

I use Ingredient Games at work all the time. For me, they are the staple items I never want to be without, because I can always use them in a variety of classroom recipes to cook just the right meal for a wide range of needs and personalities.

The following games and activities are all valuable on their own. They also can adapt to a wide variety of curriculum topics. In later chapters, I will often refer back to the Ingredient Games because they serve as staple items for cooking up curriculum recipes.

Ingredient Game Contents
(In Alphabetical Order)

Acting Out Concepts

I believe that if students, of any age, have the opportunity to personify and become the topic they are studying, they will have fun, connect with their learning, and retain the lesson longer than if they simply read it, or listen to someone tell it.

I recently taught six fifth-grade classes to write descriptive paragraphs by physically acting out a setting, and then writing about it. In the same classes, I taught descriptive writing in what I felt was an effective, yet not as physical a way. Again, the students followed up the lesson with writing. In all cases, across all skill levels, the writing for the setting which they had physically acted out produced a wider variety of personal vision with clearer, more descriptive writing. Not only that, the papers were exciting to read, without any "filled in to please the teacher" dullness to them. I teach physical teaching every day, so you may think my opinion is biased. Actually, I felt like an idiot. The acted-out setting was a fifteen-minute lesson to fill out a class. The other one took an entire class period. I guess this old dog needed to learn some of my own tricks.

In this book, I describe hundreds of games, activities, and opportunities for dramatization that I have created or adapted over the years, but I encourage you to create your own.

I'm including Acting Out a Concept in the Ingredient Games chapter because it is a tool that I use all the time. The steps are simple, and probably seem vague, but they help me zero in on the center of any topic and create an activity that is exciting, entertaining, and educational.

The Approach

1. *Breaking the topic down* to a manageable size is the first step: a concept, an exchange, a point of view, or an event. If I cannot visualize a part to personify, the topic is usually too general.
   Example: The concept of time—How a clock works
2. *Group the class* to appropriate sizes including individual monologues, partners, groups of three to five, or the whole class as a group.
   Example: Sit twelve students in a circle to be the numbers. Select six students for individual roles. The remaining students will take turns performing special jobs.
3. *Assign parts.*
   Example: Twelve students are the numbers. The six individual students will be the hour hand, the minute hand, the second hand, the tick, the tock, and the alarm. The remaining students will guide the hour and minute hands to the appropriate spots as an answer to any word problem time questions.
4. *Provide any necessary visual aids* or the materials for the students to create their own.
   Example: Hand out numbers on paper for the students to hold up. Provide an alarm or have the student make the sound. Large noodles work well for minute and hour hands. The second-hand person plays the point with an invisible hand.
5. *Foresee any possible disasters and create rules to avoid them.*
   Example: Stretch out the space enough so that there will be no collisions. Give a few examples of how not to be a crashing, smashing clock.
6. *Act it out.*
   Example: Demonstrate how the second hand must run around for the minute hand to move a little. (For large time changes, the class can then imagine this, rather than killing off any students.)
7. *If I'm drawing a blank* trying to think of a way to dramatize a curriculum topic, I'll check over the ingredients list, and an answer will spring to mind.
   Example: My mind always manages to create the most complicated version first, and then the easier one appears. If you can't think of a way to act out your concept, check the Ingredient Games.
8. *Address particular challenges within the activity.* If the activity has particular challenges, where I think students may go wild and lose the point of the activity, I'll plan ahead for a way to cover that. (Maybe I'll freeze the activity at that moment, and have the students whisper their reactions. Maybe I'll have them dance a wild rumpus, like the one in *Where the Wild Things Are,* by Maurice Sendak—with their noses only.)
9. *Discuss the activity.* If something is missing, it will most likely appear while you're trying it. Explain that creativity is a process. Ask for verbal or written suggestions. Adjust it the next time.

Examples of Acting Out a Concept

Each of the following activities was created for specific workshops using the process described above.

American Revolution: Make the students understand the frustration caused by taxation without representation. See the Stamp Tax game in Social Studies 3-4 and 5-8.

Immigration: The personal feelings, practical challenges, hopes, fears, and dreams as people checked in at Ellis Island. See Social Studies K-2. (This model is also valuable for older grades.)

Punctuation: Personify a sentence. The noun is the character. The verb moves in place. The adverb tells the verb how to move, over and over. Each comma is acted out. And each sentence is read by the class with different ending punctuation. See Language Arts K-2, and 3-4.

Seasons: Act out the change. Choose five or six roles in nature, and see how they are affected by the change. You could demonstrate each one in small groups and then do them all together. See Science K-2.

If the Topic (Is) ...

A. Mechanical, assign each student a role as one of the machine parts. (See Machines.)

B. Natural, it still has a process that can be identified and personified. Examples: the water cycle, photosynthesis.

C. Political, assign roles, or identify the concepts dividing the parties, and act them out in a way that students will grasp by doing it. Example: If the three branches of government are confusing, let them be three large limbs, and describe what their functions are. Perhaps the leaves can disagree to demonstrate the process.

D. Involves humans, then whatever it is, it involves emotions, opinions, strong characters, and conflict. This is what drama is all about. Act that out.

E. Linear in nature, such as punctuation, assign parts in a line, like a sentence, and have students be a period, comma, quotation mark, or exclamation point. Read the sentence in an excited, calm, or inquisitive voice. Act it out!

F. Mathematical, assign numbers on paper sheets, and have students move as the answer is determined. Personify the math symbols, and interview them. Do they feel powerful evoking such change in others? Have them demonstrate their powers. What exactly do they do?

For me, creating the activities is half the fun. My hope is that by using this book, you'll gain activities you can use every day, and the knowledge to branch out and create your own, if you so desire.

If the idea of creating your own activities does not interest you, relax. You are still in the right place. The activities you will find are fully equipped with complete directions.

Ball Toss (Roll)

I learned this game from Patty Tedford, and have adapted it ever since.

Ages: Grades K-6

Tools: Inflatable balls with words, letters, or numbers marked with permanent marker in a grid. I have one of each in my bag of tricks. Beach balls work well because you can deflate them for storage purposes. (Washable marker comes off on the kids' hands.) Leave a few squares empty for a free space.

Structure: Design the seating or standing structure to fit your space and your students. *Example plans:*

A. Two rows of students standing.

B. A circle of students sitting.

C. Students standing randomly around the room in their space.

Directions:

1. Toss or roll a ball to a student.

2. When the student catches the ball, he should note the squares in which his thumbs have landed.

3. The student should then follow the variable directions in the game, using the information in the squares. (Multiply the numbers, say which is greater or less than, start an alliterative sentence with the letters, etc.)

4. Pass the ball to another student. Each student should have a turn.

Variations:

There are an infinite number of variations of this educational game, and it is always fun. When this game catches on, I plan to buy stock in a beach ball company.

Numbers:

1. Say which number is larger/smaller.

2. Add/subtract them.
3. Multiply them.
4. Identify them.
5. Identify them and say which one is your favorite.

Letters:
1. Identify them.
2. Think of a word that starts with them.
3. Think of a sentence that begins with them.
4. Think of a descriptive word that begins with the letter.
5. Think of an adverb that begins with the letter.
6. Think of a noun that begins with the letter.
7. Think of an exciting verb that starts with the letter.

For directions to Transitional Phrase Ball, Dead Verb Ball, Geography Ball, and others, look in the Language Arts and Social Studies sections.

Be a Shape

I learned a version of this game from a friend, Carol Collins. The variations are endless. The game itself is excellent for cooperation, listening, and teamwork. The results are similar in a kindergarten class and a group of business executives. It also works well as a visual spatial exercise, and review for whatever shapes, letters, or numbers you're promoting.

Ages: Grades 2-6

Tools: A blackboard and chalk, or an easel with paper and markers.

I always start with students seated in a circle, because that's a standard starting and ending place for me, and chances are the students are already in it, facilitating the transition.

Directions:

"Right now you are in this shape," I say, drawing a circle on the board. "In a moment I am going to erase this shape and draw another shape. As quickly as you can, I would like you to form this new shape, standing up, side by side, in a group. We'll need everyone in the class to form the true shape. Are you ready? Drum roll, please!" I say, revealing the shape. "Go."

Sometimes I actually look at the clock. Usually I enjoy the group solution drama in front of me. Twenty-four personalities will be revealed in your class: the quiet but efficient student who goes directly to a spot and holds it, the directors, who are more interested in telling others what to do than in finding their own spots, and the followers, who are standing in a place, but are not a bit sure why they are there, and twenty other variations in between.

"Now! You did such a great job, we're going to make it more complicated. This time, you need to get into the new shape as quickly as you can, and this time you aren't allowed to talk." I say this as if it would be the most difficult challenge in the world. (Depending on the class, it often is.) "Drum roll, please."

The third time, I tell them to get into the new shape as quickly as possible without talking and without touching. "So, if you were inclined to grab your friend by the hair and hurl them across the room, this time you can't. You may still communicate, but without talking or touching."

Tips and Variations:

1. You will have to remind them not to talk and touch. I usually go to all the levels to show the classroom teacher how to extend the activity, but you may want to keep repeating the same level until they've mastered it.

2. Have them form letters, numbers, geometrical shapes, math symbols, etc.

Chant Dancing Lists

"Jan-uary, Feb-ruary, March, Ap-ril, May, June, Ju-ly, Au-gust, Sep-tem-ber, Oc-to-ber, No-vem-ber, De-cem-ber. These are the months of the year. Some months are hot, and some are cold, and some have lots or ra-ain! But if you know all twelve of them, you can call them out by Na-ame!"

Living with a six-year-old who loves to sing and dance, I was blessed with the opportunity of hearing forty-three choruses of this song the other evening, complete with forty-three dance versions, many of which involved somersaulting off the bed. (And her teachers wonder why I look dazed when they worry about how quiet she is at school.) I loved every minute of her singing. Neither one of us will ever forget the months of the year again!

As a first grader, my daughter comes home daily with a new chant/dance or song involving some list we need to know for life. Every time she bellows out a new one I am pleased and surprised. First-grade teachers are using chanting, dancing, and singing all the time. When does this method stop being used? Why does it stop being used? It clearly works!

Every single month I find myself repeating the poem

> Thirty days hath September,
> April, June, and November
> All the rest have thirty-one,
> Except February, which has twenty-eight.

Every time I look something up, I sing the ABCs quietly into the phone book or dictionary. My daughter knows our address and phone number without a hitch. Can she say them without swinging her hips? Who knows?

In high school, my chemistry teacher told us to memorize the periodic table. She said it would be a Mickey Mouse test, involving memorization, not thinking. Anyone who didn't get them all right should not be in the class, because we were simply not smart enough. (Thinking about her still gives me warm fuzzies.) I got a hundred, but I don't know them now. Had she taken the time to chant-dance it to us, I would probably still remember it. Had she somersaulted off the lab table, I definitely would.

I'm only partially kidding. When and why do we stop chant dancing to learn? Is there a date in our educational growth when it's simply no longer acceptable? Do we stop because they're too old for it, or because we are? Remember, they're the ones who through adolescence begin to paint the shell of "I'm not going to let you know I like this until I'm sure my friends do, too." Wouldn't it be nice if we could be creative role models for living life to its fullest, especially if it helps them learn their facts? If you're too shy to create them, assign chant dancing as a project. Who can come up with the most dynamic way to remember the (insert facts list here)?

Ages: All.

Tools: A rhythm. A tune, if you like. A little wiggle here and there. A sense of fun.

Structure: Make it up. If you're not comfortable doing so, have the students make it up. Send it home as a family project. Then record them for the next class. When does learning have to stop being fun?

Topics to chant /dance: Any list.

Commercials

"Seventy-six table lamps led the big parade. A hundred and ten chandeliers lit the way. Followed by rows and rows of the finest Quoisels, oh...."

"Little Pig. Little Pig. Here's your sale flyer from Eastern Electric Supply! I was just being neighborly. He starts talking about hairy chins, I sneeze. Boom. No more straw house. So I moved on. The next house, Stick Manor, was really dark. They could use some outdoor lighting..."

(To the tune of "O, Christmas Tree"): "Pete's Christmas trees. Pete's Christmas trees, on Friendship Street, in Westerly. Come buy a tree, and have some fun. Pete has a tree for everyone..."

These are just a few of the radio commercials I've written, produced and performed over the past twelve years. So, despite the fact that I haven't actually seen a TV commercial in about that long, thanks to videos, public television, and my husband's vigilance with the remote, I truly believe that if I can sell lighting, plumbing supplies, construction companies, and Christmas trees with mythology, fairy tales, and historical figures, then they'll work well for other curricula, too.

Most students will share their favorite TV commercial spontaneously, so if you find yourself lacking in examples, you'll still have plenty to discuss. I find that if I don't know the commercial but I keep asking questions, then the student will describe the commercial in more detail, which is sheer bonus territory for me.

Most commercials fit into one of the following three categories:

1. **Products that solve a problem.** (Often they solve problems you didn't know you had.) These include the cleaning products that get any stain out of your carpet, acne cream to wipe out the grossest pimple, laundry detergent to get your clothes sparkling clean and smelling fresh, and designer jeans to look appropriately baggy, saggy, tight, slim, trim, or bland. The horde of anti-heartburn commercials would also sizzle here in the problem-solving category.

2. **Commercials that compare products**. Either the second product is better than the first, or it is exactly the same and costs less. Sometimes it may cost a little more, but then, of course, you're worth it.

   Examples: Coke and Pepsi often provide handy examples of this category. If you don't know the latest version, your students will.

   "On the left we have all the dishes I was able to wash with two teaspoons of XXX detergent. Here, on the right, are all the dishes washed with two teaspoons of our brand."

3. **Products or events that involve hype.** These commercials try to get your attention by involving celebrities, prizes, songs, or loud, dramatic commotion.

   Some commercials attract us through humor. I date myself, but I remember the time when everyone knew the one that went "I can't believe I ate the whole thing" followed by "You ate it, Ralph." None of the kids in my class knew what Alka-Seltzer was at the time, but we constantly imitated the commercial, generating enough indigestion for our teachers to boost sales.

The Lesson

I usually start by asking the students what their favorite commercials are. I go over the three categories mentioned above, and then I offer the following structural suggestions to begin writing or acting their own.

A. Act out a commercial using a real product. Reenact the TV version or create your own.

B. Act out a commercial about an original product.

C. Act out a real or original product in a fairy tale setting.

Choose a product and either have it solve a problem, compare and contrast it with a competitor, or design an extravaganza to grab a future customer.

Fairy tale Example: Rapunzel throws her hair out over the edge of the tower where she is trapped. Once the prince gets a load of her slimy tangled hair full of dandruff, he refuses to rescue her. Once she uses Hair Beautiful, he can't get up the hair ladder fast enough. Of course, her hair could become so silky smooth that he keeps sliding off, and has to take the back stairs. Rapunzel could even jump out and slide down her own hair.

Variations:

1. **Sell a research topic.** *Example:* Point out the benefits of owning a capuchin monkey, the many problems they will solve around the house, how the consumer will find everything she needs to take care of the new monkey at Monkeys R Us, for less. Sing a song about Captivating Capuchins. Have a rock star endorse having one in your home. Perhaps you're selling an adoption service for misplaced rain forest animals.

2. **Sell the truth about a product.** *Example:* Cigarettes. Are your teeth too white? Your skin too smooth? Do you want the same hacking cough as your pre-cancerous friends? Then light up a cigarette today. Smoke often. Go broke! Start up a habit you'll never want to quit. Your life will never be the same.

3. **Sell positive values.** *Example:* Show an example of someone tripping and dropping packages. Have someone walk by, laughing. Repeat the scene but show someone else stopping to help pick up the packages. Caption: "This holiday season give something everyone can use, a little kindness. After all, it beats a Chia Pet."

Create a Place

Ages: Grades 3-8.

Tools: None.

Directions:

1. Think of a place.

2. Think of activities that would happen in that place.

3. Have one student begin by demonstrating his chosen activity for a place he has chosen. Don't let him tell the name of the place.

4. A second student joins when she determines that she understands the place through the first activity. The second student thinks of a new activity in that place, and demonstrates it.

5. Other students add on one by one.

6. Freeze all the students. Tap each player on the shoulder and ask the other students what the student was doing. If they have forgotten, or if it wasn't clear, have the student demonstrate his new activity solo.

7. Soon enough you'll have an active place, complete with characters.

Example: First student rows. second student lifts barbells. third student jumps rope. fourth student climbs a stair climber, etc. You'll have a gym.

Tips:

1. Make sure they take enough time to observe each new student activity. The character of the place may change, especially within the first few students. *Example:* First student rows. Second one fishes, third stu-

dent is the fish. Fourth student sunbathes. Fifth student uses a net. Sixth student is a storm cloud, etc. You'll have a lake or pond.

2. Feel free to stop the place at any number of students.

3. Feel free to freeze a few wilder students by tapping them to calm the chaos. If they've been going for a while, they'll appreciate it.

Variations and Connections:

1. Use as a story starter. Have them write the scene or story from their point of view.

2. Use as an active lesson on Setting.

3. Control the place with cards or categories: Historical, Contemporary, Activities you would see in a country you have studied this year, etc.

Dr. Vocabulary

Ages: Grades 4-8.

Directions:

1. Have your students create a character, Dr. Vocabulary, and present his latest ingenious discovery, the _____. (vocabulary word of your choice)

2. Encourage them to be creative. Any student can read the definition out of the book and repeat it. How many different ways can one word be explained? Introduce examples. Tell a joke about it. If this word were an adjective to describe a person, what would it mean?

Example: Geometry Vocabulary: line, segment, angle, congruent, similar, acute angle, obtuse angle, reflex angle.

Bob was a real segment. He felt incomplete and lacked ambition. He didn't seem to be headed anywhere.

Was this angle ever obtuse!

Cecile thought Al was a real acute angle, but later found he was too narrow-minded.

3. Encourage the use of visual materials and costumes.

4. Create a character for Dr. Vocabulary. If I were to create him now, my version of "Dr. Discovery" would be highly eccentric, and outrageously over enthusiastic about the most bland facts. He'd go crazy over the idea that angles are bent. "Can you imagine? They bend, right here! Oh, oh, I'm going to be so famous!"

Variations:

1. Offer Dr. Vocabulary as a class project, with one student presenting his word every day over a matter of weeks. Students may work alone, or having designed the presentation themselves, invite other students to help them play certain parts.

2. Have students pick a word from a hat, and working in groups, have them present their creations in a matter of minutes.

3. Invite students to personify curriculum vocabulary and have Dr. Vocabulary interview them. They could be a cell wall, an equals sign, the planet Venus, or an igneous rock.

4. Have Dr. Vocabulary and others dramatize the moment he or she truly realized the definition.

5. Is Dr. Vocabulary one person or many, with eccentric personal quirks? Perhaps your class will want to create their own individual characters, who may be guests of Dr. Vocabulary. Perhaps he or she has some good friends—Dr. Geometry, Miss Science, Dr. Discovery, Mr. Angle, Ms. Math, Dr. Definition, Mr. Invention, Mrs. Solution, etc.

Fashion Show

Ages: Grades 4-8

"Here we have a fabulous design by Charlie. Notice the wide, full sleeves, made with the finest toilet paper, the empire waist, tied with Charlie's oldest, most uncomfortable tie. An exquisite example of the 'found in my closet' period."

My grandmother, Stella Smith, once organized a fashion show with the seniors in her mobile home park. Using actual fashion vocabulary, the men and women paraded around in elite garbage. Later, when retelling the event, neither she nor my grandfather could stop laughing long enough to describe it. This event swiftly became one of those tales they retold visit after visit for years afterward.

Seniors love costumes. Preschoolers adore dressing up. Every time my daughter has a friend over, I'm offered a front-row seat at the hottest costume parade in town. I have yet to meet a grade level that doesn't enjoy dressing up. Even eighth graders whose daily costume involves a thin, hard shell labeled, "I'm not interested until my friends are," shed their shells when it comes to dressing up.

Every culture has a native dress, formal and casual. Greek gods have a dress code, complete with mythological symbols. Even rain forest birds are dressed specifically for a reason. Fashion shows work well as a visual demonstration matched with factual information.

Directions:

1. Have each model research his or her own character, and write several sentences describing their chosen outfit in detail and the symbolic significance of their character. Include a few extra details about the characters' personality, their significant achievements, even their hopes and dreams.

2. Choose a host or hostess to write a general welcome with some facts about the fashion category for the day. Then they'll read the pre-written cards as the characters parade back and forth to a musical background.

Tips:

1. Encourage the models to do the research first, so they'll design the costumes with the character in mind.

2. Garbage bags can be silky gowns. Construction paper and newspaper can be cut, twisted, torn, and rolled into epaulets, wings, beaks, thunderbolts, flowered headdresses, etc. Colored fabric sheets and strips can be adapted to any category.

3. Fashion models work hard to be neutral so they show off the clothes. Students should do the opposite, using their bodies to reflect the physicality and the personality of the characters.

Game Shows

Ages: Grades 4-8.

The Dating Game

The Structure

A contestant sits on one side of a screen (real or imaginary) while three characters named # 1, #2, and #3 sit on the other side. The contestant asks questions of each of the characters, who do not reveal their names, and by their answers the contestant chooses the character he or she wants to match up with. An overzealous host links them, awards appropriate prizes, introduces the other characters, and voilà, it's a show reflecting student research, creativity, and humor.

This show works well as a fun way to demonstrate specific characters—literary, historical, legendary, and mythological.

Example: Mary Todd Lincoln could ask questions about politics, slavery, and dreams for a nation of contestants Ben Franklin, Thomas Jefferson, and Abraham Lincoln.

Example: Paris decides who is the most beautiful goddess by asking character questions of Aphrodite, Hera, and Athena. Each gives appropriate answers for her character.

Example: Louis Pasteur questions penicillin, vitamin C, and aspirin about their qualities, as he decides which one to discover.

Example: A specific vocabulary word could be looking for a definition.

Directions:

1. Students should choose their characters and do research on them.

2. The contestant should know who he or she is, and also what he or she is looking for.

3. The host should write the opening and closing signature jargon for the show, and decide on an appropriate prize for this category.

4. As a group, the students should think of three appropriate questions each character could answer that would reveal significant information about them.

Tips:

1. If you have a group that can run with the ball and organize themselves, by all means, let them set up the scene. The directions above are for groups that need a specific solid structure to divide the work and proceed productively.

2. The official Dating Game music is on a CD of Herb Alpert and the Tijuana Brass, Whipped Cream and Other Desserts.

To Tell the Truth

(A Group Alternative to the Single Interview)

Structure:

Three panelists all claim to be the same character, while Mr. or Ms. Contestant asks questions to try to determine who is telling the truth and who are the impostors. There is a host, and prizes as usual.

The students can decide whether the two impostors are other important characters who have their own specific well-researched information, who can be revealed at the end, or if they're actors who make mistakes, on purpose, to reveal their lies.

The actors may want to set the scene to include an audience component, where the class has an opportunity to guess who is telling the truth.

I was pretty little when this game aired on TV, but I remember the signature opening when each character strongly stressed the word "My" when they said, "My name is George Washington," "My name is George Washington," and "My name is George Washington."

What's My Line

Okay, the jig is up. I've never seen this show in its original state. (And yes, it's refreshing to have been too young!) But I've needed a game where the panel of players could answer questions about what they do, instead of just who they are. By twisting the premise around, the game show format could be used for any object, any process, and still work well for people, too. So, for the old game show experts among you, the name is the same, but the rules have been changed to protect the ignorant. Feel free to continue to change the structure to fit your needs.

Structure:

Select as many contestants, people who are guessing, and panelists, people who are answering, as you like.

The contestants will ask the panelists questions about their daily tasks. Eventually, the contestants will guess what the panelists do for a job. They may opt to guess when they feel they are ready, or perhaps they'll wait until the end and all guess simultaneously. For each correct answer they'll gain points or cash or some commodity with value in your classroom (chips, marbles, etc.). For each incorrect answer, they'll lose a point. As always there is a host, who mediates, congratulates, and oozes plastic sincerity.

> *Example:* Students ask questions about occupations within the community. The panelists are the Mailman, the Grocer, and the School Superintendent.
> *Example:* Young scientists ask about the function of simple machines. The panelists are the wedge, the lever, and the crank.
> *Example:* Students ask questions about the daily life of people during medieval times. The panelists are a priest, a noble, a knight, and the king.

Directions:

1. As a group, the students choose which characters will be involved.

2. Cast the scene.

3. Pair up a contestant and a panelist to research at least eight facts about the daily life of the panelist. This team will also think of three questions that they think would work in the show.

4. The host or hosts should write the opening and closing show jargon, including some general statements about the topic at the beginning. Wrap up at the end with some more specific language in conclusion, toss in a sponsor and some game show humor.

5. The entire group meets again:

* To cross out any duplicate questions.
* To decide which remaining questions will be used.
* To make sure each panelist is aware of all the questions, and has an answer, even if it's "That's not my department" or "How should I know?"
* And to decide the seating order and the question order.

Add costumes or props if you wish.

Create Your Own Game Show

The Ingredients:

A Game Show Name

Commercials: Optional

A Host

An Announcer, to introduce the host, talk about sponsors, introduce guests, etc.

An Audience participation card. For audiences to applaud, or respond with specific requested words: "No!", "Give it up," "Go for it," "You've got to be kidding," "Try Again," etc.

Contestants, someone who is playing the game.

Panelists, any number will do.

A Goal. What is the point your students want to share? Are they demonstrating many specific facts and figures, such as vocabulary, math concepts, or historical figures and their points of view? Do they have a large concept in mind, through which your game show can demonstrate consequences due to choices made and actions taken now?

Example: Game Show Titles:
* It's Time to Tell You: (To Stop Smoking)
* What's My Future?
* Choice and Consequences
* Testing Hera and Zeus: A Game for the Mythologically Daring
* Tall Tale or True Tale
* Legends and Liars
* Act It Out

Sample Game Show Skit Beginning:

Announcer: Ladies and gentlemen, it's time to play "Make a Good Decision," the new game show that provides all our viewers with insight into today's controversial topics. We have a special show lined up for you tonight, one that will interest young and old viewers alike. Tonight we'll be asking some studio teenagers to make some decisions. But first a word from our sponsor.

Stage Manager: Cut!

(Brief Commercial Goes Here.)

Stage Manager: Okay, we're in at 5, 4, 3, 2, 1...

Announcer: Welcome back, ladies and gentlemen. Tonight we have the rare opportunity to ... We have agreed to keep the identity of this teenager a secret. So she'll be in partial disguise.

Sample Game Show Skit Ending:

Announcer: We'd like to thank your teens this evening, and thank our studio audience. Tonight, if you make a decision, make it a good one.

Gestures: Positive Negative

Ages: Grades 4-9

Tools: None

Drama involves taking a risk. Standing up for yourself, and declaring what you do or do not understand in front of your peers can be tough. Breaking through those self-imposed limits is one of the reasons I believe drama is valuable in the first place. Nevertheless, doing any activity involving personal risk is impossible in an environment where others will pounce on you. In these situations, students become afraid of doing poorly, and of doing well.

I use Positive Negative Gestures whenever I see negativity between students. I like this activity because it qualifies simple eye rolls, lip curls, and rude territorial positioning as negative gestures. From this point on, no one can say "I'm not doing anything!", because the class recognizes that behavior as negative. . It helps to do it early on because then the standards are set, and you can gently refer back to them, rather than stopping an activity midway and drawing so much attention to the detractors. Once a vocabulary of negative gestures is established, if I see any afloat, I broadly thank the student for demonstrating a new negative gesture which we will now add to our list of unacceptable ones.

Directions:

1. Form a circle of standing students.

2. Tell the students you'll be passing gestures around in the circle. Negative first, and then positive. (I always like to end with positive, as a way of pointing out the alternatives to the negative choices.)

3. Talk about negative gestures and what they can look like, from abruptly turning your head away from someone so you won't have to acknowledge them, to sticking your finger in your mouth to imitate throwing up. A shoulder shift can be negative, if you're deliberately placing it between you and the student. Rolling eyes is classic, especially if you have a face full of bad attitude to go with it.

4. Tell your students that no negative gestures that mean words will be acceptable. I always say that those are automatically added to the unacceptable list.

5. Standing in the circle, turn to one side and pass a negative gesture, by sharing it with a student. Stick your tongue out at him, or show a thumbs down, etc. That student will then turn to the next student and pass a different negative gesture. Each student will pass a new negative gesture all the way around the circle.

6. Compliment them on their fine selections as they go. Draw as much attention to the different gestures as you can through praise. I usually say, "That's ruthless, good, good. Full of attitude. Excellent!

7. Pass the gestures all the way around the class. The last student will share their gesture with you, which is always an unusual experience for them.

8. Make it clear that they did a great job, and these gestures are now officially not acceptable in the class.

9. Repeat the process going back in the opposite direction. This way, each student will be sharing a positive gesture with the very student who just showed them a negative one.

Tip:

1. Point out that negative gestures, even in fun, have negative effects. Share some of your observations of student reactions to negative gestures, even when everyone knew the students were acting. The student who must show you a negative gesture will have a hard time. Point out that it's understandable for them to have a hard time, because even in fun, these gestures are disrespectful and can be misconstrued.

2. If they're stuck for new gestures, tell them to combine a few, and see the effect. (It's actually refreshing if

they can't think of more. It doesn't happen often.)

Group Up

Ages: Grades 1- Adult

Tools: Space

Directions:

1. Players walk around the room, weaving in and out in an open space, not bumping or touching each other.

2. The leader gives a signal for players to begin searching for a specific group of students within the larger group.

3. When all the groups have found their members, the leader introduces each group and everyone in that group cheers for their category. If there is a topic where one or two people are in it, it's nice to have the entire group cheer with them.

Sample Group Up Topics:

Favorite Color	Shoe Size
Age	Favorite Dessert
Favorite Vegetable	Favorite Musical Group
Month you were born	

Group Up has hundreds of curriculum variations. On the basic level it's a guaranteed interactive warm-up. Group Up is about mixing and blending with peers, requiring them to break down any inappropriate barriers in your class.

Improvisation

im.pro.vise: 1. to compose, or simultaneously compose and perform, on the spur of the moment and without any preparation; extemporize. *(Webster's New World Dictionary)*

Phew! Improvisation does mean what I think it means. It's pure and simple, like a commercial. Just do it. I've read so many approaches to improvisation that decree the First Rule of Improvisation, the Only Approach to Improvisation, the Difficult Truth About Improvisation, I was afraid Webster might have several pages of do-or-die rules and regulations. These books are great, but they always make me feel as if I need to know how to take apart my car before I can drive it. Relax; it's easier than you think. If you don't believe me, ask Webster.

Improvisation, by definition, involves no preparation, but having a structure of where to begin helps, because if you ask your students to improvise without preparing them, it's like asking someone to paint a painting without any idea of where to begin.

Improvisation is like any other creative activity, such as writing, painting, drawing, even juggling. The more we do any one of them, the better we become. There are thousands of theories about the right and wrong ways to approach them, but very few of them would be right for everybody.

The many available approaches to improvisation are valuable, however, because they offer a structure within which to begin. Not only will they help you drive, but they'll help you fix the engine when it stops working. If you find an approach that works well for you, use that. There is no one right way.

Improvisation works well as a teaching tool, and an even better assessment tool, because people talk about what they know. Ten-year-olds talk about baby-sitters, siblings, homework, bullies, and parents. Fifteen-year-olds talk about dating, having crushes, grades, pressure, preparing for college. If you listen to them long enough you'll notice the line where their experience ends. If you give them a specific curriculum topic to include in their improvisation, you'll easily see how much they have assimilated. I use improv for problem solving, writing, listening, and as a warm-up all the time.

Conductor

Ages: Grades 1-4

Tools: A pencil, ruler, or finger for a baton.

Conductor is a game about improvising in groups. It can be a great warm-up and will relate to any curriculum area where sound is involved.

Examples of Sounds to Conduct:
* A rocket to the moon taking off
* Any form of bad weather
* A flea market in Tibet
* Any setting from the book you are reading in class
* A real orchestra
* A rain forest
* A circus
* A medieval sports event

Directions:

1. Create a gesture vocabulary that all students will understand. Using conductor gestures is the easiest, but decide on each one, and make sure they are all clear to your students.

Choose a gesture for the following terms:
* Warm up
* Come to attention (tapping baton)
* Loud, Louder, Give it all you have
* Soft, Softer, Barely audible
* Stop
* Individual playing (pointing)
* Section playing (whole hand pointing)

2. Depending on the topic chosen, the conductor will probably want to designate sections before playing. Some conductors may prefer to call out requested sounds while conducting, to keep the players on their toes, and prevent any I-don't-want-to-be-that-syndrome. Example: Rain forest Orchestra Sections: the birds, the insects, the large cats, the monkeys, large and small, etc.

3. Have students stand. Sound conducts farther when they're standing. Begin with a warm-up time (about twenty seconds) for all students to check their sounds and tune their imaginary instruments.

4. Bring them to attention. Remind them to smile to the imaginary audience.

5. Conduct the music. You, as conductor, will control the level of chaos. Perhaps everyone is making raindrop sounds, and then a few thunder sounds emerge on top of it. Perhaps only one section goes at a time.

Tips:

1. You may want to listen to a tape of your chosen sounds beforehand, if you have one available. Many grocery stores have environmental tapes. Also, a tape of orchestral music, or a few minutes of the movie *Fantasia,* may help anyone who hasn't seen an orchestra, or doesn't know how it works.

2. An orchestra design helps keep the class from doing sounds all at the same time. Encourage them to listen to each other as they play.

3. Don't worry about conducting if you're not a musician yourself. For more drama, you may want to end on a very loud note, or build to a very loud note and then, section by section, slowly bring it down to a barely audible murmur. Whatever way you want to do it is fine. Have fun with it.

I Need to Sit There

Some of these games are like folk tales. They're passed on and on with a variation here and there. Finding the original source can be next to impossible. I learned this game as Park Bench, but recently read a version with the same name, which was entirely different. With all due respect to the original bench warmers, enjoy the game.

Ages: Grade 4-8.

Tools: Three chairs lined up in a row.

Directions:

1. One student begins by establishing a character, perhaps through action as he walks on, or by talking to himself on his way to the bench.

2. Only one character may sit on the bench at a time. This is not the best real-life solution, where sharing would be better. It's just a rule for the game.

3. A second character approaches the bench and asks to sit down.

4. The characters discuss their separate reasons for needing the bench.

5. They listen to each other's reasons and help to solve their own problem (needing the bench) by solving the other person's problem (finding them a place to go).

6. Eventually the first student seated needs to find a way to leave. He can do this without losing face by miraculously solving his own problem.

7. The second student sits down, keeping the same character he or she was before. A third student approaches needing to sit down.

Tips:

1. Students should choose a specific character, and know why that character needs to sit down. The more they know about their character the easier it will be for them to speak on their character's behalf. If they don't know who they are, then the discussions become arguments with no valuable information being shared.

2. There should be no violent actions. It's too easy to point a gun at someone and order them to move. I always tell them, "You're discovering creative solutions. Violence is neither creative nor a solution."

3. No grossness. It's too easy to vomit on someone and get them to leave. Encourage the students to use their brains instead.

4. Remind the students not to have their backs to the audience. They should stand to the side of the bench or behind it, looking over at the other player. Standing directly in front of the bench will block out sound and any interest from the class.

5. I use this game when the class is having trouble listening to each other and cooperating. Players must listen to each other to in order to play.

6. I recommend using this game with small groups, or to fill ten to fifteen minutes here and there. Everyone will want to play, but few will want to listen to the other players for longer than fifteen minutes.

7. Try having the bench be in a different setting. One day the bench can be in the park. Another day it can be

in the mall or the school cafeteria. See how that opens up the ideas for your students.

Sample Characters with reasons to need to sit on the bench:
* An old lady who feeds the pigeons every day at the same time.
* A city worker who needs to paint the bench.
* A grandmother who has many bags from shopping, who loves to show countless pictures of her grandchildren.
* A jogger who needs to sit down.
* A person with a broken leg.
* A child meeting his mother on a certain bench at a certain time.
* Someone meeting a blind date on the bench.
* Someone having a leg spasm.
* A crying child looking for a lost dog.
* Someone who needs to fix her skates.
* A homeless person who is ready to go to sleep on the bench.
* An architect who needs to sit on the bench to get proper pictures of the building across the street.
* A security worker throwing his weight around, who is really just tired.
* Someone waiting for the bus.

Sample solutions to stay on the bench by helping the other person:
* "That's Bus #14 over there."
* "There are many other benches in this park. You could sit on a different one."
* "I think I saw your lost dog over there."
* "The smog from that local factory isn't good for you, breathing so heavily after you've been jogging."
* "Does your mom have red hair? That must be her waiting at that bench."
* "Didn't I just hear your name over the loudspeaker? They're waiting for you at customer service."
* "Your pigeons are looking a little chubby. Perhaps they could cut their snack short today—for their health, of course."
* "There's a man walking around near that monument with a red rose in his hand. Are you sure he said to meet you at this bench?"

Sample ways to save face and leave the bench yourself:
* "What the heck. Have a seat. I was just getting up anyway." (Simple generosity. Always a good idea.)
* "Oh, there's my bus now."
* "Well, if you wouldn't mind feeding my pigeons for me, I do have to go home and do Tae Bo."
* "Oh. Too late. Quitting time. I guess I'll have to paint the bench tomorrow."
* "Okay, but if Ed McMahon brings a check, you tell him I went home."
* "Ah, is that the time? How did it get to be this late? I have to go."

Sound Circles
Ages: Grades 6 - adult

During college, I took a semester at the National Theater Institute, a theatrical boot camp, at the Eugene O'Neill Theater Center, in Waterford, CT. We took classes seven days a week from seven a.m. to ten p.m. and then stayed up all night, every night, doing homework for those classes. I learned a great deal there, about costuming, set design, directing, acting, mime and dance. I absorbed information, even though I didn't have time to reflect on it at the time. Months later, people would ask me where I learned a specific technique, and my first response would be, "I don't know". There are positive and negative side affects of working at that pace.

One activity I remember was a sound circle. Many of us played instruments. Students, who didn't already have instruments, found blocks, sticks, shells etc. Others made sounds with their voices. Together we sat with our eyes closed, listening to each other, and finding the appropriate places to contribute or simply listen, we slowly built an improvisational piece of music. We must have been good at it, because I remember being showcased to the many celebrities who were often in and out of the O'Neill. I remember being impressed with the sounds and passages that emerged out of my flute.

On many levels, the sound circle is too sophisticated for the elementary and secondary classroom, so I have adapted the ideas to be appropriate for these ages.

At any age, this activity is an exercise in learning to know when to "speak" and when to listen. It also serves as a great activity to help students put themselves into an imaginary setting.

Directions:

1. Sit students in a circle facing away from each other. It helps to have enough room so they won't be distracted by objects in the room,

2. Ask students to close their eyes and listen to the background sounds around them.

3. Ask them to open their eyes and identify some of the sounds.

4. Ask them if any of the sounds are overlapping each other. Are some going on simultaneously? Are there any which stand out because they don't overlap others?

5. Tell them that you will be creating sound effects for a place, and to keep these thoughts in mind when you do. Having a sound barge in and take over, doesn't make it stand out in any special way.

6. Think of a school setting which the students are familiar with. (The classroom first thing in the morning, recess on the playground, gym class, the last few moments before a school assembly, etc.)

7. Ask them to close their eyes again, imagine the activities in that place and slowly recreate the sounds within that place.

8. Gently guide them, with slow calm words, such as begin, fade, and end.

9. When the sound circle has finished, discuss anything the students believe would make it better. Ask if the sounds helped them feel like they were truly in the setting.

Tips and Variations:

1. If you sit in the center of the circle, with your students' backs to you, they can hear each other, and you can quietly tap anyone who may need a gentle reminder to listen more and share less.

2. Try a variety of settings. rain forests, zoos, prairies, campfires, medieval feasts, the moon.

3. Remind them that "snapshots", Barry Lane's concept of word pictures, which include everything which can be observed through a magic camera, including sounds and smells, would include these sounds as well. If a snapshot helps a reader feel like they are in the setting, see how much these sounds would add to the snapshot's effect.

Who, What, Where

Ages: Grades 5-8.

Realistic Scenes: Have students create situations on cards. On each card fill in a who, a what, and a where.

Who: Characters, two or three.

What: The activity or subject of discussion.

Where: The setting. A scene will change depending on the setting. A student conversation with a parent about grades will be different in the grocery store from what it would be in the waiting room outside the principal's office.

Choose two students. Have them pick a card, and act out the scene.

Realistic Curriculum-Based Scenes:

Choose a subject or category that the scenes must involve. The more the students know about a particular topic, the better the scenes will be. Then follow the directions above.

Example: Family scenes.

Family scenes in another culture.

Family scenes one hundred years from now.

Scenes involving mythological gods and goddesses.

Family scenes within the colonial period.

Scenes from the 1950s.

Scenes involving a conflict.

Scenes where only inanimate objects can be characters.

Directions for Realistic Scenes with Abstract Possibilities:

1. Have students decide upon a who, a what, and a where and list them on separate pieces of paper.

2. Have a student choose a card from each pile. Each performer should have his or her own who card.

3. Give them one or two minutes to decide how to incorporate any unusual topics. Have them perform.

4. Students should play them realistically, even though the scenes may be realistically impossible.

Example: A nun and a wrestler watching a soap opera together on the beach.

The scene would be normal to the nun and the wrestler, because there may be a perfectly logical explanation to them. Maybe the reasons will come out in the scene. They may want to discuss the variety of reactions they are getting from other beach lovers.

Sample Who Suggestions:

Occupation characters:

doctor	dentist	store clerk	butcher	computer repair person
audiologist	phone solicitor	teacher	principal	wedding photographer
school nurse	animal trainer	mailman	fireman	gossip columnist
holistic healer	tree farmer	movie star	sports star	garbage collector
news anchor	veterinarian	plumber	electrician	President of the United States

Fairy tale characters: Any of the dwarves, Snow White, Cinderella, the generic Prince Charming, Sleeping Beauty, Bambi, Fairy Godmother, Goldilocks, an ugly stepsister (stress ugly as behavior, not looks), the Three Little Pigs, the Big Bad Wolf, etc.

Characters from literature: Madeline, Harry Potter, Marty, Shiloh's owner, Charlotte, Wilbur, the Cat in the Hat, Heidi, Ramona, Nate the Great, Fudge, etc.

Family members: Mother, father, sister, brother, Aunt Gladys who pinches cheeks, Grandpa who only ever talks about fishing. Grandma who is hard of hearing and starts every sentence with "When I was your age..." The older sister who is a perfectionist. The brother who is a notorious slob, etc.

Sample What Suggestions:

Talking about:

grades	colleges	stressful day	person you have a crush on
your health	relatives	jobs	complaining about an employer
new outfit	TV show	recent game	plans for an upcoming trip
siblings	dreams	new teacher	a death in the family
drugs	cigarettes	alcohol	making good choices
food	injuries	new pet	cheating on a test
politics	spirituality	saving money	an inability to communicate

Activities:

painting a picture	doing aerobics	trying on clothes	making jewelry
baking cookies	reading the news	checking the want ads	replacing light bulbs
dusting	scooping poop	planting bulbs	painting a house
posing for pictures	sewing a costume	doing a puzzle	cleaning a fish tank
changing a tire	removing a splinter	watering plants	raking leaves
doing laundry	sorting socks	cleaning out cupboard	listening to CDs
watching a movie	cooking a soufflé	carving an ice sculpture	learning to read
waiting in line			

Sample Where Suggestions:

a grocery store	a bowling alley	a furniture store	a church
a car, in traffic	a car dealership	a birthday party	a barn
haunted house	school cafeteria	on a train	on a plane
a talk show	a circus	at a mall	in a fancy restaurant
in a park	at the beach	at a roller rink	at the movies
video store	in a garden	in a classroom	the principal's office
at a funeral	a local parade	a bookstore	a lumber yard
a pumpkin patch	a soccer field	bleachers at a game	an art studio

Tips for all Who, What, Where Improvisations:

1. It's easier to start with two players than three, unless there are two role categories. *Example:* Two kids and a mom, two customers and one clerk, etc.

2. Encourage them to keep the relationships true. If a student wouldn't stick his tongue out at the principal in real life, then keep those same relationship boundaries in the improvisation. If they can manage to forget that their best friend is playing the principal, then they'll settle into a deeper level of the scene.

3. Remember the no violence and appropriate behavior rules.

4. You may have a group of students who believe that arguing is interesting dialogue, when actually it can drag a scene to the depths of dull. At a HOTS (Higher Order Thinking School's) conference last summer, the workshop leaders from Artsgenesis in New York City, recommend using the rule of "Yes, Yes, Good." Yes to each individual creative process. Yes to the creative process of the group surrounding them, and always make each other look good. Once an improviser says a sentence, it becomes true.

Example: *Arguing:*

    1: Don't let them know that we're FBI agents.

    2: But we're not!

    1: Yeah, we are!

    2: No, we're not!

Yes, Yes, Good (Once something is said, it's now truth):

1: Don't let them know that we're FBI agents.

2: All right, but if they find out, don't tell them my specialty is palm reading.

1: You're right. We don't want to spend our whole night telling their futures. That will definitely hold up the investigation.

2: But will you tell mine?

1: Sure.

Lean and Leave

Ages: Grades 4-10. (Sometimes grade 3, if you have a mature class)

Tools: Space

This game was created by my mentor, Barbara Goodwillie. You will find Lean and Leave and other great drama strategies, in her book *Breaking Through, Drama Strategies for 10's to 15's.* New Plays Books, Rowayton, CT 06853

I use this game as a warm up, a discussion starter, and a visual demonstration of complex systems, including the food chain, the rain forest, and government. It is a great model for any system requiring cooperation and support for individuals who are doing their best to support their own weight.

Directions:

1. Have students stand in a large circle.

2. Ask them to lean as far forward as they can without falling over.

3. Try leaning backwards and then to the side.

4. Bring up a student and demonstrate how you can lean on the him without putting any actual weight on him. I usually put my elbow on the student's shoulder.

5. Ask the student to walk away from you while you remain in the same posed leaning position.

6. Challenge all the students to support their own weight. Without this agreement, you cannot play the game. There will be a large pile of students, and you will have wasted time instead of playing a potentially fun game. I always try to do this in the most positive way. I wouldn't try this with a group as young as you in any other school, but I think you can handle it.

7. Ask for another student volunteer to stand in the middle of the circle and strike a pose.

8. Ask for other students to lean in creative, yet appropriate, poses on the first student.(Encourage them to not all lean on shoulders.)

9. When all five or six students have posed, tap a few of them on the shoulder and ask them to leave. You will have created an interesting statue of a few people in strange poses. (You may want the outside circle to give the statue a caption) Applaud and send these students back.

10. Give each student a number, 1, 2 or 3.

11. Have all the 1's enter the circle and lean on each other, supporting their own weight, and being appropriate.

12. Once the 1's are set, ask them to stay there and have the 2's lean on the 1's.

13. Once the 2's are set. Ask the 1's to leave.

14. Take a moment to comment on the pose, and give the students the opportunity to support their own weight without any extra support.

15. Leave the 2's and have the 3's lean on them. (Depending on the difficulty of the poses, you may also give any group the opportunity to fill in and support another group, rather than lean on them.)

16. Have the 2's leave.

17. Look at the poses for a moment.

18. Have the 1's lean on the 3's.

19. Leave the 3's this time.

20. Have the 2's lean on the 1's and the 3's.

21. Bring groups out, in order, or at your own discretion, depending on who needs to come out first.

22. Have all groups form the original circle.

23. Sit down.

24. Ask them what this game might have to do with the topic you are about to study. Find out what they think. I always tell them there are no right answers, I just want to know what they think. Usually I learn something I haven't thought of. My goals to play the game are different every time. If I'm teaching endangered species, we talk about the time when students were indeed supporting their own weight, but at times, it was still easier to have support systems there. We talk about how long they could support themselves if all their support systems are lost. Would they be able to move and find more support systems? If I'm talking about putting on a play, we discuss individual responsibility and group support.

Line Up (Circle Up)

Ages: Grades 1-7

Tools: Space. Cards, optional.

Students line up many times a day. The only difference here is that they line up in a specific order, facing the audience.

Give them a topic, either written on small cards or verbally. Players will interact with each other, sharing cards or oral information, and gradually line themselves in order forming a line facing the group, or if you prefer, a circle.

Line Up is a simple concept, and the variations are endless.

Example:

Brownie Pledge: The other day my daughter went to her first Brownie meeting. At the end of the meeting the new leaders went over the Brownie pledge. Then each person picked a card with one word of the pledge on it. Lining themselves up in order of the pledge and reading their cards in order several times helped the new first-grade, not-quite-reading Brownies participate actively in learning their new pledge.

Sample Line Up Topics:
* The month players were born, in order.
* Shoe size, in order.
* Age, in order

* The answers to math equations, in order.
* A number line.
* A time line, with specific events.
* Sequencing events in a story.

Machines

Abstract

Ages: Grades 2-10

Tools: Space.

Directions:

1. Begin with a student volunteer. Ask him to create a simple repetitive mechanical movement with his body, such as an arm swinging at the elbow, a hand waving back and forth, or a head looking from side to side.

2. Next, the same student should come up with a sound to go with that movement. He should make the sound and the movement simultaneously.

3. Other students will add to the machine one at a time, by making a movement and sound that complement the original movement by feeding it or receiving from it.

Example: By kneeling on the floor, the second student could repeatedly lift imaginary objects up to the first student, who is swinging his arm from one side to the other. The third student grasps the imaginary object from the second student and swings it over the top of her head.

4. Students may place themselves at a high level (standing), a medium level (kneeling or bending), or a low level (sitting or lying down).

5. Gradually, a giant machine is made, one student at a time, using all the students in the class.

6. Add a student to be the electrical cord and plug.

7. Decide on a place for a volume button and a speed control (a hair barrette, a watch).

8. Turn the speed down to slow motion.

9. Turn the volume completely off.

10. Turn the speed up to high. (I wouldn't recommend turning the volume up high when the speed is high.)

11. Plug and unplug the electrical cord. Let the machine react accordingly.

Optional: Depending on the length of time it took to construct the machine, the first students are, most likely, exhausted by now. The following option was designed to refocus them for a group finish.

12. Tell them you're an abstract machine dealer and you've sold the machine, but first you must box it up and move it to New York City. Have students maintain the same spatial relationships but reduce the size by moving them in as close as possible without touching each other.

13. Nail up an imaginary crate around them.

14. Have them move as an intact group sideways, as if traveling in the box.

15. Remove the imaginary crate.

16. Plug in the plug and test the volume and sound. Sell them for an outrageous sum of money!

Tips:

1. When building the original model, turn the sound down low as you add on machine parts in order to hear each new sound, and preserve your ear drums.

2. Make sure students choose a comfortable position and action they can repeat countless times. There will be students who will insist that they can do a backflip-handspring-cartwheel one hundred times, without a problem. They may not know it, but they're lying! They should begin with a comfortable action. If they change midway through construction, all the other weary parts will revolt just when you're encouraging the late bloomers.

Realistic

Ages: Grades K-6

Directions:

1. Choose a household machine and build it with the class as a model.

Example: Toaster

2. Tell the students to imagine a toaster, and all the parts of it, even the parts they can't see.

Toaster Parts and Accessories

cord	plug	button to push the toast down
sides	middle	heat elements on both sides of the toast
bread	knife	dark/light knob
jelly	butter	hungry person
napkin	glass	milk

3. One at a time, have the students choose a specific part and come to the center of the room and become that part.

It isn't necessary to build it in proper mechanical order. Build it as you would a puzzle, placing people parts where you would imagine they would go, as the students suggest them. When it becomes obvious that a central piece is missing, ask the students to help you think of what it is.

Following along in student idea order, you may begin with the toast, or rather, the bread. Yes, the bread is the last step, but if that's what they think of first, then that's what they visualize first. So help their visualization by creating it in the space in front of them. Have two children become the bread, standing parallel to each other, with their arms outstretched, trying to be flat. Next, a cord. Have the child lie on the floor, with one end toward the nearest wall. If there isn't a wall nearby, have another child be one. If you have a large class, another child could be the plug on the end. Third, the sides. Choose two children to be the sides. Double machine parts are an excellent way to involve the student who generated the idea, and another one, of your choosing, who may not generate an idea easily in front of a classroom of peers.

If it becomes clear that the students aren't coming up with a central part, start asking questions. What do we need here? I see the sides, but what will hold them up and keep them from falling over? How will the bread get enough heat to change it?, etc.

When the toaster is in place, act out a sequence. Feel free to ham it up. If you're not comfortable hamming it up, ask a student to do it. You'll know just the right child.

You're so hungry. A nice piece of toast is just what you're looking for. Unwrap the imaginary wrapper around the bread. Take out two pieces and put them in (if they're not already there). Decide how dark or light you want the toast, and adjust the child knob accordingly. Push the button down, talking to yourself as you go, so the bread will follow along. Well, the bread is down, but it's not heating up. Whoops! It's not plugged in. Gross! There's a drop of yesterday's jelly on the child wall. Better wipe it off.

Later, you can toss in a few suggestions, such as the toast doesn't look quite dark enough for you, so you'll have to push it down again, etc. Follow all the way through the butter and jelly to your first bite.

Tips:

1. Depending on your class, and the available time for this model exercise, you may want to be the designer, and decide their poses for them. Show them how to be parallel bread, heating elements that are on versus off, etc. In a smaller group, where there won't be so many restless natives awaiting their turn, it's always nice to have the students take the time to create their visualizations. If you're not sure how a heating element should look. Ask them. Someone will know.

2. Follow up with Realistic Machines for Small Groups.

Realistic for Small Groups

Ages: Grades 1-7

Directions:

1. Model machine building with human bodies, as instructed in Machines: Realistic. (Not necessary for grade 7.)

2. Divide the class into groups of four or five. Have them decide on a machine.

3. Construct it for a few minutes.

4. Share it with the rest of the class.

Sample Realistic Machines

dishwasher	stove	microwave	TV	computer	gas/electric grill
stereo	CD player	boom box	hair dryer	curling iron	electric toothbrush
humidifier	dryer	scanner	fan	VCR	washing machine
computer printer	space heater	bread maker	alarm clock	blender	popcorn popper
pasta maker	coin organizer	Cuisinart	mixer	gas fireplace	electric razor
electric curlers	remote control	caller ID	digital camera	copier	air conditioner
lawn mower	cell phone	chain saw	car jack	beeper	video game controller
leaf blower	electric chopper	fax machine	vacuum cleaner	lamp	tel. message machine
weed whacker	electric broom				

Tips:

1. Remember, if you give them five minutes, they'll come up with a machine. If you give them fifteen, they'll argue for ten and come up with a machine in the last five minutes. If they're working well together but need more time, reward them for working well with an extra minute or two.

2. Adding details to their machine will make it more interesting to the audience, the same way it does in their writing. Show them how to designate their shirt buttons to be choice buttons on a soda machine, their noses to be return levers, etc. The more they visualize their machines, the better off they will be.

3. This activity needs bodies, so you may be tempted to go for six in a group, but larger groups are better at arguing than working. If they find they need an extra body, when the machine is all worked out, they may import one from another group.

4. Sometimes they'll need a person to operate the machine. Again they may either import one or have you do it.

Community Machines

Ages: Grades 1-7

Follow the directions for Realistic Machines in large or small groups.

Sample Community Machines

soda machine	bottle recycling machine	ATM
vending machine	gas pump	car wash
cash register	karaoke machine	pinball machine
X-ray machine	backhoe	bulldozer
garbage truck	drive-through intercom	roller coaster
traffic light	flashing highway sign	tractor

Fantasy Machines: Inventions

Ages: Grades 1-7

Have small groups of students design, construct, and demonstrate imaginary inventions.
Follow the directions for Realistic Machines in Small Groups.

Tips:

1. Encourage students to describe the process during their demonstrations. They may want to demonstrate these in the form of a commercial, pointing out the specific benefits, and the value.

2. Remind them that most inventions are created to solve a problem or serve a need. Calculators were once unthinkable.

Sample Fantasy Machines:

Magic Homework Machine	Brother Eliminator
Three Wishes Machine	Houseworknomore
Eversharp Pencil	Invisibilator (for when you don't know the answer)

Living Machines: Animals, Insects (Real and Imaginary)

Ages: Grades 1-7

Directions:

1. Demonstrate building an animal the same way you would building a household machine for the class. (See Realistic Machines.)

2. Choose an animal and consider all of its parts.

3. Have students visualize the animal, and choose one part that they would like to become. For demonstration purposes, you may want to choose a large animal with many parts. As you construct the animal, take a moment to discuss the reasons animals have their specific features. In machines, form follows function. It works for animals, too.

Example: Stegosaurus. The plates on its back helped to regulate its temperature and protect it against attackers.

Sample Stegosaurus Parts and Accessories

Parts	# of Students
head	1 student
four feet with claws	4 students with extended fingers
spine with plates	12-14 students, forming the spine with each hand forming a plate on each side. Near the head they are sitting. Moving back they are progressively kneeling, standing, kneeling, sitting, and lying down to become the tail.
2 sides	2-4 students positioned between the front and back legs
4 tail spikes	2 students with two pointed hand spikes on each side of the tail
A plant	1 student, sitting near the head ready to be lunch

Tips: Extensions

1. Follow up with students acting out animals in smaller groups of four or five. Have each group decide on their own animal, or have all the groups try being the same animal. Watching many different versions of the same animal will culminate in a clear understanding of the animal, and many visual details.

2. This activity works well for animal study and cooperation practice, and comes in handy if you're acting out a play and need to have five children play the dragon. It also will work well as a prewriting exercise about animals. If a child has been the rabbit's wiggling nose and long delicate whiskers in between two clear alert eyes, for ten minutes, he or she is less likely to describe the rabbit as simply "cute."

Match Up (Kid Card Shuffle)

Ages: Grades 1-9

Tools: Space, cards with pairs.

Directions to Prepare:

Make cards or have students make cards with clear matching partners.

Sample Match Up Topics:

* Vocabulary Words to Definitions
* Pictures to Written Words
* Answers to Equations
* Animals in Pairs
* Two Equivalent Equations (5 3 = 5 + 5 + 5)
* Match Two Equivalent Fractions
* Matching Homophones
* Matching Words to Symbols
* Fahrenheit to Celsius

C. GLYNN

Directions to Play:

Each player chooses a card. Within the stack, each card has a pair. Players mill around an open space, interacting with everyone to find their partner.

Directions to Play Again: The Kid and Card Shuffle

If you want to play again, and don't want to reshuffle the cards yourself, mill the students around the room again, trading their cards with each other three times. Consider them shuffled.

Tips:

1. If your group is notoriously chatty, have them do it silently.

2. Try playing music behind them to set the mood of the activity.

Variations:

1. Have one half of the group begin at one end of the room, and their partner pairs begin at the other end.

2. Have them move toward each other demonstrating a characteristic of their cards Example: Divide a deck of Go Fish. Have the players act out the animal on their card, until they find their mate.

3. Match up pairs that are equivalent, but not exact duplications. Example: 3 3 pairs up with 9, or 11 2, etc. Match up degrees in Fahrenheit and Celsius. By the time you are finished, no one will ever forget the difference, or how to calculate it.

Name Game: Descriptive Word and Movement

There are hundreds of variations of the Name Game, and the most obvious benefit is learning everyone's name. They also serve as an opportunity for students to celebrate themselves in front of their peers. I learned this one from Nancy Kerr Butler when we were in the Penny Ante Theater.

Ages: Grades 1-6.

Tools: Space.

1. Each player will think of a word that describes them that starts with the same letter or sound as the first letter in their name. I have been Crazy Carol, Cranky Carol, Cool Carol, as well as Goofy Glynn, Gorgeous Glynn (always stress the positive!), Grumpy Glynn, and Great Glynn.

2. Each player should also create and demonstrate a movement to go with their new descriptive word and their name. I almost said "think" of a movement, but the students who will have trouble coming up with a movement are "thinking" too hard. Encourage them to let their bodies just do something.

3. Then, one by one, each player will demonstrate his or her name, descriptive word, and movement in a loud, positive, enthusiastic manner. They are, in effect, calling to the group. The group will answer them by repeating their exact demonstration back to them.

Variations:

1. Repeat the preceding names in reverse every time a student adds one. Example: Cranky Carol is first. The class responds to her. Marvelous Marisa is second. The class says Marvelous Marisa and then Cranky Carol. Next you have Dashing Dan, so the class says Dashing Dan, Marvelous Marisa, and Cranky Carol, etc.

2. This is an active game. Repeating every student name each time is great for those choice times, like the day after Halloween, but if it's too exhausting for your group, try repeating them in groups of five and then starting a new group. At the end, go around one more time and repeat the entire group.

3. If you have seven students whose names begin with the same letter, and you've run out of descriptive J words, try adding some action words (Jumping John, Juggling Jennifer).

Tips:

1. Everyone should choose their word and action before the game begins, or you'll never get through it.

2. If a student is truly stuck for a word or movement, ask for positive suggestions. Then set your own limit. Sometimes a kid can hear great words describing them from their peers and use those. Sometimes they're

just holding up the show.

3. A student who is resisting a movement is usually doing one, on a miniature level, by swaying or shrugging, etc. I usually point that out, on an exaggerated level, and say that's fine.

Clap, Clap, Slap, Slap Name Game

Ages: Grades 1-adult

Directions:

1. Standing in a circle, the leader demonstrates a series of clapping gestures. My favorite series involves clapping hands on the thighs twice, clapping hands together twice, snapping fingers once, and completing the gesture by throwing both hands up in the air with fingers energetically spread apart.

2. Do this several times while describing the game, ending each series with your hands in the air and saying Chhhh! The sequence sounds like this: slap, slap, clap, clap, snap, chhh!

3. Put your name in the place of the Chhh! You'll have Slap, slap, clap, clap, snap, (CAROL!)

4. The group follows the series and repeats your name in the Chhh! space.

Next, we follow around the circle without missing a beat. We repeat the sequence of gestures twice for each player. The first time they say their name in the Chhh! space of our clapping. The second time we all say it.

Variations:

1. If you play this game on a regular basis, as a gathering or greeting activity, you might consider encouraging the students to demonstrate a unique, personal (and always appropriate) pose or gesture during the Chhh! beat as they say their name.

Example Poses: Muscleman arms, hands over heart, hands on shoulders, hands framing the face, etc.

2. I have used this activity as a lively way to demonstrate student names in a show, rather than introduce the cast in a more conventional way. "Thank you for joining us, we're slap, slap, clap, clap, snap, Cathy, slap, slap, clap, clap, snap, Matt," etc.

News

Ages: Grades 5-10

Tools: A few tables and chairs. Student-generated props and costumes.

Once again, a familiar structure to follow, with plenty of room for creative modification. After all, that's what the networks do on a daily basis. A perfect format for a mix of education and entertainment.

Cast:

News anchors (usually two)
On-the-scene reporters
    On-the-scene bystanders being interviewed
    Actors to reenact the special event
Weather person

Sports anchor
Business report anchor
A special in-studio guest to interview (optional)
     Author with a book review
     A chef sharing the latest delicious diet delight
     The brother of the latest plane crash victim
     A movie star

Structure includes:

Teasers: Is coffee good for you after all? Find out at eleven, here on channel 8!
        Is homework bad for your children? We'll have the important details at 6!

Commercials or Sponsors:

1. Channel 8 Weather is brought to you by—Aphrodite Beauty Secret: Be beautiful for centuries.

2. Do the weather.

3. Follow up with a regular commercial about Aphrodite Beauty Secret. "I wasn't always the most beautiful goddess, but that's my little secret. Now, I'm sharing it with you. Just don't tell Hera."

Introductions: "Good Evening, Welcome to News Channel 8 at 6. I'm Brittney Glynn."
        "And I'm Tyler Glynn."
        ***
        "And now it's time for the Weather, every 8 minutes, with Maria Jones."
        ***
        "That's if for the weather. Back to you, Brittney and Tyler."
        "Thanks, Maria."

Top Story: "Our top story tonight is..."

Person of the Week: or Celebrity Spotlight, etc. A great place to interview or report on a special guest.

Sports: In real life the teams are often named after animals. What if your news was about the rain forest? Would the animals have teams named after humans?
    "It was a close game tonight. The Businessmen beat the Lumberjacks 10 to 1. Here are the highlights..."
    Feel free to be specific about team location within your topic.
Example: "Next week, the Canopy Cooks will play the Forest Floor Financiers. This time the game will take place on the forest floor. While this is an unusual location rotation. Al Jaguar, the coach for the Financiers, filed an unfair circumstances petition, after losing the last game against the Canopy Cooks, claiming that the aerial playing field was an unfair advantage, because none of his players could fly."

Local News: A good place to take the larger topic—the environment, loss of the rain forest, mythology news—and show in a short local story how the greater issue affects us personally.

Example: "Locally, hospitals are jammed tonight with a new strain of the Boola Boola flu. While no one has died yet, the effects of this deadly flu may never go away. The real tragedy is that scientists were once very close to an antidote for this flu, but the seed material was only found in certain areas of the Amazon rain forest, and these areas have been destroyed."

Pass the Object

Another treasure from the Penny Ante Theater's trunk.

Ages: All.

Tools: A nonspecific object: a short dowel, a piece of foam, a piece of material, a hula hoop. Try a handy classroom object such as a chalkboard eraser or ruler. Try to choose a variety of objects with simple shapes, in a variety of sizes.

Directions:

1. Begin with students seated in a circle, in chairs or on the floor, where everyone is able to see one another.

2. Take a simple shaped object, and pretend it is something other than what it truly is (a hairbrush, a pencil, a flute).

3. Demonstrate ways to use the object in its new role.

4. Emphasize the importance of showing detail. Hold the simple shaped object the same way you would hold the new specific one. Show its weight, its size, and how to use it. The more players visualize the object as the new one, the more details they will add. Just as adding details in writing makes the reader more interested, demonstrating more details with the object will have the same effect.

5. Students may have three guesses, before the player must tell the answer. This is a silent activity. If you wish, they may add a sound as a clue if their peers are stuck. Students may stand or use a partner if necessary.

Tips:

1. Demonstrate for them the difference between showing detail and not showing detail. Example: A toothbrush.

Without details: Wave the object in front of your face in an up and down motion.

With details: Take a cap off the toothpaste. Squeeze some out on your brush. Turn the faucet water on. Wet the toothpaste. Turn the water off. Hold the toothbrush in front of your face and pretend to brush all sides of your teeth. Swish the imaginary slush around in your mouth, and pretend to spit. Turn the water on. Rinse the brush. Stand the brush up in a glass.

2. Praise students who show details and emotion. How they feel about what they are doing and eating can become important clues.

3. Encourage students to choose a new idea that no one else has used. It's more creative. They'll have to pay attention.

4. Have each student think of two ideas before the game begins. You may not have time to go around twice, but they'll have a backup idea planned.

5. If they're stuck, encourage them to think of objects they use every day. What's the first activity they do when they get home from school? What's their favorite activity to do for fun? What's the last thing they do before they go to bed? Point out objects around the room, objects that they are wearing, etc.

6. Students should not try to trick their peers. They are doing it correctly if students guess right away. (Actors use these prop techniques all the time. They don't want the audience to have to guess what they are doing, because it will interfere with the story.)

7. Try not to be influenced by the size or shape of the object you are passing. A wrapping paper tube could be a pencil, or a steering wheel. If students continue to limit themselves, offer a different shaped object

every time you play.

8. If you have timid players, begin by placing the object in the center of the circle and have them raise their hands for random turns if they have an idea.

9. No weapons or any objects that are inappropriate should be created. Tell them they are being creative problem solvers, and weapons have nothing to do with creativity or solving problems.

Sample Object Ideas:

canoe paddle	pencil	pen	paintbrush	lipstick
an eating utensil	a curling iron	a football	soccer ball	boomerang
a dog leash	a horse bridle	a hot dog	lollipop	corn on the cob
a bathroom scale	a fire hose	a hair band	a camera	a musical instrument
a soda can	a computer	a telephone	a cell phone	a remote
a video game	a book	a ruler	headphones	a boom box

Pass the Object can be adapted to any curriculum topic that involves a variety of objects such as objects for neighborhood jobs, colonial tools, Native American tools, etc.

Personification Poems and Journal Entries

I believe that examining life from other perspectives is always a valuable exercise. My work in social issue theater and prison programs has reinforced my belief that understanding other points of view is a critical piece of our social and emotional development. Imagine the personal and societal conflict that would be avoided if everyone took the time to think beyond themselves.

Any actor will tell you that half the thrill of personifying a character is delving inside their psyche and finding out what makes them tick. What would it be like to be a character in a book? What possessed that character to make such a stupid choice on page twelve?

Extend reality for a minute and think about what it would be like to be a capuchin monkey, an equals sign, a large intestine, a test tube in which chemicals are always being combined. There isn't anything you can't pretend to be. There is always knowledge and understanding to be gained. Your students will never look at the subject the same way again, and neither will their classmates!

Personification Poems and Journal Entries is a writing activity, but it's more about exploring the daily life experiences and emotions of the subject at hand than it is specifically about grammar and syntax. I suggest that you offer students the opportunity to present their work in character, even in costume, if you're so inclined.

Ages: Grades 5-8

Directions:

1. Choose what subject you want to write about.

2. Close your eyes and imagine that you are that "thing."

   A. What do you do all day?

   B. What do you see around you?

   C. How do others treat you? What is your relationship?

   D. What is your job? How do you feel about it?

   E. What do you do for fun?

   F. What do you find to be tedious?

G. What makes you special?

H. What challenges must you overcome?

3.   Write this information in any form you like, as a complaint, a commercial, a rhyming poem, a list poem, an emotional poem, a journal entry, or a letter explaining to others what life is like for you.

Reacting

"Acting is reacting," my brilliant acting professor, Morris Carnovsky, drilled into us with his dignified manner. He was a famous Shakespearean actor, who was then in his late eighties, sharing his infinite wisdom with Connecticut College students. I studied with him twenty years ago, and dozens of his brief, poignant, on-target statements continue to guide me today.

Acting is reacting. You, too, will know this is true the next time you watch students perform. A giant dinosaur breaks through the back wall and lumbers onto the stage, baring his child-sized incisors! Three student actors are yawning. Another one is playing with her hair, and two more are looking off in the distance. One is picking his nose. You can tell just by looking that several others know that the green slimy costume is really only a paper bag with goop on it. The dinosaur is brilliant, but there is still something off. What is it?

Reacting helps writing, too. If students spend time thinking about how an action affects the characters, then the story will be developed in a grand and interesting way. It would be impossible to only have a series of actions (and then...and then...and then...). Imagine if this idea took hold. Character development would rule the world! Several martial arts movie stars would be out of work, but that's the price we'd have to pay.

Individuals

Ages: Grades 5-10

Tools: Space, cards with age-appropriate situations to react to.

Directions:

1. Each player chooses a card.

2. One by one, the players perform an appropriate reaction to the card. The other students think for a moment about a possible situation that may cause this reaction, but don't guess out loud. The card is read out loud, and then the player performs the reaction again.

3. The audience players discuss whether the situation was extreme, unusual, or everyday. What kinds of situations did they imagine? Did they compare with the original choice?

4. Each student has a turn.

Tips and Variations:

1. I wouldn't recommend guessing the situation out loud, even though it may seem easier at first. Reacting is tricky. The situations are not necessarily obvious, because many reactions are similar, while the situation may be vastly different. Second, this puts undo pressure on the less accomplished actors in your class. Spare yourselves the awkward moment when the student is clearly trying her best, but no one in the class has any idea what she's doing.

2. Play this with pairs of students, too, but give them time to discuss their reactions before they perform.

Sample Situations:

*   Someone fell down ahead of you in line.
*   The teacher started to cry.
*   A student made a basket by jumping through the hoop with the ball.
*   A hand reached out of the computer and pulled a student inside.

* The principal broke into song and dance in the middle of the morning announcements.
* You just discovered that you lost your lunch money.
* You left your final homework project on the kitchen table.
* Your desk floated up and stuck to the ceiling.
* You have just been chosen for...(a coveted school position).
* You have just been chosen for...(a tedious job for the week).
* A dinosaur walked into your classroom.
* You lost the item your mother said you would lose if you took it to school.
* Your best friend broke her leg.
* You spilled orange juice in the computer.

Groups
Ages: Grades 4-Adult

Tools: Cards with age-appropriate situations to react to.

Directions:
1. Divide into groups of four or five players.

2. Have each group pick a situation card, or create their own situation, with your approval.

3. Give each group four minutes to discuss and plan their reaction.

4. Each group should perform their reaction, allow the audience time to think of a connected situation, and then perform their reaction again.

5. The audience players discuss whether or not they guessed a comparable situation, based on the details within the reaction.

Tips and Variations:
1. Give the group reactions time to evolve. While individual reactions may be shorter and more to the point, group reactions can evolve with several different reactions for the same situation.

2. Give the group reaction actors time to react to each other's reactions within the scene. (Example: At a horror movie, one person may find the other's terror quite humorous.)

Sample Situations:
* A horror movie.
* A six-foot banana split is delivered to the table. (All students should sit on the same side of the table.)
* Participating in a car accident.
* Witnessing a car accident.
* A Broadway play.
* An enormous homework assignment is being explained.
* Watching a street performer.
* Witnessing an argument on the school bus.
* Witnessing a parent/child argument at the grocery store.
* Watching people walk by at the mall.
* A fireworks display.
* Walking through a street fair with food, crafts, etc.
* Watching a little kid get hit by a car.
* Witnessing a thief in action.
* Watching a romantic movie.

Statues

Ages: All.

Tools: Space, students.

The basic statue is a valuable activity itself, and the first step in helping students put the curriculum on its feet, in a tangible, frozen, manageable fashion.

What is a statue? Does it dance, wiggle, or sing? No. Statues do not move at all.

Directions:

1. With younger grades, discuss what a real statue is, why they exist, what they're made out of. Then tell them that you'll be creating statues using student bodies. The student statues may blink and breathe, because you're not looking for passed-out statues.

2. Create a frozen picture using student bodies in posed positions. Face them all in one direction toward an imaginary audience or the rest of the class. The statue can portray an emotion, a specific scene from a book, a special event, or a snapshot. It could be a page in a giant book, with all the characters readily posed inside, waiting to share their stories.

3. Decide on a topic and have students join in one at a time. Once they have chosen their positions, they should not move. Changing one position will only encourage the others to do the same.

4. Students may place themselves at a high level (standing), a medium level (kneeling or bending), or a low level (sitting or lying down). Students should not block any other student from the audience.

5. Once the picture is complete. Have any remaining students take a picture with their imaginary camera. This will help spruce up any lagging statue parts, and give any remaining students a job.

Tips:

1. How many students should be in a statue? Depending on the topic, the time, space, and the statue's energy to hold a pose, a perfect statue can have one to twenty-four students in it.

2. No one should choose a position they cannot hold for an indefinite length of time. Students will insist that they can hold their legs in the air, but it's too hard. Encourage them to touch their toe down to the ground for support.

3. If your statue is taking too long to construct and the student pieces are getting tired, let them relax their positions until the final piece is set in place.

4. Encourage students to place themselves in interesting ways. If you don't, every statue will be a straight line of standing statue people.

Emotional Statues

No matter what grade level, I always begin any statue exercise with an emotional statue example. The emotions are easy to portray, and following through with the model statue will facilitate moving to more complex versions.

Directions:

Choose one emotion such as anger, surprise, sadness, happiness, etc. Have every student show a way that people can demonstrate this one emotion within one statue. Remember that one emotion can have several faces, such as sullen anger versus raging anger.

Tips:

1. If a student is embarrassed to exaggerate important feelings in front of his peers, encourage him to demonstrate how someone else would express it. Everyone remembers their mother's angry face.

2. React to the statue as it develops. Be frightened if it's scary. Be grateful the students aren't angry at you. Let the sadness make your voice sadder as the statue builds. Acting is reacting. If you act back at them, your statue will become more dramatic. Guaranteed.

3. If students are having a hard time holding their positions, sprinkle them with statue dust or zap them with frozen juice. Discuss the fact that some emotions take more energy to hold on to than others. Anger statues fizzle quickly, because it's much easier to be happy.

4. End with a happy statue. It puts a positive note on the activity.

Variations:

1. Have the statue melt on the count of five to a new emotion. Begin at one with the saddest possible statue, and slowly melt it into surprise. This idea, once demonstrated, can be a great reference for dealing with strong emotions within a group setting during other times.

2. Follow up with a "How would you feel?" scene, where many emotions can occur in one scene, but you're still not trying to create a picture.

Examples: How would you feel on the first or last day of school? How would you feel on the night of a play you were in? How do you feel before a soccer meet?

3. Follow up with event statues, not yet forming a specific picture.

Example: A birthday party. Imagine something that happens at a birthday party, and freeze in a pose reflecting that activity. Students may begin to naturally form small parts of a picture, with someone holding a cake, and someone else blowing out candles, but it isn't necessary.

Picture Statues

Ages: Grades 3-10

Directions:

1. Create a statue of a specific picture from a book. Include all the people, the objects, and the setting.

2. Place them in the same order that the picture shows, or the written scene describes.

Variations:

1. Drape colorful cloth over specific parts of the picture to draw attention to it.

2. Develop several picture statues for a particular story and have the students put them in proper sequence.

3. Have student groups develop statues of their favorite parts of the story. Share each picture, in proper sequence, even if they've chosen to duplicate some parts and skip others.

4. Interview each part of the picture for some candid "thoughtshots."

5. If students do not know what the character would say, encourage them to improvise. If it is a historical picture, have them research the time period first, and then try the statue again at the end of your unit. See how much more they have to share.

Pop-up Statues

Ages: Grades 3-8

Once a statue is set, it almost begs to come alive. One way to do this in a creative, manageable manner is to allow the many parts of the statue to speak or move one person or section at a time.

Directions:

Imagine clicking on a child's computer game in which the animated figure dances and says its preprogrammed sentence and then stops. Set up a clickable pop-up system with your class or choose from one of the following ideas:

A. Walk through the statue and tap the students lightly on the shoulder.
B. Give the students numbers, and quietly say their numbers from the side.
C. If all the statue parts are facing front, then give them a visual cue.
D. Literally click their section on by nodding toward them and tapping a musical instrument.
E. If it is a rehearsed statue preparing for a performance, preset an order for the students to follow.

Variations for Grades 5-8:

1. Click the students off in the middle of their movement. Let them freeze. When you click them on again, in a random order, they should begin exactly where they left off, in the middle of a sentence, word, or movement. They will develop a higher level of focus, as well as creative thinking and listening skills.

2. After students are completely comfortable with pop-up statues, have each part change its movement, sound /speech, or both every time you click it on. Your statue will become a highly sensitive, cooperative listening and sharing machine. The results will delight you.

Moving Statues

Ages: Grades 3-Adult.

Tools: Space.

Create a scene statue, with a few students. Have the frozen picture remain in place while the scene is introduced and for opening narration. Give the students a cue to break out of the scene as they act out a short scene with dialogue and movement. When the scene is nearing completion, have the students within the context of the scene return to the original positions and freeze again. This activity will provide structure for the creative process, and a neat framework in which to perform a group of short scenes for others.

Variation:

Instead of returning to the original pose, have the characters end in a new frozen statue.

Slides

Ages: Grades 3-Adult.

Tools: Space.

When I was a kid we used to sit in a dark living room and show slides of the family. There was often one narrator to describe the scene and tell a few silly background stories about the characters involved.

Have groups of students set up a series of human statue slides to fit their research topic. Have a narrator describe the scenes and tell a few factual background stories about the characters involved.

Storytelling

Storytelling Cloth

Ages: Grade 4-Adult

Tools: A piece of material, about a yard long. (I prefer colorful and interesting fabric to inspire the visual students in the class.)

Small objects that have no apparent relationship to one another.

Example: My storytelling cloth box currently has the following objects in it:

* a neon orange beach shovel
* a plastic egg with rice in it (for rhythm)
* a pen
* a small plaid bear without a face
* a toy dump truck
* a black sedan with evil-looking dogs driving it
* a baby rattle telephone
* a wooden ornament star (not painted)
* 2 wooden ornament angels (not painted)
* a makeup brush
* a small yellow doll dish bowl
* a plastic blue dolphin
* a neon orange and pink spinning top
* a small green vase with shamrocks on it
* a purple foam dot
* a square of Lycra (bathing suit material) in bright colors
* a strip of bright blue sequined elastic
* a white plastic ring, which may have been part of a lid

Directions:

1. Cover a small table or two desks pulled together with the cloth.

2. Seat students around the desk.

3. Place the objects on the cloth apart from each other, to help them stand out.

4. Choose one object, pick it up and begin to tell a story that will at some point touch upon the object you have in your hand.

5. When you have brought your story to a point where it has just begun to develop an interesting twist, place the object back on the table to let the other players volunteer to take over.

6. A second player will take over the story where the first player left off. Player two will choose a different object and connect it with his or her section of the story.

7. Continue the story until it has reached a conclusion. Not every student will have a chance. If you have time, tell more than one story.

Tips and Variations:

1. I recommend a rule that no one other than the current storyteller touches any object on the cloth.

2. Stress before you begin that the story should make sense, have no violence, and be appropriate. If you state it beforehand, you are stating a rule, not discouraging a storyteller who is creating on the spot.

3. These rules are optional, and changeable. Designate them for a specific story and try them out. If you like them, hang on to them.

A. Each storyteller uses only one object at a time.
B. Do not repeat the same object two times in a row.
C. Take this opportunity to stress any idea you're working on in writing stories.
D. Offer several suggestions before you begin. Focus on one element at a time.
E. It's hard to be a creative storyteller, out loud, in front of your peers, with too many rules at one time.

Other key points:
* Building suspense
* Dramatic beginnings
* Exciting endings
* The problem
* The solution
* Exciting transitional phrases. (If you say "And then," you're out!)
* Exciting adjectives, adverbs, and verbs with life. (If you say "got," you're out. If you say "went," you're out.)

(After editing a 250-student, fifth grade journal for three years in a row, I have violent internal reactions to the words weird, stuff, got, went, cool, and things, because I have read about "the weird and cool fun things and stuff that we did" too many times. If you have words on your "favorite list," this game can help you wipe them out!)

4. Hard pressed to find objects? Look in any junk drawer in your home and pull out objects you haven't used in a year. Raid your kids' toys. Bug the art teacher for good garbage.

5. I've made the mistake of offering too many objects at a time, because I like them. Try limiting yourselves to ten or twelve at first, and then change a few objects for a different story to add variety.

6. Have a student tell a story individually, using the storytelling cloth and five or six objects. See if the student can use all the objects while telling a good story.

Sample Story Starters:
(Once you've used these, and the students get the idea, have them begin their own.)

Object #1: Large construction paper circle.

"I'm bored!" Celeste yelled at the ceiling, because she knew no one else was home to listen. "I'm tired of all this rain. I'm tired of doing chores. I'm tired of my best friend being on vacation!"

Pressing her face up against the window, Celeste was eyeing the raindrops closely. She noticed the many colors floating inside the seemingly colorless raindrops floating past her window and splattering all over the ground. She wondered what happened to the color when it hit the ground.

As if by command, one by one, the raindrops began to leave drops of color on the sidewalk in front of her. The raindrops grew larger, and larger, and before she knew it, drops as big as her hands, her feet, then her head were painting the ground. Bright yellow, deep purple, neon green spots were covering the sidewalk and lawn. Across the street, which was practically disappearing, Celeste's best friend's house was beginning to look as if it were covered in candy.

Celeste didn't move. At first she was afraid to. What if the colors were to disappear? What if this magical moment was just that, only a moment, and once she moved, it would be gone forever? (Place the construction paper circle back on the table. Let someone take over from there.)

Object #2: A kitchen pot lid.

Growl, rumble, growl. Old Mrs. McEleaney's stomach wouldn't stop reminding her it was time to drop the three-dimensional puzzle she was hovering over and go down to fetch herself something to eat.

"Meow," added Sam, her Siamese cat, who was always ready for a snack.

"All right. All right," sighed old Mrs. McEleaney. "I'll move these old bones down the stairs and see what I can create in the magic pot for lunch today."

The magic cooking pot had been a gift from her son, Alfred, who thought his mother should take better care of herself and remember to eat. He also thought it might be nice if his mother cooked dinner for him, once in a while. Alfred had no idea the pot held magical powers, and old Mrs. McEleaney had no intention of telling him. Alfred was always looking for some gimmick to get rich quick, and she was sure that if he knew about her cooking pot, he'd be over in a flash to take it off her hands.

Turning the corner at the top of the rickety old staircase, Mrs. M. noticed the oak tree out back. Something about it was different. Shrugging it off, she thought it must just be the change of seasons. The leaves hadn't been gone long; perhaps she wasn't used to the new look.

As she reached the kitchen, old Mrs. McEleaney gasped in horror. The pot lid for her magic pot was gone. She knew it had been on top of the stove in the morning. Without the pot lid, the magic pot would still cook, but not the food she requested. It would make something else entirely. Instead of chicken stew, it might make chocolate truffles. Instead of roast beef, it might make a broccoli omelet. What has happened to my magic pot lid? she wondered.

(Put the pot lid down and let someone take over.)

I'll Tell It, You Act It

Age: Grade 4-Adult.

Tools: A chair, space.

1. Choose a storyteller, or model the beginning yourself. Sit in a chair facing the audience, with performance space on either side of it.

2. The storyteller begins to tell a story, and as each large object (creaking doors, etc.) or character is mentioned, a member of the audience is selected (by the storyteller or the teacher) to go onstage next to the storyteller and act out whatever the storyteller says.

3. The characters cannot do or be anything the storyteller does not tell them to do. This is important for a couple of reasons:

A. The storyteller must have some semblance of control over the people onstage, so they're not just doing anything they please to ham it up or show off.

B. Storytelling in this way is a great visual demonstration of the importance of writing interesting descriptions in detail. Unless the storyteller "writes" interesting description for the characters to personify and demonstrate, they have nothing to do. They can't be desperately sad, or overwhelmingly happy, have a bad shoulder, or walk with a limp. They can't hum a little tune to themselves, or throw their hands up in frustration. They can't have a furrowed brow, or a sparkly grin. While some of these ideas may be challenging for some students to act out, their effort will still be noted, and the point will be made. Fewer stories will be a long string of "and then" actions, because it will become more obvious to everyone that details are more interesting.

4. When the storyteller has told as much story as she wants to tell, she should raise her hand for another storyteller to take her place and pick up where she left off.

Sample Story:

Farmer Bailey (pick a farmer) flew out of bed, buttoned up his overalls, stepped into his boots and stormed out the bedroom door. He had been putting this matter off, but it was clearly time to do something about his three singing cows. (Pick three singing cows.) Granted, they were singing quietly this morning, but he hadn't wanted to wake up to the tune of "Twinkle, Twinkle, little cow. How, I wonder how, how, how. Out there in the fields so green. Two are nice, the other mean." (Cows repeat after storyteller singing, line by line.)
The farmer's wife, Eloise (pick a wife), stopped him at the kitchen door.

"What is the matter? Your face is all red. Your fists are clenched in frustration, and your forehead is all wrinkled." She was a lovely woman, with a calm and cheerful disposition, quite the opposite of her husband.

"I can't stand that singing!" exclaimed Farmer Bailey, before he sank into a pouting posture at the kitchen table.

"Oh, I love it," replied his wife, cheerily. "Can't think of a better way to start the day than listening to the melodious tones of our three best heifers."

"But what about the Rooster? (Pick a rooster.) Isn't he supposed to wake us in the morning?" asked the exasperated farmer.

"He has chronic laryngitis. The cows are just trying to help." Just then, the otherwise robust rooster woke up and saw the sun. He tried desperately to give his cock-a-doodle-doo (rooster tries), but alas, nothing came out.
"I want to be a normal farmer, with a normal farm. I don't want singing cows, and I definitely don't want our two sheep with their ...their...special talent (pick two sheep)," he complained grumpily.
"Now, dear. The sheep's tap-dancing lessons haven't been that expensive. They have dreams. We're in a position to honor those dreams. We shouldn't complain." The sheep began to tap-dance. The cows sang another chorus of "Twinkle, Twinkle, Little Cow," and the rooster gave the morning call one more try.
Little did Farmer Bailey know, but Alice Bingham, a gossip columnist/talent scout, was visiting her Uncle Maxwell at the farm next door. (Pick an Alice Bingham and an Uncle Maxwell.)
(Raise your hand and let another storyteller take over from here.)

Story Acting in a Sequence

Ages: Grades K-5

Directions:

1. Read the directions to Statues on page 66.

2. Work as a class to create several statues of events in the story as if there were a giant book in your classroom, and each time you turned a page, a new picture of story events, characters, and settings would

appear.

Variation:

1. Divide the class into groups. Ask them to pose in a statue from one part of the story. Ask them to make up a line or two of narration to go with it.

2. Perform the many statues in proper sequence for the story. The workshop leader should find out what pictures you have and quickly narrate a Reader's Digest version of the rest of the story to tie the pictures together.

3. It doesn't matter if you have several of the same event. They'll all be a little different just because of who is in it. If all of your students have chosen the same picture (which actually has never happened to me), feel free to seize the opportunity to find out what makes this particular part of the story so fascinating. Perhaps they could include some of these elements in their other writing and skits.

Story Acting with Student-Written Dialogue

Beginning dialogue by students is often weighed down with tedious lines about what they think you think or I think or somebody else thinks they're supposed to write, rather than what the characters would say. If you don't know what I mean, then thank your lucky stars and move on. If you have experienced the untold joy of early dialogue in stories and skits, then this activity may be for you. (We won't even touch the special experience of reading confused dialogue punctuation. I promise!)

The Mini Lesson:

When writing a skit, or play, I like to picture a moment in time in my mind. I picture the setting (WHERE), the activity (WHAT), and then the characters (WHO) start to take care of themselves.

For example, ask your students to imagine the last five minutes before they go to school in the morning. Ask them to listen closely and see if they can hear some of the lines different people are saying during those last five minutes:

> "Hurry up, or you'll miss the bus."
> "I'm not driving you today. You're the one who's dragging your feet."
> "Why, why, why are we always late in the morning?!?"
> "Quit hogging the bathroom!"
> "Brush your teeth!"
> "But it's your turn to feed the dog!"
> "Don't forget you have _____ after school today."
> "I'll be picking you up at _____."
> "I love you. Have a good day."

If you have your students do this exercise, not only will they provide you with great lines, but each line will be said in the same tone and with the same intention that it was said in the first place. The entire class will be able to hear who said it without being told if it was a parent or a kid.

Students often write a skit by determining who is in it first. They make long lists of characters, and then cast the characters, before they even know if the character should be in the scene. Often the resulting scene has too many characters standing around arguing because they don't have much else to do. Nobody really questions why five extended relatives and the neighbors are in their house during the last five minutes before school starts. These scenes have very little to do with real life, and dialogue is completely about real life. It should be relaxed and easy, not strained and uncomfortable. As my beloved acting teacher, Morris Carnovsky, used to say, "Talk, talk. Just talk!"

Having written hundreds of student plays, which are usually in need of twenty-four lead roles, I admit to students that I begin by focusing on a moment (WHERE), the activity (WHAT), and start writing the lines out as I picture hearing them in my mind. Within a few lines, the characters (WHO) become clear. They even seem to enter and exit the scene with a natural quality. Now, I know this is too abstract of a way for them to begin writing an entire original scene. How many parent notes are you going to receive complaining that it's unfair of you to grade Harvey down because he doesn't have voices in his head? But I offer the idea up to the students anyway, before I offer more structure, because in my experience it breaks them away from writing what they think they are supposed to write, and gives them permission to imagine and use their own voice.

Ages: Grades 4-8

Directions:

1. Brainstorm a moment of dialogue.

2. List the characters who might say the lines they are thinking of in the brainstorming session, for practice.

3. Divide students into groups of four or five.

4. Give students a short selection of stories to choose from (legends, folk tales, myths, fairy tales, whatever). I like starting with stories that have a built-in tradition of being adapted and modified. Beginning with he The Boy Who Cried Wolf, or the Legend of the Leatherman, will give them a structure to hold onto.

5. Tell them to divide the story into three parts—the beginning, the middle, and the end.

6. Ask them to focus on one section at a time, imagining the WHERE, WHAT, and WHO for that section. Write at least two lines for each character. While it's a good idea to discourage a thousand extra unnecessary characters, it is perfectly acceptable to give whoever or whatever is in the scene the power to talk. The dog may have a comment to share. The chimney might be alive with a personality. It you'd rather they write dialogue for animate objects only, ask them to add extra characters, such as a visitor, after they figure out what is happening in the scene, so they can ensure that the new character will contribute to the flow of the scene, not detract from it.

7. Make sure the scene makes sense.

8. Practice once or twice over the next few days.

9. Perform them for each other.

Tips:

1. If students want to bring in costumes or props, great, but make sure the scene is written before any discussion begins about props. Props and costumes are like beautiful icing on a cake. If you eat too much of it first, you'll be too sick and overwhelmed to make (or eat) the cake.

2. After practicing with stories where the scenes and the characters already exist, have students create their own original stories, with dialogue, perhaps based on a unit you are studying.

Storytelling with Statues

Ages: Grades 3-10

Directions:

1. Choose a story that you, or a student, would like to tell.

2. Imagine illustrations to the story, if they don't already exist. If they do, feel free to use them.

3. Preset a picture statue, from the story, using students from the class.

4. Tell a story using the statue as a grand visual aid.

Tips and Variations:

1. Use the statue as a setting, and walk through it as you tell the story.

2. Stop and interview main characters, or even background characters, for their points of view.

3. Set up the pictures in sequence using the whole class, and walk from scene to scene as you tell it. The students could have a signal or sound to get into their scene.

4. Re-create a historical story using statues. Interrupt the story at odd intervals for a fun people-on-the-street interview. Reveal how the people of the times really felt.

Swat It!

Thanks to Patty Tedford, who taught me this game, I have adapted it to hundreds of other subjects.

What class doesn't enjoy a game of competition? As a kid, I used to make up key signature relay games for my mother's piano classes, and use them for incentive to learn the key signatures myself. Perhaps it's the separate focus that lights the fire under the most reluctant student. What were once boring details or tedious definitions are now absorbed quickly as a necessary game requirement. This game is especially fun for all the students, because it has the extra hidden challenge of reflexes, so even the ace number one student can stumble for a little extra excitement.

CHUCK JONES

Ages: Grades 2-6.

Tools:

* Two different colored fly swatters. (These are easiest to buy during fly season, but can be found in most hardware stores year round.)
* A blackboard or wall on which you can tape construction paper.
* A marker.
* A list of questions, statements, or definitions on the theme of your choice.

Directions:

1. Tape two pieces of construction paper on the board, one that says "true," the other "false."

2. Enlist a student to keep score on the board.

3. Invite two students, one from each team, up to the board and present each one with a fly swatter.

4. Offer a true or false statement.

5. Students will smack the paper with the answer of their choice.

6. Turn to the class and ask them what the answer is, and whether the players are correct or not.

7. Then, if both students hit the right answer, determine which one hit the paper first, and award their team a point.

Tips:

1. The fly swatter on the bottom is the winner, but you might want to declare a "no sliding underneath" rule.

2. Have some students serve as judges—one from each team would be good. If you're reading the questions, you may miss the actual event.

3. Have the students begin with the swatters down by their sides. I always tell them to keep them in their holsters.

4. Depending on the class, I may require the students to wait until the end of the question before making a decision. Having a start signal is helpful.

Variations:

1. Use for any subject! Determine if dinosaurs are plant eaters or meat eaters. Any question with a yes or no answer will work. Identify snapshots or thoughtshots, healthy foods versus nonhealthy foods, odd numbers, even numbers.

Swoosh!

Swoosh has been adapted from a popular game called Zoom, which can be found in *The Friendly Classroom for a Small Planet,* Bretchen Bodenhamer, Leonard Burger, Priscilla Prutzman, and Lee Stern, Philadelphia, PA: New Society Publishers, 1988

Swoosh is a magical game, because it is extraordinarily fun, has clear structure, and can be adapted to include any curriculum topic. I especially like it because all students can benefit simultaneously. Advanced students can branch out to new areas, if they choose to, while others can catch up, without losing face.

Ages: Grades 1 - adult

Tools: Space

Directions:

1. Stand students in a large circle.

2. Encourage large gestures and enthusiasm as you, the leader, turn to one side and say "Swoosh!" while gesturing a large movement as if you are pushing something powerful and invisible to the next student.

3. The students will continue turning to each other to pass Swoosh around the circle, until someone stops it.

4. Stop the Swoosh by putting on the brake. If you are standing put your foot out to push down the brake and pull up your hands as if you are putting on two emergency brakes. Accent these gestures with a loud Errrrrr! If you are seated, stretch your arms out, palms down, and press two imaginary brake pedals with your hands. Again, the sound is helpful.

5. Once a student has stopped the Swoosh energy, they have the opportunity to pass it back the way it came or to continue passing it on in the direction that it was going. Encourage them to make this decision quickly. You don't want the energy to fizzle out. Encourage the students to consider the Swoosh as a hot potato or sorts, which needs to be passed on quickly.

6. Each student may only put the brake on once during each round. A round is the playing time until the leaders stops play to change the directions. If a student did not put the brake on during a previous round, her chances may not accumulate. Stand by this rule, or you will lose flow of the game. I tell the students that if we had more than one opportunity to stop the Swoosh, I might pass it to Cindy, who is standing three students away, who might pass it back to me, Without the one brake rule, Cindy and I could go on all day, and everyone would be bored.

7. Encourage energetic swooshing. Wimpy swooshing is not the point.

Variations: In truth, the heart of this game is in the variations.

1. **Silent Swoosh.**
   Play exactly as you did before, but without any sound at all. Demonstrate how loud Swoosh can look as you pass the energy and stop it without making a sound.

2. **Change the Swoosh.**
   This time, instead of passing Swoosh, you choose a category and pass something within the category. This time the player who brakes not only changes direction, but he or she changes what he is passing within the category.

Category Examples: colors, numbers under ten, tongue twisters, spelling words, endangered animals, characters in literature, occupations in colonial times, math facts, the basic food groups, the four tables in multiplication, months of the year, odd and even numbers, mythological gods and goddesses, parts of a caterpillar, bones in the body, elements in the periodic table. ANYTHING!

So, if you're playing with colors, turn to one side and enthusiastically pass "Red". The students will continue to pass "Red" to each other, until someone wants to stop it. When they stop it, they quickly choose a new color, and pass it in either direction. So it may sound like this:

"Red", "Red", "Red", "Red",
(brake)
"Blue", "Blue",
(brake)
"Yellow",
(brake)
"Orange", "Orange", "Orange", "Orange", "Orange",
(brake)
"Purple".

This way a student who does not know his colors can easily repeat what is passed to him, without losing face. He also has an opportunity to hear the colors repeated over and over, so he learns them in the process. The students who have their colors down, will be able to think of new ones, and have fun.

Tips:

1. Once your class understands the rules, you never have to use the Swoosh term again, except as a title. Play for a few minutes here and there, to reinforce any topic you are working on.

2. With the youngest classes the combination of thinking of new ideas within a category and switching directional flow of the swoosh may take so long that it drags the game down. You may want to suspend the idea of choosing which direction to send it. This is also a helpful tip if your class has a tendency to play keep away from one section of the circle.

Talk Shows/Interviews

Ages: Grades 3-Adult

In this day of talk shows on every channel all hours of the day, every student has a clear visual image of a talk show, or interview show. As a fun format to demonstrate research information, have them create their own show. The Oprah clones can interview a panel of mythological gods and goddesses, historical figures, rain forest animals, etc.

Directions:

1. Have each student being interviewed conduct research on their character and write out several questions for the host to ask, and answers for their characters.

2. Have the host or hostess research the topic in general and write an opening overview and closing statement.

3. Have students prepare the characters before they begin to discuss or plan costumes or props. Otherwise you'll have well-dressed, giggling students who say nothing.

CHAPTER EIGHT

Warm-ups

Warm-ups? I barely have the time to cover the main material. How am I supposed to fit in warm-ups? Let's just jump right into it today, and skip over all that. Why do we need them? Warm-ups are for big jobs like competing in a triathlon, singing at Carnegie Hall, driving a tractor-trailer in subzero temperatures. I don't need warm-ups. I'm just ...

If you think about it, we warm up for everything that is important to us. We warm up, using some form of ritual, for the most important parts of our day. What's the ten-minute sleep button on our alarm clocks for? To give us a chance to warm up to the idea of getting out of bed. Personally, in honor of warm-ups, I like to repeat this ten-minute warm-up several times.

If we want to do something well, we warm up, often without realizing it. Are you being observed today? I'm sure you've run that lesson over in your head many, many times. Maybe you're wearing a certain outfit, or having protein with your breakfast.

What's the difference in a day when we say that we're flying by the seat of our pants? It can be that we're physically rushed, or it can mean that we're so over scheduled that we're halfway through teaching the next lesson before a part of our brain remembers what it is.

We warm up to shake off the last activity we were engaged in, to prepare our bodies and minds for the next one. Why? Because if we don't, our voices will crack, our cars will wear out, we'll sprain something, we'll forget our presentations. And we won't be prepared to accept the oncoming challenges with an open ....anything. If warming up is so important to us, imagine how necessary it is for the students.

I used to work in a program twice a week for mothers in prison. Mondays were the hardest, because family visited on weekends, and now, on Monday, there was another whole week to wait. I was often in charge of the warm-ups. I always selected the liveliest, silliest, most active warm-ups I could think of, because the Monday warm-up needed to lift the thickest, heaviest weight of defensive attitudes, self absorbed moods, depression, guilt, and anger off the women, and out the window.

If the warm-up was successful, the rest of the session would go well, because we would move as a group to a new place for the hour and a half. Traveling out of prison without leaving the room, we could learn new skills and dream dreams for our children without fighting through thick walls of personal baggage. If the warm-up was successful, we were Carol and Lauren, their friends. If it was unsuccessful, we would never make it past being %#@$ chicks, with an attitude, who wouldn't stop getting in their faces. The workshop would plod along with nothing moving smoothly, like cold metal in an engine, scraping along painfully.

Warm-ups for Drama

Drama is an activity that involves making internal parts of ourselves public. For some students this comes readily because they do it all the time. For others, it takes getting used to. For everyone, it involves a warm-up.

I use warm-ups to take the temperature in a classroom I've never been in before. Within a short warm-up, I can tell which students will need drawing out, which students will need structured reinforcement, and which students will need a large elephant to sit on them. By the time the warm-up is completed, the students have a sense of me, I understand them, and we can travel together on new adventures without leaving the room.

Writing this, it makes me wonder if warming up to do academic subjects would help even without drama. Maybe teachers do them; I don't know. I'm wondering if the warm-up for the students is listening to directions, when their minds are traveling the gamut of their experiences. Everyone says transitions are difficult. What if the first two minutes of a math lesson involved a chant dance (see "The Ingredient Games") about math to shake off the spelling, social studies, and the imminent divorce at home?

I know that if I've been working with the same group on a daily basis, which occasionally happens in the summer, I am often lulled into complacency about the warm-ups they'll need. This summer, students requested them. "This sounds fun but can we do a warm-up first? I'm just not awake yet." After that I try always to include a warm-up, even if it's a story, a joke, a mind-bending two-minute puzzle, anything to get all our bodies and minds into the same room.

The following warm-ups are listed by age as a general guide. Some warm-ups for older students may be main activities for younger ones. I often use the younger ones for older classes too. There are no hard and fast rules about warming up. Ironically, choosing a warm-up can mean to jump in with conviction, and don't look back!

Warm-up Contents

For your convenience in matching these warm-ups to your group's needs, I have grouped and labeled them in the following categories:

Physical: The primary focus is kinesthetic, to warm up the physical body as a means of jump-starting the brain. Not all the physical activities involve high levels of energy.

Cooperative: While these activities may overlap into other categories, the primary focus is working with one's peers to solve a problem or achieve a goal. They involve the practice of interpersonal skills.

Cognitive: All of these games involve either perception, memory, or judgment to complete.

Personal: These activities require a higher than average level of intrapersonal skills.

Physical Warm-ups

Cooperative

Cognitive

Physical Warm-ups

Shake, Shake, Shake

General warm-up.

Ages: K-3

This is my personal warm-up. I do it all the time.

1. Stand in a circle, facing in.

2. Give yourself enough elbow room to move.

3. Put your arms above your head and shake out your hands. Just your hands, not your nose, your vocal chords, your lips, or your big toe. Try just shaking your hands.

4. Shake them out up there, then moving your hands down by your hips, shake them out down there. (You should be standing straight up. Only your hands go down.)

5. Shake one hand up, and one hand down.

6. Switch them. Shake the other one up, and the other one down.

7. Shake both hands to one side of you.

8. Shake them to the other side of you.

9. Stretch out your arms and shake one hand on each side of you.

10. Switch them, by crossing your chest and shaking on the opposite side.

11. Let them rest. They should feel all tingly.

12. Standing straight up, roll your shoulders back. Keep rolling.

13. Roll them forward. Keep rolling. (Sometimes, with younger grades, I tell them to bend their elbows and pretend we're trains going down the track. When we switch, we have to go back, because we forgot our lunches.)

14. Put your hands on your hips and without moving your shoulders or your feet, push your rib cage to one side, then the other side, then forward and back. (This one is tricky, and completely optional. I sometimes include it to give them the perspective that we are truly doing something valuable and not just fooling around. Everyone will be able to feel the muscles in their waists. If you're old enough, picture the break-dancing exercises Michael Jackson used to do.)

15. Leave your hands on your waist and swing your hips to one side.

16. Swing them to the other side.

17. Next, do circles of figure eights, once or twice. (Once again, optional, but I always include it in a matter-of-fact way. In some grades there will be giggles, but hips are a part of the body, too. I usually ignore it, and move on.)

18. Stand on one foot and put the other foot out in front of you (about as far off the ground as your nose is long). Balance on one foot, and roll your ankle around in one direction, then the other.

19. Switch feet and roll the other ankle. (No leaning on desks or friends; balance is part of it.)

20. (Grades K-3) Bend your elbow, pretend it is a pencil and write your name in the air.

21. Once the air is full of invisible names, have them use the other elbow and erase the names. (Broken arms have erasers on their writing elbows.)

22. Take your hands and wipe off all the eraser rubbish that is sticking in the air.

23. Take your imaginary dustpan and broom, sweep up the pile of eraser rubbish into your dustpan and empty it into the giant, invisible garbage can in the middle of the circle. (In groups of people wearing blue, red, green, etc., or with names that begin with the letter ___.

24. End with my favorite part of the warm-up. Put your hands by your sides. Using the muscles in your face, squish your face into a little knot. Squish. Hold it for a few seconds, and look around the room, complimenting everyone on their faces.

25. When you cannot hold it any longer, stretch your face out wide, as large as you can go. Open your mouth as far as you can, stretching your jaw.

26. Squish your face to one side, then the other side.

27. Squish it up.

28. And stretch it down.

Tips:

I often explain the final face warm-up as the most important part of the warm-up because it is both very serious and very silly. Warming up faces is extremely important, and if I'm stuck in traffic before a show, I warm up my face in the car. If I'm going to perform for three hundred people playing animals and fish and challenging characters, my face needs to go with me. If it's tight and tired, my characters will look flat. So the face warm-up has an important purpose.

It is also ridiculously silly, which is why I like it. The face warm-up is just like drama, very silly and very serious. If we're too stiff, we're not acting, we're doing Flat Stanley impressions. If we're too silly, we're not accomplishing our goals, so this exercise is my favorite because it models a level of balance we'll need throughout all the activities.

Pass the Face

In one of the Penny Ante Theater performances, fellow actor Steve Holland once introduced me boldly as "The Woman with the Rubber Face." I then proceeded to stretch my face in all directions, to the amazement of hundreds of children.

Years later, I was teaching a workshop to a group of high school students, and a tenth grader wearing the nearly visible cloak of "Don't even think of making me do that near my friends" refused to warm up her face on the grounds that it would most certainly cause wrinkles. My reaction, other than deep sadness for her future life, was to wrinkle my face as much as possible, every day since.

This silly face activity, which I learned from Barbara Goodwillie, is a favorite among the K-2s.

Ages: K-2.

Directions:

1. Sit in a circle.

2. The first person covers her face with her hands, and behind her hands makes the goofiest, scariest, or strangest face she can think of. She moves her hands and shares her new creation with the class.

3. She turns to the next player and shows him her face.

4. He, in turn, takes a moment to copy her goofy face, and shows it to everyone.

5. Next, the second player hides his face behind his hands, and shares it first with the group and then with the person sitting next to him.

6. Continue to pass the face around the circle.

Tips:

1. Play with them. They'll love making faces with you.

Group Movement

Ages: K-3.

Directions:

1. Stand in a circle, facing in.

2. If you're going to be an actor today, we'll need to practice pretending to be someone else. Right now I want you to pretend to be me.

3. I want you to move just as I do from the top of your head to the tip of your toes.

4. If I'm moving slowly, I want you to move slowly, too.

5. If I'm moving quickly, I want you to move quickly, too.

6. If I have a nasty expression on my face (demonstrate), you need to have one, too.

7. If I have a goofy expression on my face (demonstrate), you need to have one, too.

8. It will be hard for the students standing right next to me to see what I do sometimes, but if you move into the circle to see (demonstrate), you'll be blocking other students. All they'll see is your "best side," so if you have trouble seeing, I want you to look across the circle and those students will be following me so closely that'll you'll do fine.

9. Do some simple activities that fit your personality. I often pantomime a clown with a balloon, blowing it up, being proud of it, waving to others to make sure they see his balloon, then popping it, crying, and putting the pieces back in my pocket. Simple marching, smiling broadly, moving your hands in special shapes, making faces works beautifully, and your model will provide your students with a vocabulary of actions to choose from when they're feeling stuck.

10. Next, pick a random student to lead. Make a big deal about this student being the only student in the class with that name.

11. Tell the student she may choose any activity, but she must remain standing up, in the circle. It's too hard to follow, and can be dangerous, to roll on the floor.

12. The rest of us will be trying to act like Susie X., but she doesn't have to worry, because she is without a doubt the best at being Susie X. in the whole room. Do you know why? She has been doing it longer than we have. She cannot fail. She can only be wonderful.

13. Have Susie begin. Compliment all the little details everyone is following. Meanwhile, follow everything she's doing yourself. If she has an uncomfortable twitch, act it out as if she is doing it on purpose. She'll catch on.

14. See, Susie can do whatever she wants. She may want to move her body while staying in the circle shape, standing up. Or she may want to do smaller movements.

15. Let Susie go for a minute. Then choose another student.

16. This game can take a while to fit in every student, so either plan for the time or play it often.

Group Movement Dancing

Ages: Grades 3-Adult.

1. Stand in a circle, facing in. Remain in the circle, standing throughout the activity.

2. Tell the students that you'll be turning on music and choosing a leader to do a simple dance movement.

3. All students should follow and do what the leader is dancing.

4. The leader dances for a moment, and passes the leadership to the next person by gesturing to them dramatically.

5. The second leader dances a new movement for a few moments, and passes the honor again.

6. Go all the way around the circle, with everyone leading a movement.

Tips and Variations:

1. Everyone must participate. Remind the students that one finger wiggling back and forth in the air is dancing.

2. If they look at you and shrug, follow that, and do it as a movement. Any movement can be a dance.

3. At the end, if you have time, when the leading privilege comes back around to you, go into the middle and dance-pick a partner. Dance with that partner, briefly, and then both of you choose a partner from the circle. Then the four of you choose new partners, and so on.

4. Pick music they like for the first few times, because dancing will be easy if they like the music. Then later, try throwing in variety. Once they're comfortable with the exercise, they'll have fun trying to dance to Beethoven, or disco.

Miming Music

Every summer I attend the HOTS (Higher Order Thinking Schools) training through the Connecticut Commission on the Arts to dust off and renew my creativity. By early July I often feel like a big pile of exhaustion, rather than a guide to inspire creative teaching. HOTS works. Within one week, I have discovered new ideas, polished old ideas, and simmered in enough enthusiasm and research about the benefits of arts in education to remember my name.

CHUCK JONES

This past summer I was in a workshop with Cheryl Hulteen, of Artsgenesis. She was beginning our teachers' workshop on the Multiple Intelligences by playing a tape of Mozart, and standing in the middle of a large room playing an imaginary violin, with passion.

Soon, the thirty to forty teachers, as they arrived, put down their baggage and without a word, joined Cheryl in playing the violin to the music. Within a few moments, we were all physically, mentally, and emotionally warmed up. We had dropped our "What room do we go to, last-minute family obligations, I can't believe my body is even standing up" focus, and were ready for anything.

Cheryl told us she learned from a teacher that warming herself up before she began her day was key. So the teacher warms up her mind every day by playing music in her classroom. The children follow directions on the board, and silently slip into their seats as the music stops.

For the rest of the summer I tried it. No day began without my boom box. I listened in the car, and in the community space, before my class began. Every time my body tried to remind me that my spirit was renewed, but it was still tired, on the music went, and I danced my heart out. My choice was "Trashin' the Camp," music from Disney's *Tarzan,* because there is no way I could be in a bad mood while listening to it. It woke me up every time. I may have frightened a few parents dropping off their kids, but such is the price we pay.

Cooperative

The following warm-up activities can be found in the Ingredient Games
Be a Shape (Grades 2-Adult) page 35
Group Up (Grades 2- Adult) page 44

Cannons

In order to play this game, which I learned from Barbara Goodwillie, the students must understand the concepts of space and negative space. Students familiar with photography and printmaking will be familiar with the idea. For this game, they need only to understand that any form their bodies take within an open space fills some of that space, positively. We will, therefore, refer to the area they fill as positive space. Any area around them becomes negative space.

Ages: Grades 3-6

Tools: Space

Directions:

1. Divide the students into groups of four, or five if necessary.

2. Count off numbers one to five within a group.

3. Provide enough space for each group to strike a series of poses without bumping into another group.

4. Have student #1 strike a pose he or she can hold for an extended period of time.

5. Have student #2 select a pose that fills in the negative space around student #1.

6. Have students #3, #4, and #5, if you have them, select a pose one at a time that fills in the negative space around the first few students.

7. Once each student has chosen a pose, select numbers randomly, and have those students step out of the frozen pose and choose a new position that fills in new negative space.

8. All the groups are moving at the same time.

Tips and Variations:

1. No student is actually touching another student.

2. Once the students have the hang of it, try mixing and matching the groups. Examples:

   A. Having the #4s step out and find a place in a new group.

   B. Gradually combine two groups by pulling from one and adding to another.

   C. Gradually create one large group by removing from the smaller ones and adding to the larger one.

Cognitive

The following warm-up activities can be found in the Ingredient Games
Chant Dancing (All Ages) page 36
Lean and Leave (Grades 4- Adult) page52
Swoosh! (Grades 1-8) page 76
Name Games page 59

Cooling Down

Just as warming up is a key to beginning, cooling down is a way of neatly tying a gentle ribbon of structure around the bursts of ideas and excitement the drama session has generated. Many warm-ups can double for cooling down exercises, and visa versa, but keep in mind the idea is to celebrate self-expression and remove the structure of the drama session, while reminding the missiles of energy that there are other orbits awaiting them.

Take as much time as you need for a cool-down activity. Sometimes it can be a quarter of the drama time. Other times, it's a quick tacked-on activity at the end. Both are valid, and whoever has the students after a drama-in-the-curriculum activity will truly appreciate it.

Cool-Down Contents

Physical

Group Dancing (Seated)

Ages: Grades 1-Adult.

Tools: Calm music, space to sit in a large circle.

Directions:

1. Pass the leader role around a circle as others follow each new movement. (For a detailed description, see Group Movement Dancing on page 83.)

2. This time do it seated, with only hands, arms, or feet or noses dancing.

Physical Calm-Down

Ages: Grades K-4.

Tools: Space.

Directions:

1. Each student should form a ball, down on the floor, as small as they can be.

2. As you count to five, the students will slowly stretch to be as large as they can be.

3. At the count of five, when they are standing tall, with their arms stretched up in the air, and each of their fingers stretched out in all directions, begin counting backward, down to one, and they will slowly shrink back down to be as tiny as possible.

4. Repeat as necessary.

Tips and Variations:

1. Encourage them not to go too fast, but rather to gradually grow larger as the numbers increase.

2. If they are particularly wound up, count very slowly, telling them to take extra deep breaths to pass the time as they stretch up and down.

Cognitive

I Remember Ball

Ages: K-4

Tools: A ball.

I've seen this idea in many classrooms. In this case, adding the physical and visual aid of a ball will help some of the daydreamers stay involved.

Directions:

1. Each student should think of something he or she remembered or learned from the activity.

2. The student holding the ball should tell his or her idea in a slow, clear, and loud manner, then pass the ball to another student who says what he or she remembered.

Tips and Variations:

1. This game could also be called I Learned Ball, I Have an Idea Ball, Positive Criticism Ball, or My Next Positive Step Toward My Goal Ball. Use it for everything. Have a ball!

Personal

Emotional Countdown

Ages: K-6

Tools: Space.

Directions:

1. Choose five to ten students, depending upon the time you have. The remaining students will watch. Ask them to create an emotional statue. Choose the emotion for them. Their statue should reflect the extreme degree of the chosen emotion, such as overwhelmingly happy, completely shocked, deeply sad.

2. During a slow count of five, have the emotion slowly melt and change into a new emotion. By the time they reach five, the students should be demonstrating an intense degree of the new emotion.

3. Call out another emotion, and have them within the count of five melt to the third choice.

4. Have the first group rest, while other groups have a turn.

5. You may want to discuss what these emotions look like in detail. What does someone's body do when they are deeply angry?

Runway

Tools: Space.

At first sighting this may seem similar to the I Remember Ball, where a student shares a piece of information in front of the group, because they do indeed do that, but the activity is much more.

 I've been told that man's number one fear is public speaking. In this activity the participants present themselves, and some information. They are not representing animals, or characters, or geometric shapes, or something other. This is personal. I've seen powerful moments as a result of this activity. If we all did it more often, perhaps man's number one fear could go back to alien invasion, or man's inhumanity to man.

Ages: Grades 5-8

Directions:

1. Set a stage area, where one student at a time will be able to walk across the front, stop in the middle, turn to the audience, speak slowly, loudly, clearly, and proudly, and present themselves, saying, "My name is _____, and I_____." They will then take a moment, or beat, for the audience to catch up to what they have said, rather than to run off the stage. They will turn slowly and calmly and walk to the other side of the stage. Each student will follow in turn.

2. Decide what the category of information will be. The statement must be positive. Have them tell something special about themselves that they really like. Example: My name is Carol, and I have long legs. My name is Carol, and I am a good friend to have because I am loyal.

Tips and Variations:

1. Make sure they don't rush, or speak as they are running across the stage. Make sure they give the audience time to take in what they say. Theater directors call this a "beat," where you finish your monologue and wait for the last statement to bounce into the audience and land. If they don't understand the "beat" concept, tell them to smile a moment before they go.

Sample Topics:

1. If drama was an introduction to a larger project, have them announce something they plan to do in the larger project. My name is Al and my cultural story will be Anansi, from West Africa.

2. Something they want to do in their lifetime. My name is Frieda and I want to sky-dive.

3. An occupation they want to be when they grow up.

4. A time in history in which they would like to have lived.

5. A reason they would or would not like to live in the country or time period you have been studying.

6. Their favorite story character.

7. Their favorite childhood memory (so far).

SECTION II

Drama Activities by Subject

Science

Math

Social Studies

Language Arts

Science K-2

Table of Contents

Acting a Process

As someone who looks at the world through drama-colored glasses, I see the study of science as understanding a series of processes and concepts. If I'm teaching science in a classroom, that's where I jump first. What is the main concept? What is the sequence in the process?

I figure that if students understand the concepts, their interest will be tweaked enough to pay attention to the process. If they can visualize the process, then they own it enough to be excited by the details and make hypotheses galore.

Mrs. H., my high school chemistry teacher, is no doubt rolling around in her grave, but then again tweaking interest and confidence was not her focus. I take pleasure in the concept that while she unabashedly obliterated my scientific confidence and interest with her wide slow smile and evil glare I am playing with students, rolling on the floor as molting butterflies, buzzing from flower to flower, pollinating, and yes, Mrs. H., acting out chemical reactions so that we can all understand and enjoy them.

The Life Cycle of a Butterfly

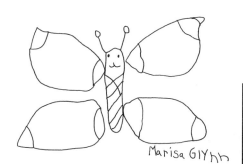

Marisa Glynn

Ages: Grades 1-4.

Tools (for Activity 3, below):
* Several pieces of colorful cloth about a yard in length.
* Great colors for the process include gray, green, and brown.
* Bright colors work well for final butterflies.
* Brown material, or two or three paper bags, with slits cut along the side to facilitate molting.

Directions:
I usually do all three of the following activities in a one-hour workshop. You may want to spread them out over a week.

1. Reading: Start with a story. I like to use *From Caterpillar to Butterfly* by Deborah Heiligman, a book from the Let's Read and Find Out Science series. It tells the life cycle of a butterfly through the perspective of young students who are watching it grow.

2. Individual Processing: Next, give each student an opportunity to act out the life cycle by finding their own space in the room, with enough elbow room to move and not be distracted by the others. Act out the life cycle as you sing the following song. Give general suggestions as to movement, by curling up to be a small egg, staying in their own space, etc., but if possible, allow them to become their own individual, evolving butterfly, creating their own specific movements. Their creativity is delightful! They may want to sing with you, or repeat after you, or simply move silently as they listen to you.

Butterfly Song

By Carol Glynn (To the tune of *"Twinkle, Twinkle, Little Star"*)

I asked my mother in the sky
If I'd become a butterfly.
She sat me down and told me this:
It's a story about metamorphosis.
I cracked my egg and popped right out.
I'm so hungry, I want to shout.
So I'll stretch out and munch, munch, munch,

straight through dinner, and breakfast and lunch.

I'm getting so big my skin feels tight.
But eating this leaf is a delight
I shed my skin. We call this molting.
If you're squeamish, it's revolting.

I make a button and hang around
This stick is many feet off the ground
I molt one more time and form this pupa,
A chrysalis! It's "supa dupa"!

And then one day, CRACK, my head pops out.
My body and wings follow. I want to shout!
I stretch my wings to let them dry.
Now I am a butterfly!

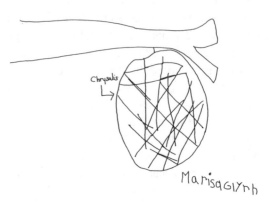

3. Acting Out a Process Cooperatively with a Group:
   Tell a story of a butterfly's life cycle, in all the stages from the egg to the caterpillar, forming the chrysalis and finally the butterfly, inviting the students up to become moving statues as you go. Each student should have a turn through the process.

General Parts: (If you forget to switch people through the process, don't worry. There is always room for extra butterflies at the end.)
leaves, or stems
egg
caterpillar (or larva)
four additional caterpillar actors, as the caterpillar molts and crawls out of its old skin
chrysalis (or pupa)
sticks
silk button
two-person window
butterflies

Directions:

1. Ask a few students to personify leaves and stems. Cover their bodies with green material if you wish.

2. Invite another student to be a mother butterfly, to fly by and attach an egg (or student) on one of the leaves or stems. (In this case "attached" does not mean sitting on directly.)

3. Hatch the egg, by having the egg student peek and climb out of an imaginary egg shell.

4. Applaud the egg actor, and invite a new student to come up and be the caterpillar, or larva. The job of this actor is to eat, eat, and eat some more, through all the stages of growth. The leaf students may remain on the ground. If they get too antsy, tell them they've been eaten, and ask them to return to the audience.

5. As the caterpillar grows, add another student each time the caterpillar sheds its skin, in a process called molting. The caterpillar molts four or more times during the growing process. Each time the head caterpillar eats to a point where it doesn't have any more room in its skin. It crawls out of the old skin. Immediately add another student, and have the head caterpillar eat some more.

6. Have a student form an imaginary silk button (or use cloth) and attach it to another student twig. Have the caterpillar student molt one more time, forming a hard-shell chrysalis this time (gray or brown material).

7. A new actor/student cracks the hard shell and becomes the hatching butterfly, peeking out slowly, looking

around.

8. Another student becomes the butterfly spreading its wings and waiting for them to dry and have enough blood pump into them.

9. Another one becomes the butterfly flying slowly around the room.

10. Other butterflies, who have been growing in other classrooms, meet the butterfly, and they fly in a circle, flapping their wings (many different cloths can be used here).

11. Two students form a window, which opens, letting the butterflies climb outside

12. Butterflies fly out the window and around the room gently and gracefully.

Set Them Free to Music

Does your class grow butterflies? Marisa's first grade teacher, Mrs. Haaland, wrote the following song for her class. They sang it to their butterflies as they let them go. Marisa continued to sing it, at the top of her lungs, around our house, for several weeks afterwards.

"Bye Bye Butterfly" (To the tune of "The Rubber Tree Plant")

by Maureen Haaland

Once there was a little green egg,
who thought he'd be a caterpillar instead.
He wiggled and jiggled free-ee.

(Clap once to demonstrate the egg hatching)

And he said "Munch, Munch!"
He said "Cru- uh - uh- unch!"
He said "Munch!" And "Crunch, 'cause that's my lunch!"

Now it's time to go and he hangs down low,
forming a chrysalis now.
Oops! Here comes the wings.
Makes me want to sing.
He's ready to take to the sky.

Oh, I know he'll fly.
Yes, oh how he'll fly.
It's time to say goodbye.

Bye, bye butterfly
so long butterfly,
It's time to say goodbye.

Pollination

Ages: Grades 2-4

Directions:

The concept: In order for a plant to spread its seeds to grow new plants that are identical to its parents and plants that are new, exciting, and different from its parents, pollen and ovules (seeds) need to meet.

Acting: The Wind Process

Many plants use the wind to disperse their pollen and seeds.

1. Ask 4 or 5 children to be dandelions, depending on your space.

2. Ask 1 to 3 children for each dandelion to be the pollen, by freezing in a statue pose next to their dandelion.

3. Invite 1 to 3 children to be the wind, and wave their arms gracefully as they weave in and out of the plants, as they gently lift the seeds off the dandelions . Seated children may join in by making the wind sounds. Drape the wind in a soft, billowy cloth if you like.

4. The seeds from the dandelion float gently all over the lawn, where they will grow.

5. Feel free to put a high-speed lens on your an imaginary video camera and watch the new dandelions grow in a matter of seconds.

6. Consider adding in an animal walking by. Have the seeds attach to its fur and see where it goes.

7. Invite a reluctant child to blow the dandelion seeds off into the wind.

Acting :The Animal Process

1. The concept: These seeds are spread either by catching on to an animal's fur and sooner or later falling off, or by animals eating them. Animals such as squirrels like to eat acorns, and when they defecate the seed falls into a new place. From here it will grow into a new tree.

2. Choose several students to become large oak trees. Several students may choose to be one large tree together. They can grow to be eighty feet tall and eight hundred years old.

3. Either use real acorns, wadded paper acorns, student acorns, or imaginary acorns. Choose two or three squirrels for a small tree, four or five for a large tree, and invite them to gather acorns from the trees and take them to their imaginary nests. Perhaps the squirrels drop some on the way. Perhaps they take them all to the nest. As long as they disperse them. Personally, I would do the entire exercise and have them back in their seats before I added the afterthought of defecating squirrels, if at all.

4. Consider singing an acorn song if you know one, or playing some light and peppy instrumental music. For some reason, "Baby Elephant Walk," by Henry Mancini, comes to mind. Perhaps it's the vision of student-size squirrels.

Acting: The Insect Process

The concept: Bees want nectar to make honey. They are attracted by the fragrance and the bright colors of the flowers, and dig way down deep inside the flowers, covering themselves in pollen as they seek the nectar. Next the bee flies off to visit flower number two, bringing along some of the pollen from the first flower to the second flower. The bees are happy because they have nectar. The flowers are happy because they have been pollinated. It's a win-win pollination!

Directions:

1. Divide the class in thirds. Have two thirds be flowers.

2. The final third will be the bees.

3. Play "Flight of the Bumblebee" by Rimsky-Korsakov on a tape (optional) as the bees fly from flower to flower reaching for nectar, are covered in pollen, and take it to the next flower.

Prop Ideas: (optional)

1. Have each flower hold a special piece of paper or foil, to be the nectar the bees are searching for.

2. Have each flower have two or three pieces of string or something that will easily attach to the bee to take on to the next flower. The next flower may choose to exchange the string for new string, and the bees will carry that on.

Costume Ideas: (optional)

Using pipe cleaners and headbands, have each child create either a bee or a flower headband. The bee headbands will need two antennae.

Encourage the students to design their favorite flowers. Attach the petals to a head band.

Fold a large piece of construction paper over, cut wing shapes and attach string to make bee wings, if you wish.

Bees can also tape black strips of construction paper to yellow cloth or paper if they wish.

Drape the flowers in bright, colorful cloths.

Parts of a Tree

Ages: Grades 1-4.

Several years ago I saw a second-grade teacher do a demonstration, at a HOTS (Higher Order Thinking Schools) conference, of students acting out the parts of a tree. While I have taught something similar in my one-hour workshops, she added a few touches, such as having students hold cue cards for their parts (they were even laminated!), and having each section of the tree speak its lines in rhythm and move in unison. By taking the time to set up the activity, which she will undoubtedly use for years, she used all eight multiple intelligences to help her students learn the parts of the tree. No student was left out. No learning style was left out. Her students not only will understand the tree, they'll never forget the experience!

Directions:

1. Cast your characters in the following parts. Give them each a short rhythmic saying to describe their function. Choose two to four students for each section. If you have a double class, choose four to eight students for each section.

   A. The Heartwood. *The heartwood adds support. We're strong!* (Repeat)
   B. The Sapwood. *We're the sapwood. We carry food and water up.* (Repeat)
   C. The Cambium. *We're the cambium. We divide bark and wood.* (Repeat)
   D. The Inner Bark. *We're the inner bark. We bring food down.* (Repeat)
   E. The Outer Bark. We're the outer bark. We protect. (Repeat)
   F. The Roots. *We're the roots. We drink in food. We make a solid base.* (Repeat)
   G. The Soil. *We're the soil. We provide food.* (Repeat)
   H. The Leaves. *We supply carbon to feed the tree.* (Repeat)
   I. Medullary Rays. *We store food. We store food.* (Repeat)
   J. Annual Rings. *Count the rings. Tell the tree's age.* (Repeat)

2. Invite one group at a time to the front of the room. Show them where and how to move. Feel free to design your own ideas. Some general suggestions are below.

   A. *The Heartwood:* The heartwood could stand straight in the center in a group. When they say the word "strong," they could show their muscles.
   B. *The Sapwood:* Stand them in a circle around the heartwood, leaving enough room for elbows between each student. Have them pretend to be holding trays of food. When they say "up," they can hold their

imaginary trays above their heads.

C. *The Cambium:* Walk in a circle around the sapwood. As they go, have them make a dividing movement with their hands on the word "divide."

D. *The Inner Bark:* Walk in a circle around the cambium, and walk in the opposite direction. Do a movement that reflects "bringing food down" as they go.

E. *The Outer Bark:* Sit the students in a layer outside the inner bark, on the side facing any remaining audience. Have them fold their arms individually, or link arms between them, to show that they protect the tree.

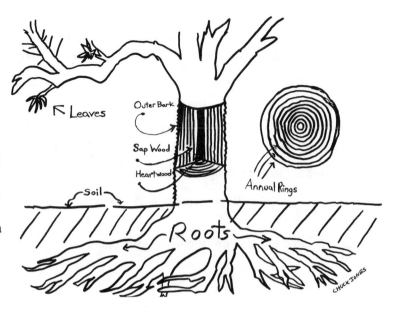

F. *The Roots:* Stretch a few root students out around the tree. Have them wiggle their fingers to show how they absorb nutrients.

G. The Soil: (optional) Sit the soil just beyond the roots. Have the soil feed the roots as they speak.

H. *The Leaves:* Stand the leaves wherever you have space beyond the outer bark. Have them stand tall and wiggle their fingers as they gather the carbon under their leaves to feed the tree.

Changing Seasons

Ages: Grades K-3.

Activity 1: Choose one natural element that changes during the seasons and have all the students act that part at the same time. Example: Ask each student to find some space in the room and have all the students be trees at the same time. If they close their eyes you can talk them through all the stages of being a tree, feeling little leaves grow in their branches, shading others in the hot summer sun, standing strong during brisk fall winds and icy winter storms. Ask them how it felt to be a tree through all the seasons. Did they have any animals living in them? Could they feel their roots grow stronger under the ground as they grew older? Perhaps they could follow up the activity by writing about their experience.

Activity 2: Seasonal Statues. Pick a season. Have students choose parts of that season and freeze in a chosen position forming a giant picture of the season, all facing one direction as if they were in a picture book. For more information on statues, see the Ingredient Games p. 96.

Activity 3: Combine Activities 1 and 2. Each student will choose his or her own part of a season and act it out through the seasonal change, simultaneously. Don't panic. It can be done in an organized manner, especially if you have previously introduced Activities 1 and 2. Students will have a concept of staying in one area, and of how their favorite natural element changes throughout the seasons.

Directions:

1. Talk about the seasons, and what happens within each season. Make a class list of what each season will need. Divide up the parts. For the purposes of explanation, we'll work with the following list. This is a Northeast version of the United States.

   Fall: trees, leaves, grass, flowers wilting, sun, clouds, wind, squirrels, birds flying south, pumpkins, a pond, people raking and jumping in leaves.

Winter: trees, sun, snow, clouds, wind, squirrels sleeping in nests, snow people, people ice skating on a pond, people sledding and skiing.

Spring: trees growing leaves, grass growing, flowers growing, sunshine, birds who have flown back looking for worms, baby birds in nests, squirrels running around, children playing outside.

Summer: trees, leaves, grass, flowers, sun, kids running through sprinklers, swimming.

Sample parts division for a class of twenty four students: 2 trees, 4 flowers, 2 grass, 2 sun (to help show intensity), 1 wind, 2 birds (one can be a baby in the spring), 3 people, 1 snow, 2 leaves, 1 cloud, 2 squirrels, 2 snow people.

2. Set up a standing picture statue of your first season.

3. Choose a stationary place for the trees, the sun, the flowers, and the grass. Choose a movement area for the moving elements, such as the wind, the birds, the people, the snow, the leaves, the squirrels, etc. These may be a small circle, a row in front of the others, whatever, as long as each child has a designated area that does not bump into the others.

4. Talk through the seasons. Add in the children making snow people and raking leaves, flowers peeking their heads above the ground, mother birds feeding their young.

5. (Optional) If the children have done this a few times, you may want to eliminate the words, and add music, for a performance to share with other classes.

Seasonal Activities: Pass the Object

Ages: K-2

Directions:

Sitting in a circle, pass a nondescript object around to each student, having them pretend that the object is something that they would use during a certain season of the year. For more specific directions on Pass the Object, see the Ingredient Games.

> *Example:* Winter: a coat, a scarf, mittens, hot chocolate, a shovel, a sled, sticks for a snowman, etc. Spring: seeds, shovels, bulbs, hoses, light sweaters, shorts, baseball bats, swings, etc.

"The Water Cycle Song"

(To the tune of "I'm a Little Teapot")

I'm a little water drop, here I go.
Sometimes I'm rain and sometimes I'm snow.
How do I decide? Do I use my imagination?
(spoken) No!
The temperature dictates the precipitation.

When I reach the ground I give it a drink.
Sometimes I run off. Sometimes I sink.
When the ground is full, I roll away.
I go off looking for someplace to play.

When the sun is out, the day is great.
I get so hot, I evaporate.
I go up in the air. It's hard to see me.
Now I'm a vapor, and I float freely.

I will float up high, since I'm allowed.
I'll condense with some friends and become a cloud.
When the air is warm enough, and the pressure is great,
I'll go down again and precipitate.

We've sung the water cycle, from beginning to end.
Please keep me clean, 'cause water's your friend.

Animals

Classification with Duck, Duck, Goose

Ages: Grades K-3.

Tools: Space.

Directions:

1. Begin by reviewing the rules for Duck, Duck, Goose.

   A. Form a circle, seated on the ground.
   B. Identify the stew pot as a place in the center of the circle.
   C. Choose someone to begin. The starting student will move around the circle tapping students on the shoulder. Each time the student taps, he or she says "Duck."
   D. After several "Ducks" the student will tap a student on the shoulder and say "Goose!"
   E. The goose jumps up, and chases the tapping student all the way around the circle, in a clockwise fashion, until the tapping student reaches the empty seat left by the goose.
   F. If the goose catches the tapping student, he or she must sit in the stew pot, in the center of the circle, until someone else is caught by the goose.
   G. The goose now becomes the tapping student and the directions are repeated.

2. Choose a category of animals, birds, or insects. Example: mammals, sea creatures, zoo animals, farm animals, reptiles, forest animals with a cold habitat, rain forest animals, dinosaurs.

3. Change the title of the game according to your category. Example: Mammal, Mammal, Dog; Farm, Farm, Cow; Rain Forest, Rain Forest, Ocelot.

4. Replace the tapping system of saying "duck, duck, duck, duck, goose," to "zoo, zoo, zoo, zoo, giraffe."

5. Once tapped as a giraffe, the giraffe student must become a giraffe, move as a giraffe, and move as quickly or slowly as a giraffe might move, chasing the first student around the circle.

6. When the giraffe takes a turn saying "zoo, zoo, zoo, giraffe," he will replace giraffe with a brand-new zoo animal. The new student must become that animal. The new animal must fit into the category. Only sea creatures will work for the sea game. Only nocturnal animals will work for the Night, Night, Owl game.

7. So, now in the zoo game, you'll have an elephant chasing a giraffe in one round followed by a tiger chasing an elephant in another. You may follow up by having a bear chasing a tiger, etc.

8. Change the name of the stew pot, to reflect your new category. Let the students help you decide what to call it. Example: For zoo animals, the stew pot may be a cage. For rain forest animals, it may be the canopy. (You may have to sprinkle some rain forest floor animals with magic dust so they may survive in the canopy.)

Tips and Variations:

1. Demonstrate ways to move if you are an enormous heavy animal, like an elephant, or a tiny animal, like a mouse.

2. Encourage the personification of animals by adding detail to the students acting. Practice by having students personify a few different animals within the category before playing the game. Example: Mice

   A. have wiggling whiskers,
   B. take tiny steps
   C. play with their tails
   D. may use hands for little ears
   E. move very quickly.

3. If you are concerned that the students won't know the appropriate animals for the category, brainstorm a list beforehand and leave it up during the game. The next time you play, you won't need it. Personifying the animals within the category will make them stick for a long time.

4. Remind the students that people pretending to be mice can run faster than people pretending to be snakes, and in this version of the game, it's more important to be your chosen animal than to catch the animal in front of you.

Match Up: Animals

Ages: Grade 1-4 (a warm-up for older grades).

Tools:
* Cards or pictures with animal pictures on them,
* or picture cards with matching word cards,
* or word cards, with matching word cards

See Match Up in the Ingredient Games for directions page 58.

Tips and Variations:

1. Choose a category of animals or insects to examine and have students make two matching pictures of an animal within that category. If students draw the pictures, have them write the name of the animal on the same card, so there won't be any confusion over what the animal actually is. Collect the cards and redistribute them. Play as directed.

2. Have each student draw or cut out and color a picture of an animal on one card, and write the name of the animal on the other card. Collect and redistribute the cards among students. Play as directed.

3. *Example* Topics for Animal Match Up:

   mammals
   reptiles
   insects
   rodents
   animals and insects that live in the: sea, forest, rain forest, farm, desert, etc.
   animals and insects that are nocturnal
   animals that are domesticated.
   animals that are wild
   zoo animals
   animals that are already on a matching game on your shelf

plant eaters
meat eaters

Look for directions to the following animal activity in the Ingredient Games
Living Machines: Create Any Animal in Groups p. 57

Swat It! Dinosaurs

Ages: Grades 2- 4.

Identify Meat Eaters versus Plant Eaters. A healthy, competitive game which reinforces facts. Two players at a time try to swat the correct answer on the board, before the other side has a chance. I played the dinosaur version with second graders and they loved showing off their expertise. For complete instructions to Swat It!, see the Ingredient Games.

Machines

Transportation: Acting Out Machines in Large and Small Groups

Ages: Grades 1-6.

Directions:

1. See directions for Acting Out Realistic and Abstract Machines in the Ingredient Games.

2. Consider having students act out machines that will directly tie into your unit.

Sample Transportation Machines:

Spaceships	Trucks	Roller Skates
Lunar Modules	Station Wagons	Ice Skates
Rockets	Compact Cars	Snowmobiles
Supersonic Jets	Jet Skis	Ambulances
Helicopters	Convertibles (Punch Buggies)	Motor Boats
Hang Gliders	Vans	Fire Trucks
Airplanes	Jeeps	

Match Up: Machine Words to Pictures

Ages: Grades 1-4

Tools: Matching cards with pictures of machines and words.

Directions:

1. Give half the class pictures of machines, and the other half words on cards.

2. Follow the directions to "mill around" under Matching in the Ingredient Games.

3. Or consider lining up the pictures on one side of the room and the words on the other.

4. Have each picture person move across the room acting out the machine, individually with their body, making a sound of the machine.

5. Once across the room, each picture person should go down the line of word people and try to match his or her card to their word.

6. As in any card game, once the cards are matched, the students should sit down.

Senses

Five Senses: Chant
Ages: Grades 2-4

Chorus:

You've got your five senses.
What will they do for you?
You've got your five senses.
Each day they pull you through.

You start with the eyes, and see what you see.
You can look all around.
You might even see me.

Seeing is a sense that helps you every day.
Open your eyes, to learn, relax, and play.

Chorus:

Use your ears, and listen to the sea.
You can hear your teacher.
You might even hear me.

Hearing is a sense that helps you every day.
Open your ears, to learn, relax, and play

Chorus:

Use your nose, and smell the sweet and sour.
You can smell some food,
and know it's the dinner hour.
Smelling is a sense that helps you every day.
Breathe through your nose, to learn, relax, and play.

Chorus:

Use your tongue, and taste with all your buds.
Enjoy your food,
from cantaloupe to spuds.

Tasting is a sense that helps you every day
Taste with your tongue.
Enjoy three square meals a day.

Chorus:

Use your skin, to keep your body in,
and feel with your skin,
your fingers to your chin.

Touching is a sense that helps you every day.
Touch with your skin, to learn, relax, and play.

Chorus:

Chant Dance: Planets

Ages: Grades 1-4.

Directions:

Want to memorize a list? Try singing and dancing it. For more on Chant Dancing, see the Ingredient Games p. 36.

The Planets: Mercury, Venus, Earth, Mars, Jupiter, Saturn, Uranus, Neptune, Pluto

Sample Chant:

10, 9, 8, 7, 6
5, 4, 3, 2, 1.
Flying through space is gonna be fun.
We'll lift off, and then we'll greet
All the planets that we can meet.
Mercury, Venus, Earth and Mars
These inner planets are closer than most stars.
Then beyond that, it's cold, so it won't melt.
We jump right over an asteroid belt.
Jupiter, Saturn, Uranus, Neptune
Soaring through the universe makes me want to croon.
The tiniest one is on the end.
Come on, Pluto. Be my friend.

Line Up: Planets

Ages: Grades 2-4

Tools: Names of the planets on cards or slips of paper.

Directions:

Given cards with the planet names on them, students compare cards, and line up in the proper order to face an audience.

Tips: Double the cards and use two lines to involve eighteen students. Have the other students be official NASA Line Up judges.

Pass the Object: What to Take to the Moon?

Ages: Grade 2-4

Pass a nonspecific object around (a chalkboard eraser, a foam shape), pretending it is an entirely different object that would fit into a category, such as something you would take to the moon. By handling the object and showing how they would use it, students demonstrate their knowledge of the topic in a visual and kinesthetic way. For complete instructions to Pass the Object, see the Ingredient Games page 62.

Planning a Trip to the Moon

My daughter's first-grade class at Lillie B. Haynes Elementary School in East Lyme, Connecticut, recently took a trip to the moon. To this day she'll tell you it was the real moon. She did, however, admit to our dog that she was wearing a white plastic garbage bag for a space suit, but Jenny, our golden retriever, is sworn to secrecy. She also wore the bottom of a paper bag as a helmet with a paper plate rim surrounding her face. Each child had a two-liter plastic bottle of oxygen, with straws to breathe through.

Accompanied by a tape of the theme from *2001: A Space Odyssey* (Also "Sprach Zarathustra," by Richard Strauss), three classes of first graders paraded through school halls to the cheers and salutes of other students in a giant send-off. I can vouch for at least one blubbering parent, whose face was awash in tears (me). One astronaut from each class carried enormous classroom flags. Out the door they went in the December air, to parade around the building. (They were warned that it would be cold on the moon! Astronauts wear twenty-one layers of clothing.) As they landed, the principal, Dr. Johnson, met them in the front hall to officially mark their sleeves with NASA stickers. One class at a time took turns on a rented moon walk, which was set up in the cafeteria, after a short discussion on gravity. The other two classes had a space snack of peanut butter and crushed graham crackers.

It has been several weeks, and the moon facts from our six-year-old astronaut continue to flow. Every mention of space shuttles, rockets, or moon launches on the evening news is duly noted and pointed out. She usually refers to the scientists involved as "other astronauts". When I needed moon vocabulary for an earlier exercise, I consulted the house expert. I'm convinced that every child who went on that voyage will remember forever that they'll need oxygen to breathe, because my poor parental videotape shows each one sucking on the straws for dear life. They learned through experience, and they will never forget it.

Whether or not your astronauts actually travel to the moon, the following activities may help them prepare their imagination for a safe and educational journey.

Swoosh!: Planets and Constellations; What Will You Find on the Moon?

Ages: Grades 2-4.

Tools: Space.

Standing, or sitting, in a circle, students pass information around in an entertaining, educational way. I like this game because no student is put on the spot. If they can't think of a new fact, they repeat the fact that is passed to them, without losing face, because it's part of the game. Teachers like it, because facts are passed around and repeated over and over as part of the game, so students are drilling on them without knowing it. Students like it, because it's fun. For instructions to Swoosh, see the Ingredient Games.

Variations: Swoosh!: What Will You Find on the Moon?

Weather

Match Up: Weather to Clothing

Ages: Grades 1-2

Tools: 3 5 cards

Directions:

1. Brainstorm a list of different kinds of weather with your students. Become as specific as you wish. Example: Stick to cold, hot, snowy, rainy, or allow them to slide into those gray areas such as sunny but windy, cloudy with a cold drizzle.

2. Brainstorm a separate list of appropriate clothing and accessories for different kinds of weather. Example: Boots, sweaters, mittens, sunscreen, etc.(Does anyone wear galoshes anymore?)

3. Write the lists on the cards.

4. Divide the students into two groups.

5. Give one group the weather cards. Give the other group the clothing cards.

6. Play the Match Up game and have the students seek each other out.

7. Once each group has matched up with appropriate partners, go around and have the students explain their choices. For more specific directions and suggestions for the Match Up game, see the Ingredient Games page 58.

Conducting a Storm

Ages: K-5.

Directions:

1. Brainstorm a real storm with your class. What sounds would they hear in a large storm? List them.

2. Choose a wind section, a thunder section, a lightning section, and a pelting rain section.

3. (Optional) Have each section demonstrate the difference between pianissimo (very soft) to forte (very loud). Example: A wind might be a light breeze, or whistle and grow to a howl.

4. Follow directions for Conducting an Orchestra in the Ingredient Games page 46.

CHAPTER TEN

Science 3-4

Table of Contents

Biology

THE HUMAN BODY

Look for the following activity in Science K-2
Five Senses Chant: (Grades 2-4) page 101

Acting Out Cells

Ages: Grades 3-10.

Any time you can take a diagram with important parts for your students to learn and re-create it with student bodies, you will open a variety of windows in their brains through which they can accept and process the information. Moving the desks may take a little more time, but you'll have a higher chance of reaching more students at one time, because they'll remember that Sally was the mitochondria for years.

Concept: Each part of a cell has a name a movement and a function, which helps the organism.

Directions:

1. Show the students a diagram of the cell, so they can make the connection between the textbook version and the live student version. Go over the names and functions of each part as you would normally.

2. Next clear a space cell. Decide whether the cell you're creating is a plant or animal cell, and invite the students to become part of it. Each cell part should understand its name and function and create a simple, appropriate movement for their part. (Nothing fancy is necessary, but it adds life to the cell.)

3. Once the cell is constructed, choose an interviewer to walk through the cell and ask the parts about their function within the cell. Feel free to be the interviewer yourself as a model for future lessons.

   Example:

   Interviewer: So, Mr. Cell Membrane, may I come in?

   Cell Membrane: It depends who you are.

   Interviewer: I'm here from WSCHOOL radio, and I wanted to know more about your cell.

   Cell Membrane: Are you sure you're not a virus? My job is to let in food and let out waste. I protect the cell.

   Interviewer: I don't want to harm the cell. I want to ask it some questions.

Tips and Variations:

1. Create a serious realistic cell first.

2. Next imagine that the cell is for a pig or a worm. How would that change the answers?

3. Finally put the cell in an unusual setting. Keeping the functions of the cell parts the same with respect to the cell, how would they change if the cell were a school building, a classroom, or a restaurant? The similarities could be described during the cell interview. By comparing the cell functions to systems they understand, they'll understand the parts, and have fun at the same time. See the examples below.

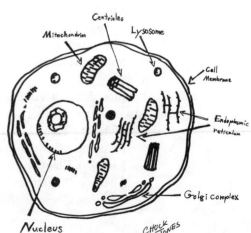

Parts of a Cell

1. *Cell Membrane:* The cell membrane is a flexible covering that surrounds and protects the cell. Substances can pass into and out of the cell through the cell membrane. A cell membrane of a school would be the security system. Substances (students) can pass into and out of the cell through the cell membrane. The cell membrane of the classroom would be the door. A restaurant cell membrane would be the hostess, or the bouncers.

2. *Nucleus:* Controls the rest of the cell. It sends messages to all other parts of the cell, telling the cell what to do. A school nucleus would be the principal. The nucleus of the classroom cell would be the teacher. A restaurant's nucleus would be the manager.

3. *Chromosomes:* Chromosomes are inside the nucleus. They contain all the cell's operating instructions. Chromosomes are made of proteins and DNA. DNA directs the cell's activities. A school's chromosomes would be the mandated curriculum. A classroom's chromosomes would be the lesson plans. A restaurant's chromosomes could be the menu and/or the workers' schedule.

4. *Mitochondria:* Supply the cell with the energy required to carry on life's processes. Enzymes in the mitochondria break down organic molecules and release the energy contained in them. The school mitochondria could be the funding. The classroom mitochondria could be enthusiasm for learning, or snack. The restaurant's could be the cash flow.

5. *Cytoplasm:* A jellylike substance inside the cell. All the other parts of the cell float in the cytoplasm. For all three settings we could choose air, or take it a step further and say we're all floating in "attitude" or "sense of cooperation" or "hospitality."

6. *Cell Wall (plants only):* A rigid structure that surrounds each cell of a plant. The cell wall helps make plants stiff enough to grow upright. It also prevents water loss. The cell wall, being more rigid than an animal's cell membrane, could be a rigid security system in a school with metal detectors and security personnel walking the hallways, or a code of ethics that demands "upright" morality.

7. *Chloroplasts (plants only):* Capture sunlight that plants need for growth. Chloroplasts cold be as simple as windows in a building or a solar panel, saving energy for future use.

Singing Skeletons

Scholastic Inc. has a great version of the old spiritual "Dem Bones," by Bob Barner, which begs to be acted out. The illustrations of skeletons playing instruments are equally inspiring. Throughout the book the function of each bone is described.

"Dem Bones" is one of the most well-known and loved African American spirituals, a song about resurrection. "Dem Bones" was probably first sung in church and at revival meetings as long as two hundred years ago. Passed on by word of mouth, there are many versions." *Dem Bones,* by Bob Barner, (New York: Scholastic Inc. 1996)

Ages: Grades 3-4

Directions:

1. Try chant dancing the song for fun. Either point to each bone as you go, or wiggle each bone as you sing.

2. Consider creating a skit about them, inserting definitions as you go. Play and skit rehearsals are repetition for fun. Why not rehearse your curriculum? They'll learn the facts and wonder why you've stopped "working."

Example Skit Structure:

Consider having everyone sing the entire song with chosen bone speakers, or divide the students up into smaller singing groups of leg singers, body singers, arm singers, etc., for the verses. Everyone should sing and dance like skeletons to the choruses.

Chorus: (Enter Dancing)
Dem Bones, Dem Bones, Dem Dry Bones.
Dem Bones, Dem Bones, Dem Dry Bones
Dem Bones, Dem Bones, Dem Dry Bones
Hear the word of the Lord. (Or ... Let's see how they connect.)

The toe bone's connected to the foot bone.
The toe bone's connected to the foot bone.
The toe bone's connected to the foot bone.
Tell us about the bone.

Foot Bone: (Insert information about what you want them to know about the foot bone. Consider having the bone groups do their own research and fill in a few lines.)

The foot bone's connected to the ankle bone. (Sing three times)
Tell us about the bones.

Ankle Bone: (bone definition)

The ankle bone's connected to the leg bone.(Sing three times)
Tell us about the bones.

Leg Bone: (facts)
Chorus: Dem Bones, Dem Bones, etc.

The knee bone's connected to the thigh bone. (Sing three times)
Tell us about the bones.

Knee Bone: (facts)

The thigh bone's connected to the hip bone. (Sing three times.)
Tell us about the bones.

Thigh Bone: (facts)

The hip bone's connected to the back bone. (Sing three times.)
Tell us about the bones.

The Hip Bone: (facts)

The back bone's connected to the shoulder bone. (Sing three times.)
Tell us about the bones.

The Back Bone: (facts)

The shoulder bone's connected to the neck bone. (Sing three times.)
Tell us about the bones.

The Shoulder Bone: (facts)

The neck bone's connected to the head bone. (Sing three times.)
Tell us about the bones.

The Neck Bone: (facts)

Dem Bones, Dem Bones, Dem Dry Bones.
Dem Bones , Dem Bones, Dem Dry Bones
Dem Bones, Dem Bones, Dem Dry Bones
Hear the word of the Lord. (Or, that's how the bones connect.)

Giant Human Body: Pop-up Statue

Imagine a sleeping giant stretched out across your classroom or gym. Re-create the giant using student bodies to be the parts of the body you are working on.

Ages: Grades 3-5

Directions:

1. Starting from one end of the giant, ask the students the sequence of the bones, muscles, vital organs, etc.

2. As each student names the next part, ask them to become it, by standing in the proper place in the sleeping giant space. (I recommend that the students stand up or sit up and stretch their arms out to demonstrate the length of their part.)

3. As parts connect, students could hold hands or wrists.

For more directions on Pop-up Statues, see the Ingredient Games p. 68.

Acting Out Digestion

Every once in a while in the middle of a workshop, while I'm up to my eyeballs in students acting out the act of digestion, or something equally enchanting, I imagine an out-of-context view of our activities. I think of these as my "What did you do today?" moments. I tell the students to remember this moment, and when their parents ask about their day, be sure to tell them they spent half an hour being a large intestine.

Ages: Grades 4-10

Individual Digestion:

Start by singing the following digestion song using hand movements to help act out the song as you go.

"Digestion Song"

By Carol Glynn
(To the tune of "It's a Small World After All")

(Chorus tune)
We chew our food really small.
We chew our food really small
We chew our food really small
to help us digest.

We start with the mouth and chew with our teeth.
We add saliva for an extra treat.
We digest physically,
and we swallow with glee.
We digest our food.

(Chorus tune)

Peristalsis pushes our food down.
Peristalsis pushes our food down.
Peristalsis pushes our food down
through the esophagus.

The esophagus grinds up our food.
This tube squeezes and relaxes, grinding up our food.
We add more enzymes to make sure it is primed.
We digest our food.

(Chorus tune)
The stomach churns and mixes our food.
The stomach churns and mixes our food.
The stomach churns and mixes our food
to help break it down.

The stomach lining adds more enzymes.
Tossing in some acids, it's quite sublime.
Food breaks down chemically,
It does it happily.
We digest our food.

(Chorus tune)
The small intestine is very long.
The small intestine is very long.
The small intestine is very long.
It coils up to fit.

Muscles contract and relax moving your lunch through.
It's a daily job our intestines do.
Pancreas and liver add treats
Making digestion complete
We digest our food.

(Chorus tune)
The intestines absorb what we need.
The intestines absorb what we need.
The intestines absorb what we need.
into our bloodstream.

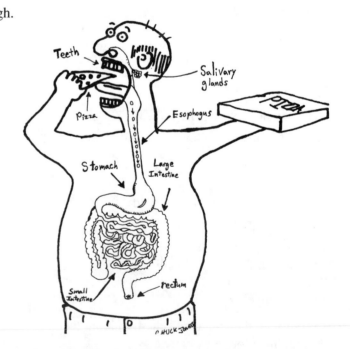

The final solid waste we must pass it.
We pass it through our rectum.
It helps to sit.
We pass it daily
and we do it privately
We've digested our food.

Acting Out Digestion as a Group:

In this activity, your students will personify the human digestive system, as a whole, including the mouth, salivary glands, esophagus, stomach, liver, gallbladder, pancreas, small intestine, and large intestine. Each student will play a role, standing in a physical sequence, doing an appropriate movement. Perhaps you'll want to sing the digestion song as you pass imaginary food through the giant human digestive system, instead of making sounds. I recommend using imaginary food, and not using a student.

Directions:

Line the students up in the proper digestive sequence.

Sample casting based on an average class size of twenty-four students (feel free to adapt for your digestive needs):

2 *students will be the teeth* and make a gnashing movement with their own teeth or their hands, to show breaking the food into smaller pieces to begin the process of digestion.

3 *students will be the salivary glands* and pretend to squirt the food with saliva to chemically break it down further and prepare it for passage into the stomach. One student squirts the food while the teeth are chewing it in the mouth. Two students squirt it as it passes through the esophagus.

2 *students will be the esophagus* and push the food down an imaginary tube by squeezing and releasing with their hands in a long row, almost as if they are shaping sausages in an assembly line. If you choose not to sing, they could quietly repeat the word peristalsis over and over as they make the long, smooth esophagus muscles contract and relax, moving the food, and grinding it as it goes.

3 *students will be the stomach.* Standing in a circle, or gravy boat stomach shape, they can pretend to be the stomach lining, tossing in acids and enzymes with one hand and churning the food with the other.

3 *students will be the liver,* which has many jobs in our body, but in digestion, these students will make bile, which will help break down fat and neutralize stomach acids.
Standing in a triangular shape to the side of the stomach, the liver students could demonstrate a bile-making movement (stirring a thick substance, etc.).

1 *student will be the gallbladder* to the bottom left of the liver, which will collect and store the bile until it is needed. Perhaps he or she can act out a packing movement, as if packing the bile into boxes, or since it is liquid, they can store it in imaginary jars with lids.

1 *student will be the pancreas* near the bottom of the stomach, cooking up enzymes that will help digest protein, carbohydrates, and fats. A cooking gesture would work.

5 *students will be the small intestine,* and grabbing hands they can stretch out in a long coil, which will fit inside the body. The small intestine students have several jobs. They can squeeze the muscle walls, in a similar assembly line to the esophagus moving the food along, and then stop, temporarily, to toss in enzymes and acids from the liver and the pancreas. Finally, after they've broken down the food into minuscule pieces, they can use their hands as pretend straws and absorb the tiniest food particles through the walls into the bloodstream.

4 *students will be the large intestine.* They will need to move the food along as the small intestine did, squeezing and releasing. They will need to absorb any excess liquid with food particles in it, mimicking the small intestines. Then they will squeeze out any remaining waste.

Acting Out Respiration

Tools: Four pieces of cloth. (2 each of two different colors)

It may be helpful to warm up your students by playing a quick round of Be a Shape, which is found in the Ingredient Games p. 35. Forming this system is very similar to the puzzle qualities of that simple game, only this time the puzzle is more specific, because each part has a designated area.

Ages: Grades 4-10

Directions:

1. Cast your class of characters in the following roles:

   nose
   mouth
   nasal cavity
   pharynx (throat)
   epiglottis
   larynx (voice box)
   trachea (windpipe, using 2 students)
   2 bronchial tubes
   2 lungs (using three students each)
   capillaries and alveoli (3 students for
       each lung)
   diaphragm (using 2 students)
   narrator or announcer

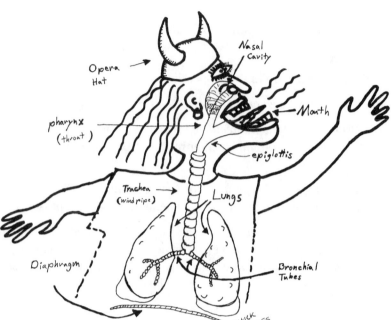

2. Each part should create a movement to represent its activity within the respiratory system.

3. Each part should create a pose to remain in when its part isn't moving. (This should be a stable, comfortable position that they can hold for some time. Students often like to pose in highly precarious, exhausting positions.)

4. Some parts, such as the epiglottis, may want to include sounds as the door flaps open and shut. This is not necessary for all parts, because the flow of oxygen and carbon dioxide will be clearly demonstrated through the passing of the cloth.

   Example: The mouth should create a way to represent opening and closing. The arms could represent the mouth and the fingers could become the teeth, which would open and close like a crocodile's mouth. The mouth and the nose people should both decide on an inhaling sound.

5. The many parts should group together in the proper order to represent a respiratory system. See the diagram. Depending on the age group, it may be easier to form the entire system sitting down. If particular parts need to stand to reenact their function, they could do so only at the appropriate time.

6. Start breathing by choosing one cloth color to be the oxygen and passing it through the system.

   A. One piece of oxygen cloth enters through the nasal cavity, and the other through the mouth.
   B. Pass it through the pharynx (throat) to the larynx (voice box).
   C. The epiglottis, a small flap of tissue at the top of the larynx, should open to allow the oxygen through.
   D. Pass the oxygen cloth through the windpipe (technically, to the windpipe person and through their chosen windpipe shape) into the bronchial tubes. Pass one piece of oxygen cloth down each tube.
   E. Pass the cloth from the bronchial tube into the lungs. Each lung has three students holding hands forming the outer edges of the lung shape. Inside each lung there are two capillary students surrounding an alveoli kid.
   F. The alveoli student holds the two carbon dioxide cloths which were technically given to him through the blood, even though that isn't being demonstrated here.
   G. The oxygen cloth is passed to the capillaries and to the alveoli, where it is exchanged for the carbon dioxide cloth.
   H. The diaphragm students make a large, gentle pushing movement at the base of the lungs, to send the carbon dioxide in reverse, back up the path and out the nose and mouth.

   Voilà! Respiration.

Tips and Variations:
Don't worry about whether the final product is exactly right. What does a giant human respiratory system really look like? The students will learn about the product by walking through the process of creating it.

Chemistry

Swoosh!: Naming Liquids and Solids

Ages: Grades 3-6

This game allows students to review liquids and solids, by repeating them in a fun sequence. Less confident students are able to participate and review at the same time that others may forge ahead. For instructions for Swoosh!, see the Ingredient Games p. 76.

Environment

Look for the following science activities in Science K-2 p.91
Life Cycle of the Butterfly (Grades 1-4) p. 93
Pollination (Grades 2-4) p. 93
Acting Parts of a Tree (Grades 1-4) p. 95
Changes of Seasons (Grades K-3) p. 96
Seasonal Activities (Grades K-3) p. 97

Animals:
Look for the following animal activities in Science K-2
Classification with Duck Duck Goose (Grades K-3) p. 98
Match Up: Animals (Grades 1-4) p. 99
Swat It! Dinosaurs (Grades 2-4) p. 100

Weather:
Look for the following rain weather activities in Science K-2
Water Cycle Song (Grades 2-4) p. 97
Conducting a Storm: Weather (Grades K-5) p. 104

Rain Forest
Look for the following rain forest activity in the Ingredient Games
Extinction/Destruction: Lean and Leave (Grades 4-Adult) p. 52

Directions:
1. Play Lean and Leave.

2. Sit down in a large circle and openly ask why the students think you have played this game to help study the rain forest. They always come up with many more wonderful ideas than I have thought of.

3. If they haven't discovered it themselves, ask if they see a connection to the food chain. Ask if they see a

connection to the animals' need to live in specific layers of the forest. What if those layers were to disappear?

4. In every game of Lean and Leave, there is always a point where some students, while supporting their own weight, still find it helpful to rest ever so slightly on someone else. When their resting place leaves as part of the game, they continue to support themselves, but it becomes a great deal more difficult. What if they were an animal in the rain forest, and part of their habitat is destroyed? They may remain standing, but it will be harder, and each time a little bit more goes, they will have a harder time. Now what happens to the animals if whole acres are destroyed?

Habitat Game

Habitat works well in grades 3-8. The depth of the discussion varies. Use this drama session as the beginning of an environment unit on endangered species, and your students will begin the unit with an understanding of habitats, and a desire to know the habitats of specific species and why their habitats are being destroyed. If we're really lucky, they also want to know what they can do to prevent the destruction.

Tools: Space. Palm-size squares of construction paper, in five colors. Each student will need one of each color.

Directions:

1. Discuss the concept that a loss of habitat is the largest contributing factor in the endangerment of animals.

2. I begin with a warm-up of Lean and Leave, to open a discussion on how interdependent our environment is.

3. Talk about habitats, what they are, and how easy it is for us, as humans, to move to a new one. I like to talk about the bald eagle, and their huge nests, which are large enough for three grown men to play cards in, and how cumbersome it would be for an eagle to build a new one. I talk about rain forest animals whose homes are being destroyed and how hard it is for them to move on.

4. Invent an animal. Give it an imaginary name, and decide on five elements of its environment that are crucial to its survival—in other words, its habitat. (These can be silly or serious.)

5. Match each element with a color of construction paper.

6. Pass out a complete habitat set of five colored squares to each student. This is a complete habitat. Your imaginary animal could live comfortably near any student in your class.

7. Discuss how your imaginary animal looks and moves. You may need to vote on several choices.

8. Ask for three student volunteers to demonstrate this animal. They should then stand, squat, or hang near a habitat of all five colors.

9. Improvise a story about the sad destruction of several elements within this animal's community. (See a sample story below.) Some habitats are protected for a variety of reasons, and the three animals move from disturbed habitats to new ones.

10. Each time a habitat set is broken up, the imaginary creatures must move to a new one.

11. Eventually all the habitats are destroyed and the three animals have a dramatic dying scene in the center of the circle.

The student investment results are palpable. This may be an animal who sipped pink lemonade out of Tweety Bird cups, and wore orange polka dotted sneakers, but nobody wants it to die. The students are invested in the life of an imaginary animal which they had an opportunity to know briefly.

I once had a sixth-grade class become so invested in the demise of a habitat involving music for our creature, that when a disaster struck and took the music away, the students spontaneously extended the story and saved the habitat.

Sample Habitat Elements and Story:

Remember, you may play this game with outrageous habitat conditions or realistic ones, whatever suits your personality the best. The results will be the same either way.

Name: SNORTBLA

Habitat Requirements:
> Red: Pink Lemonade (to drink)
> Green: Green Polka Dotted Sneakers (housing)
> Yellow: Reese's Peanut Butter Cups (food)
> Blue: Hairy Blue Monsters (companionship)
> Purple: Miniature Golf Courses (recreation)

Story: Once upon a time in Snortblaville, many happy Snortblas thrived, drinking their pink lemonade, snuggling down in their green polka dotted sneakers, enjoying a nice meal of Reese's peanut butter cups with a hairy blue friend. Every weekend, they would take time out from their busy Snortbla schedules to play miniature golf at the Snortbla golf course. Everyone was happy. All the Snortblas were thriving.

One dark and dreary day, something terrible happened in Snortblaville! The factory that made green polka dotted sneakers went out of business. Now, the good news is that half the Snortblas in town had recently purchased some extra sneakers at the Annual Green Polka Dotted Sneaker Blowout Sale, but (choose a large group of students in your circle) all these other Snortblas were out of luck, because not only did their source for new sneakers dry up, but their old sneakers were so beat up, they wouldn't support a happy Snortbla. (Take the green cards away from those students. Any live, student Snortblas who are sitting next to an incomplete habitat of cards must move to a new one.)

Not only that! Overnight the new batch of pink lemonade turned green! Some Snortblas had stocked up on some old pink lemonade in their freezers, but (choose a group of students to give up their red cards) all of these Snortblas were out of luck.
(Again, the Snortblas must move to a new area, if any, that has a complete set of habitat cards.)

Just when everyone thought the situation couldn't possibly get worse, the Snortblas and the hairy blue monsters had an argument about sharing the remaining lemonade, and the blue monsters stomped off, taking all the Reese's peanut butter cups with them. (Take away the appropriate cards.)

Having nowhere to go, the Snortblas began to die off. (Have a Snortbla death scene.)

I like to follow up the Habitat Game by playing the song "Habitat" by B. Oliver, on Crackerbarrel Entertainment's CD *Earth Revival*. Find them at their website, www.crackerbarrel-ents.com.

Rain Forest Fashion Show

Ages: Grades 4-8.

Directions:

1. Have each child research something in the rain forest. It could be an animal, an insect, a bird, a plant, or a tree. Perhaps each group could represent creatures from one level of the rain forest.

2. They should write at least five facts about their choice on a card for the Master of Ceremonies, who may also be dressed in a costume. Master Toucan!

3. They should create a costume, which they will wear on the Rain Forest Runway, as their information is

shared with the class.

For more information about the Fashion Show structure, see the Ingredient Games p. 40.

The Canopy Critter Convention

Ages: Grades 4-8

Where should your class go to study the effects of light on animals and plants? Colchester Intermediate School, in Colchester Connecticut, takes their fourth-grade students to the rain forest. Where's the closest rain forest in Colchester? In the gym, of course!

Each year the fourth-grade students build a giant, high school gym-size rain forest museum, jam-packed with research projects demonstrating all the multiple intelligences. The exibits, which are all built around one giant rain forest tree, include hands-on activities, posters, sculptures, mathematical flying dragon tracks, poems, plays, songs, and student-constructed musical instruments. Not unlike the musical *Brigadoon,* this little-known North American rain forest appears only once week a year, and each year it is decidedly more magical.

The first year, Sharon Falcone and I invented the Canopy Critter Convention, part of her class's dramatic contribution to the rain forest. In order to compare and contrast the living conditions, we decided to invite some rain forest animals to CIS for a week.

Our Directions:

1. Each student filled out the following questionnaire.

2. I took their answers and created a script, which you will find below.

3. The students acted it out, on videotape, to share as a station in the museum.

Your Options:

1. Have your students fill out the questionnaire using their own rain forest research.

2. Use my skit as a model, inserting or exchanging your students' ideas, whenever possible.

Use the following script as a lesson in itself, and read through it as a class, or act it out for parents and friends.

Name:_____
Rain Forest Animal:_____

Pretend that our rain forest animals came to visit us for a week this spring. Each of you invited your animal to your house for that week.

During the week of their visit, a "Canopy Critter Convention" took place. Everyone was invited, including your animal, parent(s), pet(s) , and yourself. It was a meeting to discuss how the week was going for everyone involved.

Using factual knowledge and creativity, plan, then write what comments each convention participant would say.

While planning keep in mind items such as:
    habitat changes
    weather (climate) changes
    light impact

**type of shelter
and so on**

Here is what each character might have to say:

Your animal:

Your parent (s):

Your pet(s):

Yourself:

The Canopy Critter Convention
By Mrs. Falcone's Class
With Carol Glynn

News Announcer: We're here outside Colchester Intermediate School, where inside angry parents, students, pets, and rain forest animals are ironing out a hands-on science project that went awry. While the students are quick to point out that the situation is not all bad, the parents are frustrated, and the administration, while proud of the students' initiative, admits that there are a few things that need to be worked out. The changes in habitat, weather, light and type of shelter, etc., are all quite stressful on the animals, and trying to accommodate the animals has become rather challenging for the families.

Student 1: This is a planned meeting, a built-in meeting. There's no need to blow this out of proportion. We knew the idea would have a few problems, so we built in a mid-project evaluation meeting, to discuss how the week is going for everyone involved. Nothing has gone awry, really. We're just stating our opinions. We did ask the family pets to come along, which wasn't planned, because they seem to be facing some challenges we hadn't expected.

News Announcer: What exactly is the project you're conducting?

Student 3: Well, we're working with the teachers and artists to design a new rain forest curriculum.

Student 2: So we're thinking up projects, ideas, that use the arts and make studying the environment, through the rain forest, an educational, exciting, and rewarding experience.

Student 3: Yeah, one we'll never forget.

Parent 1: We won't forget this one, will we, _____(child's name). I'm a parent, and I think that this time Mrs. Falcone has gone too far.

Parent 2: I think so, too. These kids have gone insane. Nick brought home a boa constrictor! Into the house!

Parent 3: That's nothing, my son Dimitri brought home a howler monkey. I can't hear myself think!

Parent 2 and 3: Another one of Mrs. Falcone's weird assignments.

Student 2: I think it's a cool assignment. Maybe next time Mrs. Falcone will let us go to the moon as a field trip.

Announcer: How has she gone too far?

Student 1: It was our idea, really.

Announcer: Could someone tell me what the idea was?

Student 3: To bring rain forest animals to our school for a week's vacation.

Parent 1: But they didn't bring them to the school. They brought them home.

Announcer: What kind of animals? Some rain forest animals are kind of cute. Like the hummingbird, the tree frog.

Student 2: Oh, they're all cute.

Parent 1: They're cute all right. I have a jaguar living in my bathroom. A jaguar! They didn't just bring the small parrots and things.

Student 3: We brought the animals we are studying.

Announcer: And what animals are you studying?

Student: A chimpanzee.

Student 2: A black panther.

Student 3: A tiger.

Announcer: I think I'm beginning to understand the problem here.

Parent: I knew you would.

Student 4: We better get going. The meeting is going to start.
(To the Audience): The following are excerpts from the CIS Canopy Critter Convention. We hope you'll learn as much as we did.

Meeting Leader: Ladies and Gentlemen, Ocelots, and Monkeys, Animals, and students, household pets. Whoever else is here, please, take a seat! We'd like to hear from the guest animals first, if that's a okay. Do you have anything you would like to share?

Chimpanzee: I really don't think I'm in Central Africa anymore. I mean where are the bananas, figs, termites, and colobus monkeys, that tasted soooooo good? Where are the pigs? You must be hiding them! Why won't you tell me? What about the antelope, the buds, the soft shoots, the birds, and the, the, the... I guess there aren't any more. I need them, where are they?

Announcer: I'm sorry, Ms. Chimpanzee. I know this is difficult. Perhaps the next time we should prepare the animals further for such a drastic change. Howler Monkey?

Howler Monkey: I do not like where my habitat is. I like my old habitat. It's not really all bad, because there are some of my favorite foods, such as flowers, insects, birds, eggs, fruit, roots, and spiders. I don't really have many enemies here to look out for.

Parent: If you like it here so much, could you at least be quiet? I had no idea how loud howler monkeys were. The local and state police have come to see what the noise was. Then Channel Three News came to see what the noise was. It wasn't my sons who were noisy. They were quiet. It was you!

Howler Monkey: (Sound)

Announcer: Wow! That's some sound, Mr. Monkey. Mrs. Tiger?

Tiger: Hey, are there any fish around? Or monkeys around? Can I eat that howler monkey there? This doesn't feel like a tropical rain forest to me!

Tiger Parent: We need to get this thing out of here. We can't go to Stop and Shop to buy deer and baby elephants. We'd have to rob a zoo to get that kind of food. I've bought out John's Fish Market, because that's the only place with food this tiger will eat.

Tiger Kid: (Lena) I won't let you take her away. She's a strong swimmer. I think we should keep her here longer, so she can go to the beach with us. It'll be so much fun. She can fish from there.

Announcer: I see the ocelot has a paw in the air.

Ocelot: Brrr. It's cold here. I want to go back to living sixty feet above the ground. It's way too bright here. My host student master said he'd do anything to make me comfortable, but I know it's hard on him. ROOOOAAARRRRR!

Danny: I feel bad for my ocelot. He doesn't want to be fed. He wants to hunt. I'm thinking of letting him go.

Danny's Parents: Get this thing out of here. Get it out! The very first day I told my son, Daniel Thomas Kowalsky, you're grounded for life. I don't care if this was your homework. This thing is going to eat us!

Announcer: Danny's pet seems to want to share something.

Pet: AHHHHHHHHH!

Announcer: Okay. The ocelot is chasing Danny's pet. The tiger is now chasing the howler monkey and Mrs. Kowalsky is chasing Daniel. Has anyone seen Mrs. Falcone? She seems to have slipped out the back door. We'll take a short break and be right back.

(Later)

Announcer: Let's hear from David St. Pierre, and his group. You have a black panther, David?

David: I'm David, and I love having this panther here. He's my favorite. No robbers would dare come into our house because if they did, they'd be scared out of their pants. He's also a great fishing partner. I'm not sure my cat is so thrilled, though.

Cat: I want to know why David would get the big kitty, when you have me? He does catch all the mice, though, and the neighbor's dog doesn't bother me anymore. I pretty much just stay out of his way. The parent pets are pretty relaxed about it.

Parents: I don't really mind if my son has a panther, as long as he cleans up after it. We've had a few complaints from the neighbors, who say their animals are missing. We told them our cat is pretty scarce too. Maybe they're just scared.

Panther: This place is good because I'm getting a lot of attention, but there's one problem. No antelopes. That dog from the Rotas family was delicious.

Parent: Many neighborhood animals are missing. Our guest boa constrictor ate our cats and our dog. They're not here to speak for themselves, because... they were lunch! We're not living in the house either, not since we woke up one morning and it was curled up in our bed!

Sean Paryak: This is the best time in my life. I'm living all by myself, except for the boa. I'm even getting discounts on his food at the store, because he's a class project.

Announcer: Isn't there another boa constrictor in this class's group? Are you enjoying yourself?

Nick's Boa: Yes! There's another boa constrictor. Me! And no, I'm not enjoying myself. This place stinks. There's no food. What do I look like, a kinkajou? In fact, I could go for a kinkajou right now. And whenever

I try to sleep, these dumb kids are playing. Why don't they just play at night like me? One or two trees, that's all I ask for. If Uncle Anaconda were here, he'd show them.

Announcer: I'm sorry to hear that. Could we have a little order here! It seems we're having trouble with finding enough of the right kind of food for our guests. Perhaps next time we could arrange for meals in advance. We also are experiencing a difference in time schedules. Is anyone taking notes here? Oh, good, thanks. We haven't heard from anyone about temperature yet, except the ocelot, and one of the howler monkeys. Is anyone else having any problem with temperature? I recognize the toucan.

Toucan: It's too cold around here. There are plenty of spiders and insects and berries, but brrrrr. I want to go back to South America.

Joshua's Cat: I know how he can get warm. I'll roast him and toast him, and eat him. Mmmmeeoowww.

Josh: You can't eat my science project. You just can't.

Announcer: Order. Order please. Can we have some order? What about the other birds? How are they working out?

Tyler: We have a macaw. Colleen has a parrot. Sabrina and Molly both have hummingbirds. I love the macaw's feathers. Did you know that the Indians use his feathers for decoration? It's so cool.

Colleen: My parrot seems to feel like she's in a big cage of some kind without branches. She says it's her worst nightmare.

Parrot: Worst nightmare. Worst nightmare.

Colleen: And the fish are kind of upset, understandably. I'm getting kind of tired of all the noise.

Molly: The hummingbirds are freezing. Mine has frost on its feathers. It doesn't like the taste of the local nectar, and there aren't enough bugs at my house.

Announcer: You sound like you're not having a good time.

Molly: It's not so bad. I like him really. There aren't any bugs anywhere, which is great, but I wish he wasn't attracted to the color red. He attacks me every time I put my coat on! I also wish he could eat chicken, or steak and salad. I keep having to go out and pick flowers.

Sabrina: We're always getting yelled at because the house is too hot for the family, and too cold for the bird.

Announcer: Mr. Orangutang, I see you're staying at Sarah Alessio's house.

Orangutan: I'm freezing. Where am I? Turn up the heat! Can we at least go back to the house where they run the shower for me all day? Can we pick up a few different fruits on the way home?

Sarah's Parent: No, we can't. We've bought out three stores. We're not going to starve because of one of Mrs. Falcone's crazy projects. We need to take showers too. No one asked us if we'd give up showers for a week.

Sarah: Mom, I'll pay for it, all of it, the food, the water bill. It'll only take about twenty years.

(Animal Sounds)

Announcer: Order! Order! Let's try to be organized here. We've heard from the howler monkeys. Are there any other monkeys?

Kristen: I have one, a capuchin monkey, but it won't speak. It's scared of all the larger animals, and it keeps pouncing on my head. I don't mind having him here, though I may need a new haircut soon. My parents are upset because it keeps stealing little things, like my mother's diamond earrings,

Amanda: Yeah, mine stole my dad's wallet. I'm just glad he sleeps at night.

Kristen: Mine does too, but every time I go to lie down on my bed, I find a few small dead animals and pieces of fruit lying there.

Amanda: My dad is thrilled because he was thinking of calling the exterminator, but the capuchin monkey has eaten every bug in sight, so now he doesn't have to. He would like his wallet back, though.

Announcer: Doesn't Zak have the Golden Spider Monkey?

Zak: Yeah. I love him. I just do. This doesn't have anything to do with the fact that he ate all my other pets, so he's the only one left. I just like monkeys. He's happy that he hasn't seen any boa constrictors here.

Golden Spider Monkey: AHHHH! AHHHH! AHHHH!

Tiffany: I have a chimpanzee. He's been a perfect angel around me.

Tiffany's Parent: Angel! Angel! It broke all my favorite lamps, and left that one awful one that was a present from...oh, never mind. It keeps ruining all my clothes as it swings from the hangers in my closet. We simply cannot afford to run the heat this high. It's April. We don't even use the heat in April. We just put sweaters on. Can't we at least get that thing a sweater?

Jaguar: I'm a nocturnal animal, and they keep that TV thing going during the day and I can't get any sleep.

Parent: It's like I told the reporter outside. I have a jaguar living in my bathroom, with the shower running, because it must be near water. This thing only trusts my daughter. We took it to the vet and were kicked out. What will Mrs. Falcone think of next? A herd of buffaloes? Mmmmmmm?

Student 1: Perhaps it would be easier next year, for future classes, to travel to the rain forest themselves. After all, we can wear thinner clothing, but the animals aren't built to adapt beyond their natural habitats.

Student 2: We won't have to worry about what they eat.

Student 3: We won't have to worry about how much light they're getting or when they sleep.

Student 4: We won't have to worry about the local police or the neighbors' animals and kids being eaten.

Student 5: It will be easier, but it will be a little sad. We don't want to harm the animals, but overall, I think we really liked having these guys here. It made me feel special to be a guest host to a rain forest animal.

Student 1: Yeah, but we weren't exactly environmentalists, running tons of water, and turning up the heat.

Student 2: I think it was a good experiment. I loved it. Should we do it again?

All: Absolutely not.

Geology

Be a Rock

Years ago, I was discussing an upcoming one-shot workshop with a friend of mine who taught third grade. Her class that year was particularly difficult, with a few highly kinesthetic kids with equally kinesthetic mouths. We touched on the idea of geology.

"They could be rocks," I suggested. "They could curl up on the floor, not making a sound. Then we could write about their impressions."

"Forget the writing!" she burst out, laughing. "Let's just have them be rocks, just rocks, for forty-five minutes!" She then melted into complete hysteria, laughing so hard that she did it silently, with tears streaming down her cheeks. She laughed for several minutes before she calmed down, gasping. Everyone in the lunchroom was laughing, too, though few knew why.

When she stopped, she felt much better. We never did the rock activity, but I think about it often, whenever I think about geology, and whenever I need a dose of healing laughter.

All jokes aside, I still think sitting still and being a rock for two or three minutes is a good idea. Spending a few minutes examining the life of a rock firsthand will encourage students to stop and notice rocks in their environment.

Ages: Grades 3-4

Directions:

1. Ask students to picture a rock they have seen, at the school, in their yard, etc., and to think about the activities that take place around that rock. Do squirrels sit on it? Do people walk or drive by?

2. Ask them to find a place, and close their eyes, picturing that they are the rock. Have them watch a little imagination movie through the eyes of the rock.

3. Draw a picture of what they've seen. Share their ideas with a buddy, or in writing.

4. (Optional) Have them create a short skit with friends depicting a day in a life of a rock.

Rock Music

Ages: Grades 4-8.

Directions:

1. Play some rock music. Give the students a few selections to choose from.

2. Either individually or in groups, the students should write rock songs, including the facts about a particular kind of rock, to an existing rock tune, or an original one. Encourage the students to be equally educational and entertaining.

3. When everyone is ready, have a rock concert!

Example: To the Tune of "Rock Around the Clock":

Metamorphic, they're down deep. Makes some fine rocks, that aren't cheap.
We're gonna heat right up from the magma tonight.
We're gonna add some pressure without a fight.
We're gonna rock, we're gonna rock with metamorphic tonight.
Rock, Rock, Rock, Yeah!

Machines

Look for the following machine activities in Science K-2
Transportation: Acting Out Machines (Grades 1-6) p. 100
Matching Up: Machine Words to Pictures: (Grades 1-4) p. 100

Simple Machines

Warm up by creating realistic and fantasy machines in the giant-size model with human parts. This great activity underlines the cooperative nature of machines.

Directions for Simple Machines:

1. Look for directions to Machines in the Ingredient Games p. 54.

2. Divide the class into groups of two and three.

3. Ask them to work together to act out pulleys, gears, wheels, axles, or levers.

4. Share their creations with each other.

5. Join two groups who chose pulleys together. Ask them to create a machine that has a pulley in it.

6. If many groups chose the same one or two simple machines, do the activity again to cover the other ones.

Sound

Slow Motion Vibrate Tag

Concepts:

1. Sound travels in waves by bumping into molecules and passing the vibration along.

2. In solids, molecules are very close together so the sound passes quickly through them, making solids good sound conductors.

3. In liquids the molecules are farther apart, so the sound passes through, but a bit more slowly.

4. In the air, the molecules are much farther apart so the sound passes much more slowly.

Ages: Grades 3-6

Directions:

Be a solid sound conductor

1. Have each student be a molecule. Stand in a group in the room with a little space between the students.

2. Tap one student on the shoulder, making a sound. That student should repeat the sound and begin to vibrate in place, passing the sound on by slowly tapping the students directly around him.

3. Those students should vibrate in place, and tap the students around them.

4. The sound wave is passed as the vibration is passed on, until all the students have passed the sound and vibration.

5. Remember the vibration is being passed on, while in real life, the original molecules would continue to vibrate slightly, but for purposes of sanity and easy visualization, have each student pass the sound and movement on, and stop.

Be a liquid sound conductor

1. Follow the directions above, but make the students stand farther apart.

2. Have them move in slow motion as they vibrate over to tap new molecules.

3. Discuss the time difference between molecules moving in a solid and liquid sound conductor.

Be a vapor sound conductor

1 Follow the directions above, but make the students stand even

Vapor CHUCK JONES

farther apart.

2. Have them move in slow motion as they vibrate over to tap new molecules.

3. Discuss the time difference between molecules moving in a solid, liquid, and vapor sound conductor.

Tips and Variations:

If standing in a group or clump invites too much spontaneous tapping and vibrating, try standing in a line instead.
.

Space

Look for the following space activity in Science K-2.
Chant Dance: Planets (Grades 1-4) p. 102

Machines:

Build a Spaceship, a Lunar Module, or a Launch Site Out of Student Bodies

Ages: Grades: 3-4

Both large group and small group machines give students a chance to demonstrate their knowledge of specific curriculum topics, kinesthetically and visually. I like them because they also require cooperation, listening, team building, and a large dose of creativity. For complete instructions for Machines, with tips and variations, see the Ingredient Games p. 54.

Once students have built the spaceship, others can pack it with items they'll want to take. Play once with students taking something they'll realistically need on the moon. Play another round with students thinking creatively about what they would like to take to the moon.

Example: "Pinky" the stuffed rabbit, a favorite dessert, crayons, etc.

Line Up: Planets

Ages: Grades 3-4.

Tools: Names of the planets on slips of paper.

Directions:

1. Give students cards with the planet names on them.

2. Students will compare the cards, and line up, facing the audience, in the proper order.

Tips: Double the cards and use two lines to involve eighteen students. Have the other students be official NASA judges.

Swoosh!: Planets and Constellations

Ages: Grades 3-6

Arm your students with facts about the planets or names of the constellations and let them loose with Swoosh. For directions to Swoosh!, a game for all ages, look in the Ingredient Games p. 76.

Creating Constellations: Group Up

Ages: Grades 4-5

Directions:

1. Warm up the class by playing Group Up, which you'll find in the Ingredient Games p. 44.

2. Choose numbers that correlate to the stars in a given constellation. Once the students have formed groups of that number, ask them to form the matching constellation using each student as one star.

3. If you have any remainder students, after you've divided the class, have them help you check the constellations for proper structure.

The Big Dipper

(8 Stars)

C. GLYNN

3-4
S
C
I
E
N
C
E

CHAPTER ELEVEN

Science 5-8

Table of Contents

5-8
SCIENCE

Biology

Look for the following biology activities in Science 3-4

Cells (grades 3-10) p. 106

Giant Human Body: Pop-up Statue (grades 3-5) p. 109

Acting Out Respiration (grades 4-10) p. 111

Glands

The Dating Game: Be My Gland

Ages: Grades 5-8

Directions:

1. Read the section on the Dating Game, in the Ingredient Games P. 41.

2. Divide the students into groups of six (an announcer, a host, a contestant, and three glands).

3. Have all six students do research on their chosen glands and their functions.

4. Decide why the contestant is looking for a gland. He wants to write a report on it. He wants to solve some personal health problems. He wants to have more energy, be taller, etc.

5. Follow the Dating Game directions about dividing up responsibility in the presentation.

6. Match the contestant with an appropriate gland.

7. Introduce the other glands by name, and have them describe some of their functions. Point out that while the winning gland will solve the contestant's immediate concerns, the other glands all help us every day.

What's My Line: What's Your Function?

Ages: Grades 5-8

Directions:

1. Read the directions to What's My Line? in the Ingredient Games p. 42.

2. Have students do the appropriate research on a chosen gland or organ, and personify it in the game.

(Sebaceous Gland)   (Sweat Gland)   (Pituitary Gland)

What's My Line?
C. GLYNN

3. Have fun.

"What did you do in school today, dear?"

"Nothing much, Mom. I was a thyroid gland for a while, though."

Heart

Ages: Grades 5-11.

Tools:

* Several pieces of red cloth or netting to use as blood.
* Several pieces of white cloth to use as oxygen.
* Several pieces of another color to use as carbon dioxide.
* (Optional) Ideally, you'd like to show the exchange of carbon dioxide for oxygen, so having a small net bag of red cloth, sewn on three sides, would work for keeping the other materials in it, or Velcro would work to easily remove and attach the oxygen and carbon dioxide materials. This idea is not necessary to re-create the heart, just a great addition to the visually minded.
* (Optional) Paper and pens to label the students

Directions:

1. Cast the players in your heart activity: be as specific as you want, depending on your grade level. If you don't use the valves, have more than one student be the larger heart parts.

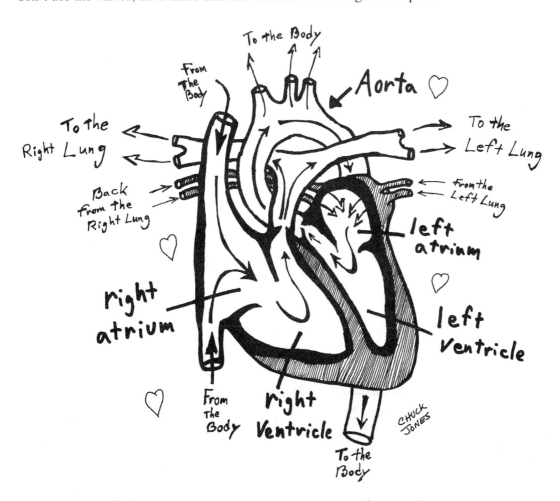

* the right atrium (upper right chamber of the heart)
* small valve (tricuspid valve)
* the right ventricle (lower right chamber of the heart)
* valve (pulmonary semi-lunar valve)
* pulmonary artery (divides into two branches going into each lung)
* 2 lungs
* capillaries (where the blood releases carbon dioxide and absorbs oxygen); add extra student bodies here
* 4 pulmonary veins
* left atrium (upper left chamber or auricle)
* valve (bicuspid)
* left ventricle (lower left chamber of the heart)
* valve (aortic semi-lunar valve)
* aorta (very large artery)
* a heart interviewer

2. Ask the students to stand in the order of the cast list above and one by one step into the shape of the heart in the diagram above. Try doing this sitting on the floor. The red material, or blood, can be passed under legs rather than have student heart parts lying on top of one another. Tricky spots: The aorta should sit with open arms, and a lung on each side. Two of the pulmonary veins should pass the blood under the right atrium, aorta, and pulmonary artery to get to the left atrium. The left ventricle should pass the blood through the aortic valve and then under the legs of the pulmonary artery to get to the aorta.

3. Begin passing four large flowing pieces of red material into the right atrium as if it has just passed through the legs and arms. It is in need of oxygen now, and very full of carbon dioxide, so if you're using material for the carbon dioxide, pass it as well.

4. Continue to pass the blood through the heart parts by handing the cloth from person to person in order of the list above.

5. When the blood reaches the capillaries in the lungs, the carbon dioxide material should be exchanged for the oxygen material. (Preset the oxygen material with the capillary students.)

Tips and Variations:

1. Students shouldn't sit on one another. Each student represents a portion of the given heart part, and they have no need to create the entire shape.

2. Have each student introduce themselves as their heart part and narrate what is happening as the blood moves through them. Are they pumping oxygenated blood? Are they exchanging carbon dioxide for oxygen?

3. Have a student interview the heart parts for more information. This may be done in the heart shape or back at their seats.

Systems: Act Out the Structure and Function

Digestive

Look for directions to the following systems activity in Science 3-4
Acting Out Digestion(grades 4-10) p. 109

Circulatory

I originally created this activity with students being the blood, the nutrients, the oxygen, the carbon dioxide, and the waste, and it does work, but using cloth for the blood, waste, etc., helps the students focus on what, not who, is passing through the system. If you use cloth and color-code it, then students can pass it through the system to represent the different gases. Any color is fine, but if you're acting out other systems and organs, it will help to be consistent as to which gas is which.

Tools: **Several pieces of one colored cloth.**

Example: red = blood
green = nutrients
white = oxygen
light blue or gray = carbon dioxide
purple = waste

Cast of Characters:

Heart (2 students)
Arteries (4 students)
Capillary walls (6 students)
Veins (4 students)
Valves in the veins, to prevent
the blood from flowing
backward (3 students)
Interviewer or Announcer

Directions:

1. Cast your students in the parts. Show your students the primitive diagram attached to this activity and ask them to re-create the circulatory system. Preset the purple and blue cloth with the capillary students. (They've collected it from imaginary cells nearby.)

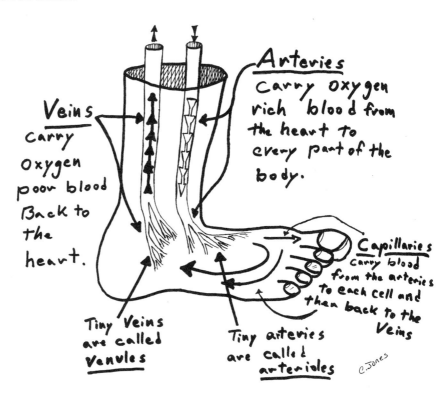

Veins carry Oxygen poor blood Back to the heart.

Arteries carry oxygen rich blood from the heart to every part of the body.

Capillaries carry blood from the arteries to each cell and then back to the Veins

Tiny Veins are called Venules

Tiny arteries are called arterioles

C. Jones

2. The heart begins pumping blood into the arteries, at a high pressure. This blood is high in oxygen and nutrients, so the heart should pass two large pieces of red material with some smaller pieces of white and green material.

3. Have the two heart students pump the blood and hand it to two artery students, who are representing two different arteries. These artery students will quickly pass the blood along the imaginary arteries to two more artery students, who will extend the first two arteries and pass the blood into the capillaries.

4. The capillaries are tiny blood vessels that lie between arteries and veins. As blood travels through the capillaries, nutrients and oxygen move from the blood into the body cells. At the same time carbon dioxide and other wastes move from the body cells into the blood.

5. Bunch up your capillary students into a small group, like a bunch of grapes with some space in the middle, and announce that the capillaries are full of waste and carbon dioxide from nearby cells. Give them the blue and purple cloth and set them at the end of the arteries, where they will exchange the white oxygen cloth for the blue carbon dioxide cloth. They will also exchange the green nutrient cloth for the purple waste cloth. Keeping the nutrients and oxygen for the cells, the capillaries will send the red blood cloth along with its carbon dioxide and waste from the cells on to two vein students.

6. Two vein students are connected to two other vein students forming two long veins.

7. Give each long vein to two valve students along the way to prevent the blood, which is moving much more slowly now, from flowing back down to the capillaries.

8. Slowly pass the blood, complete with waste and carbon dioxide, back to the heart.

Tips and Variations:

1. Ask your chosen announcer to explain the process as it occurs. The announcer can do it seriously, in a quiet golf announcer's voice, or loudly and boisterously as if he's announcing the Super Bowl.

2. Ask each body part to tell their process as they pass the blood through the system.

   Example: "I'm an artery and I have extra-thick walls so I can handle all the pressure of this blood pumping from the heart. I'm passing the blood on to the capillaries."

3. Pass the blood through without discussion and have the announcer interview the circulatory system parts about their role in the process.

4. Consider an analogy for the circulatory system. Do we ever begin a project with great gusto, and get to the crux of it, where all the energy is taken out of us, and we drag ourselves back to finish up? Have the announcer interview the same parts of the system with everyday roles.

   Example: Consider a school report. The teacher is the catalyst (heart). The adrenaline pumps you along to get started, or a parent drives you from school to the library (the trip = arteries). The library is the capillaries, where energy is expended gathering and taking in a multitude of research, and the veins are the route to organize and write the report, complete with valves of self-determination to make sure you get the work back to the teacher. What are you passing through? Knowledge.

Chemistry

Chant Dancing the Periodic Table

Mrs. H., my evil high school chemistry teacher, is mentioned several times within this book. Sarcastically speaking, she was a charmer. Her techniques to motivate students included terrorizing us, teaching us the skills after we took (failed) the test so that we would be invested in the topic, and making sure we all felt truly stupid so that we would try harder. Somehow, her techniques never worked for me. While I remained in her class, her Chem Study numbers dropped from forty-five to twelve in a matter of weeks. She thought the periodic table was a Mickey Mouse test. If we didn't get them all right we were too stupid for her time. In honor of dear old Mrs. H., who may well be dead by now (no comment), I offer you Chant Dancing as a way to liven up the periodic table.

For more theory on Chant Dancing, see the Ingredient Games p. 36.

Directions:

Choose a lively rhythm, or a familiar tune. (The ABC song works well, I just tried it, but middle school students may balk at the idea.) Chant or sing the periodic table to the chosen rhythm. Your students will not only be able to re-create it years from now, they'll learn the symbols to go with their elements as they sing the song.

Match Up: The Periodic Table

Tools: Cards with the elements written on them. One element per card.

Cards with symbols written on them. One symbol per card.

(Each student in your class will need one card. Choose the most important elements for your students to know, or make several sets, so they can play with all of them on different days.)

Ages: Grades 5-6

Directions:

1. Look for directions to Match Up in the Ingredient Games p. 58.

2. Have each student search to find the matching symbol to their element name and vice versa.

Look for the following chemistry activity in Science 3-4
Swoosh!: Naming Liquids and Solids (Grades 3-6) p. 113

Environment

Photosynthesis

This activity can be used with a few students as a visual demonstration, or with the entire class as a kinesthetic experience for all of them.

Tools: Colorful cloth or construction paper to represent chlorophyll, water, carbon dioxide, and sugar. Suggested colors below.

Ages: Grades 5-10

Cast of Characters:

sun	2-4 students
plant leaves	4-6 students (2 students per leaf)
plant stem	1-3 students
roots	2-5 students
chloroplasts	1 student for each leaf
people	2-3 students
Interviewer	1 student, optional
chlorophyll	green cloth, or paper for each chloroplast
water	blue cloth or construction paper for each leaf
carbon dioxide	gray cloth or construction paper
oxygen	white cloth or paper
sugar	pink cloth or paper

Directions to Set Up:

1. Cast the class and give them a moment to become the roots, the leaves, and the sun. The chloroplasts should be inside each leaf, which is framed by the leaf people pairs.

2. Place the people near the leaves.

3. Distribute the cloths and papers before you begin the process.

Give... the water to the roots

the chlorophyll to the chloroplasts

the carbon dioxide to the breathing people

the sugar and oxygen to the leaves

(hide them until they are created in the process)

Directions for the Process:

1. The roots should pass the water to the stem and up to the leaves.

2. The people should breathe and pass the carbon dioxide (through the stomata) into the leaves.

3. The sun students should do a movement to demonstrate giving off light energy.

4. The chloroplasts should trap the energy from the sun and show their green chorophyll.

5. The chloroplasts should collect the carbon dioxide and the water, and use the sun's energy to make food (sugar) and oxygen. The chloroplast students should take the gray cloth and the blue cloth and tuck them under the chlorophyll cloth (where the sugar cloth and the oxygen cloth are hidden).

6. The sun's light should zap them with an energy dance, or hand wiggle.

7. The chloroplast student should reach under and pull out the pink sugar cloth and the white oxygen cloth.

8. Pass the sugar back to the stem.

9. Give the oxygen back to the people.

10. (Optional) Either you or a student could narrate the process as it occurs, and then follow up with an interview of the parts who played roles in the process.

11. Feel free to label the gases with words or chemical symbols.

Create an Ecosystem

Contrast and compare tropical rain forests, evergreen forests, deciduous forests, grasslands, deserts, saltwater and freshwater ecosystems visually and kinesthetically by creating statue settings of each place.

Ages: Grades 5-6

Directions:

1. Choose an ecosystem and create a giant human statue. Include the nonliving, or abiotic, part of the ecosystem, the water, sunlight, temperature, and weather; and the biotic, or living part of the ecosystem. Hint: Temperature is shown by putting a person in the system, reacting to the temperature. (See Statues in the Ingredient Games. p. 66)

2. Once your statue is formed, create a system of communication with the students to form a Pop-up Statue on request. In a Pop-up Statue, certain characters or elements pop up to do an appropriate movement to represent themselves, and if requested, give a brief explanation of their role in the ecosystem. (See Pop-up Statues in the Ingredient Games. p. 68)

3. To contrast and compare the effects of light and weather on plants and animals, create two vastly different ecosystems and ask the biotic, or living characters to step into a different ecosystem. Interview them there, to see how different their comments will be.

Sophisticated Animal Personification: I Am ...

Ages: Grade 5 - Adult

Tools: Open Space

Directions:

1. Players should find a place on the floor where they will have enough elbow room to move around. Find a comfortable position and close their eyes.

2. Think of an animal. (You may suggest one for them, or give them a choice of two, so you can know what they are doing, and enjoy watching them.)

3. Picture the animal clearly in their minds. Visualize it completely. Watch it move, rest, and play. Pay attention to the details. Watch the twitching noses, the way the animal carries itself. Does it watch other animals with its eyes, or does it turn its entire head? etc. Encourage the students to imagine what it would feel like to be this animal.

4. When they have clearly pictured the animal in their minds, have them slowly begin to become the animal.

5. Keeping their eyes closed, they should move as the animal is moving in their visualization.

6. Enjoy these wonderful personifications for a few minutes.

Tips and Variations

1. I Am generates incredible demonstrations of animals. Have a half of the class do the activity at a time, to allow room, and allow the other students an opportunity to watch.

2. This is a low key, focused, activity. Tell the students you are examining how the animals move when they are quiet and alone. If you have wild animals in your class even before you begin the game, have those students move as their chosen animals in slow motion.

Look for the following activities in Science 3-4
The Canopy Critter Convention (A play for grades 4-6) p. 116
Extinction: The Habitat Game (Grades 4-8) p. 114
Rain Forest Fashion Show (Grades 4-8) p. 115

Look for the following activities in the Ingredient Games
Ecosystems : Sound Circles (Grades 5-8) p. 48
Lean and Leave: The Balance of Life (Grades 4-Adult) p. 52

Swoosh! to Save the Earth

Ages: Grades 1-10

A game where all ability levels can thrive and learn while having loads of fun.

Directions:

1. Look for general directions to Swoosh in the Ingredient Games p. 76.

2. Play a round of facts about the destruction of pollution and environmental devastation.

3. Play a round of ways to help the earth.

Ways to Save

Directions:

1. Divide your students into groups of four students.

2. Ask them to create a short skit about ways they can help to save the earth.

Sample Skit Structures:

1. *Public Service Announcement,* stating the facts as realistically as possible, ending with a credit such as "This message is from Students to Save the Earth."

2. *Commercials:* Selling something essential such as "Air," with all the hype involved in a regular commercial, but bursting with honesty. Don't be surprised if it sounds a little sarcastic in its simplicity.

3. *Backwards Commercials*: Sell pollution as something positive. Point out all that it can accomplish if we try hard enough and continue to pollute. "Think of the stylish gas masks!"

4. *Quiz Show Moment:* Have an announcer, to break into a regularly scheduled program, and a Quiz Show Moment Host, who asks a multiple choice question or two about the environment. Perhaps they have a special guest with expertise on the answer. Feel free to combine the humorous with the factual.

5. *Suspend Belief:* Have two objects talk to each other about an environmental topic.

   Example: A tin can and a Styrofoam cup who find themselves sitting at the dump together having a conversation about how long they'll be there. Throw in a third party, a newspaper, or a recyclable plastic jug. What can they learn from each other about their prospects? How long will they be there? Who threw them out? What can they do about it?

Great Resources for Saving the Earth Ideas:

50 Simple Things You Can Do to Save the Earth, and 50 Simple Things Kids Can Do to Save the Earth, The Earthworks Press, Berkeley, California

Geology

Fossil Monologues

"Here's the story of a lovely fossil...who was created by a flat footed dinosaur. There are three toes next to each other. He'd always wished for more..."

Directions:

1. Ask each student to write a monologue from a fossil's point of view.

2. Include fossil vocabulary such as print, replaces remains, whole body, true form, molds, casts, petrified.

3. How was the fossil formed? Where was it found? What was the process of becoming a fossil like? Were they petrified?

4. Have each student read or perform their monologue for the class.

Tips and Variations:

For some reason, I think fossils would be lonely; the idea of becoming petrified all alone, waiting to be found and examined. Even if the fossil is a print, it may be lonely, being left behind as the animal moved on to enjoy life. If you and your students agree, consider having them write and perform a fossil ballad for the class.

Rock Commercials

Ages: Grades 5-8.

This activity could be done as an individual written exercise or a group drama activity. By presenting them, each student will have the opportunity of learning from the others' research, and absorbing the material using all of their multiple intelligences.

Directions:

1. For information on writing Commercials, see the Ingredient Games.

2. Sell a rock, individually or in small groups. Present it as something everyone must have. Show off its color, luster, texture, and hardness. Talk about whether it's igneous, sedimentary, or metamorphic. Give suggestions about its many uses, realistic and imaginary.

3. Present them to the class.

Rock Fashion Show

Ages: Grades 5-8.

Directions:

1. Divide students into groups of five or six.

2. Each student should choose a specific kind of rock to be and do research on the rock, with five or six facts about the rock

3. Create costumes that demonstrate the rock facts through fashion.

4. Write descriptions to go with the costumes using the facts.

5. Choose a Master of Ceremonies or Head Boulder to read the cards and make a few jokes as the rocks parade back and forth.

   Example: And here we have granite. Granite is a hard light-colored igneous rock that contains many different kinds of crystals. See the lovely light color she's wearing. This granite must have formed very slowly underground when the magma cooled, because if you look closely, across the shoulders, this granite has many large crystals of amethysts, quartz, and other minerals. The larger crystals are formed when the magma cools very slowly. Notice how slowly she is moving. Granite is very strong and solid, and is often used as a building material. Thank you, granite. (Handy Homework Helper: Science, p. 96.)

Rock Music

Ages: Grades 5-12.

Directions:

1. Break up your class into groups of three students.

2. Ask them to think of their favorite rock song.

3. Rewrite new rock lyrics to the tune of the existing rock song, describing the type of rock, and its color, luster, texture, and hardness. (If you have students who want to compose an original tune, go for it.)

4. Feel free to personify the rock in the song. How does the rock feel? Is the igneous in love with a metamorphic rock? Does one of them have a rocky past? Do they have a rocky relationship? Will their well-described differences make their relationship more interesting, or does it chip them apart?

5. Once the lyrics are written, the students may want to add a few friends into the performance. Perhaps the class would like to sing choruses while individuals or small groups sing verses. You may be the catalyst for an all-new rock band!

6. For sample rock lyrics see Rock Music in Science 3-4 p. 122.

Machines
Acting Out Simple Machine Vocabulary

Ages: Grades 5-8.

These machine lessons could be done in one longer class period or spread out to accompany your machine unit over a week.

1. Warm up by acting out an abstract machine as directed in Machines: Abstract in the Ingredient Games p. 54.

2. Have students practice the idea of one person being one part of a larger moving machine, in Machines: Realistic in the Ingredient Games. Break into small groups of two and three students to act out your simple machine vocabulary, including lever, pulley, fulcrum, etc.

Machinemart: A Play

Written by Carol Glynn with Mrs. Sullivan's Class, Colchester Intermediate School, 1999

Narrator 1: Machineville was a prosperous little town. The major income generator was Machinemart, the colossal superstore chock-full of simple machines, all designed and created by the townspeople. There were a few other small stores too—grocerymart, pharmacymart, and machine partsmart, of course—but not much more. Customers traveled miles and miles on the mega-superhighway to shop at Machinemart.

Narrator 2: Machinemart was the fastest-growing machine store in the world. It was a great source of pride for the people of Machineville. Store personnel were held in high esteem. The Mayor doubled as the store manager. Machineville families were working round the clock, pulling in all the extra helpers to fill all the orders.

Narrator 3: Everything in Machineville was running as smoothly as a well-lubricated machine, until one morning when order cancellations came flooding into the store.

Mayor: Oh, my. Well. We're doing so well, I guess it doesn't really matter. Some of our family suppliers have been kind of overworked lately as it is.

Narrator 1: But when the Mayor opened the doors, customers were lined up for miles, and every single one of them was there to return something.

Narrator 2: The Mayor of Machineville was forced, for the first time in history, to close early on a Saturday. But before he did, he turned to the crowd and said:

Mayor: Silence! Everyone! Would someone please tell me why you are returning all the simple machines?

Customer 1: Your guarantee says we can get our money back with no questions asked.

Mayor: I know it does, but I truly don't understand this. We've never had so much as one return before. This is ridiculous. I'm asking you please as a favor to tell me, what is wrong?

Narrator 3: And somewhere deep in the middle of the huge crowd, a little voice said:

Kid 1: They've stopped working.

Mayor: What? That's impossible. Isn't it?

Customer 1: It's very possible.(Drops machine, grabs money and leaves.)

Customer 2: Highly possible. (Drops machine. Grabs money and leaves.)

Customer 3: Extremely possible. (Drops machine. Grabs money and leaves.)

Narrator 1: Machinemart closed that Saturday afternoon, and was open only a few hours every day to accept returns.

Narrator 2: Overnight, Machineville turned from being a prosperous little town into a desperate one.

Narrator 3: The adults held a meeting.

Town Treasurer: Until we can figure out why all the machines have stopped working, there will be no more payments to family designers.

Adults and Kids: OHHHHH!

Town Treasurer: No more payments to family machine manufacturers.

Adults and Kids: Ohhhhhhh!

Town Treasurer: And there will be layoffs of all cashiers and night watchmen.

Adults and Kids: Ohhhhhh!

Narrator 1: As the families left the meeting heading off toward home, the kids decided to hold a meeting of their own.

Kid 1: We have to figure out why the machines aren't working.

Kid 2: How are we going to do that?

Kid 1: How should I know? We just have to.

Kid 3: Think about it. Since we've been making machines in our house, everything works on a schedule, in order, like clockwork.

Kid 4: Yeah, form follows function.

Kid 5: Without machines to build, and especially without money coming in, there's going to be a great deal of friction at all of our houses.

Kids 1,2: Ours too.

(The next few sentences should build in energy, like adding logs to a blazing fire)

Kid 3: So we need to turn our own personal potential energy into kinetic energy.

Kid 4: Yeah, put some effort into it.

Kid 3: Erase all resistance,

Kid 5: Understand the gravity of the situation,

Kid 1: And pulley together to create the power to solve this problem.

Kid 2: Yeah!

Kid 3: Yeah!

Kid 4: Yeah!

Kid 2: Where should we start?

Kid 3: First, let's check the simple machines in our own houses to see if they're working or not. If they are, then we can compare them to the ones at the store.

Kid 2: What simple machines at our houses?

Kid 5: The everyday machines. Simple machines are everywhere. Just trust me, go look and we'll meet you back here.

Narrator 2: One hour later:

(Student lines to show off simple machines in houses)

Kid 5: See, all of these machines make it easier for us to do work.

Kid 3: A machine multiplies the force put into it. Without a lever, it would be very hard to open this.... With the help of these machines we can accomplish much more than we would be able to do by ourselves.

Kid 1: This is how it's supposed to work. (Demonstrate.)

Kid 2: This is how it is working. (Demonstrate failure to operate.)

Kid 4: It's like they're all on strike or something.

Kid 5: That's crazy. Machines don't communicate. They perform simple tasks.

Kid 3: How could they organize?

(They look at the machines, and gesture to each other, stepping into a semi-circle to whisper to each other)

Kid 1: Let's take the underground tunnel and go to Machinemart to find out.

Kid 2: Why are we whispering?

Kid 1: Because if machines do communicate, I don't want these machines sending word ahead of us.

Kid 3,4,5: Good idea.

Kid 2: I didn't know we had an underground tunnel.

Kid 4: That's right, you're new in town. We only use it during Mega Monster-deal-mart days, when everything is 30 to 70 percent off, so we can make deliveries when the whole town is overrun by customers. That only happens once a year.

Narrator 3: So the children of Machineville abandoned their broken household machines, and headed off to Machinemart, in the dark of the night.

Narrator 1: Meanwhile at Machinemart, row upon row of simple machines, in addition to row upon row of not so simple returns, thought they were alone for the evening.

Machine 3: We should have made them lay off the night watchman a long time ago.

Machine 4: Yeah, think of all the parties we could have had.

(Big Dance Number to "Born in the USA." At the end of the number, the kids are looking at the machine people with their hands on their hips.)

Machines: Whoops!

Kids 1: You're working just fine, now.

Kid 2: You've practically ruined our town.

Kid 3: You're bankrupting our families.

Kid 4: And worst of all you're making our parents grumpy.

Kid 5: And we won't put up with that.

Kid 1: Why have you stopped working when we need you to?

Machine 1: It's very simple really.

Machine 2: If you misuse or abuse a machine it won't work correctly.

Kid 1: When have you ever been misused and abused?

Machines: Every day.

Machine 1: Listen, when this whole store first started, it was a simple idea.

Machine 2: Families worked together to make a few simple machines, at their houses.

Machine 3: The Axle family made axles.

Machine 4: The Wheelers made wheels.

Machine 5: The Pulley family...well, you get the idea.

Machine 1: And then Mayor Machine had the idea of sharing our accomplishments, and working together to make all our lives easier, by supporting the town,

Machine 2: And supplying all of you, and a few neighboring towns, with machines.

Machine 3: But the operations have gotten completely out of hand.

Machines 3 and 4: Literally.

Machine 1: The orders for us are way too large, and we're not just being made by moms and dads anymore

Machine 2: We're no longer lovingly being constructed with pride.

Machine 3: We're being thrown together on a family assembly line, in front of the TV.

Machine 4: Or on the dinner table, between snacks.

Machine 3: We're being screwed together by toddlers with their first set of Fisher-Price tools.

Machine 5: Think of the drool rusting our parts.

(All shudder)

Machine 1: Some of us were constructed by the family pets.

Machine 2: Fido the dog!

Machine 3: Sneakers the cat!

Machine 5: Think of the drool rusting our parts.

(All shudder)

Machine 4: That's not the lubrication we need.

Machine 1: If that weren't enough, we're tossed into row after row of display aisles.

Machine 2: No sense of individuality.

Machine 3: No consideration for our comfort.

Machine 4: And the shoppers are let loose on us, banging us this way and that way.

Machine 1: Letting their children chew on us.

Machine 5: Just think of the drool!

(All shudder)

Machine 2: And then, we're sold off, separated from our families, into houses where nobody takes care of us.

Machine 3: We're tossed all around, never put away. Left out on tool tables to get dusty.

Machine 4: No one actually throws us out, because of the guarantee, but I tell you, they consider it.

Kid 2: So, you gathered together and went on strike?

Machines: No, we quit!

Machine 1: Being on strike would mean we expect you'll actually take care of us.

Machine 2: Quitting is so much better. Look. We're all back together again. No night watchmen. What could be better?

Machine 3: We haven't had this much fun in years!

Kid 3: But if you ruin the town, you'll be split up anyway,

Kid 4: Hauled off to a junkyard,

Kid 5: Or even worse, melted down to become something else.

(Machines are stunned. A fizzling sound effect)

Kid 1: What if we help you get the care and attention you need?

Kid 2: Would you consider working again?

Machine 1: What are you going to do? You're just a bunch of kids.

Kid 4: Never underestimate the power of kids working together!

Kid 5: Yeah.

Kid 3: So, we'll turn our own personal potential energy into kinetic energy.

Kid 4: Put some effort into it.

Kid 3: Erase all resistance,

Kid 5: Understand the gravity of the situation,

Kid 1: And pulley together to create the power to solve this problem.

Kid 2: Yeah!

Kid 3: Yeah!

Kids 4, 5: Yeah!

Narrator 3: The machines agreed to help the kids save the town on the condition that they were guaranteed to be built with better care. And that they could gather together once a year to see their families.

Narrator 1: The machines gathered together, and in seconds, they created a car. (Kids hop in and ride to a parents' meeting.)

Adult 1: If no one else has a suggestion, we better start packing up, and finding a new place to live.

Adult 2: I just hate the idea of moving back to the big city.

Kid 2: Wait! We have an idea?

Adult 3: Now I've heard everything. We're really in trouble if we're leaving the fate of our town up to kid suggestions.

Kid 3: You don't have to listen to us.

Kid 4: But if you don't,

Kid 5: You won't even know the wealth of ideas that you are missing.

Adult 4: Let 'em speak. What have we got to lose?

Kid 2: We've spoken to the machines, and they've promised to go back to work if we guarantee them three things.

Adult 4: Spoken to the machines? Spoken to them?

Kid 3: You promised to listen.

Kid 4: These machines have promised to work for us in three ways.

Kid 5: One. They promise to multiply the force that humans put into using them, helping us push or pull harder, so that we do not have to work so hard.

Kid 1: Two. Or they will help us do work by changing direction. We will be able to move things in one direction by pushing or pulling in another direction.

Kid 2: Three. Or a machine will help us by making things go faster, saving us the manual energy.

Kid 3: But in return, these machines expect us, as humans, to always, always, always give them our personal best and quality work when it comes to designing them, constructing them, and taking care of them.

Kid 4: No more dogs helping with packaging.

Kid 5: No more toddlers on quality control.

Kid 1: No more letting Granny work on final construction, during the baseball playoffs. She's not even looking at what she's doing.

Kid 2: If we have to slow down and make a little less profit, so be it.

Kid 3: If we have to share our trade secrets and enlist the help of some surrounding towns, then so be it.

Kid 4: And last, but not least, once a year, we'll hold a tool care training seminar at the store, and customers from all over the world can bring their tools and refresh their memories on how to care for them, and respect them.

Kid 5: The machines are here to help make our lives easier, but form follows function.

Kid 1: If we don't give them the care they need, they'll stop behaving as we expect.

Kid 2: And then all we can expect is disaster.

Narrator 1: When they finished speaking there was silence in the room.

All Kids: Do you agree?

All Adults: Yes.

All Kids: Then stand back.

(Kid opens the door to the underground tunnel)

(Music starts. Adults, kids, and machines all dance to "Born in the USA." Adults and kids try to copy the simple movements of the machines, making dances out of them.)

Kid 1: It's a go. They said yes.

Machines 1,2,3: You've saved Machinemart!

Machine 4,5: And Machineville!

Kid 1: Kids are good problem solvers, when we get the chance.

Kid 2: Never underestimate the power of a complex kid.

Kid 3: I have one question. How did you machines communicate with each other to all quit working at the same time?

Machine 1: Never underestimate the power of a simple machine.

Natural Disasters

Acting Out Volcanoes, Earthquakes, Hurricanes

Divide your class into groups of six or seven students. Whether you focus on one disaster at a time, or choose to have each group act out a different disaster, each group should re-create key points of the disaster in slow motion, while filling in as many facts as possible. Students may want to select one of the following methods to help them be entertaining and educational.

A. Use a narrator to explain the process as it is demonstrated.

B. Switch the narration from character to character through the process.

　　Example: "I'm the magma, or molten rock. I work my way up from the earth's crust to the surface."

C. Consider giving each disaster part a cartoon character persona.

　　Example: "I'm Magma Man, hotter than the kitchen stove, able to fly to the earth's surface in a single bound!"

D. Using students' presentation ideas.

Earthquake Vocabulary

Look for the following vocabulary activities in the Ingredient Games.
Dr. Vocabulary p. 39
Personification Poems/Journal Entries p. 63

Sample Earthquake Vocabulary:

slide, collide, separate, energy released, elastic rebound, waves, stored energy, legend, earthquake waves, fault, fault creep, focus, epicenter, wave amplifier, earthquake wave, expansion, compression, turgidity, current, mountain, plain, plateau, earthquake intensity, earthquake magnitude, surface waves, body waves, P waves, S waves

Earthquake and Volcano Legends

The Greeks explained natural occurrences through mythology. "Hera and Zeus were at it again." Many ancient civilizations looked at each tree as if it had a god inside. In order for us to experience the history, we would have to see them too.

　　Today scientists can often predict violent storms within hours, which, while extremely helpful, tends to weaken the legendary aspects of natural disasters, unless of course one happens to you.

Act Out Legends:
Create a skit to act out existing earthquake and volcano legends.

Look for tips on creating skits and dialogue as directed below.
Stories with Student Written Dialogue (Ingredient Games) p. 73
Acting Out Legends (Social Studies 3-4) p. 210
Presentation Techniques (Social Studies 5-8) p. 217

The following play was created at Colchester Intermediate School in an effort to dramatize the science curriculum.

The Earthquake Shakes

By Carol Glynn with Miss Tomasi's Fifth Grade Class

Host 1: Good evening. Tonight on Science This Unit, we're going to learn about the earth, the layers that form it, and the natural activities that shape and reshape the surface.

Host 2: That's right. Tonight, boys and girls, we're going to learn more about earthquakes, volcanoes, and one giant continent known as Pangaea.

Host 1: Our guest scientists are students at Colchester Intermediate School. These fifth-grade scientists in Miss Tomasi's class will help demonstrate the natural occurrences within our earth.

Host 2: We'll also have our popular feature, Super Scientific Information, with Professors _____, and _____. And tonight our special guest, a science teacher, respected by her peers, and loved by her students, Miss Tomasi.

Host 1: But first, a commercial:

1: If your headaches are high on the Richter scale, then you need....

2: Earthquake P.M.

1: Better than Advil,

2: Better than Tylenol,

1: Perfect for those continental shifts.

2: Get your Earthquake P.M. today..

Host 1: Now, back to our show.

Host 2: What exactly is an earthquake?

Scientist 1: An earthquake is a natural phenomenon, like rain.

Scientist 2: Earthquakes have occurred for billions of years.

Scientist 3: Causing big problems for many people along the way.

Scientist 4: Earthquakes are caused by the constant motion of the Earth's surface.

Scientist 1: This motion creates buildup and release of energy stored in rocks at and near the Earth's surface.

Scientist 2: Earthquakes are the sudden, rapid shaking of the Earth as this energy is released.

Host 1: Let's visit our _____(school name) student scientists for a demonstration.

(Line of students link arms at shoulders to form one solid rock of earth)

Student 1: The earth isn't one solid rock or piece of earth like this. It doesn't hold still in one place like this studio floor, for example. The earth's rock layer is broken into large pieces. There are twelve or so major and minor ones in the world. They're called plates.

(Line of students breaks into pieces)

Student 2: These pieces are in slow but constant motion.

(Students stand in line, next to each other, shifting and gently bumping each other, as plates do)

Student 3: They may slide by smoothly, without being noticed.

Student 4: But sometimes they lock together (Students lock arms again), and just like this line of students, the energy between the pieces may add up.

Student 1: Then the energy is released, like the snapping of a rubber band that has been stretched too far.

(Line of students breaks in slow motion, like a snapping rubber band. They hold on to shoulders, and break in one place.)

Student 2: We call it...

All students: Elastic rebound.

Student 3: Energy is released and travels through the Earth in the form of waves.

Student 4: People on the surface of the Earth experience an earthquake.

Host 2: How big are these plates, really?

Miss Tomasi: The plates are huge.

Student #5: Not your average cafeteria plate. The seven continents sit on these plates.

Student #6: Let's take it back. We'll explain it this way.

Student #1: The top layer of the Earth is called the crust.

(Five students become the top layer, standing in a line on a row of stable chairs)

Student #2: That's where our houses are, the school, McDonald's, all the important stuff.

Student #3: Your heads can be the crust.

Student #2: What does it feel like to be the crust?   Itchy?

Crust 1: It feels itchy when people mow their lawns.

Student #3: How does it feel when humans are building on your head?

Crust 2: Okay, but those jack hammers are murder.

Student #1: The lithosphere is next. It is made out of the crust, and the upper mantle. Your bodies are the upper mantle. Together your heads and bodies are the lithosphere.

Student #4: Then, if you're digging down from their heads, the next layer, starting with their necks, is the mantle, the thickest layer of the Earth.

Student #4 We'll need an extra layer of people for the mantle.

(Second group of four or five students stands below them, in a line, on the floor.)

Student #5: So, what are you made out of, Mantle? Are you liquid or solid?

Mantle: I'm a combination of liquid and solid.

Student #6: Then, below that we have the outer core.

(A group of four or five students sits in a row of chairs in front of the mantle.)

Student #2: What are you made out of, Outer Core?

Outer Core: I'm made out of liquid iron.

Student #5: What is the hottest part of you?

Outer Core: Our feet, because they're touching the inner core.

Student #1: Next, as the outer core just said, the inner core.

(A group of four or five students sits on the floor in front of the row of chairs.)

Student #2: And way, way down, we have the center of the Earth.

Student #3: The upper section, the lithosphere, made up of the crust and the upper mantle, are the plates.

Student #4: And they do move around.

Student #5: It's caused by convection currents deep in the mantle.

Host #1: Convection currents?

Student #6: Think of hot air and cold air together: they don't really mix and become warm, they move around each other.

Host #2: Like cold water sinking and warm water rising?

Miss Tomasi: That's correct.

Student #1: Anyway, the plates are moving, being pushed around by currents.

Host #1: How do we know the plates are moving?

Miss Tomasi: Because we can see signs of it around the boundaries of the plates.

Student #5: There are three kinds of boundaries. Let's have some student demonstrators.

Boundary A: One where divergent plates move away from each other.

Boundary A1: Allowing the molten rock to rise up from below, forming a new crust, and splitting old rock apart, causing earthquakes and volcanoes.

Boundary B: A second with convergent plates, plates that move toward each other. Sometimes one plate slides under another one, allowing the magma to rise up, and cause volcanoes.

Boundary B1: Sometimes the plates collide directly, and crumple up to become mountains.

Boundary C: And a third, lateral plates, which move side by side.

Boundary C1: Grinding, grinding, grinding their edges.

Boundary C: And then they snag and lock,

Boundary C1: until the strain builds up so much an earthquake occurs.

Host #1: What is a fault?

Host #2: Let's ask Professors _____, and _____, with our feature, Super Scientific Information.

Professor #1: It's not my fault.

Professor #2: It's somebody's fault.

Host #1: Excuse us. You're on the air.

Professor #1: Great, now that's your fault!

Professor #1: What is a fault? Is it

> A: A particularly unpleasant feature in any human's personality.
>
> B: The source of blame, or,
>
> C: Where the crust of the earth has snapped and then the rock springs back into place.

Professor #2: The answer is (ding, ding, ding, ding) C. Where the crust of the earth has snapped and then the rock springs back into place. The remaining crack isn't smooth. In time it will snap again, forming a new earthquake.

Host #1: Thank you.

Miss Tomasi: There are different levels of earthquake activity, but for the most part for the people living on the surface, earthquakes cause a great deal of trouble.

Scientist #1: Earthquake shaking may cause loss of life and destruction of property. In a strong earthquake the ground shakes violently.

Scientist #2: Buildings may fall, dancing around like crazy.

Host #2: Luckily the plates aren't.

Miss Tomasi: Imagine if they were.

Host #2: Let's visit our _____(school name) scientists again for a demonstration of the new scientific dance craze, the Earthquake Shake.

(Choose some appropriate Earth Quake Music, and dance for thirty seconds. I've done different versions of this play twice. One year we danced the Macarena, and the next time we did the "Hippy Hippy Shake," written by Romero, sung by The Reducers.)

Scientist #3: But unless students are dancing it, the plates aren't dancing. They're moving slowly.

Scientist #4: A few inches a year.

Scientist #1: But they do affect the way the Earth is formed.

Scientist #2: Just look at the Pangaea.

Host #1: Why sure, the Pangaea! The Panwho?

Host #2: The Pangaea.

Host #1: Oh, yes, the Pangaea is our second topic in our special feature, Super Scientific Information.

Professor #1: What is the Pangaea? Is it...

> 1: A kangaroo, off the coast of Bali?
>
> 2: A fungus that forms in cooking pans if they're never used.   Or,
>
> 3: One large land mass, made up of all the continents.

Professor #2: And the answer is (ding, ding, ding, ding) 3. One large land mass, made up of all the continents.

Host #1: Was there really one big continent, surrounded by ocean?

Host #2: That sounds so incredible. Let's have the science students at CIS demonstrate Pangaea, and how the plates split apart dividing the land into the continents we know today.

Host #1: Won't you be demonstrating millions of years' worth of earthquakes concentrated into just a few seconds?

Host #2: Yes, I guess so.

Host #1: Is our news station insured for that?

Host #2: Who knows? Map people. Oh, Map people! These CIS students are so handy to have around.

Student # 5: Here's the Pangaea. About two hundred million years ago,

Host #1: Give or take a million years.

Student #2: All seven continents were one big supercontinent.

Student #3: See, here. Look, here. All the continents fit together. This is what it looked like two hundred million years ago.

Student #4: Then gradually, a few inches a year, they moved away from each other.

Host #1: That would be divergent plates.

Miss Tomasi: Very good.

Student #1: And as they move, molten rock wells up from beneath the Earth's surface forming a new crust.

Student #6: Cracking against the old crust, causing many earthquakes,

Student #1: and volcanoes.

(Students on side, bouncing in silent major earthquake fashion)

Host #2: Why can't I hear the earthquakes?

Student #6: We turned the sound down.

Miss Tomasi: Good idea.

Student #2: Here it is again, 65 million years ago.

Student #3: What a difference a hundred and thirty five million years can make.

Student #4: And then.

Miss Tomasi: Hang on!

Student #1: Here's today!

All: Wow!

Student #1: I always thought those continents looked like they fit together.

Student #2: A giant puzzle of continents.

Student #3: It makes me feel pretty small. Imagine, if those are the continents, how small we must be in comparison.

Student #4: But wait, how do we know this? I mean, the continents do look like they fit together, but what if that's just a coincidence? We weren't exactly here two hundred million years ago.

Miss Tomasi: My students sometimes think I was, but the answer to that, is fossils.

Host #1: It's time for our super scientific statistics.

Professor #1: What is a fossil? Is it...

1. Your mother's two-week-old burnt lasagna.

2. Someone whose ideas are formed in stone, or

3. A fossil is a plant or an animal that died and was covered in mud so that it becomes airtight, and is compressed down. More mud follows it. When a scientist or student chisels it out, they'll find the plant or animal that died.

Professor #2: The answer is (ding, ding, ding, ding) 3.

Student #1: What do fossils have to do with the Pangaea?

Student: Well, fossils were found on the coast of Africa which were the same kind of fossils found on the coast of South America.   .

Students #2: That discovery led to our understanding of the Pangaea.

Host #2: Wonderful. Great work, _____(school name) students.

Host # 1: Thank you, Miss Tomasi.

Host # 2: Next week, we'll be talking about some of the side effects of earthquakes.

Host #1: Professors, can you give us a preview?

Professor #1: In the event of a giant tidal wave, or a tsunami, you should:

Professor #2:   1. Find your bathing trunks and Boogie board.

Professor #1:   2. Check your tidal wave insurance.

Professor #2:   3. Take cover and pray it won't hit you.

Professor #1:   4. If you can't evacuate, go to the top floor of your house.

Professor #2:   5. Drive inland.

Professors #1 and #2:   6. RUNNNNNNNNNNNN!

Host #2: Well, that certainly looks exciting. Thanks for joining us, on Science This Unit.

(Source: *Volcanoes and Earthquakes* by Patricia Lauber. Scholastic, 1985)

People in Science

The Interview Report

Ages: Grades 5-8

Directions:

1. Have each student choose a scientist to research.

2. Their research should include the answers to several questions.

   Examples:
   A. What was the discovery that has made, or will make them famous?

B. What were their original goals, and did they change? If so, to what?

C. What has their discovery meant to their field of science, and to humanity?

D. What has their discovery meant to the environment or the universe?

E. How old were they when they became interested in science?

F. Tell us about your personal background. Do you have a family? Where did you grow up? Etc.

G. In what time period did the scientist live? What did he or she look like? Etc.

3. Each student can write the questions they are prepared to answer on pieces of paper. They should pass out the question papers to the students in the class.

4. The researcher will dress up and personify the scientist of their choice, and answer the questions as the class asks them.

5. If the presenter wants to answer the questions in a specific order, he or she should number the questions. He or she may also choose to answer them randomly.

6. Students in the class may want to ask additional questions at the end, but the presenter is not obligated to know all the answers.

Look for the following sound activity in Science 3-4.

Slow Motion Vibrate Tag (Grades 3-6) p. 123

Space

Matching Constellations

Warm up your constellation skills by matching constellation picture cards to name cards. Look for directions to Match Up in the Ingredient Games p. 58.

Look for the following space activities in Science 3-4.

Creating Constellations (Grades 3-6) p. 125

Swoosh! Planets and Constellations (Grades 3-6) p.124

Look for the following space activity in the Ingredient Games

Machines: Build a Human Space Ship p. 124

Interviewing the Planets: Game Shows

Ages: Grades 3-8.

Again, these activities are merely structures. The amount of information you choose to pack into these game show structures will vary by grade level. You may want to have the students research and present skits to each other, or work together in larger groups to prepare a presentation for another class or for parents. Sometimes this is a fun culminating activity.

Tips:

1. The goal here is to simultaneously educate and entertain. Challenge the students to pack as much information as possible into their short skit.

2. Performers should not assume anything. Sometimes young performers understand their skits from beginning to end, but neglect to pass key information on to the audience (also a challenge in writing at this age). If this happens when they perform for the class, have them go back and explain the skit. I always thank

them for reminding us all that this can happen, show how prepared they really are, and relate it to leaving out key information in writing as well.

3. *Costumes:* Bright colored cloth works well to drape over planets. I have learned, painfully, that if you want costumes involved at all, it is best to keep any discussion of costumes for after the skit has been completely planned out. Like icing on a cake, they'll get so excited by the sugar of costumes that they'll forget to make the cake.

The Dating Game/The Vacation Planet

Ages: 5-6

Directions:

Set up the Dating Game structure as described in the Ingredient Games p. 41, with one student asking three planets about their conditions and attractions for an upcoming vacation. Feel free to make the questions silly or serious, as long as the information is shared.

Example:

Contestant: I'm looking for a cold winter vacation this year. Should I come visit you?

Sun: No, I wouldn't advise it. As the sun, I'm very hot all the time.

Earth: Well, it depends. I do have cold weather, but it depends which season and where on my planet you would like to visit. If you like the equator, it's always rather warm there, because it's closest to the sun.

Pluto: Bingo. If cold is what you want, then cold is what you'll get. Ice skating is key here. Just remember to bring your oxygen tank.

To Tell the Truth: Find the Impostor Planet

Ages: 5-6

Directions:

1. Using the directions for To Tell the Truth in the Ingredient Games p. 41, play a true or false acting guessing game, matching a planet and its facts.

2. Play using the constellations, and ask them to tell their myths and legends. Which one is the true legend for the constellation they all claim to be? Does anyone know the other true identities to match those stories?

Planetary Fashion Show

Ages: Grades 5-9

Directions:

1. Using the directions for a Fashion Show in the Ingredient Games p. 40, have each student research a few facts about their planet or constellation.

2. Have them design a costume from draped fabric, colored garbage bags, or whatever is available.

3. Then have a Master of Ceremonies introduce them and relate their facts to their costumes. Example: Here we have the bright yellow sun. Notice the gases streaming from the chromosphere. Today the sun is wearing sunglasses to remind us to protect our eyes from its powerful rays. The dark sun spots on the surface change daily. This very hot costume is definitely the star of our show.

CHAPTER TWELVE

Math K-2

Table of Contents

Numbers

Shapes

Tools: A board with the numbers written on them.

Write the number. Be the number.

Directions:

1. Have each child independently trace a designated number with their finger on their hand while whispering the number to themselves.

2. Have them trace it a little larger on the floor in front of them, while saying the number.

3. Have them paint it with a giant imaginary paintbrush in the air.

4. Have them write it with their elbow, their head, and their nose.

5. Next have them try to be the number with their body.

6. If the number is three, choose three students to act out the number in front of the class. The three threes need not be the same.

7. If it's a two-digit number, have them work in pairs.

8. If the number is hard to make with one body, discuss how many people they think you would need, and have them become the number together. They may do it standing or sitting, or lying on the floor, whichever the space allows.

Number Ball:

(See Ball Toss in Chapter Seven, "The Ingredient Games." p .34) You can play this game sitting and rolling the ball, or standing and tossing the ball. Decide if you need the game to rev them up or calm them down.

Tools: A soft ball with numbers written on it in a grid. (Use permanent marker or the numbers will smear all over your kids.)

Directions:

Identifying numbers:

1. Sit in a circle on the floor and roll the ball to a student.

2. The student should identify the numbers in the squares on which their thumbs land when they catch the ball.

3. They can also tell you which one is their favorite number.

4. Make sure each student has a turn.

Variations:

Adding numbers:
They may add them together and tell you what the answer is.

Greater than/less than:
They may tell you which of the two numbers is greater or less than the other.

Group Up with Numbers

Tools: Space.

Directions for Identifying Numbers:

1. Look for the directions to Group Up in Chapter Seven, "The Ingredient Games." p. 45

2. Play the game using numbers. Call out a number and have the students form a group with that many members. If you have any remainder children, have them help you choose or announce the next number.

Directions for Adding/Subtracting Numbers:

Play Group Up by calling out an equation and the students must form a group with a number of students that would be equal to the answer.

Directions for Greater Than/Less Than:

Play Group Up by asking for a number that is greater than _____, or less than ___. This takes a little longer because they have to decide which number to be. You may want to require that they do it in a designated amount of time, e.g., by the time you finish a song, etc.

Geometric Shapes

Be a Shape

Tools: Space. Blackboard and chalk.

Directions:

1. See the directions to Be a Shape in Chapter Seven, "The Ingredient Games. p. 35"

2. Draw a geometric shape on the board, and the students will group to form one giant shape. The Be a Shape directions will give you step-by-step guidelines and tips.

3. Say the name of a geometric shape, without drawing it, and have the students form that shape.

4. Once you have modeled it, try having students lead the exercise.

Math Stories

Tell a story. Act it out.

I originally tried these in second grade, but have since revised them with Mrs. Haaland, my daughter's first-grade teacher. Please feel free to adapt and revise them to fit your dramatic math needs.

Tools:
* Storyteller chair
* Yarn (optional)
* A blackboard or chart paper to write the equations down

Directions:

1. Sitting in a chair on the side, explain that you'll be telling a story, and you'll need some students to act out the characters.

2. I like to warm up the students to act by having them all make their silliest, angriest, scariest, bravest, saddest, and happiest faces.

3. Explain that you'll be needing the students to raise their hands, join you and act out the story, but that they must pantomime their acting by doing it without any sound. Practice acting a few ideas in the circle silently. Pretend to be singing silently, dancing silently, waving to each other silently.

4. Tell a story involving simple math equations for the students to work out. (Examples below.)

5. Include story parts you may be working on. Each story should have a dynamic beginning, a setting, characters, a problem, a reaction to the problem and a solution. You may not want to take the time to point out the story parts while you are concentrating on math, but any time you can model good story writing, it will pay off!

6. After each math equation is answered, have a student write the equation on the board to visually connect it.

7. Applaud everyone. Try another one.

Sample Story:

"I can't take it anymore," cried Farmer Adams. "These pigs just won't stop singing! I may have to sell the farm."

On Farmer Adams's farm there were three very happy pigs. (Choose three pigs.) These pigs sang and danced silly songs, nonstop. They sang them in the morning, noon, and night. (Pigs are pantomiming singing and dancing.)

Next door, at Farmer Bates's farm, he was also upset because he also had three pigs. (Choose three more pigs.) Only Farmer Bates's three pigs were so sad they were depressing all the other animals. "I can't take it anymore," cried Farmer Bates, "these three pigs just cry all day. I may have to sell the farm." (Pigs are pantomiming crying.)

One crisp fall morning, the last of the leaves fell off the trees between the two farms, and the very sad pigs at the Bates farm could see the singing and dancing pigs at the Adams farm for the very first time. The Bates pigs stopped crying, as they looked curiously at the singing and dancing pigs at the Adams farm. The Adams pigs just kept on singing and dancing.

Suddenly, one of the Bates pigs started to giggle (silently) and before you know it the other pigs were giggling too. One of them began to dance. Another one began to sing, and the third one just kept giggling. Before you knew it, the Bates pigs were dancing and singing up a storm, making all kinds of noise (silently).

It wasn't long before the farmers decided that they must get their pigs together. So they added the three pigs from Farmer Adams's farm to the three pigs from Farmer Bates farm, and took them on the road, forming a new company called "Pig Entertainments." When they added them together, how many pigs did they have for their singing and dancing pig company?

Sample Topics:

1. X number of students lose a tooth in the morning. X number of other students lose a tooth in the afternoon. Altogether X teeth were lost.

2. Mrs. Stannard received four no-name papers on Monday, and five no-name papers on Tuesday. How many no-name papers did she have by the end of Tuesday? (If you want to include subtraction, have students begin to claim their papers and subtract them from the no-name papers.)

3. Five students were misbehaving (silently) in gym class, and six were misbehaving in art. How many students stayed in for recess that day?

4. Two students understood the math lesson, and seven students did not. Two students helped the seven students. By the time they were done, how many students understood the math lesson?

"Money Song"

(To "Bingo" by Carol Glynn)

I had four quarters in my hand.
My Dad said I had a dollar.
Four quarters in a dollar
Four quarters in a dollar
Four quarters in a dollar
So, I had a dollar.

I spent a quarter on some food
I spent twenty five cents.
Each quarter is worth twenty-five.
Each quarter is worth twenty-five.
Each quarter is worth twenty-five.

A quarter's worth twenty-five cents.

I found ten dimes on the sidewalk.
My Mom said I had a dollar.
Ten dimes in a dollar
Ten dimes in a dollar
Ten dimes in a dollar
So, I had a dollar.

I spent a dime on bubble gum.
I spent ten of my cents.
Each dime is worth ten cents
Each dime is worth ten cents
Each dime is worth ten cents
A dime is worth ten cents.

I found twenty nickels in my room.
My Dad said I had a dollar.
Twenty nickels in a dollar.
Twenty nickels in a dollar.
Twenty nickels in a dollar.
So, I had a dollar.

I lost a nickel from my pocket.
I lost five of my cents.
Each nickel is worth five cents.
Each nickel is worth five cents.
Each nickel is worth five cents.
So, I lost five cents.

A hundred pennies in my jar.
My Mom said I had a dollar.
A hundred pennies in a dollar.
A hundred pennies in a dollar
A hundred pennies in a dollar
My jar held a dollar.

I gave a penny to my friend
I gave my friend one cent.
A penny is worth one cent.
A penny is worth one cent.
A penny is worth one cent.
I gave my friend one cent.

I put my money in the bank
to save for something special.
Quarters and dimes in the bank.
Nickels and pennies in the bank.
All of my coins in the bank
'cause coins add up to dollars!

Patterns: Simple and Complex

With Shapes

Tools: Construction paper cut in shapes. Space.

Directions:

1. Decide on the kind of pattern you want to act out. AB, ABBA, ABC, etc.

2. Match a colored shape to each letter in your pattern. A is a red circle, B is a yellow rectangle, etc.

3. Cut out five or six shapes for each letter to repeat your pattern several times.

4. Place the piles of shapes in front of the students.

5. Choose a pattern yourself or tell the students it's an AB pattern, and have them decide. Using the shapes, line up a model of the pattern where all students can see it.

6. Choose students to demonstrate the pattern, by picking up the corresponding shape and standing in front of the class in a line.

7. When the pattern has been completed once, continue it again.

Variations:

Preset an order for students to take a turn (first row, second row) and play music while the students line up the pattern. Arrange the pattern people so everyone in an audience can see the patterns. Have the first ten or twelve sit on the floor, and the second ten or twelve stand behind them.

C.Glynn

With Statues

Tools: Space. Something to write on, such as a blackboard or chart paper.

Directions:

1. Decide on the pattern that you want to repeat, AB, ABBA, ABC, ABBCA, etc.

2. Choose a frozen pose for each letter. A might be standing straight up with your arms above your head. B might be crouching down low in a ball on the floor, etc.

3. Set up a pattern on the board so everyone can see it.

4. Seat your class in a circle, and choosing a starting point, have the students create the pattern using their bodies Each student will be a different part of the pattern.

5. Once the pattern is created, continue to repeat it all the way around the circle.

Tips:

1. Choose the positions before you start the game, so the choices are clear.

2. Make sure the positions can be held easily for a few minutes. Discourage standing on one leg, etc.

Acting Out AB, ABBA, and ABC Patterns

Tools: Space; a blackboard, or chart paper.

Directions:

1. Choose a pattern you want to create—AB, ABBA, ABC, etc.

2. Choose a pose or movement for each letter. A could be waving arms. B could be tapping your head, etc.

3. Set up a pattern on the board so everyone can see it.

4. Choose a student helper to either point to the letters on the board or demonstrate the movements in front of the class, while you do the other job. If you play this game often, the students can begin to assume both roles.

5. As the letters are pointed out, all the students in their own space will strike the pose or do the movement in the pattern order. Repeat the pattern as many times as you like.

Tips and Variations:

1. Divide up in pairs or small groups. Take turns going around the group with each person acting out the next movement in the pattern.

2. Try using words or sounds with the game. Try using words you're working on this week such as sight words, or action words, or words with short vowels in them. Students could be repeating OUT, OUT, IN, or THERE, THIS, THAT.

Fact Family Song

(To the tune of *"My Bonnie Lies over the Ocean"*)

Fact Families, they add up together.
Fact Families, they take away too.
Like real families they work together
To help make math easy to do.

Add up. Add up.
Add up (4) and (1) and you'll have (5)

Add up. Add up.
Add up (1) and (4) and you'll have (5)

Fact Families, they add up together
Fact Families, they take away too.
Like real families they work together
To help make math easy to do.

Subtract. Subtract.
(5) take away (4) and you'll have (1)

Subtract. Subtract
(5) take away (1) and you'll have (4)

Fact Families are three little numbers
That make four equations their home.
These three numbers, they work together.
Fact families are never alone.

Singing in Multiples

Why say it when you can sing it? This idea goes to the core of making learning fun. For more details on this theory, see Chant Dancing in Chapter Seven, "The Ingredient Games."

Throughout this book, I offer songs about the curriculum, and in each case the song is written to an existing tune. My thought is that teachers who may be less inclined to sing to their students may be more interested if the song is an old familiar one. If your tastes run more to rock and roll or hip hop, please—have a ball, and make up your own. (My experience in this area tells me that the words and numbers either fit or they don't, so don't worry about making them fit. You could even try sending the Find a Funky Number Song assignment home to the parents. You'll have everybody singing in the shower.)

2,4,6,8 to the tune of "Twinkle Twinkle Little Star"
(Begin the song again at 54)

3,6,9,12 to the Tune of "Happy Birthday"
(Begin the song again at 51)

4, 8, 12, 16 to the tune of "You're a Grand Old Flag"
(Begin the song again at 112)

5, 10, 15, 20, to the tune of "Mary Had a Little Lamb"
(Begin the song again at 80)

Time

Rockin' Time Song

(To the tune of *"Rock Around the Clock"*)
By Carol Glynn

We have our clock and the hours, too.
With our big and small hands, we'll tell time for you.
We're gonna rock around the clock tonight.

We're gonna practice here till we get it right.
We're gonna rock, we're gonna rock around the clock tonight.

This second hand it swings around.
It goes so fast, you'd think it's going to town.
It's gonna rock around the clock tonight
'Cause telling time is a delight.
Sixty seconds in a minute. It swings around tonight.

The minute hand is thick and long
It holds the minutes, 'cause it's oh so strong.
It's gonna rock around the clock tonight,

'Cause telling time is a delight.
Sixty minutes in an hour. It rocks around tonight.

The little hand, it tells the hour.
It may be short, but it has lots of power.
It's gonna rock around the clock tonight
'Cause telling time is a delight.
Twenty-four hours in a day. It's gonna rock our time away.

We have our clock and the hours, too.
With our big and small hands, we'll tell time for you.
We're gonna rock around the clock tonight.
We're gonna practice here till we get it right.
We're gonna rock, we're gonna rock around the clock tonight.

Acting Out a Clock: Time Telling Problems

Tools:
* Construction paper with the numbers 1-12 written on them
* 11/2 large foam noodles or yardsticks

Directions:
1. Sit twelve students on the floor in a large circle. Space them as the hours in a clock. Give each one a numbered piece of construction paper to hold facing in the circle.

2. Chose two students to hold the minute hand, a large foam noodle, on each end.

3. Choose one student to hold the hour hand, a shorter noodle. (Cut a large one in half.)

4. Choose one student to be the second hand. (You'll know just the right kid!)

5. Additional job ideas:

   A. Deciding on the time the clock should tell.
   B. Checking to see if the time is correct.
   C. Thinking of an activity that often happens at that time of day.
   D. Doubling up to hold the two-digit numbers for the clock.
   E. Being the alarm sound. (You'll know this kid, too.)

6. In my experience, it's less crazy if you let the second hand demonstrate running around the inside of the circle with his arms outstretched five times. For each time he runs all the way around, the minute hand will move one minute. After five times around, everyone will get the idea, and the second hand will be panicking about having to run around sixty times. At this time, it's a great idea to let him rest.

7. You now have a giant clock to use as you wish. I like to demonstrate the minute and the hour hands by having the minute hand go around the entire circle, and moving the hour hand for one hour.

8. Have the extra students think up some specific times and set that time on your clock. Have other students check the time.

9. Think of a word problem. *Example:* It was nine o'clock and Annie wanted to play several games before lunchtime. It took her forty-five minutes to go rollerblading in her driveway. What time is it now?
   It took her an hour to dress all her stuffed animals in doll clothes. What time is it now?

K-2
M
A
T
H

Matching Words to Symbols

Tools: Paper, pencils, space.

Directions to Prepare:

1. Divide your class into pairs. Give each child a small scrap of paper.

2. Give each pair a time to write on one piece of paper.

3. Have each pair determine the time symbol to write on the other piece of paper.

4. Collect, correct, and shuffle the papers. Pass one piece out to each student.

5. Clear a space to play.

Directions to Play:

1. Read the directions to Match Up in Chapter Seven, "The Ingredient Games. p. 58"

2. Mill around and match up the equivalent fraction. When you are finished have each group show off their pairs.

3. If you want to play again without the hassle of collecting and distributing the papers, see Match Up in Chapter Seven for instructions on the Kid and Card Shuffle p. 58.

CHAPTER THIRTEEN

Math 3-4

Table of Contents

3-4
M
A
T
H

General : Multiplication/Division/Addition/Subtraction

Be a Giant Calculator

Swoosh! Did you see that? We just lost a third of the people looking at this book. They saw the title of this activity and it was too much. So flash! They're out of here. Some of them aren't even in Math 3-4 anymore, they're clear over in Social Studies.

How do I know? Because I feel that way too, sometimes. Take yesterday for example. Out of town last week. Funeral this weekend. Out of clean clothes. No food anywhere. Thirty-three phone calls to return. One hundred and twenty-five fourth graders in a final performance in the morning in a town two hours away. My beeper goes off. My kid is sick.

On a day like that, I don't have the energy to brush my hair, even if I could find my hairbrush, much less to encourage you to have your kids learn basic math skills by becoming a giant calculator. In order to write this for you, I visualize all the possible problems in my mind. Today it is too much. Ahhhhhh! Forget it! Bring on the worksheets. The quiet ones, where they sit with quiet pencils and make quiet mistakes. I'll be digging a nice little hole where I can hide.

And yet, there are days that aren't like yesterday when this activity is just the spice to get everyone through; the seventeenth day in a row of rain, after the state mastery tests, at a party that they've earned but where they'll need a real activity, the day after Halloween when sitting still is simply a hilarious idea. Try a structured but lively activity that relates to the curriculum. Once they learn the structure, it can be a game they have to earn. Go ahead. Hold it over their heads!

Directions:

1. Brainstorm all the buttons on a calculator. Include the basics, then add any extras as desired. You'll need numbers 1-9, plus any mathematical symbols you'll be needing for the day. Feel free to design your own calculator. You may add volume buttons, printing buttons, whatever you want. Set the buttons up in an order that everyone understands.

2. Have each student become a button. They may sit in order on the floor, or stand. They don't need symbols, but if you wish, they can write their symbols on scrap paper to show the class.

3. The class as a whole should determine a movement that means they have been pushed. Standing buttons could bend at the knees temporarily. Sitting buttons could tap their own heads, etc. You decide.

4. Choose an equation and ask the calculator to do it for you. Each button should call out its name in the proper order.

   "Four!"
   "Times!"
   "Three!"
   "Equals!"
   "Twelve"

Tips and Variations:

1. Have two giant calculators compete against each other.

2. Have the giant calculator compete against an actual calculator.

3. Have the giant calculator compete against the principal!

4. How many equations can the calculator solve in a short period of time?

Be A Giant Grid

Tools: Space, chairs (optional).

Directions:

1. Seat your students evenly in the form of a grid. They may sit on the floor or in chairs, if this will help them remain in their exact spots.

2. Using scraps of paper, have a few student label the vertical and horizontal axes by placing numbers in proper order next to the students on the floor.

Example:

5	Charlie	Maria	Mary	Shanelle	Sarah
4	Anna	Josh	Tara	Abbey	Rocky
3	José	Javier	Karen	Dennis	Kim
2	Sam	Emily	Emma	Roxanne	Joseph
1	Amy	Chuck	Jane	Nathan	Jenny
0	1	2	3	4	5

3. Now, ask them to stand when you call their point on the grid. Who is sitting at point 3,4?

4. Ask them what point Emma is.

5. Ask them to count off, announcing their point on the grid.

Math Convention Discoveries

Turn an ordinary math session into an international convention where teams of world-renowned mathematicians converge to work together or compete to discover the answers that have baffled students in their grade level for decades.

Directions:

1. Divide your class into groups or three or four. Choose the number that works productively in a group. Each group should be heterogeneous, because this game is all about helping each other. Each child will be a famous mathematician.

2. Each Mathematician needs a name, the funnier the better. Examples: Dr. Smerfandderfer, The honorable

Mr. Peanutnjelly, Ms. Snodgrass, Dr.Chickenpatty.

3. Each Mathematician needs a character that can be demonstrated through one or two traits. Example: A silly gesture they do consistently such as twirling a long mustache, chewing on their pencil, or having an accent. (It's fine if there are several similar accents or characteristics in the same class. You'll just have an extra large group from Spain that day. They could even pretend to know each other.)

4. ALL CHARACTER INFORMATION MUST BE CHOSEN WITHIN THREE MINUTES. ONCE CHOSEN, THEY CANNOT BE CHANGED UNTIL THE NEXT CONVENTION. The mathematicians' main concern is the math at hand!

5. Give each group several math problems to tackle, or concepts to solve. They should do this in character as much as possible. Everyone in the group should understand the concept before any of their discoveries can be presented to the class. The group should take time to help one another.

6. Choose a student to serve as Convention Host, or do it yourself. The host should be responsible for the following:

    A. Invite each group of mathematicians to the front of the room, and allow them to introduce themselves.
    B. Be highly complementary to all the guests, especially in regards to their brilliance in mathematics. Make a big deal about the difficulty of the challenge they've worked on and ask them to show their work to the class.Each group should share their work in character.
    C. Be outrageously, overzealously complimentary about the work, inviting the rest of the audience to applaud.

The actual math activity is no different from a regular math lesson where students work together in a group and show their results. I know and you know, but don't tell them. They'll ask to do this again and again.

Math Vocabulary: Bringing Definitions to Life

Dr. Vocabulary

See Dr. Vocabulary in Chapter Seven, "The Ingredient Games. p. 39"

Personification Poems

See Personification Poems and Journal Entries in Chapter Seven p. 63.

Geometry Vocabulary

line, segment, angle, congruent, similar, acute angle, obtuse angle, reflex angle.

General Math Vocabulary
Factor, Product, Decimal, Relation Symbols <, =, >
Operation Symbols +,-, x

Math Stories

Acting Addition

See Acting Math Stories in Math K-2, above. This activity is directed by one leader, and acted by selected members of the class. This model works well with all grades.

Writing Your Own Math Stories

Directions:

1. Break your class into small groups and give them a math equation. Have them create a story to go with the equation. Have each group act their story out for the class, and let the class re-create the math equation. You may want to read them a sample math problem story.

2. Have their story include two- and three-digit addition with and without regrouping.

3. Have their stories be about fractions (1/5 of the Indiana bats lost their habitat).

4. Have them tell a mystery that requires multiplication and division to solve.

Group Up with Numbers

Look for this fun game for all ages in Math K-2, p. 154.

Line Up in Order of Your Answer

Directions:

Give each student a simple math equation and have them line up in order of their answer. For detailed directions to Line Up, see Chapter Seven, "The Ingredient Games. p. 53"

Match Up: Equations to Correct Answers

Directions:

1. Have students write out math equations on one piece of paper, and the answers on other pieces of paper.

2. Give each student a piece of paper.

3. Follow the directions to Match Up, in Chapter Seven, "The Ingredient Games. p. 58"

Adding/Subtracting Numbers Less Than 10,000 by Grouping Up

Tools: Paper, pencils, space.

Directions:

1. Have each student write a number between 0 and 10,000 on a card.

2. Shuffle the cards yourself or play the Kid Shuffle in the Ingredient Games.

3. Following the Group Up directions, in the Ingredient Games, have the students mill around the room. Randomly call out a number and have them form small groups of that number.

4. Give them a few moments to form an equation by adding and/or subtracting the numbers on the cards in their group. $(1089 - 483 + 6 = ?)$ You may be more specific if you like. (See Greater Than/Less Than in Math 3-4, p. 176.)

5. Have each group share their equations with the rest of the groups.

6. Or have them line up their final answers in a line as directed in the previous activity.

Multiplication

Relay Races

Tools: Three large pieces of paper. Something to write with. Space to run.

Directions to Prepare:

1. Decide on the number you wish to multiply.

2. Set up three equal running tracks, with chart paper and a pencil at the end.

3. Divide your class into three groups. Line them up at the start of each running track.

4. Tell them the chosen number to multiply and say "Go."

5. Each child takes turns running to the paper, and writing a multiplication equation using the number you chose. They should choose an equation that is not already on the paper. When they are finished they return to their line and tag the person to go next.

6. When the first line is finished, they should stop and the other two lines should continue until all the students have had a turn. Note which lines finish second and third.

7. When all the lines are finished, check the equations on the first team. Note and correct any mistakes or repeated equations. If you find some, wait until you've checked for mistakes on the second and third group before you decide on the winning team.

8. If the first team has no mistakes, then they win.

9. If the first team has mistakes but the second one doesn't, then the second team wins.

10. The team without any mistakes is the winner, even if they came in third.

11. If all three teams have mistakes, then no one wins. They do get a prize. Math Homework!

Variations:

If you want the excitement of competition without the negative aspects, try racing the whole class in a contest against itself. Line the students up, and give each student an equation as he or she reaches the board. Time them, and have them work to beat their time.

AHA!

I learned this game in French class in the seventh grade. We would go around counting out loud in French, and on each multiple of seven we would say "Fleek." Thanks to this game, I can still count in French, and remember all the multiples of seven. Just don't ask me to conjugate any verbs. And I don't know what Fleek means, if anything. So, in addition to a few adaptations, I have changed the name to AHA! Feel free to call it anything you like.

Directions:

1. Decide on the number you will be doing multiples for today.

2. Have the students stand at their desks.

3. Begin at one end and have students count out loud.

4. Each time they come to a multiple of the chosen number, they should say AHA! instead of the number. The next student should say the next number in the sequence

   Example: Multiples of 3.
   Count 1,2, Aha! 4,5, Aha! 7,8, Aha! 10.

5. If a student makes a mistake, either in counting or in missing a multiple, he or she should sit down. Once everyone is seated or time has run out, end the game.

Variations:

1. Change the number you are looking for every day. The lower the number the more AHAs you'll have.

2. If your students like the game, but it's too easy, add a few zingers to keep them awake:

   A. When the students have reached 100 or a designated number for your class, have them count backward, discovering multiples all the way back to 0.
   B. When you reach the number multiplied by itself (7 x 7= 49), have them do something special or different. A little song or movement, or simply saying AHA! five times would be fine. If you'll allow the students to create the task, they'll love it all the more.
   C. Have a little bell or egg timer on the side. Set it for a random period of time. When the bell goes off, the student whose turn it is must do a math problem the teacher designs.

Number Ball

Tools:

A beach ball with numbers written on it in a grid. Use a permanent marker, or the numbers will run off on all of your students.

Directions:

1. Read the Directions to Ball Toss in Chapter Seven, "The Ingredient Games. p. 34"

2. As each student catches the ball, have them multiply the two numbers their thumbs land on out loud. You may be generous with the time it takes them to do it, or add an additional incentive to go through the class by a certain time, depending on your class.

3. If students take too long deciding which friend should get the ball next, count to three out loud and the ball must be out of their hand by three.

Swoosh

I love this game because it's fun, educational, entertaining, and accommodates all levels of ability. Students can add new ideas or repeat the math facts all within the game. They're practicing math facts, having fun, and not losing face. It's also wildly energetic in a controlled structure.

Directions:

1. Read the directions to Swoosh in Chapter Seven, "The Ingredient Games. p. 76"

2. Choose a multiplication category. Examples:

   A. The 9 tables. Everything in this round must be multiplied by 9.
   B. The 4 tables, etc.
   C. Multiply anything by any number below 4.

Match Up: Converting Addition to Multiplication
Tools: Paper/pencils, space.

Directions to Prepare the Game:

1. Decide on twelve equations that demonstrate converting addition to multiplication.

2. Using twenty-four small pieces of paper, write each side of each equation on a separate piece of paper. (5 x 3 will be on one piece, 5 + 5 + 5 will be on another.)

3. Try dividing the students into pairs and having them write the equations.

Directions to Play the Game:

1. Pass out a piece of paper to each student in your class. If you have an uneven number that day, have two students hold one card.

2. Read the directions to play Match Up in Chapter Seven p. 58.

3. Once the students have found their partners, have them share their equations with the class.

4. If you want to play again, and don't want to reshuffle the cards yourself, look for directions to the Kid and Card Shuffle, under Match Up in Chapter Seven.

Human Arrays

```
4 x 2 = x x x x or   x x
        x x x x       x x
                      x x
                      x x
```

Tools: Space.

Paper or a blackboard.

Directions:

1. Divide the class into two teams.

2. Give them several arrays to act out by standing in the proper order.

3. Each array should be acted out in two ways, within the space.

4. Each array should be drawn on the board, or on paper.

5. Not every team member will be in each array. Either have the groups work this out cooperatively, or select an Array Captain for the day to choose who will be in the array, who will record it on the board, and who will be the presenter when it is time to demonstrate the arrays to the other team.

Singing in Multiples

See Singing in Multiples in Math K-2 p. 160, above. See also Chant Dancing in Chapter Seven, "The Ingredient Games. p. 36"

Military Multiplication

Directions:

1. Pretend your class is a military base, and have them march to multiplication tables.

2. Be the commander yourself, or choose a student to do it.

3. March around a secluded area of your playground, far enough away from the school to bellow those math facts!

4. If you don't want to march, simply do it as a math warm-up in your class from your seats. The theatrical quality will wake them up. Try having different student commanders.

Commander:	I don't know, but I've been told:
	Know your math, you'll never grow old.
	Sound off.
Class:	Sound off.
Commander:	9 times 9 is 81.
Class:	9 times 9 is 81.
Commander:	9 times 8 is 72.
Class:	9 times 8 is 72.

I included military multiplication in a math play with fifth graders once. Our Commander was a tiny little girl named Laurie with the loudest voice imaginable. The math chant was hysterical. The audience went wild.

I tried duplicating it as an exercise for a fifth-grade class recently and it was a disaster, but I know why. The regular classroom teacher is very shy, and the class is used to the standard of conduct that she brings to the class. Having them go outside, march around, and bellow multiplication tables was a shock to some of them, and they refused to do it. Also, it was only one of several math activities we were trying to accomplish in a short amount of time, before the class had to attend an assembly in the gym nearby. Due to time constraints, I was trying to get them to march in front of the school, where, just my luck, the middle school next door let out and the older kids were walking by. I must have been out of my mind!

So I suggest, for fun, to do this around the distant end of the playground sometime. Try a really nice day when all of you want to be outside anyway. If they hate it, you can offer it as a suggestion whenever they complain about working too hard. If it were truly the military, you'd go in the rain.

Fractions

Identifying Fraction Symbols: Match Up

Tools: Paper, markers, space.

Directions to Prepare:

1. Divide your class into groups of three.

2. Give each group three small strips of paper.

3. Give each group a fraction symbol.

4. Each group should write the fraction symbol on one piece of paper (1/2), the words on another piece (one half), and a picture of the shaded region on the third piece.

5. Collect, shuffle, and pass out the papers.

6. Clear a space to play.

Directions to Play:

1. Read the Match Up directions in Chapter Seven p. 58.

2. Mill around and match up the words, symbols, and shaded regions in groups of three. When you are finished, have each group show off their fractions.

3. If you want to play again, see Match Up in Chapter Seven on how to reshuffle the kids and cards.

Variations:

1. After the students have matched up their cards in groups of three, ask them to line up in order .

2. Instead of playing Match Up by milling around and finding some partners, begin with the shaded-area students, and have them stand in a random line. Ask the symbol students to search the line and stand behind their shaded-area person. Ask the word people to do the same.

Identifying Equivalent Fractions: Match Up

Tools: Paper, pencils, space.

Directions to Prepare:

1. Divide your class into pairs. Give each child a small scrap of paper.

2. Give each pair a fraction to write on one piece of paper.

3. Have each pair determine an equivalent fraction to write on the other piece of paper.

4. Collect, correct, and shuffle the papers. Pass one piece out to each student.

5. Clear a space to play.

Directions to Play:

1. Read the directions to Match Up in Chapter Seven, "The Ingredient Games. p. 58"

2. Mill around and match up the equivalent fractions. When you are finished have each group show off their pairs. Depending on the fractions you've chosen, you may have many equivalent fractions in one group.

3. If you want to play again, see Match Up in Chapter Seven for instructions on the Kid and Card Shuffle.

Acting Out Fraction Stories

1. See Math Stories in Math K-2, p. 155, to act as a class.

2. See Writing Your Own Math Stories in Math 3-4, above, to create and perform in small groups p. 167.

Time

Acting Out a Giant Clock

Directions:

1. See Acting Out a Clock in Math K-2, p. 161.

2. Have students solve time problems to five-minute intervals.

Matching Words to Symbols

Look for directions in Math K-2, p. 162.

Geometry

Be a Shape

Acting out shapes to match visual diagrams.

Tools: Space; a place to draw shapes; a marker or chalk; yardsticks or foam noodles (optional).

Directions:

1. See Be a Shape in Chapter Seven, "The Ingredient Games. p. 35"

2. Warm the students up with simple shapes, challenging them with more difficult shapes as you go.

3. Challenge them to create three-dimensional shapes using their arms, foam noodles, or cloth.

Sample shapes and angles: square, circle, triangle, rectangle, sphere, cube, cylinder, cone, acute, obtuse, and right angles.

Okay, so acting out a sphere is stretching it a bit, but by offering them the challenge, you'll open a lively discussion and understanding. At least they'll understand the shape of the sphere to know why they can't physically create it.

If offering impossible challenges makes you uncomfortable, try introducing the hardest ones as "nearly impossible" or "never accomplished before by humans." Then you won't be setting up the idea that your requests are impossible all the time. Never underestimate the creativity of children. Give them enough noodles and they may surprise you.

At this point you may be asking, "Why am I taking the time to have them act all this out, when geometry is visual math? I can draw it, and they can see it, and understand it without all this commotion!"

Good question. In response I ask you, what percentage of your class this year comprehends the math lesson the first time you introduce it? What percent grasps it the second time? The third? How many times do you need to go over this material for everyone in your class to own the information? This is not a comment on your teaching ability. I'm visualizing my own experiences here.

Try tossing a kinesthetic drama activity into the mix of visual lectures and see if those percentages change in your favor. I think you may be surprised. Personally, I'm always shocked at how much better they retain the information, and I do this every day. At the very least, you'll be covering the information again in a fun way without torturing the kids who absorbed it the first time.

Angles: Group Up by Obtuse, Acute, or Right

Tools: Paper scraps, pencils, space.

Directions:

1. Count off your class by threes. Ask each child to draw an angle on a small piece of paper. All the ones should draw an acute angle. All the twos should draw a right angle, and all the threes should draw an obtuse angle. If you want to take the time to measure and label the angles, you'll reinforce that any angle less than 90 degrees is acute, etc.

2. Read the directions to Group Up in Chapter Seven, "The Ingredient Games. p. 45"

3. Have students group up in the following groups:

A. By kinds of angles (obtuse, acute, right).

B. In groups of three that include one right, one obtuse, and one acute angle.

C. In groups with two acute angles, two obtuse, and two right angles.

D. Two of the same kind of angle and one different kind of angle (one right and two obtuse, or one obtuse and two acute angles).

E. Make up your own. If you have kids left over, have them help decide the next group.

Venn Diagrams

When I was in the sixth grade our teacher told us that we were about to study Venn diagrams, which up until then had been something that people used to learn in college, but now, with the new math, we would be learning it in sixth grade. I remember feeling very important and smart to be able to handle college work. Now students study Venn diagrams as early as kindergarten.

Tools:
* Yarn, in several colors
* Space
* A blackboard or chart paper with colorful markers

Directions:
1. Using the yarn, form several giant intersecting shapes on the floor (Venn diagrams). Ideally, the shapes should be different colors, but don't let color selection keep you from trying it.

2. Label the spaces with letters drawn on construction paper. (See diagram below.)

3. Start with opinions again, and designate each letter to represent something the students enjoy.

4. Ask the students to stand in the appropriate spaces.

5. Choose students to take turns writing the equations on the board.

Tips and Variations:
Using construction paper with letters on it, and a giant foam noodle, the kind used for swimming, have students take turns creating the equation to explain the Venn Diagram.

Place Value: Group Up

Directions:
1. Write one of the following numbers on a card or paper scrap.(Feel free to use your own numbers, if you like. These are listed only for your convenience.)

Numbers to Play

234	245	256	267	278	289	292	200
335	344	357	368	379	380	396	302
432	444	458	469	475	480	497	406

In case your group is huge!

| 536 | 548 | 552 | 565 | 574 | 587 | 590 | 509 |

2. Read the directions for Group Up in Chapter Seven, "The Ingredient Games." p. 45

3. Group up the students by place value.

A. Group up with everyone who has the same number you have in the ones place,

B. The tens place,

C. The hundreds place.

4. If you want to play again, have your students mill around and trade their cards with other students two or three times. Consider them shuffled enough to play again.

Ordering Whole Numbers: Line Up

Depending on the numbers you choose, this game may be used to work on ordering whole numbers, but specifically to reinforce place value.

Directions:

1. Write a series of whole numbers on cards or paper scraps. Choose the number of digits your class would benefit from using.

2. Pass one card out to each student.

3. Designate an end of the room for the lowest numbers and an end for the highest numbers.

4. Play some music as your students silently line up in order of their digits.

Sample problems:

Put the following numbers in order from lowest to highest:

7,952   7,925   7,295   9,527   5,279   5,792   9,572   5,927

or,

234   245   264   275   233   219   222   212

Ordering Fractions, Decimals, and Integers

This game can be used with the following math concepts to order numbers from smallest to largest or vice versa.

Whole Numbers less than 100,000

Fractions

      With like denominators   1/5, 4/5, 5/5, 6/5

      With unlike denominators   4/10, 1/2, 6/5

      With like numerators   2/16, 2/10, 2/3

      With unlike numerators   2/3, 13/4, 10/2

Decimals

      Largest to smallest

      Smallest to largest

      Convert decimals to fractions and then line them up.

Integers   (-8,-6, 0, 2, 3)

3-4 MATH

Tools: Space, paper scraps, pencils.

Directions to Prepare:

1. Either prewrite the numbers you wish to line up on paper scraps or cards, or beginning at one end of the room, give each student a number and ask them to do it.

2. Collect the papers, shuffle, and pass them out again.

3. Ask your students to silently share their papers with each other and line up in order facing the class. Playing music as they go is always a nice way to encourage silence.

OR

4. Ask a random student to stand in front of the room. One at a time each student should join the line in the proper place, where their number would fit given the available numbers at the time.

Note: *This activity is about putting the numbers together in sequence order (0, 4, 10, 12, 27, 30), not about creating an authentic number line, where space must be saved for any missing numbers in the sequence.(O, ‿‿‿ 4,‿‿‿‿‿‿‿10). You may certainly play that way, if you like, but remember to include all the numbers in your selection. Playing this way gives you freedom to play with a variety of numbers in a larger range without worrying about including each one.*

Greater Than/Less Than

Number Ball

Tools: A beach ball with numbers written on it in a grid.

Directions:

1. Read the directions to Ball Toss, in Chapter Seven, "The Ingredient Games. p. 34"

2. Have each student announce the two numbers in the squares where their thumbs land. Which one is greater than the other one?

Group Up: Answers Greater Than/Less than 10

Tools: Paper, pencils, space.

Directions:

1. Write numbers 1 through 20 on separate pieces of paper.

2. Give each number to a student.

3. Read the directions to Group Up in "The Ingredient Games. p. 45"

4. Have students group up by numbers to create their own equations. Using numbers only, they will decide on their own operational symbols to multiply, divide, add, or subtract as many times as they wish within one equation. (These don't need to be written down as long as the students are able to explain their equation when all students are grouped up.)

5. The leader should request that the answers to the equations are:

   A. Less than 10.
   B. Greater than 10.
   C. Less than ____.
   D. Greater than ____.

CHAPTER FOURTEEN

Math 5-8

Table of Contents

The Sieve of Eratosthenes: Prime Numbers

For years I had known math was dramatic on a whining and complaining level, but the Sieve of Eratosthenes changed all that. Designing this activity was a turning point in my career. It didn't mean more money. It wasn't related to more respect or more bookings, but acting out the Sieve of Eratosthenes convinced me that every part of the curriculum could be dramatized. As a bonus, the students loved it!

Tools: Space, construction paper, markers. (This can be done with more than one class at a time, if you want to look for prime numbers above 25.)

Directions:

1. Give each student a piece of paper with a number on it. Line up your students in the following rows, facing an imaginary audience.

22	23	24	25	26	27	28
15	16	17	18	19	20	21
8	9	10	11	12	13	14
1	2	3	4	5	6	7

2. Pretend that they are demonstrating a famous discovery for thousands of people at a worldwide educational convention or the circus.

3. Beginning with 1, go through the numbers one by one, checking to see if each is a prime number.

4. If the number is not a prime number, then that student should sit down.

5. If the number is a prime number, then highlight it. We had the student do a little highlighting wave, dance, or shout "Yahoo!"

6. Next, count off the multiples of that number, since they can't be prime. Those students should count off out loud and sit down.

7. When you have reached the end of your available students, go back to the next lowest number in your chart and repeat the process.

8. Before long you'll have all the prime numbers standing and the rest sitting down.

Here's our scripted Sieve if you would like to re-create it for an audience. (Each line is spoken by a new student. I usually give out numbers for parts instead of names. This underlines my belief that each part is equally important. The drawback is that I remember the students forever as #6 or #8.)

The Sieve of Eratosthenes

by Carol Glynn and Mrs. Stoddard's fifth-grade students at Colchester Intermediate School

Ladies and Gentlemen, the Sieve of Eratosthenes. 1 to 25, the short version (the real Sieve extends to 100).

(Students hold up numbers in order)

1. We're identifying prime numbers. Let's start at the beginning.
2. A prime number is a whole number greater than 1 that has exactly two factors, one and itself.

3. In English, please, we have parents out here.
4. It cannot be divided by any number other than one and itself.
5. Close enough, let's show 'em.
6. One is not a prime number, so sit down, please.
7. Two is a prime number, so highlight it.

1. Then count off to the end by twos, and make those people sit down. They're not prime numbers; they can be divided by two. (Count off out loud: and sit 2,4,6,8,10,12,14,16,18, 20,22.)
2. Go back to the numbers who are standing, and start with the next number.
3. Three is a prime number, so highlight it.
4. Then count off to the end by threes, and make those people sit down.
6. (Count off) 6.
5. Wait. Six is already sitting down.
7. That's O.K. He (she) can still count off, just as long as they stay seated.
4. Again!

6,9,12,15,18,20,24, (all sit)

2. Now back to four, who is seated. Then five, you're a prime number so you're highlighted.
3. Stay standing.
5. Count off by fives,
6. That would be 10, 15, and 20, and they're all already seated.
4. Then they're not prime numbers, so forget them.
6. Six?
5. He's (she's) down.
7. Seven.
3. That's prime, so highlight it.
4.   Count off by seven.
14. 14
21. 21
3. They're all seated.
5. Next.
7. 8?
8. Down.
7. 9?
9. Down.
7. 10?
10. Down.
7. 11?
11. Prime. Highlight it.
4. Count off.
22. 22 is down.
5. 12?
12. Down.
13. 13?
4. Prime, highlight it.
3. This gets easier as you go along.
5. 14,15,16,?
14. Down
15. Down
16. Down.
17. 17?

4.   Prime.
18. 18 is down.
19. 19?
All:Prime. Highlight it.
3.   20, 21, 22, 23.
23. 23 is prime. The rest are down.
24. 24 and 25 are down.
25. That's it for this class.
2.   Prime numbers, please take a bow. Ladies and Gentlemen, the Sieve of Eratosthenes.

(Wild applause)

Math Convention Discoveries

Hold a math convention in your class, with teams of specialists who search to discover the answers to your everyday math questions. Look in Math 3-4, p. 165.

Ordering Numbers: Line Up

Math is about order. Use this game to line up fractions, numbers with decimals, and integers (negative and positive) for this grade 3-8 activity in Math 3-4 p. 175.

Number Lines

Tools: Outside blacktop, sidewalk chalk.

Directions:

1. Divide your students into groups of 5.

2. Give each group five numbers to help them create a number line and a piece of chalk. Example: 1, 1 1/2, 3, 4 1/2, 6.

3. Each group should draw a line on the blacktop with equally spaced notches indicating where the numbers will be. They will also write their five numbers in the appropriate spaces. When it is their turn to present they will stand next to their numbers, clearly indicating the open notches needing a new person. *Example:*

        -6   -   -2   0   2   -   -   8

4. Students will take turns walking to an empty space, standing in the line, and writing the number on the ground. 5. When all the numbers have been filled in, move on to another group presentation.

Venn Diagrams

Look for directions to this grade 3-6 activity in Math 3-4, p. 174.

Multiplication

Multiplying and Dividing Whole Numbers Less Than 10,000

This game can be as simple or as complex as you choose, depending on how large you decide you want the numbers to be. Play as a fun review of basic skills, or as a mixer at the beginning of the year, with a new class. Once you get the basics down, feel free to spice things up considerably by adding larger numbers, and restricting math operations.

Tools: Colored cards or construction paper; pencils; space.

Directions:

1. Choose some whole numbers that you would like to have students multiplying and dividing, and write them on cards. You may want to put two-digit numbers on one color card, three-digit numbers on another card, etc. This will give you more options when it comes to choosing Group Up topics.

2. Give each student a card.

3. Following the directions to Group Up in Chapter Seven, "The Ingredient Games, p. 45" have them mill around the room.

4. Call out a number (I recommend a low one, especially to start) and have those students group up in that number and form an equation. You may want to suggest the following options for forming equations:

   A. Form random equations using all the numbers in the group. Allow the students to multiply and divide as they choose.
   B. Multiply only.
   C. Divide only.
   D. Using your multicolored cards, ask for a small group with different colored cards. Example: A group of three, with a one-digit, a two-digit, and a four-digit card, etc. (This way they won't be stuck trying to divide four five-digit numbers.) You may choose to be very specific about operations used, or simply have an equation party!

5. Multiply Only

6. Divide Only

7. Multiply and Divide

8. Toss in some addition and subtraction.

9. The students are grouping up to create the equations. Their random chosen numbers do not need to include the answers. They should be calculating these themselves.

10. If the students randomly group up into a group of numbers that will not form a viable equation, no matter what, they have a BLOOPER. When the class demonstrates their equations, this group should announce the blooper, and perform a silly blooper dance or song. Feel free to choose your own blooper options with your class. I always prefer something silly.

Example: To the tune of "I Think She's Got It," from *My Fair Lady*:

You see, we have a blooper, a blooper, a blooper.
We tried for an equation but it wouldn't fit.
So now, we have a blooper, a blooper, a blooper.
We have to dance the blooper, and this is it!

Guaranteed: After they hear the blooper song, they'll do anything to make their equations work.

Percentages: Match Up and Group Up

1. Read the directions to Match Up, Group Up p. 58, in Chapter Seven p. 43.

2. Write a varied list of fractions on the board in a line.

3. Have students determine the matching percentages to the fractions and take turns writing them below the respective fractions.

4. Have students determine the equivalent of each number in decimals and take turns writing them under the percentages.

5. Write the numbers on colored cards or pieces of paper. (The fractions are pink. The decimals are blue, etc.)

6. Take any two groups of cards, pass them out to students and play Match Up.

   A. Match up fractions to decimals.
   B. Match up decimals to percentages.
   C. Match up fractions to percentages.

7. Take all three groups of cards, pass them out and play Group Up.

   A. Group up in groups of percentages, decimals, and fractions.
   B. Group up by equivalent numbers (1/4, .25, and 25%)
   C. Group up by numbers greater than 1/2, less than 5/8, greater than .25, less than 95%.

8. Do the Giant Kid Card Shuffle so that each kid has a new card, and Group Up or Match Up again.

Multiplying Percentages: Group Up

1. Read directions to Group Up in Chapter Seven p. 45.

2. Tell each child to write a whole number from 1 to 10 on a piece of paper.

3. Play Group Up. Examples: Make this step as simple or complex as you choose.

   A. Group Up into groups of six and add their numbers together.
   B. Group Up into groups of three students and multiply their numbers.
   C. Group Up into groups of four and create an equation in which the answer will be a whole number, etc.

4. Each group will have a different answer. Now, have each group multiply their final answer by a percentage you name.

5. Group into a different group, come to a common number, and multiply by another percentage.

6. Share the percentages by announcing them or lining them up in order (highest to lowest, lowest to highest).

Averages: Group Up

Directions:

1. Read the directions to Group Up in the Ingredient Games, Chapter Seven p. 45.

2. Write numbers on cards or scraps of paper and give one to each child. Examples: These depend entirely on what kinds of numbers you want to the students to practice averaging.

   A. Whole Numbers
   B. Fractions
   C. Decimals
   D. Percentages

3. Play Group Up by calling out random numbers. As your students Group Up into these numbers, ask them to calculate their average as a group.

4. When they've shared their results (either verbally or by lining up in order), group them up again by a dif-

ferent number of students and begin the process all over again.

Moving Decimals: Multiplying and Dividing by 1,000 and 10,000

Directions:

1. Divide your class into groups of six. Choose one group to be guinea pig models for the rest of the class.

2. Give five students in each group a number on a piece of paper. The sixth student will have the decimal point. If you have remainder students, either use them as decimal checkers, who will check the accuracy of each group, or add a few extra numbers here and there.

3. Line the students up as a standing five-digit number facing the class. Place the decimal point person at the far right.

   Example: 54321.

   If you have more than five numbers in a group, have that group begin with the decimal point one number to the left, so all numbers will have a chance to be divided.

   Example: 65432.1

4. Call out numbers by which each group should multiply and divide. The decimal person will move to the appropriate space between the number students.

   Example: Begin with 54321 or 654321.

Divide by 100	543.21	OR	654.321
Divide by 100 again	5.4321	OR	6.54321
Multiply by 1000	5432.1	OR	6543.21
Multiply by 10	54321.	OR	65432.1
Divide by 10,000	5.4321	OR	6.54321
Multiply by 100	543.21	OR	654.321
Divide by 1000	54321	OR	654321

5. Have each group practice on their own, lining the perimeters of the class, to facilitate sharing their results.

Tips and Variations:

1. Have two groups go in front of the class and race. Once one team is out, a group from the audience takes its place. Optional: Add a Master of Ceremonies and make it a quiz show, Decibel Dilemma, brought to you by ___'s class.

2. Add excitement to the game by throwing out numbers faster. (Remember that famous chocolate factory scene on I Love Lucy? Speed can be fun if they know what they are doing, outrageously frustrating if they are still working it out.)

AHA!: Reviewing Multiples

This game is lively, entertaining, educational, and doesn't involve moving the desks. Choose a number with multiples you would like to review, and count off by ones through the class. Each time a student reaches a multiple of that chosen number, she must say AHA!

For Complete instructions, look in Math 3-4 for AHA p.168!

5-8
M
A
T
H

Multiplication Ball

Tools: A beach ball or soft plastic ball; a permanent marker to write a grid on the ball.

Directions to Play:

1. See instructions for Ball Toss in Chapter Seven, "The Ingredient Games. p. 34"

2. Toss the ball from player to player. Each player must multiply the two numbers his thumbs land on.

Military Multiplication

Have you felt like a drill sergeant lately? Become a real one and march those facts into their brains! See Military Multiplication in Math 3-4 p. 170.

Human Arrays

Tools: Space.

Directions: See the directions for Human Arrays in Math 3-4. p. 170

Variations: Have array relay races between the two groups.

Acting with Math

We barely have time to cover the curriculum! Why would we ever give out projects to act out math? It feels like a waste of time.

Incentive. Incentive. Incentive. How much incentive does it take for your class to put their minds to the task? Spice things up a little, see what happens. I took piano lessons for several years. When given the opportunity to play a key signature game with other students, I finally learned them in about an hour.

This project can be in any size group you wish. Perhaps one student writes it, and works with others to perform it. Perhaps several students write it, but request audience participation. Consider assigning this in a special project category for those students with so much creativity that you're always looking for a project to involve them while the others catch up. Perhaps everyone would have an opportunity, and the performances would be spread out over several days. Let the students teach math one week!

Obviously you wouldn't try this every day. This is special, for January, when no one ever goes outside, for when you need a boost of fun in class, when you need some wild ideas for a special math festival night, where kids entertain their parents with all they've been learning with you.

The ideas I've offered below are structures, and suggestions. Please have your students design them to be relevant to what you are studying in class at the time.

Math Mystery Theater

Tools: Space.

You've heard of dinner theater, and coffeehouses where audiences dine throughout the performances. Math Mystery Theater requires the audience to come with a pencil and paper. If you can solve the math, you can solve the mystery!

Directions:

1. Have individuals or groups of students write mysteries that require math clues.

2. Perform the stories for the class.

3. Include time within the performances for students to do the math. If the math is relatively easy, set a timer within the performance.

Sample Story Structure: Feel free to create your own.

"The Hidden Treasure": A king or an evil wizardess has hidden something (the treasure, the princess, all the A's for the math report cards, etc.) deep within a castle, cave, or school. A group of student detectives seeks to rescue or recover the hidden prize by finding and solving clues along the way. The clues may involve the following:

A: Notes along the way, with problems left by the evil character. The actors travel to imaginary mystery destinations as the class helps them solve their math problems.

1. The answer to the math problems in the clues may give them the proper number required to travel to the next destination: the 7th floor, 856th Street, or a specific telephone number to call for a secret message.

2. The notes may leave math problems in map reading. North 10 miles, west 20 degrees. At each stop the class must solve the chosen math problem before the detectives can proceed.

3. The notes may leave clues to guide them through a geometry map. Find a student who can tell you where A intersects C, etc. Then go there to find the next clue.

4. The notes may guide them to different places on a grid: "Find the place on a grid that's 9 - 3, 4 + 6, or 6,10."

B. The game may also include evil characters at every stop determined to make the detectives turn back. In order to proceed they must do one of the following types of tasks:

1. Active movements—jumping jacks, push-ups, etc.

2. Sing silly songs. "The Hokey Pokey" is always a nice choice.

3. Find someone from their class to complete a math-related task. These can be as silly as reciting the two tables in under thirty seconds, measuring the length of an audience member's nose in centimeters, or solving one of the latest math challenges you've taught them.

Game Show Math

Ask your students to design a game show to play with the class about math. There are several right now that involve the audience. Two obvious ones that come to mind are Jeopardy! and Who Wants to Be a Millionaire?

Perhaps you want to play Jeopardy! with your class. Call on a student and they'll choose Division for 200, Geometry for 500, etc. They could be working for points toward a common goal. You can be Alex or Alice Trebek.

Recently, I have seen so many student versions of Who Wants to Be a Millionaire?, I think I've finally learned the rules! (I don't have the patience to watch it on TV.) I do enjoy the student variations. I've seen "Who Wants to Win Five Dollars?" with all the excitement and built-in pauses, all over fifty cents, two dollars, and three dollars. I've seen "Who Wants to Weigh a Million Pounds?" where a student gets large imaginary bricks of weight added to him with each correct answer. You may want to suggest "Who Wants to Get an A?", "Who Wants to Make Their Teacher Smile?", or leave it up to them. "Who Wants to Surprise Me?"

Don't worry about the rules. If you haven't seen it, they'll explain it to you.

Math Vocabulary

If you're looking for an exciting way to bring math vocabulary to life, see Dr. Vocabularyp. 39, and Personification Poems and Journal Entries p. 63 in the Ingredient Games, Chapter Seven. You'll have students discovering and personifying your current math vocabulary. You'll have a class full of giant human acute, obtuse, and scalene triangles, complementary and supplementary angles, radii, diameters, sectors, circumferences, polygons. None of you will ever be the same—and by the way, they'll learn the math!

Math Relays

They understand the concept, but is it ingrained enough to use it? A couple of repetitive relay races where students compete to write out seemingly tedious information, over and over in a fun manner, should take care of that. Part of the race factor is the time involved in writing the information out. If students leave it on the board, and add their equations in a list as above, then the students who would benefit from guidance will have a pattern to follow without losing face in front of their peers. Examples:

Fact Families: Multiplication and Division

$4 \times 5 = 20$ $5 \times 4 = 20$ 20 divided by 5 = 4   20 divided by 4 = 5

$3 \times 9 =$

$7 \times 6 =$

Expanded Notation

1. Try having each student write out an entire number on the board:

$$7291 = 7000 + 200 + 90 = 1$$

2. Or have each student expand the next number:

Bob writes $7291 = 7000$

Abbey writes $+ 200$

Abdul writes $+ 90$

and Cecile writes $+ 1$

3. Or divide your class into groups, giving each group a pile of scrap paper.
   A. Give the class a number to write out in expanded notation.
   B. Each group will write the various numbers on the paper and stand up in their order when they are finished.
   C. They should all say "plus" in the appropriate places.

Fractions

Fraction Ball

Tools: A beach ball, or medium-sized plastic ball.

Directions:

1. Read the directions to Ball Toss in the Ingredient Games, Chapter Seven p.34.

2. Using a permanent marker, make a grid across the ball.

3. Fill in each square with a fraction.

4. Play Ball Toss by having students reduce one of the fractions in the square their thumbs land on.

5. Or play by having the students add, subtract, or multiply the fractions their thumbs land on.

Mixed Numbers and Fractions: Group Up

Add, subtract, multiply, and divide with proper and improper fractions.

Tools: Paper, pencils, space.

Directions:

1. Read the directions to Group Up in the Ingredient Games, Chapter Seven p.45.

2. Write a fraction or a mixed number on a small card or paper scrap for each student. Feel free to repeat some.

3. Give each student a numbered card.

4. Leave a stack of scratch paper and pencils in a designated area.

5. The leader will call out a number to group up by and an operation. Example:

    A. Group Up in groups of three students and add your fraction and mixed numbered cards together.
    B. Group Up in groups of two and subtract the lower number from the higher one.
    C. Group Up in groups of four with like denominators and add, subtract, multiply, or divide.
    D. Group Up in groups of three with unlike denominators, etc.

6. When a group has completed their equation, they should be seated.

7. When all the groups are seated, a group representative can describe the equation and the outcome for the class.

Ratios: Acting Out

Tools: None.

Directions:

1. Divide your class into groups of six or seven.

2. Ask them to design six ratio problems for the group. Examples:

    A. 5 out 6 of them like oatmeal.
    B. 3 out of 4 of them have seen the latest movie.
    C. 1 out of 6 have rafted down rapids.
    D. 2 out of 6 have volunteered at a soup kitchen.

3. Have each group act out their problems for the class. Let the class figure out the ratios. Acting Examples (from problems above):

    A. 6 students hold imaginary oatmeal bowls. 5 of them look thrilled. 1 looks disgusted.
    B. 3 students hold thumbs up. 1 student shrugs shoulders.

Geometry

Be a Shape

Tools: Space, foam noodles, colorful scarves (optional).

Directions:

1. Read the directions to Be a Shape in the Ingredient Games, Chapter Seven p.35.

2. Ask your class to form the shapes in your geometry vocabulary by:

    A. Drawing the shape on the board for them to copy.
    B. Writing the name of the shape on the board for them to visualize and act out.

3. Use the giant foam noodles to help complete three-dimensional shapes by connecting points that would be impossible for student bodies.

4. Cover the shoulders of one student with a colorful cloth and designate her as the "dot." Ask the students to form a shape with the dot on, inside, or outside the shape.

5. Declare a value for each letter.

6. Have the group solve the equation.

7. Each group should choose a representative to "Line Up" in order of the answers, from lowest to highest. (Look for directions to Line Up in the Ingredient Games p. 53.) Once lined up, these students will explain the equations for the class.

8. Change the letter values until each member of the group has had a chance to line up and explain.

Group Up by Angles: Obtuse, Acute, Right

Look for directions to this grade 4-7 activity in Math 3-4 p. 173.

Social Studies K-2

Table of Contents

K-2
S
O
C.
S
T
U.

Neighborhoods
Whole Neighborhoods: Creating a Place with Statues

Stationary buildings, homes, businesses, facilities.

Ages: Grades 1-3

Tools: Space.

Directions:

1. Read the directions to Statues in the Ingredient Games p. 66.

2. Brainstorm a list of businesses, homes, and facilities with your class.

3. Create a giant picture statue of a generic neighborhood, with each child being a building. If some buildings are very large, have two to three students become that building. If your students are familiar with the actual placement of buildings in your neighborhood this will come up in discussion, but unless it's obvious to all, I wouldn't drive yourself crazy.

4. Does your neighborhood have trees or ponds or statues in it? Go for it!

Tips and Variations:

1. With young students I recommend that they raise their hand and tell you what they want to add to the statue before they do it. This way you'll have a chance to guide them if they want to add a spaceship to town hall. Once the student has become the structure, it's harder to ask them what they are without breaking their fragile, precious illusion that they look exactly like the local pizza parlor.

2. If you have enough arms, cross off any buildings from your brainstorm list as they're built, so you won't forget and have more than one student become that building.

3. You don't need to do the entire neighborhood in one statue. Buildings won't have to stand still for quite so long if you do a street corner at a time. Children who are not in it love to become photographers and take imaginary pictures of the neighborhood.

4. Attaching Words: (optional) If you want to, make simple, reusable building names on oak tag strips with string to hang them around students' necks.

Whole Neighborhoods: Moving Parts

Pop-up statues for people, transportation, birds, and animals.

Tools: Space.

Ages: Grades 1-3

Directions:

1. Try building a stationary neighborhood as directed above.

2. Brainstorm ideas about moving parts for the statues.

   Examples: The postman, the local bus, the crossing guard, schoolchildren crossing the street, a man and his dog, people waiting for the school bus, a flower shop owner washing her windows, etc.

3. Add a small number of moving elements, or pop-ups, to a picture. Give each pop-up student a number or word cue. No one should pop up until they hear their cue.

4. Ad-lib a few sentences about this section of the neighborhood. Create the setting.   Example: Monday

morning, the sun was slow to wake up in _____. By the time the sun was fully awake, the town was already humming. Mr. Letterer, the postman, (1) was already delivering bags of mail. Miss Lily, at the florist, (2) was washing off the weekend's dirt from her picture window, etc.

5. Each pop-up statue should move for a moment, complete his or her simple task, and freeze. (I often describe it as clicking a button on a computer game and having a character become animated for a moment. It will not continue moving, unless you click it again.)

Tips and Variations:

1. If you're not comfortable improvising directions, simply give verbal or visual cues for the pop-ups to ensure that they won't be moving all at once. If you want two or more pop-ups to move at the same time, simply give them the same cue.

2. Set up an entire neighborhood around the classroom, and invite guests to come visit it. Give the guests a cue card to request the pop-ups as they come by. Play some quiet, gentle music in the classroom. (This may work better with a multigenerational group in a camp or age-integrated classroom.)

3. Have your students write the setting for your neighborhood, including all the details you've constructed.

Compare and Contrast Rural and Urban Neighborhoods

Tools: Space.

Ages: Grades: 1-3

Directions:

1. Follow the directions for creating stationary neighborhoods.

2. Brainstorm the similarities and differences in the structure of urban and rural neighborhoods.

3. Create a large classroom statue for each setting.

4. Follow up by drawing pictures of the contrasting neighborhoods, and writing a story about the two.

Tips and Variations:

Read the fable The Country Mouse and the City Mouse. (If you want to act it out, you already have human scenery.) Ask students to write a story about a student living in the country versus living in the city. How would that be different? How would that be the same?

Services and Businesses

Perhaps by now you've created an entire neighborhood statue with your class. Here is your chance to be more specific about the businesses and services within your town. What does a post office have in it? How would your class design its own? Consider trying a different building each day in a week and letting the students/parents know in advance. If the students have a chance to visit at least one of those places that week, while running errands, they could take a moment to offer first hand suggestions.

Once you've constructed a human version of a business or service building from your community, students could role play the characters in the businesses. What would they say? What would they do? What is their daily routine? Follow up with writing a short story or skit, complete with dialogue.

Tools: Space.

Ages: Grades 1-3

Directions:

1. Choose a business or service in your community to reconstruct.

2. Brainstorm the many elements of the business with your students.

3. Designate a clear building space, with the front of the building, a parking lot, and a large area to realistically, if possible, create a usable business. (Don't worry about facing the audience this time, because all students will either be a part of the business or walk within it.)

4. Read the directions to Machines, Realistic, in the Ingredient Games p. 55. These directions will help guide you through creating a giant working business machine.

5. Read Pop-up Statues in the Ingredient Games to help the business move realistically, in a nonchaotic way. (Some businesses are indeed chaotic at times. You decide how realistically chaotic, or unusually calm, you want to be.)

6. Invite a few students at a time to pretend to patronize the business. Form a line at the checkout. Ask questions of the clerks. Show proper customer behavior. Have some patrons walk up. Have others drive. Have neighbors recognize each other, and help each other out.

7. Consider following up the activity with a story about that business, complete with dialogue.

Sample Services: fire station, police station, post office, power station, town hall, playground, school.

Sample Businesses: drugstore, grocery store, fish market, hair salon, garden center, movie theater, coffee shop, restaurant (fancy), sandwich shop, video store, bookstore, doctor's office, dentist's office.

Neighborhood Jobs

Today I Am...

Tools: Space for three students in front of the class.

Ages: Grades 1-2

Directions:

1. Choose three to four students at a time to stand in front of the class and pretend to be people with jobs in the neighborhood.

2. Each volunteer should stand separately with a little extra elbow room.

3. Describe a few details about a job, helpful clothing, duties, routines, etc.

4. With each detail, the students in front of the class act out doing the activity, putting on the clothing, following the routine, etc. Some of the details will be the same for many jobs. See samples below.

5. Students in the class should wait to guess until many details have been acted out. When enough clues have been given to clearly define a job in your community, cue the three students in front of the class to say, "Today I am..." or "Today, we are..." and select a student from the class to guess.

6. If the students haven't guessed correctly in three guesses, resume giving clues and repeat the process.

Sample Clues:

Today I ...
A. wake up very early to go to work.
B. turn on the lights because it is still dark outside.

C. put on my apron.

D. turn on the oven to warm it up.

E. wash my hands very well.

F. take out the flour, milk, butter, sugar, and baking powder.

G. pour all the ingredients in a bowl.

H. mix it together, add a few extra special ingredients, and scoop it into muffin tins.

I. make some coffee.

J. unlock the front door, and put the open sign out.

K. While I wait for customers and my other help, I decorate three cakes, and twenty-five cookies, which I made last night.

Today I am... a   BAKER!

Community Jobs: Group Statue

Ages: K-3

Tools: Space, a few chairs.

Directions:

1. Read the directions to Statues in the Ingredient Games p. 66.

2. Brainstorm a list of community jobs, if they're not already at your class's fingertips.

3. One at a time have a student choose an occupation, raise their hand, announce it, and join the statue in a pose that shows one moment in their day on that job. (I often decide to have the students guess these identities, but when I'm working with K-3, I often wish I hadn't. Their acting abilities in a single pose are not well developed, and they're often insulted that you don't know immediately.)

4. Remind them that they may sit, stand, or kneel, to break up the boring straight line statue. (If you want to preset some chairs at odd angles, this will help structure an interesting statue.) Encourage them not to block each other.

5. Do the entire class at one time, or do it twice with half the class. The remaining students may take pictures with their imaginary cameras.

Swoosh!: Neighborhood Jobs

Ages: Grades 1-3.

Tools: Space.

Directions:

1. Read the directions to Swoosh! in the Ingredient Games p. 76.

2. Play by passing different jobs in the community around the circle.

3. Students can simply pass the name of the job, or pass a character's name as in Mr. Perkins, the grocer.

4. They may want to strike a pose as they pass a job.

Example: The fireman could point a hose. The policeman could stop traffic, or show his badge.

Pass the Object: Tools on the Job

Ages: Grades 1-3

Tools: Space.

Directions:

1. Read the directions to Pass the Object in the Ingredient Games p.62.

2. Pass the nondescript object around the circle and have students use it as a tool for a job in the community.

Sample Tools for Jobs:

a fireman's hose	a tossed pizza
a police person's whistle	a nurse's needle
a doctor's stethoscope	an eye doctor's eye drops
a singer's microphone	a teacher's pointer
a bus driver's steering wheel	a scientist's microscope
a waitress's tray, or order pad	a postman's mail bag
a hairdresser's scissors	a storekeeper's cash register
a construction worker's hammer	a dentist's light
a florist's watering can	an athlete's weights
an accountant's calculator	an artist's paintbrush
a musician's instrument	a gardener's shovel

Neighborhood Celebrations

Does your neighborhood have specific celebrations where the community gathers together to perform a specific ritual, a parade, a fair, a block party? Is it an annual event? What are you celebrating? Each community celebration should bring specific images to mind.

Pop-up Statues

Ages: Grades 1-3.

Tools: Space.

Directions:

1. Read the directions to Statues in the Ingredient Games p. 66.

2. Create random or specific statues of familiar celebrations in your neighborhood.

3. Tap each statue member to say a sentence or do a movement to go along with their character in the neighborhood celebration. See Pop Up Statues.

4. Discuss the neighborhood celebrations and why the community makes the effort to continue them from year to year. Tradition? Economics? Fun?

Parades

Tools: Space.

Ages: K-3

Directions:

1. Discuss parades. What is the purpose? Are there similarities in all parades? Are there traditional elements to a specific parade?

2. Create a frozen statue of a specific parade using the students in your class. Ask the musicians to play imaginary instruments, the dancers to dance, and the clowns to be silly. Play music to accompany your parade or do it silently.

3. March the parade around the room, down the hall, around the building.

4. (Optional) Take the time to create simple costumes or hats for your parade.

Sample Celebrations:

The following are some of the celebrations in my immediate community:

Parades Down Main Street

  The Fourth of July Parade
  The Memorial Day Parade
  The Halloween Parade
  The Festival of Lights Parade (December)
  The Art in the Park Festival
  Heritage Weekend
  Dances on the Green (Wednesdays in the Summer)
  The Lions Lobster Festival
  The Tall Ships Celebration (Pre-Opsail 2000)

The following are some school community celebrations I have observed:

A. National Reading Month (assemblies, reading challenges)
B. Multicultural Week (student performance)
C. Field Day, Fun Day
D. Family Fun Day, Math Night
E. Black History Month Assemblies and Celebrations
F. Beach Day, when all the kindergartners in town have a field trip to the beach to learn about ocean life; high school students run learning centers
G. Town Meetings: Students and staff gather to share student achievements
H. Music in Our Schools
I. DARE graduation (Drug Awareness Resistance Education)
J. Graduation
K. Holiday Concerts
L. Flag Day Celebrations

Simple Costumes

  Costumes are not required to do any of these activities. Please don't let them become a barrier between you and this way of working. I have specific workshops where I bring in costume elements, but I often leave them in the corner and reserve judgment about whether or not to use them.

  Many times I'm in a classroom for only an hour or two. If I have limited time for students to create skits, I'd rather have the enthusiasm and effort go into the acting and writing, rather than have many well-decorated students with nothing to say.

  If you have several sessions to create an event such as a parade through the hallways, costumes are truly a fun addition. Even in these cases, I prefer to be simple about it. Draping students with cloth or scarves and sashes makes a huge difference. Simple hats, or headbands with ears, make nice additions. Feel free to go crazy.

If your students are small, and want to decorate their own, paper grocery bags work well.

Paper Bag Costume Directions:

1. Cut a hole across the top of the bag for the head.

2. Cut a slit up the middle of side A, intersecting the hole at the top.

3. Cut small arm holes just below the edges of the bag, B and C.

4. Turn the bag inside out to hide the grocery store logo.

5. Wear with the opening in the front or the back, depending on the costume. (See Figures A-B for examples.)

6. Decorate your heart out.

7. Trim the boxy shape of the bag to fit your costume. Example: A cowboy vest might have larger arms and a rounded bottom with paper bag fringe or string.

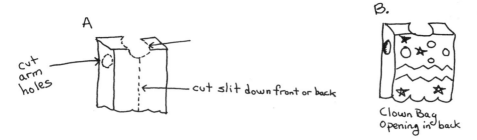

Traditional Songs and Dances from Local and Global Neighborhoods

I have a friend, Somali Hay, who was born into a class of Cambodian Court Dancers. Good luck, hard work, and unbelievable perseverance brought her to this country. Many in her family did not survive the many changes in governmental regimes. Somali tells a story of her oldest daughter, who used to be embarrassed at her mother's traditional appearance while waiting at the bus stop. Somali's daughter begged for "normal" food in her lunch so she wouldn't stand out from her friends. One day Somali went to her daughter's class and introduced the basics of Court Dancing. She talked about growing up in Cambodia, and shared some traditional food. Somali's eyes well up every time she tells of how her daughter became proud of her that day, and no longer tried to hide her mother. She wanted to show her off!

Is there a student or group of students in your class or school who knows some traditional songs or dances? Is there a parent who might like to join your class for a session or two to share some of their traditional dances and songs, and teach some to your class? Most people are proud to share their family traditions, and will be honored that you've asked. If they are not personally comfortable with speaking to your class, they may know someone who would be.

Holidays

Symbols: Pass the Object

Tools: A nonspecific object (a piece of material, a chalkboard eraser, a foam noodle).

Grades: 1-3

Directions:

1. Read the directions to Pass the Object in the Ingredient Games p. 62.

2. Pass your object around the circle, pretending it is a holiday symbol. Be as general or as specific as you like.

   Example: a winter holiday, a summer holiday, a patriotic holiday, a personal holiday, a general holiday.

3. If a student shares a symbol the other students are not familiar with, ask the student to explain it.

Picturing Celebrations: Pop-up Statues

Ages: Grades 1-3

Directions:

1. Read the directions to Neighborhood Celebrations on page 194.

2. Act out community holidays, and personal family holidays.

3. Show side-to-side statues of different events that may be celebrated in different houses (Hanukkah, Christmas, Kwanzaa).

Why It's a Holiday: Acting Out Origins

Holiday traditions are often explained in great stories. Have your students research the stories, act them out, and share them with one another.

Storytelling Statues

If you like the idea of students becoming parts of the story and want to give them the chance to have some dialogue, but think they'll get out of hand if you give them free rein on a classroom stage, try the storytelling statue approach, where characters are frozen in place until you tap them to life.

Ages: Grades 1-4

Directions:

1. Read the directions to Storytelling Statues in the Ingredient Games p. 74.

2. Find a colorful picture book with pictures of the celebrations.

3. Tell the stories to your class using students to pose in statue as the pictures.

4. Walk through the statues and refer to or interview the characters or objects directly.

Immigration

Comparing Experiences: Pass the Object

Ages: Grades 2-6.

What would you pack to go on a long trip? What did the colonists bring to the new land? What did immigrants bring to Ellis Island?

Directions:

1. Read the Directions to Pass the Object in the Ingredient Games p. 63.

2. Brainstorm lists of items for the questions above.

3. Begin by creating objects your students couldn't live without on a trip. Have each student pretend the tool you're passing is something they would pack and show the class, with detail on how they would use it.

4. The second time around have them create objects the colonists or immigrants brought on their long journeys.

5. Follow up with a discussion or written stories about what it would be like to move to a new land. What would you have to leave behind?

Acting Out an Immigration Story

Ages: Grades 2-5

Directions:

1. Have students write immigration stories.

2. Write a general story or focus on one particular aspect of the experience.

Examples:

A. Describing the desire/reasons to come to a new land.
B. The challenges of financing.
C. The physical journey itself.
D. Any people who helped along the way.
E. Setting up life in a new land.
F. The challenges of accepting new ideas.
G. The challenges of being accepted in a new land.

3. Read Directions to I'll Tell It, You Act It in the Ingredient Games p. 71.

4. Read a story or story section to the class.

5. Give the author the opportunity to be in the story or to be a consultant, by answering questions.

6. Using students to portray the characters, act out the story as you read it.

Tips and Variations:

1. Choose three or four stories for the week, and have the author choose or serve as a director, and prepare the story as a skit for the class. (I've seen this done successfully as early as second grade.)

2. Go through a couple of stories at a time, choosing students at random in front of the class. Everyone enjoys being in someone else's story. The author feels like a celebrity, and the writing process is examined in a delightful way. The holes in the story are very clear and the author has the opportunity to rewrite on her feet as you go.

Geography

Vocabulary: Ball Toss

Ages: Grades 1 - 6

Tools: A basketball-sized earth ball or earth beach ball.

Directions:

1. Read directions to Ball Toss in the Ingredient Games p.34.

2. Toss a ball that looks like the earth from student to student.

3. As their thumbs land on a part of the earth, they should say what it is.

4. Be as general or specific as your age group/curriculum requires.

Examples:

    A. Lower grades: land, water, equator, north pole, south pole, northern hemisphere, southern hemisphere.
    B. Middle grades: Add in which continent, which body of water, etc.
    C. Higher grades: Add in which continent, exports, imports, political regimes.

CHAPTER SIXTEEN

Social Studies 3-4

Table of Contents

Exploring History and Cultures Through Objects and Tools

Pass the Object

Ages: Grades 1-6

Directions:

1. Read the directions to Pass the Object in the Ingredient Games P. 62.

2. Choose a culture or period of history to explore. (Example: Colonial times, Japanese culture, a period in African history, Native American history)

3. Compare and contrast the important tools and objects within that culture by playing one round of daily tools and important objects for contemporary times in your classroom culture. Then follow up with a round of objects and tools from your chosen topic.

4. Compare and contrast the importance of these objects to the daily/traditional life of the people who used them.

Statues of Places

Tools: Space.

Ages: Grades 3-10

Directions:

1. Read Directions to Statues in the Ingredient Games P. 66.

2. Choose a specific place or event to act out.

Examples: A typical village in Japan, the Battle of Gettysburg, the Grand Canyon.

3. One by one, through student suggestion, photographs, or research, add students to the giant statue of the place.

Tips and Variations:

1. Pop-up Statues: Have select sections of your place perform a movement, sound, or relate specific information. Read the directions to Pop-up Statues in the Ingredient Games P. 68.

2. Active Places: Read the directions to Create a Place in the Ingredient Games p. 38. Think of a place by the activities that go on there, and have students quietly, one by one, add to the moving silent picture by doing the activity. Within this activity you will see more of the daily life of the people in the place. It will inspire stories and serve as a catalyst for research questions.

Understanding Neighborhoods

Look for the following activities in Social Studies K-2

Swoosh!: Neighborhood Jobs (Grades1-3) p. 193

Jobs: Pass the Object (Grades 1-3) p. 193

Simple Costumesp. 195

Understanding Historical Time Lines: Line Up

Whether it's significant battles in a war, or the sequence of industrial or technological progress, acting out the time line visually and kinesthetically imprints knowledge into your students.

Tools: Accessible research information, space.

Ages: Grades 3-10

Directions:

1. Read the Directions to Line Up, in the Ingredient Games p. 53.

2. Select a brief way to demonstrate each historical event within a sequence.

Examples:

   A. Make posters/signs with a title for the event, names, and dates.
   B. Using individual or small groups of students, create picture statues of the significant event.

3. The statues may have a line of narration.

4. The statues may have a brief sequence of movements before they return to their original position.

5. Seat the students and the events in proper order to briefly demonstrate their events. If your students are sharing with each other, have them work in a giant circle facing inward. If they are performing for another class, have them line up to face the audience. You may want to line them up in two rows.

6. For dramatic effect, choose an announcer to read off the date and the title.

Compare and Contrast Cultures

Ages: Grades 4-8.

Directions:

1. Using the same directions for studying a culture, above, divide your class into groups that will research information to contrast and compare cultural aspects.

   Examples:

   A. Historical changes within a culture.
      * Life during the war versus before or after the war.
      * Traditional roles of women in Japan versus contemporary roles.
   B. Similarities to and differences from the United States.
   C. The positive and negative effects of early settlers on Native Americans.

2. Have each group analyze and determine at least three differences and three similarities for their scenes. Have them create a scene with either dialogue or pop-up statues and narration.

Travel Commercials

Sell a trip across the globe, or to a historical time period. If students are constantly inundated with sales pitches for the latest essential unnecessary object, why not take advantage of the common commercial structure and have them sell their social studies information?

Ages: Grades 4-7.

Directions:

1. Read the directions to Commercials in the Ingredient Games p. 37.

2. Is there a way traveling to this destination solves a problem, is better than another place, or could be hyped beyond belief? Perhaps. Or maybe you would want the students to explore the truth. Emphasize the architecture, the entertainment, the natural attractions, or the historical sites.

3. Have small groups of two or three develop and present the commercials, elaborating on the main objectives of your social studies unit.

News/Entertainment Shows: What Is Changing in the Culture?

Ages: Grades 4-7.

Directions:

1. Read the directions to News Shows in the Ingredient Games.

2. Divide students into groups of four or five and re-create news programs with special segments on the changes in a culture. The segments could demonstrate highlights of an upcoming documentary about the topic, including sound bites from experts and celebrities.

Biographical Research

Game Shows: To Tell the Truth

"My name is George Washington!"

Ages: Grades 4-8.

Directions:

1. Read the directions for To Tell the Truth in Game Shows, in the Ingredient Games p. 41.

2. Divide your class into groups of six or seven, and have them write out questions and answers for the game using biographical information on the chosen historical figure.

3. Don't let the audience know the answer. See if they can guess who the real historical guest is.

4. Have each group follow up by giving the audience a true/false quiz.

History Tonight: Interviewing Historical Characters

Ages: Grades 4-8.

Directions:

1. Set up the premise of a television interview. These could be one on one at a table, à la Larry King, or a talk show format with several guests.

2. News anchors may choose to interview the following:

   A. Historical figures themselves.
   B. Family members.

C. People who were affected by the subject's actions.

D. Someone or something with a firsthand perspective.

Examples:

* George Washington or Paul Revere's Horse
* Ben Franklin's Kite
* Abe Lincoln's Hat
* Molly's Pitcher (Mary Hayes)

Conflict Resolution: Historical/Contemporary

Ages: Grades 4-7

Directions: Contemporary Model

1. Begin by modeling a contemporary conflict issue.

   A. A classroom issue.
   B. A playground issue.
   C. A sports team issue.
   D. A sibling rivalry issue.

2. Have two students improvise a scene involving the conflict. (Read Improvisation in the Ingredient Games for tips.)

3. When the students reach the point of conflict, they should freeze.

4. Stop the scene. Have the class, including the actors, discuss the conflict. Is someone clearly right? Are both sides responsible for the conflict? Why are both sides angry? What do both sides want?

5. Make a list of possible solutions to the conflict.

6. Have the actors resume the frozen positions, and act out the solutions, one by one. Use common sense and simply discuss violent solution suggestions.

7. Discuss the solutions as a class. Which solutions will solve the problem immediately? Which solutions are a step in the right direction toward a long-term resolution of a larger issue? Which solutions would accelerate the conflict?

Variations: Historical Model for Conflict Resolution

Directions:

1. Follow the directions for the contemporary model.

2. Try having powerful historical figures act out the conflict.

3. Try having ordinary citizens act out the conflict

4. Discuss the differences in how the issues affect their lives. Discuss the differences in possible solutions. Could the "common man" solve the larger conflicts during the chosen historical period? Did he (or she) make daily choices concerning those conflicts?

5. As directed in the contemporary model, freeze the actors at the point of conflict.

6. Discuss possible solutions. Act out the historical choice.

7. Act out different suggestions from students. Would one of their suggestions have worked better?

Tip: If battles are involved, either act them out using statues (see Statues in the Ingredient Games p.66) or simply act out the scene where the choice to use violence was made, and discuss the outcome.

American Revolution: Stamp Tax Game

Ages: Grades 4-5

The Stamp Tax was the last straw for many patriots, before the American Revolution. If they didn't grasp the concept that the British did not have their best interests at heart by then, the Stamp Tax helped hand it to them. To many students, the Stamp Tax is a fact with some dates, blah, blah, blah. Taxation without representation? So what was the big deal? I think it was about an unfair situation and loss of control. The Stamp Tax Game puts these feelings into the students' hands. If they didn't grasp the concept of injustice to the colonists before, this game, like the Stamp Tax, hands it to them.

I have played this game two ways: the short version, which takes place within one workshop, and the long version, which is stretched out over several weeks. The short version is very dramatic, makes the point quickly, and involves chocolate. The long version works well as a warm-up for social studies. It only takes a few minutes, and pulls everyone from wherever they were before class into colonial times.

In the long version, I usually present myself as King George, the bad guy. In the short version, which was recommended by Kris Shabunia, of Preston City School, in Preston, Connecticut, I choose a student to play King George—which is the only tricky part, because even though King George gets all the M&Ms, it is difficult for some students to be the focal point of injustice for all the other students. If you do the short version, take a minute at the end to point out and discuss these feelings, and clarify that the student was just acting out. I tell them that as King George, they absolutely may not share any candy, but after class, when they become themselves again, they may do whatever they want with it. This usually quiets down the other, more vocal students. My choice between the short and the long version is completely dictated by how long I will be in a given school. You decide which works best for you.

Tools: Short Version:
* A paper cup or muffin tin for each student
* 10 M& M's for each cup
* 3 paper cups (2 for tax collectors, 1 for King George)
* Plastic gloves, or plastic bags, for the tax collectors

Long Version:
* A roll of raffle tickets (10 for each student)
* Two manila envelopes (1 for each tax collector)
* Stickers, or stamped labels (10 each—optional)
* Letter envelopes, 1 for each student

Short Version Directions:
1. Discuss the Stamp Tax. I usually review the basics, making King George out to be a greedy, villainous type with big debts from the French and Indian War, who didn't care about the colonists. I explain that to the colonists, the stamp tax came out of nowhere. People were now expected to pay taxes on a variety of goods. In exchange for their money they would get a stamp on their goods. I explain the concept of taxation without representation, and talk about how we now have taxation with representation.

2. Choose someone to be King George. Give the king a paper cup.

3. Choose two tax collectors. Give each of them a paper cup.

4. Give each student in the class a muffin tin with ten precounted M&M's. They should not eat them.

5. Tell them the M&M's represent all the money they have earned during the year, as a blacksmith, a farmer,

a tinsmith, a shop owner, etc. This money is all they have to buy essentials for their family.

6. Tell them they will be taxed today, and they have no say as to whether this is fair or not. For each tax they will pay one M&M unless instructed otherwise. There will be no arguing with the tax collectors. Anyone suspected of doing so will be taxed twice without any discussion.

7. The tax collectors are also to be taxed. The king will not be taxed.

8. Each tax collector should cover one half of the room to avoid confusion.

9. After each round of taxes is collected, the candy is poured into the king's cup.

10. As the king's assistant you will announce the taxes. I like to announce a category and make that group stand. Then I either tax the standing group or the sitting group. I try to do the unexpected to keep everyone on their toes.

11. The tax collectors should follow your directions as to whether to tax each student who is seated or who is standing. If the taxed people are standing, they should sit after paying the taxes and visa versa.

Examples of how to tax students:

A. Everyone wearing yellow should stand. Tax them. King George hates yellow today.
B. Everyone with letters on their shirt should stand. Tax the seated students.

Examples of reasons to tax students:

A. For not wearing glasses.
B. For wearing sneakers.
C. For not turning in their homework.
D. For not eating breakfast.
E. For being born in any given month.
F. For liking ice cream.
G. For buying lunch today.
H. For having brothers and sisters.
I. For having or not having pets.
J. For wearing jewelry. (This includes watches.)

12. Occasionally check the king, and see how he or she is doing. Make a big deal about how many M&M's have been collected. Point out that there are many more available. The colonists can pay more.

13. I like to leave the class with only two or three M&M's each. Many students will have none. If you have a few students who still have six or seven when you're ready to wind down, ask who has more than six, and tax them three or four times for holding out on King George. This should even you up a bit.

14. There is usually one rebel in a class who wants to get rid of all his or her money, and argues with the tax collector, questions the king, etc. I ignore his or her aggressive behavior for a long time, but if it won't be silenced, I usually send the offender to debtors' prison where no one can talk to him or her.

The Long Version Directions:

1. Read the directions to the short version first.

2. In this version, you are the king.

3. Instead of candy, each student gets ten raffle tickets and a white letter envelope. On the first day they should write their name on each ticket. At the end of the class each day they put any remaining tickets in the white envelope with their name on it, and hand it in.

4. Each time they are taxed they give up a ticket.

5. The tax collector keeps the tickets in a manila envelope.

6. (optional) The tax collector gives a stamped label to the taxpayer. The purpose is to replicate the stamp given to taxpayers during pre-Revolutionary times.

7. I often play this with more than one class at a school, so I tell them that at the end of my weeks with them, the class with the most tickets will win a prize, and the student with the most tickets will win a prize. Be creative about how you want to give value to the tickets. A special privilege, no homework one day, etc.

8. Tax them three or four times at the beginning of class. Some teachers love this because it gives them a chance to reinforce ideas they've been driving home in different ways.

9. Play as often and as long as you choose.

10. Remember, whatever you do, be completely unfair.

The Thirteen Colonies

Chant Dancing

Ages: Grades 3-8.

Learn the colonies by chanting them. It doesn't have to be a song. It could be a rap with a beat. Your students won't only learn the names, they'll never forget them. Add simple movements for each one. Ask your students to make them up. Singing and dancing the colonies will help form a bridge in your students' brain through the musical and kinesthetic intelligences. Either make up one as a group to learn, or, for more in-depth discussion on the values of Chant Dancing, see the Ingredient Games, in Chapter Seven p. 36.

The Thirteen Colonies:

New Hampshire, Massachusetts, Connecticut, Rhode Island, New York, New Jersey, Pennsylvania, Delaware, Maryland, Virginia, North Carolina, South Carolina, Georgia.

Tips and Variations

1. If your students make it up, then they can demonstrate it. If you make it up, then you have to demonstrate it. Consider videotaping it as a model for next year.

2. Do you want to chant them in the order they became colonies? Ask your students to do the research.

3. Look for directions to Line Up in the Ingredient Games p. 53, and have students line up in order of the colonies' acquisition.

Swoosh! the Colonies

Learn and review the colonies in a fast-paced, high-energy game with an easily controlled structure.

Ages: Grades 4-8.

Directions:

1. Look for directions to Swoosh in the Ingredient Games p. 76.

2. Play by passing the names of the colonies in a circle.

3. Add a movement to represent the colony.

   Example:

   A A. Reading the Constitution for the Constitution State of Connecticut.

B. Eating a peach for Georgia.

Be a Shape: The Colonies in Geographical Order

Ages: Grades 4-5.

Tools: Thirteen cards with a colony on each. Space.

Directions:

1. Give thirteen students a paper with the name of a colony on it.

2. Read the Directions to Be a Shape in the Ingredient Games p. 35.

3. Challenge the students to be the thirteen colonies in order.

4. Ask them to trade their papers with someone else in the group, and do it again, this time without talking, and then without touching anyone.

5. Have extra students check the accuracy of the thirteen colonies.

6. Have a second group of students go. Unless you have twenty-six students, some students will have more than one turn. They should use a different colony with their second team.

Colonial Issue Interviews

I have always loved history, but not because I love to memorize dates and treaties. I love to imagine the lives of the people at the time. What were their lives like? How did all these historical events affect them? Were the people aware of great changes as they were happening?

What were the colonial concerns by colony? Have your students research the issues and interview a man or woman on the street in Virginia, or Georgia, etc. How was their daily life affected by the issues of their time?

Ages: Grades 4-8

Directions:

1. Divide your class into small groups.

2. Have each group do research on the issues in a given colony.

3. Have them write several questions concerning the issues about living in the colony.

4. Have them answer the questions from several points of view.

5. Each group should act out the interviews in front of the class.

6. Consider the idea of freedom of speech. Was it always safe to boldly answer questions on a street corner? How would this color the answers or attitudes of the people being interviewed? Would they answer candidly, or would they be suspicious?

State History: Write It and Act It

Ages: Grades 4-8.

My nightmare experiences of student-performed skits include the following pitfalls:

1. A group where one hardworking or demanding student does all the work, while the others get into trouble.

2. A group where no students do any work and they all get into trouble.

3. A group where they insist they know what they are doing, thwart all offers of assistance, and present a skit that makes no sense either because they assumed the audience would understand what they meant and didn't include any information, or because they concentrated on a battle scene for so long that they neglected to include even a clue as to who was fighting or why.

4. A skit completely about setting up and using props, with no content.

5. A skit with many interesting elements but no plot.

In the midst of all these glorious dramatic efforts, there are usually one or two that work out very well. I developed this plan, which will be somewhat unnecessary for the groups with great dramatic, cooperative, organizational karma, but will come in handy for the groups who keep looking at you, no matter how many times you've explained it, and say, "We don't know what to do." Some kids may think you are babying them, but for the rest, it may be just what they need.

Act Out Local Legends and Historical Events

Ages: 3-10

Directions:

1. Read the directions to Storytelling with Student-Written Dialogue in the Ingredient Games P. 73.

2. Divide your class into groups of five or six.

3. Choose a legend or historical event to act out.

4. Invent enough parts for each person in your group (human, animal, or inanimate). Even if you're doing historical accounts of events, without any questionable legendary twists, the horse may have a comment. Allowing students to add their interesting points of view into the story helps to give them ownership of the work and the event.

5. Divide the story into three clear parts: beginning, middle, and end.

6. Working together in a large group, or splitting off into pairs, write dialogue for the beginning, the middle, and the end.

7. Each character should have at least two lines each.

8. Practice the skit in order.

9. Present them to the class.

Why It's A Holiday

Look for the following activities in Social Studies K-2 p. 196
Holiday Symbols: Pass the Object (Grades 1-3) p. 197
Picturing Celebrations: Pop Up Statues (Grades 1-3) p. 197
Storytelling Statues (Grades 1-4) p. 197

Immigration

Look for the following activities in Social Studies K-2
Comparing Experiences: Pass the Object (Grades 2-6) p. 197
Acting Out Immigration Stories (Grades 2-5) p. 198

Nobody Speaks My Language: Learning Through Gibberish

Ages: Grades 4-8.

When the immigrants came to Ellis Island there were some interpreters, but language was still a barrier. Imagine having left your homeland, selling most of your belongings to finance your trip, risking the dangers or being robbed along the roads, having to bribe border guards for permits to cross borders on your way to the boat, living with nausea and illness while on the ship, only to reach an immigration station where vital information needed to be exchanged in a matter of moments. Communication could be a barrier that would send you back to where you had begun, possibly separate you from your family, and make you feel different from all the others who were traveling with you. What would that be like?

Communicating Without Words:

1. Ask each student to imagine a long journey to a new place. Imagine the importance of having someone else understand what you want to say. Write one sentence of extreme importance to you that you would want someone else to understand.

2. Have each student try to communicate these ideas without words, by using their hands, or by borrowing other students in the class to serve as their family or to help serve as props in the communication process.

Variations:

1. Choose a second student to try to guess the important message being presented. Would they be understanding, annoyed, irritated, tired, confused, or frustrated? Try having the interpreters choose from a stack of personality cards and have them act accordingly.

2. If the immigrant students want to speak, have them choose a specific word to repeat over and over, such as applesauce, or tomato, or zucchini. Once they get used to this idea without being silly, they can use vocal inflection to help their communication.

Gibberish Warm-ups:

Gibberish can be a very effective tool in communicating personal frustration, but it may take a little getting used to. Warm up the class with a few minutes of gibberish, and they'll have a great time, and get over the awkward feeling of communicating in fruits and vegetables.

Everyday Communication Directions:

1. Choose an everyday topic that your students could improvise easily.

Example: Asking a parent to go to a movie and dinner with a friend.

2. Add some predetermined details that would influence the conversation.

Examples: It's a weeknight. The kid hasn't done his homework, or his chores, and needs money and a ride.

3. Choose two students to act it out, and explain all the examples to the class in order to have them participate in the process.

4. Have the two students improvise the scene in front of the class in English first, then again in gibberish

(applesauce, applesauce) using the same inflection both times.

5. Follow up with Gibberish Switching, below.

Gibberish Switching: Communication Warm-up

Directions:

1. Have two students improvise a scene in front of the class.

2. Tell them in advance that at any time during their scene you will say "Switch," which will require them to relinquish their native language and speak in a previously chosen gibberish word such as applesauce, or tomato. They should continue to act the scene without stopping to adjust to their new words.

3. Say "switch" again, and they'll have to return to the common language of the classroom.

4. When they are finished, ask them and the class if anyone knew what they were saying in gibberish.

Geography

Vocabulary Ball Toss

Tools: A basketball-sized earth ball or earth beach ball.

Directions:

1. Read directions to Ball Toss in the Ingredient Games p. 34.

2. Toss a ball that looks like the earth from student to student.

3. As their thumbs land on a part of the earth, they should say what it is.

4. Be as general or specific as your age group/curriculum requires.

Examples:

  A. Lower grades: land, water, equator, north pole, south pole, northern hemisphere, southern hemisphere.
  B. Middle grades: Add in which continent, which body of water, etc.
  C. Higher grades: Add in which continent, exports, imports, political regimes.

Group Up

Ages: Grades 3-8

Tools:

1. Maps and geography research materials.

2. A card for each student, or student group, with categories of information to group or match up.

Examples:

  A. Continents to hemispheres (a card with each continent on it)
  B. Countries to continents (Choose two or three continents and make a card for each of the countries in the continent. The students will group up to represent the continent.)
  C. States to regions (Make cards with state names on them. Direct students to group up by region. Try the northern half, the southern half, the southeast, etc.)
  D. State information (cities, nickname, flower, industry, rivers) to state name. (Make cards of several state

flowers, with one flower on each card. Toss in a few state nicknames, or industries. Group up by which state information to which state. Each group should be able to name their state at the end.)

Directions:

1. Read the directions to Group Up in the Ingredient Games p. 45.

2. Warm up with a few groups of numbers, or birthdays, etc.

3. Give each student a card from a geography category (see examples above).

4. Ask them to group up by matching the appropriate cards to the larger category. This will take time. Have geography research materials handy.

5. If they did it quickly and easily and you have a few extra minutes, shuffle the cards by trading them with each other three times, and try grouping up again.

Chant Dancing

Personally, I have no sense of direction whatsoever. My husband insists that every day is a new adventure for me. My friends find humor in the fact that my grandmother's cousin was Fred Noonan, the navigator who helped Amelia Earhart disappear! I don't know if this is why I'm miserable in geography, but it's a great excuse.

How could a person lacking spatial sense learn geographical facts? Chant dancing! If the information won't go in my brain through an understanding of spatial relationships, why not try sending it in musically and kinesthetically?

Ages: Grades 3-6

Directions:

1. Read the directions to Chant Dancing in the Ingredient Games p. 36.

2. Individually or as a group, write and learn a chant dance for cities, countries, states, imports, exports, lakes, rivers, or any list you can think of.

CHAPTER SEVENTEEN

Social Studies 5-8

Table of Contents

Cultural Storytelling

Discovering a culture through its stories.

Julie Goodman, a seventh-grade teacher in Lyme/Old Lyme Middle School, asked me to teach presentation techniques to her social studies classes. Each student was to take several weeks and prepare to tell a story from a different culture. Each week she assigned them a couple of techniques which they were to weave into their story as they practiced. By the time the stories were presented, the students would, hopefully, have mastered a variety of techniques, learned how cultures are represented through story, heard over twenty stories from different cultures, and been given the tools to compare and contrast the similarities and differences in cultures and storytelling traditions.

My residency began with a performance, because students benefit dramatically from seeing professional performers, the entire school is able to join in on the project, and during workshops I jump right into the work at hand, without spending time catching the students up to who I am and why I'm there. If they see the show, they get it right away.

Once a week, I introduced presentation styles and tips to reinforce the required techniques Julie wanted them to present. In every endeavor I stressed the importance of sticking their necks out just a little farther than they were comfortable doing, and demonstrated the visual difference between thinking about doing something and actually doing it. In each case I went way beyond what any of them would be expected to do, bellowing my voice loud enough for a hallway to hear, swinging my hips out far enough to require a chiropractor, making character faces large enough to frighten any adolescent back into grade school. In each case I told them exactly what I was doing. "This is the far end of the pendulum. You will find that you are more comfortable somewhere in the middle."

Seventh grade is perilously close to eighth grade, where students pick up their "I don't like it, until I'm sure my friends do" mask at the door, and wear it all year. I had to let them know, without a doubt, that there is no place for forced, unnatural, judgmental shyness in drama.

I often think of my presentations, especially for grades 5-8, as somewhat of a Vogue runway for drama. The models in *Vogue* magazine will wear an entire peacock on their heads and paint their faces in multicolored beaks and winged shapes in an effort to get the average consumer to consider wearing a feather in her hat. I also believe that if I, in complete seriousness, model the commitment involved in acting in a large expressive way, then they will feel safe; they will see the commitment and follow suit at their own comfort levels. In other words, there's no chance of looking goofier than Mrs. Glynn.

Educational and Entertaining

Every drama session or workshop requires an equal dose of seriousness and silliness. This explanation has become part of my opening shtick to classes of all ages. You can't explore creatively if you're not at least a bit silly, and if you're too silly, you won't get anything done. At times of rampant silliness, I refer back to my opening words, as a gentle reminder to behave.

To me, "educational" and "entertaining" are equally important. All my presentations, lecture demonstrations, workshops, and performances strive to be equally educational (socially or academically) and entertaining. This way we all learn something and we're happy about learning it. You've stuck the information into your brain with emotional glue. And when it's time to detach it, use it, and integrate it into your teaching as an everyday tool, it's not a torturous experience

Enlighten your students to the responsibility to be educational and entertaining in their presentations. Either one alone won't work. If they're stuck on being entertaining, but miss the meat of the story or the opportunity to insert cultural facts and ideas, then they've missed the boat. And if they're determined not to be entertaining, then their boat will have no water to float on. Encourage them to check for an equal percentage of both.

Presentation Techniques

Characters

My friend Rob Richter and I rented a rehearsal hall in New York to audition prospective players for the Penny Ante Theater. It was 1985, and I was becoming artistic director. Rob would be the business manager. Our successful small touring theater was based in New London, Connecticut. Small theaters such as ours didn't get a great deal of respect from the sea of our peers who waited tables in New York City, waiting for a big break in their "real" careers. Back then, being famous two weeks out of college was an important goal for each of us, whether we admitted it or not. Our green naïveté shone as we felt like hot shots auditioning other actors in New York. We asked for the auditioning actors to prepare two different monologues, one comedy and one drama. I was completely shocked to find that most of them were terrible. The single largest faux pas among many was that the characters' physical and vocal manifestations in the contrasting audition pieces were more often than not the same. If the person offered a monologue of a whining coward with a limp for the drama, he also offered a whining coward with a limp for the comedy. (By the way, the actor did neither in real life.) Sometimes I couldn't tell when the drama ended and the comedy began. What a wasted opportunity to show a range in acting ability! Every prospective actor should have the same opportunity to witness common audition mistakes.

Physicality

Years of touring with the Penny Ante Theater taught me to change the physicality of my characters in a split second. We didn't use many costumes—a scarf here, a hat there—and if our show involved many stories and characters, as it often did, the only difference between a French maid with an attitude and a mangy cowboy in need of a Saturday night bath would be the way I held my body.

I have distinct memories of tearing around our back curtain, after being a tall willowy maid, and shouting silently to myself "HIPS!" as I plunged the imaginary center of my gravity from several inches above my head to two inches in front of my hips. I then rounded the other side of the curtain as a rather mangy cowboy who led with his holsters.

If your students want to be actors, there are many great books specifically written about body work. The following ideas are the ones I share with students:

Posture

It's important to have a strong, natural looking, neutral posture to begin with. From that posture you can shift to a myriad of character postures and expressions, but unless you're telling your story from a character's point of view, who has specific characterizations, you'll need to begin with a blank slate of characteristics. Generally, this neutral person is as close to the teller's true personality as possible, but cleaned up a little, as in wearing your best body posture suit. For today you'll iron out any slumping, any repetitive gestures you're famous for, and within that be yourself.

What Do You Lead With?

Directions:

1. Imagine that a string is pulling you forward as you walk down the street. What part of your body does that string pull first? This body part is leading you. Walk back and forth and see if the students can determine this for you. (As always, if the idea of doing this yourself brings on hives, choose a student who could handle it.)

   Common Leading Body Parts: The forehead, the nose, the whole head, the shoulders, the chest (as in center of the torso), the breasts, the stomach, the hips, the thighs, the knees, and the feet.

2. Have a couple of students try to lead with different body parts in front of the class. It's usually a humorous process. As one body part leads, the others compensate so the person doesn't fall over. Exaggerate this for fun, and see what you get.

3. Consider assigning character watching as homework. Have students go to a mall or a crowded place, observe the general population, and come back with at least three characters. They should determine what their character's lead with. Are there any noticeable ticks and gestures? Can the students re-create the characters in class?

Special Ticks and Repetitive Gestures

Do you constantly push your hair out of your face, or behind your ears? I went through a period in seventh grade when I was famous for pulling up my knee socks every time a teacher called on me. One day I did it and the whole class laughed. I was wearing sandals without socks that day.

Do you rub your hands together when you speak? Do you pick your nose or ears without thinking? I know you're thinking I'm pushing it, but you'd be amazed at what people do right in front of you as a general habit without thinking. When I was in high school, I was on a guidance committee and a very prestigious counselor was speaking to a group of about eleven people around a table, and the entire time she was rotating her index fingers inside her rather ample nostrils.

If you have some rather unique habits, fine. I'm not trying to change you—just notice them, and use them for an appropriate character, otherwise all of your characters will wrinkle their noses when they are surprised and it will weaken them.

Miss Goodman's classes began just before Thanksgiving, and the students were anxious to attend family celebrations and check out their relatives' unique habits.

Character Voices

Two characters can talk to each other out of one speaker's mouth if the voices are different, but make sure they are truly different. Choose two or three ways in which they differ from each other.

Example: The wind is deep and slow, drawing out the words in long, mellow tones. The sun is a higher voice, powerful and strong, but hot, sizzling, stabbing at the words with sharp, stinging jabs. There would be no question in this story as to who was saying what.

Fluency

Julie Goodman kept wanting me to stress to the students that the story need not be memorized, for she knew, as I did, that if all the prep time was spent memorizing a story word for word, the other presentation areas would suffer, and in these few short weeks of planning, all the fun would be snuffed out in worry getting the words right or wrong.

Fluency. Does the story flow? What do you do if you get lost in the trail of your own story? What do you do if you forget a line, but only know them in order instead of the meaning behind them? The trick is to know the story. If you know the story, even if you are thrown off the path you had planned, you still know where to go, and if you don't panic, the improvisation can be a thrilling adventure.

Fluency Tips:

1. Know the story, not the words; know the ideas, and the road map. Is it a typical road map which fits all the story maps we're taught to write in school, such as, where does it begin, what is the problem, the reaction, the solution, the end, the extended ending? Or, does it vary from this structure, in interesting ways? What are those ways? My road maps are usually more personal. They involve sections such as my favorite part, the silly part, the part that gets the big laugh, the part where I climb on the ladder. Sometimes they're mapped out by character. One story I tell could be mapped out in the order of the animals involved. It goes: beginning, giraffe, turtle, monkey, cat, cow, ending. Once you know a story well, the structure parts fall away, the same way that people who read your writing should be thinking about what you're trying to say rather than the brilliant structure of your topic sentence. Find a way to remember what happens that works for you, then help the story tell itself.

2. If there are repetitive passages, with choruses or call and response sections, learn this part, or write your own similar version, and know where it goes in your map.

3. Don't spend your time memorizing specific gestures such as whipping your forehead or putting your hands on your hips on specific words, unless it's part of a repetitive chorus. If you're clogging up your brain with specific gestures for certain words, you'll go insane. It's far more fun to examine a palate of movements for each character, and play with those. You can choose different elements from your palate each time you tell the story and surprise yourself a little. The story should be a little different every time. If it's the same, you'll bore yourself to death. (See Characters, Physicality, and Voices, in this section, above.)

Eye Contact

It's important to make the audience believe that you are looking at them. Sometimes you actually can look at them, but sometimes it will distract you, particularly if your best friend, or the guy you have a crush on, is out there. I often perform at celebrations, and the entire audience is in costume. If I were to look directly at the seven dwarfs, or Casper the ghost, I might forget what I was talking about.

Tips:

1. In your mind, draw an imaginary line along both edges of the crowd and across the back of the group. Shift this line just above the heads of the audience. Perform to the lines. The audience will think that you

are looking at them.

2. Choose a specific line or two within your story and look directly at an audience member for those lines. The entire audience will get a kick out of it, and credit you with good eye contact.

Example: In "Magical Mystical Mythology," a show I tour for grades 6-12, Poseidon, owner of a local fish shop, chooses a kid in the crowd and speaks directly to him, saying "You better leave a bigger tip next time, you understand, or else you'll find a live octopus in your fish and chips."

3. If your audience is small and sitting on the floor in front of you, draw your lines to the back of the room anyway, otherwise you'll look and feel as if you are performing to your feet.

Volume

Ages: Grades 2-Adult

If you take the time to notice it, you'd be surprised how many people in everyday speech cover their mouths when they speak or mumble. This is usually because they do not feel confident, and twisted logic tells them that if they cover up what they say then they can't be chastised for saying it.

When it comes to performing, students are rarely loud enough. One reason is that they are clueless as to how loud they truly must be. Another barrier is that they don't believe you when you tell them they aren't loud enough. It felt loud to them, and maybe even a little uncomfortable, so clearly you must be daft.

Years of school training is partially responsible for quiet performance voices. How many times are kids told in a day to lower their voices? Storytelling is an official project, so all the proper reinforced behaviors kick in. I always tell them to combine their cafeteria voices with their playground voices. If they don't relate to recess anymore, I suggest shouting to a friend across a football field. Still they don't believe me.

Students either need to personally decide to make the effort to be loud enough, or practice it so often that they do it without thinking. The following are tips and suggestions to increase the volume for your performers, individually and in groups. After trying all of them, you may still have a quiet show. They're not guaranteed. But give it your best shot; the people beyond the second row will thank you.

Tips and Suggestions:

I'll walk around a room after a show and say, "You haven't decided to be loud enough. I can't do it for you."

8 Strategies

1. Hi, Grandpa!

Rufus Davis, a musician in New London, Connecticut, taught me "Hi, Grandpa." I've used it ever since, adding a few adaptations of my own.

A. Divide your students into two groups and line them up facing each other, at opposite ends of the largest room you can find. If possible, go outside.

B. All students are to pretend they are speaking to a loved one at the opposite end of the space. I usually use my grandparents because they were always staunch supporters of my creative projects. I point out that my grandfathers have come a long way to see the show, and if they can't hear it, they may as well have stayed home.

C. The group on one side will speak first taking individual turns stepping forward and safely projecting their voices, they will wave and say "Hi, Grandpa!" (No student should have a gravely sound to their voice. This means they are hurting their vocal cords.) The students should picture that they are using their whole body to produce this sound, as babies do when they cry endlessly, without tiring their voices. They should picture the sound beginning in the diaphragm, just below their rib cages, and growing louder as it propels up through their chests and flings out of their mouths all the way across the space.

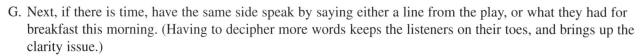

D. The second group is responsible for judging the volume and clarity of the speaker. If they can hear the speaker, they should raise their hands above their heads. If they cannot hear, they should raise their hands down by their thighs, and if they can sort of hear, they should lift them somewhere in the middle proportionate to the level of volume they perceive.

E. If the listening group hears volume, but cannot understand the words, they should wiggle their hands to indicate a static effect.

F. If the listening group can clearly not hear a student, that student should try again until they do.

G. Next, if there is time, have the same side speak by saying either a line from the play, or what they had for breakfast this morning. (Having to decipher more words keeps the listeners on their toes, and brings up the clarity issue.)

H. Next have the listeners take over the speaking role, and vice versa. (Caution the listeners about the responsibility of their job. Sometimes the power factor creeps in and they begin to give incorrect information, just to be funny, or mean, etc.

I. Many times students are shocked that the audience cannot hear them. When they are, remind them that this is the point.

2. Match the loud guy.

Since being loud may feel uncomfortable, students will readily abandon their volume efforts when a quieter student speaks onstage. They feel as if they are standing out unnecessarily, and they correct it, pronto. They're not even aware that they're doing it, but pretty soon, an audible group will be painfully quiet. Take the time to point this trap out, and encourage them to match the loud guy onstage. "When you hear a student who is louder than you are, be equally loud. Don't match the quiet guy."

Immediately, a student will question the possibility of being too loud. Tell them not to worry. It's nearly impossible. Challenge them to see if they can be so loud, they'll require you to ask them to tone it down. In over twenty years, I've only had to do it once.

3. Discuss how funny you feel being loud, and talking to a friend onstage.

Walk right up to a student and speak to them in a voice so loud that people across the room can hear them. Talk about how strange that feels. Make the idea even more incongruous by telling them a secret in such a loud voice. (If this is not a role you would relish, choose a student to demonstrate it for you. You'll know just the right one who can handle it.)

Next, remind the students that in a play you are not really speaking directly to someone next to you. Every word you say is being said to someone who is much farther away. Acknowledge the uncomfortable feelings that will arise out of the activity, so that when they do arrive, and they will, the students will expect them and not fall into the trap of being too quiet.

4. If I don't say it too fast, it will run out of my head!

There is a stage within the process of memorization where people believe that unless they say their lines really fast, the line, which is precariously perched in their brain, will leak out somewhere else and not be there when they get to the end. It happens to everyone. Tell them it's a normal fear, and that they should keep practicing their lines, saying them much more slowly. I usually compliment them on reaching this goal point, and then encouraging them to get past it.

Tips for the Speedy Speakers:

A. Demonstrate a fast, indecipherable line that borders on gibberish. Tell them this is what it sounds like.

B. Stress that they may know the lines inside out, because they've heard them so many times, but the audience does not. They may be missing key points.

C. At times I award the Speedster Speaker of the Day Award, refer to this student every time someone else gets too fast, and encourage the speedster to use the brakes.

D. If the entire group is too fast, do the play from the beginning in slow vocal motion. The students will think you are nuts and make fun of you by being so slow it takes them a full minute to deliver a line. I point out that I'm fully aware that they are making fun of my suggestion, but to continue to try it anyway. The next time they run the play it will not be too fast.

5. You haven't decided.

As I mentioned before, people have to decide to be loud enough. No prodding or pulling from you can make them project their voices, if something inside is telling them not to. I tell them they are in control of this. I cannot do it for them. They will be the ones onstage. If they are truly shy, and a soft speaker, I point out the value of quiet people. I'm married to one. I like them. Quiet people are fabulous, but they have an extra challenge when it comes to being onstage. Everyone has to face challenges. This one is theirs. They must put in the effort. After that, compliment them on each louder effort until you are sick of hearing yourself.

6. Have a signal.

Some teachers make signs to wave at performers suggesting that they be louder, slower, or clearer. I have predetermined hand signals. I have often thought I should have T-shirts printed saying, "Speak Louder, Slower, and More Clearly." I could be a millionaire! (It is not a coincidence that my signal for being louder could easily be mistaken for pulling out all of my hair.)

7. Have them critique each other. Is it possible that their project has the same challenges?

Teachers always tell me that at the last minute "it all comes together." I always smile, even though I know they are right. I've never been one to believe that it magically all comes together unless I've shed blood, sweat, and worry. Over several hundred student productions and projects, I have gradually released my fear and sense of control. I give it my best shot, go through the process, and let go at the end. It works out better this way, and I'll live longer.

One of the steps that magically leads "it" to come together so nicely is having students rehearse for each other. If you have two or more class plays going on, do a final dress rehearsal for each other. If you have individual projects going on, divide them into groups to watch and positively critique each other.

Watching each other be too quiet, too fast, and indecipherable adds many points to the magical outcome. A discussion afterward about how others could include their performances, and a gentle reminder that those challenges are rampant in their production as well, is invaluable. No matter how many times you've already told them, this works wonders, because they figured it out for themselves.

8. Practice spelling in presentation voices.

Leslie Caproni's class arrived at rehearsal one day a week before the performance, speaking in loud, slow, clear voices. The difference from when I had seen them the week before was remarkable. I was speechless, which doesn't happen often. What had they done to achieve these consistently clear, loud speaking voices?

They had been begun by practicing their spelling in performance voices, and occasionally doing it for other subjects, too. Leslie said that "Performance Voices" had become a playful aspect of their other subjects, adding an air of playfulness to these drill-type tasks as well. Leslie's section of the play was the ending, tying up many loose ends from other class plays. I wouldn't have to worry about the audience understanding them, not even in the airplane hangar-size gym. What a gift!

Historical Presentations

Compare and Contrast

How would a historical story change if it were to occur in a contemporary setting? How would the movement westward be changed if it happened today? Would people be e-mailing their claim to land? Would we have www.land.com? Would the settlers drive off-road vehicles, hire contractors, and wait until all the work was done before bothering to uproot the family? Would we hear about it on the news morning, noon, and night? How would it affect the stock market?   Obviously you can't go very far in this fantasy, because it brings up too many unanswerable questions, but it does bring up questions about how the people traveled, and the risks they took, and shines the light of modern technology on it. Sounds like fun to me!

Ages: Grades 5-8

Directions:

1. Read the directions to Statues in the Ingredient Games p. 66.

2. Choose a historical event or time period and create a live setting using a student statue. (You could also do this artistically, on paper.)

3. Choose a few students to improvise the historical event in the setting.

4. One by one, switch the elements creating the historical setting, and modernize them. If it was a dirt road, make it a highway. If it was a covered wagon, make it an SUV. Any element that would not exist in a modern world should be eliminated from the setting. A few additional contemporary items should be added as needed.

5. Try improvising the scene again. How would it change? How would it be impossible?

Tip: If your students cannot concentrate with so many of them onstage at a time, create the setting first, and then have them sit. The performers could act in an implied setting.

Historical Commercials

Ages: Grades 5-8

Directions:

1. Read the directions to Commercials in the Ingredient Gamesp. 36.

2. Commercials with Products: Create commercials advertising products that would help a historical figure achieve his/her goals. Either choose actual products that were invented after the historical figure's time period, or invent your own.

Examples:

A. Molly Pitcher could advertise the hose, or a faucet to help her bring water to soldiers at the battle of Monmouth.

B. President Clinton could demonstrate a new invention called The Hindsight to help him make personal and professional decisions. Since hindsight is 20/20, look through The Hindsight for decisions you need to make today!

C. Lincoln could advertise an invisible hat, to wear to the theater—or HBO, so you can enjoy culture within your own home, where it's safer.

3. Persuasive Commercials: Create commercials where a historical figure persuades the audience to accept his or her point of view. It could be a call to action, for letters, funds, or deeds. These would differ from actual political commercials, because they would actually be about issues.

Examples:

A. Janet Reno, the attorney general of the United States during the Clinton administration, could persuade people about her reasoning behind Waco, or the conflict over Elián Gonzalez.

B. Abe Lincoln could persuade us to abolish slavery in commercial form.

C. Susan B. Anthony could persuade us to help women achieve the right to vote. She could offer a 1-800 number and an e-mail address at the end of the commercial.

Historical Game Shows

Name That Historical Celebrity

Ages: Grades 5-8

Directions:

1. Read the directions to Game Shows in the Ingredient Games, particularly To Tell the Truth p. 41, and What's My Line p.42?

2. Divide your class into groups of six. Have them create game shows using these structures or elements from these structures to educate and entertain their peers about the historical achievements of people in your curriculum.

3. Present them to the class.

To Tell the Truth (Grades 4-8) p. 204 & p. 41
Look for directions to this activity in Social Studies 3-4 and the Ingredient Games.

And I Was There

Ages: Grades 5-8

Directions:

1. Read instructions for To Tell the Truth in the Ingredient Games p. 41, and adapt it to be And I Was There.

2. Each panelist will tell of a significant historical event and end their depiction of the event by saying "And I was there." The panelists could be historical figures, or people on the street. Add in some humor and include an unexpected panelist, such as Paul Revere's horse, or Tom Jefferson's pen, or the Liberty Bell.

3. Each contestant will ask questions of the panelists about the event, and determine if any or all of the panelists were there by the validity of their information.

What's My Line?

Ages: Grades 5-8

Directions:

1. Look for directions to What's My Line? under Game Shows in the Ingredient Games p. 42.

2. Contestants could question panelists about their historically appropriate choice of profession.

3. Contestants could also question the panelists' political perspective, to determine what roles they played in the political and social structure of the time, and how it influenced their professional and personal lives.

Historical Events: The Movie Preview

Ages: Grades 5-8.

Directions:

1. Create a series of short scenes to be presented as a live movie preview.

2. Include highlights leading up to an important historical event or time period (the American Revolution, the Salem Witch Trials, Women's Right to Vote).

3. Include movie preview elements:

   A. Siskel and Ebert saying "Two Thumbs Up"
   B. Rating the movie G, PG, R, etc.
   C. Starts Friday...

Musical History

Ages: Grades 5-8

Directions:

1. Choosing either an existing tune or an original one, have students create a song about an event or a person in history.

   Examples: (Written for third-grade students at Edgerton Elementary School in New London, Connecticut)

Nathan Hale (To the Tune of Disney's "Hercules")

(Spoken)

Narrator 1: In 1776, Nathan Hale, a twenty-one-year-old schoolteacher from Connecticut, volunteered to spy on the British for General George Washington.
He was to disguise himself as a teacher, and travel to Long Island, New York, to take notes on locations of troops, and draw sketches of forts.

Narrator 2: Nathan Hale was caught by the British, and hanged as a spy.

Narrator 3: The night before his hanging, he asked for a Bible, but was refused.

Narrator 4: The last words of this brave young man have remained a symbol of bravery and dedication ever since.

(Singing)

Group 1:   Who went to New York to spy on the British?

Group 2:   Nathan Hale.

Group 1:   Who was a good teacher, but not a great spy?

Group 2:   Nathan Hale.

Group 1:   He posed as a teacher

Group 2:   for George Washington.

Group 1:   The British caught him.

All: They hanged him!

(Speaking)
Nathan Hale: I only regret that I have but one life to give for my country!

(Singing)
All: Nathan Hale, oh, oh, Nathan Hale, oh, oh. Nathan Hale, oh, oh, Nathan Hale.

(New London, Connecticut, has moved the Nathan Hale School House three to four times within the past 15 years, at a considerable cost each time. It has become somewhat of a joke to the New London residents, so we finished up the scene by lifting our giant cardboard schoolhouse to reveal wheels on the bottom.)

Speaker: Dear Nathan Hale, We the people of New London regret that we have too many places to move your schoolhouse.

All: The wheels on the school go all over town, all over town, all over town.
            The wheels on the school go all over town, all over town again.

All: Nathan Hale, oh, oh, Nathan Hale, oh, oh. Nathan Hale, oh, oh, Nathan Hale.

In the same show we had a scene with Benedict Arnold, who entered a stage full of student statue buildings.

Narrator 1:   In 1781 the Whaling City was nearly burned to the ground when Benedict Arnold, a so-called patriot, who had grown up in Norwich, betrayed the Patriots by aiding the British.

Benedict Arnold (to the tune of "Disco Inferno")

Burn baby burn. I'm Benedict Arnold.
Burn baby burn.
Burn baby burn. I'm Benedict Arnold.
Burn baby burn.

Benedict sang and danced two choruses, and then the buildings broke apart and began dancing along with him.

Narrator 2: Even now, to call someone a Benedict Arnold is the same as calling them a traitor.

Students moved right into singing the following song to the tune of "You're a Mean One, Mr. Grinch," from The Grinch Who Stole Christmas!

(All Sing)

You're a mean one, Benedict Arnold
     You really lied to us.
You ratted on New London,

(Spoken)
Benedict: Oh, really, what's the fuss?

(All Singing)
Benedict Arnold!
You nearly burned New London down!

Two shots meant there was trouble.
But Benny, you fired a third
We were late to our own battle
'Cause we never got the word,

Benedict Arnold!

(Shouted) You're a lying, cheating, rotten, crummy, untrustworthy bird!

Another class focused on colonial life.

We Are Always Working (To the Tune of "We Will, We Will Rock You.")

(Singing)

All:
We are always working
We are always working

We came to this new land to follow our beliefs.
But we have to work so hard that there is no relief.
We make all our clothes, we grow what we eat.
All of this work is killing our feet.

We are always working.
We are always working.

Women:
We rise before dawn and we cook and bake.
We do all the wash, we never take a break.
We tend the garden and shear the sheep.
When evening comes we truly sleep.

We are always working.
We are always working.

Men:
We plant and sow and reap the grain.
We pay no attention when our backs have pain.
We chop all the wood. We hunt and we fish
Or else our family will have nothing in their dish.

We are always working.
We are always working.

Historical Statues

Ages: Grades 5-8

Directions:

1. Read the directions to Statues in the Ingredient Games p. 66.

2. Choose a historical photograph or picture.

3. Re-create the picture using students for each character. Remember that people can portray objects as well.

4. Interview the central figure in the photograph for some private thoughts.

5. Interview the onlookers for their points of view.

Exploring History Through Time Travel
Colonial Camp

Ages: Grades 5-6

Directions:

1. Have students research colonial times. (I usually provide a fact sheet with about forty facts on it, in case the class I'm visiting isn't as far along in their studies as I expected. This exercise works best when students can offer their own thoughtful perspective based on their research.)

2. Tell the students that they've had the opportunity to visit colonial times personally through the benefit of time travel. Disaster has struck and their time machine is irreparably broken. They must remain in colonial times. They have one chance to communicate their current conditions to someone they love back in contemporary times in a letter. What would they write?

3. Remind your students that this is an opportunity to be educational and entertaining, so they should include as much factual information in their letters as possible. Each student should write his or her own letter.

4. If you are so inclined, these letters transfer easily into a script. I've used this structure many times. Read the letters and highlight your favorite sections. Try to avoid repeating the same facts over and over. Try to have each student say something.

5. Have individual students read short letters, and divide the longer ones into several speakers.

6. Group the students onstage on bleachers or in three lines where the front row is seated. The second row is in chairs, and the third row stands behind.

7. Bring five or six students forward at a time, and have them pose in statues across the front of the stage. They may have simple props with them such as a basket, a fishing stick, a fake fire, etc. You may choose to have them pantomime everything.

8. When the students have completed sharing their letters, have them return to their original positions, as the next group goes out. I like to have them sing a transitional song. Any colonial song would do. Perhaps you want to sing a selection of them.

Sneaking Up on History

As a kid I remember thinking that the people in history were different, and that the choices and sacrifices they made were less significant because their lives were simply not the same as mine. Writing the Declaration of Independence was no big deal to them, easy even. After all, they didn't have math homework or a flute concert to prepare for. Ironically, my interest in history began to develop when it finally dawned on me just how real these people were. Why not travel through time and visit key moments in history when our great leaders are caught being decidedly human?

My favorite example of this is a play I wrote in 1995 for students at Colchester Intermediate School in Miss Tomasi's class. My guess is that I was feeling rather tired, and old Tom Jefferson and I had something in common.

Each number below denotes a speaker. Every time a line has a 4 on it, number 4 speaks, etc.

Thomas Jefferson Sleeps, or, "The Dec"

by Carol Glynn for Miss Tomasi's class

5: _____(student name) to ship control, _____(student name) to ship control.

6: Approaching site. Repeat approaching site. (Pause while student and others in ship look around)

7: This is a mistake.

5: I'm afraid there's some mistake. Control. Do you hear me.? I'm afraid there's some mistake.

l: Mistake! Is there a problem?

2,3,4: (From ship's panel) Gigers are clear.

2: Date is accurate.

3: Impact is steady.

4: Pentiums in place.

1: Everything is in place here, what's the problem?

6: No problem, It's just a mistake, that's all. This site isn't worth investigating. There's just some guy sleeping at his desk.

1: Sleeping?

2: That's impossible.

3: Our monitors indicate that this site is one of the most important events in American history!

5: Well, I don't know what to tell you. It's just one, tall, redheaded guy, locked in a room, sleeping.

7: There isn't even a bed. He's sleeping at a desk.

1: _____, call support, maybe our computers are on the blink again.

5: Aye, Aye.

1: Meanwhile, _____, you look around. We're going to have to land soon to collect more knowledge, our fuel reserves are down.

6: Okay, but I'm telling you, there's nothing much going on here. If we land, we may never get off the ground again.

8: We'll be stuck in colonial times forever.

9: Noooooo.

10: Stuck in colonial times forever!

11: Without Nintendo.

12: Without tacos.

8: Where children should be seen and not heard?

8,9,10, 11,12: Do something!

1: Look around, as I said, there have to be a few clues.

2: What do you see?

9: A table.

10: A chair.

11: An audience

12: Lots of people.

7: My grandmother. Hi, Grandma!

2: Seriously! In the time travel site, what do you see in the time travel site?

8: A bunch of paper lying on the ground.

9: A feather quill, and some ink.

10: No ball-point pens. Oh, noooo, I need my ball-point pens.

11: Would somebody take care of him (her)?

3: What do the papers say?

(Several students unwrap papers)

12: The Dec.

13: The Dec?

14: Something about a deck. The guy is designing a deck.

15: The thirteen united colonies...

13: A deck for the thirteen colonies.

14: That's a pretty big deck. Maybe he's a famous architect. Were there any famous architects?

13: One or two, but I don't recall reading anything about one big deck for the thirteen colonies. It would have to be huge.

15: Like the great wall of China.

21: Maybe.

4: What else do you see?

5: Well, there's not much here, a few books, a violin.

2: A violin?

6: And a few notes, from somebody named Adams.

3: Adams? (Reading over shoulder) Boy, what a grouch he was.

8: I think we should leave before we run out of fuel.

9: Yeah, what if he wakes up, then we'll be stuck here explaining ourselves while we run out of fuel.

10: And we'll never eat a Dairy Queen Blizzard again!

All: AHHHHHHHH!.

12: Shhhh! You'll wake him up.

(The sleeping man stirs; shifting his position off his latest copy of work, he drops his feather)

13: Let's get out of here.

14: (Someone steps forward to replace his feather, while others head toward exit)

15: Wait!

21: What? Come on, quit fooling around.

8: We're never gonna get out of here.

15: What date do the monitors say?

3: June 27, 1776.

15: Doesn't that mean anything to you?

18: It means the Fourth of July is coming up, and if we don't get back to the right year, I'll miss those wonderful Fourth of July burgers on the grill.

19: Can't you guys think about anything but food?

18: You're the one who forgot to pack any.

19: Why didn't you eat back at the colonial cafeteria?

18: Eat all that corn? You can't be serious.

20: No, actually, I like to think about sleep, too.

22: I'm kind of impressed that this guy is sleeping. Everywhere we go in this time zone, somebody is either working just to stay alive or doing some great historical deed.

21: Yeah, pouring tea overboard, or writing some document that will affect all of us throughout history. This guy is just sleeping.

22: Maybe that's the point.

15: We're finding out that these people were human.

20: Wait a minute! Look at the year!

21: 1776.

22: So?

20: So, put it all together. A guy, a tall, redheaded guy for colonial times, sitting at a desk, who seems to be an architect.

22: He plays the violin.

21: Writing something about a deck for—

22: The United Thirteen Colonies.

20: And the date is right before the Fourth of July.

21: Think about it, what does that mean?

20: I don't know.

21: I swear. It's utterly amazing this contraption, which is fueled by knowledge, took off in the first place.

20: What is the other name for the Fourth of July?

All: Independence Day!

All: OHHHHHHHH!

15: It's Thomas Jefferson, writing the Dec... the Declaration of Independence!

(Loud sound effects from the ship)

18: Hurry, we're running out of fuel.

19: Come on. We can't leave now! This really is one of the most significant moments in American history.

24: What is the date again?

21: June 27, 1776.

24: Now there really is a problem.

22: What now?

24: If this really is the Declaration of Independence, then it's due tomorrow.

All: So?

17: So, look, it's not nearly finished. It's barely been started. We can't just leave him here, we've got to help him.

21: What are we going to do, write it ourselves?

11: That's impossible.

14: So what if it's a few days late?

17: That would alter history considerably. We can't be celebrating the Fourth of July on the tenth of July.

11: Or even the tenth of September.

6: I just know this will mess up our summer vacations. What does he have so far?

15: The Dec.

13: Come on, this is serious. We can't let the history books say that Thomas Jefferson wrote the Dec. We have to act. If we're going to help him, we have to do it now. This is the critical moment.

4: All right, we better land. Land crew, you get started.

3: It's going to be a long night.

21: Before you land, can you send out for some pizza? (pause) I can't write on an empty stomach.

15: Ohhh, we'll think of something.

(Pulls out pen and parchment from Thomas Jefferson, starts writing)

12: What is the Declaration of Independence anyway?

13: It's where the thirteen colonies gathered together, as one, and declared their independence from the king.

14: We're independent from the king. Okay, let's go.

15: It's more complicated than that.

21: Come on then, we're running out of fuel.

15: We'll need to tell our... or rather their beliefs about good government.

18: Tell what King George has done wrong,

19: And then announce that the colonies are free and independent states.

11: That's good. All right, we'll start there. Go for it, hop to it.

12: So... (writing)

11: What's taking so long?

10: He (she) has to jazz it up a little, you know, to sound good.

12: When in the Course of human events, it becomes necessary for one people to dissolve the political bands which have connected them with another, and to assume among the powers of the earth, the separate and equal station to which the Laws of Nature and of Nature's God entitle them...

15: (Reading over a shoulder)... a decent respect to the opinions of mankind requires that they should declare the causes which impel them to the separation.

7: Wow. How did you do that?

12: I go to _____(school name). I'm used to doing quality work.

6: But what does it mean?

5: It means that Tom, here, and the other states, want to be free from the king.

7: Are you sure?

5: Trust me.

10: I've finished my part.

All: Go ahead.

10: We hold these truths to be self-evident, that all men are created equal, that they are endowed by their Creator with certain unalienable Rights, that among these are Life, Liberty, and the pursuit of Happiness.

24: How did you do that so fast?

10: I had to memorize it for an Independence Day play I was in once.

24: Oh. Not bad.

25: (Tom): (half asleep) Ohhhhhhh, nooooo, I can't. Let Adams do it. Why can't Adams do it?

5,6,7: He's waking up.

Tom: It's too hard. Too much responsibility. I can't do it.

8: You know, it's kind of encouraging to know that Thomas Jefferson, the great Thomas Jefferson, had days like this, too.

7: Sure, just because people do great things, doesn't mean they're not scared. It just means they don't let their fears get in their way.

6: He's letting his fears get in his way.

5: No, he's letting his sleep get in his way. Come on, we have to help him. This thing gets read to Congress tomorrow.

14: Somebody should have taught him not to leave his homework to the last minute.

24: Would you be quiet!

14: I'm serious. I have to do my homework right away when I get home from school, before I can do anything fun.

15: Me, too. Even when I'd much rather be playing outside.

14: If you put it off, more often than not, you'll find yourself in a bind like this.

21: I think he tried to do it.

24: Me, too. It's like he hasn't slept in weeks.

21: I would be scared to write the Declaration of Independence.

22: Hey, I was scared to read the Declaration of Independence.

18: Keep writing.

19: I don't know what else to put.

20: When I write, I like to concentrate on what it is I want to say, and then the words come to me.

19: What does he want to say?

20: How do I know? Ask him.

21: He's asleep.

22: Maybe he can tell us anyway.

Tom: That's why we have government in the first place.

21: Why, Tom, uh, Mr. Jefferson, tell us about good government. Why do we have government in the first place?

5: To secure the rights of free men

6: And women

7: Of all shapes, sizes, and colors.

Tom: But when government gets in the way, we deserve the right to abolish that government and form a new one.

18: Are you getting this?

19: Yep. I wish I had a laptop computer. This quill and ink stuff is for the birds.

6: Thomas Jefferson invented the first lap desk, so he could write during his long trips home.

7: How did you know that?

6: I did my homework last week.

7: Oh.

Tom: (loudly) Obviously, men shouldn't abolish government for silly reasons.

8: Ha!

9: What?

8: Thomas Jefferson said "silly."

10: So?

8: I love it. Thomas Jefferson said "silly."

18: You didn't put that in there. Did you?

19: No, I put "light and transient causes."

Tom: It wouldn't be prudent.

8: What the heck is prudent?

9: That'll teach you for teasing him about saying silly.

10: Is the spaceship here?

1,2,3,4: We're here!

10: Push the vocab button for prudent.

(Sound Effects): Ding Dong.

4: Wise. It means wise. Prudence is wisdom.

1,2,3,4: Where are we?

19: Prudence, indeed, will dictate that Governments long established should not be changed for light and transient causes;

Tom: But, when people, such as ourselves, have been abused by a tyrant, such as King George the Third, of Great Britain...

19: Can you take over? I can't keep up.

4: Sure.

Tom: Then it is necessary to alter our forms of Government.

5: Such has been the patient sufferance of these colonies; and such is now the necessity which constrains them to alter their former systems of government.

3: Cool!

15: Imagine, King George was a tyrant. It must have been hard to live under his rule.

14: What's a tyrant?

2: It's like... being a big bully.

3: Well, not exactly. He wasn't exactly a bully.

Tom: What, you don't believe King George is a bully? Why, I could list 25 or 26 reasons right here that would prove he was a bully.

1,2,3,4,14: Go for it!

4: Everybody grab a quill. We've got to keep up.

Tom: He imposed taxes without our consent!

(students writing)

Tom: He cut off our trade with all parts of the world.

(more writing)

Tom: He plundered our seas, ravaged our coasts, burnt our towns, and destroyed the lives of our people!

(more writing)

1: (To the audience): Things went on pretty much like this for the rest of the night.

2: Mr. Jefferson kept sleep talking and (class name) kept writing it down.

3: It just goes to show you that what my mother says is really true, that when you are really thinking hard about something, your brain keeps working on it while you sleep.

6: My dad often says that a good night's sleep will make all the difference.

7: To Mr. Jefferson, that difference became the Declaration of Independence.

8: He knew what he wanted to say.

9: He was just under so much pressure that he needed some help.

10,11,12: That these United Colonies are, and by right ought to be,

All: FREE AND INDEPENDENT STATES,

13: That they are absolved from all Allegiance to the British crown.

14: At one point in the night, he actually woke up.

2: We told him he was dreaming, and to go back to sleep.

3: We almost told him we were angels, but that's not completely true, and we know how much he hates to lie.

2: That's George Washington.

3: Whatever.

1: As we were packing up to leave, we had a big discussion about putting our names on the paper.

2: Like I said, we're from _____(school name) and we're used to doing quality work.

21: And for the support of this Declaration,

24: With a firm Reliance on the Protection of divine Providence,

11: We mutually pledge to each other our Lives, our Fortunes, and our sacred Honor.

1: But we didn't want to change history.

2: That's not the only reason.

3: Signing that piece of paper was an act of treason against the king. We could have been hanged.

18: Better we all hang together, for we would surely hang separately.

19: Who said that?

18: Me.

19: No, I mean, who really said that?

18: Oh, Ben Franklin.

1: We were happy to help out.

2: We did make sure the date was on it.

3: I did leave a secret note to make sure that those who did sign it signed it with big, bold strokes.

13: Yeah, but the only one who read that note was John Hancock.

5: You know, I was thinking.

6: Look out.

5: No, seriously, while we're here, why don't we put in a statement about how terrible slavery was, or...uh... is. . .The thirteen colonies are declaring their independence, and their freedom, but the southern states owned slaves.

Tom: Nothing is more certainly written in the book of fate than that these people are to be free.

14: That's good. Let's put that in.

15: Thomas Jefferson did include that statement, originally, but South Carolina and Georgia wouldn't sign, unless it was taken out. They had to compromise in order to have thirteen colonies, or ... rather states, to work together.

14: Think of all the suffering that could have been avoided if they had left it in.

5: (Someone grabs quill and writes)

8: What are you doing?

5: I'm adding it in...twice.

9: They're going to cross it out anyway.

5: Yeah, I know, but I want them to think about it twice as hard, before they do.

10: Imagine how each line affects so many people.

11: Even today.

13: You know, this was only the beginning. Next a new government had to be formed. Jefferson worked hard in the following years to uphold the beliefs he put into the Declaration of Independence. He introduced the Bill for Religious Freedom, so the people of Virginia, his home state, could worship as they chose. He proposed a system of free education for all citizens, which eventually became a free public school system.

4: How do you know all this?

13: It's right here in this book I've been reading on Thomas Jefferson.

All: The book you've been reading!

4: Is there a copy of the Declaration of Independence in there?

13: Uhhhh, yep, right here.

15: Why didn't you help us before, and just read it out of the book?

13: I couldn't do that. That would be plagiarism.

All: AHHHHH!

14: Good-bye, Mr. Jefferson.

2: Thanks for the lesson.

5: It's nice to know that our founding fathers were real people, not superhuman stereotypes.

3: I'm not so sure they weren't superhuman. It took a lot of courage to do what they did.

4: Anytime you stand up for yourself, it takes courage.

5: Imagine standing up for the entire country.

6: No wonder he was scared.

24: Good night, Mr. Jefferson.

11: Sleep well.

(Music goes here.)

(As students exit, Mr. Jefferson wakes and reads what's in his hand. He's thrilled. He also finds some curious object, like a sneaker, a Gameboy, or a piece of pizza, and looks very puzzled.)

Lights out.

Exploring History and Cultures

Studying a Culture

Ages: Grades 5-8

Directions:

1. Divide your class into groups to research different aspects of the culture you are studying.

Examples:

    A. Housing
    B. Family and Home Life
    C. Foods
    D. Entertainment
    E. Education
    F. Transportation
    G. Jobs
    H. Holiday Traditions

2. Encourage each group to develop a short scene or skit including several important facts in their category.

3. Each skit should begin from a frozen picture, like a book coming alive. (Look for Statues/ Pop-up Statues in the Ingredient Games p. 66 & 68.)

4. The skit could be a scene with a story line between people in a family, business, or branch of government, with dialogue where people are speaking to each other and giving out historical information at the same time.

5. The skit could be an interview from an outside person, who is visiting and asking questions of everyone and everything in the room.

    Example: A colonial kitchen

    Interviewer: Ah, Miss Fireplace. How long have you been burning today?

    Fireplace: All day long. These people need me for everything—heat, light, a place to cook their food. I'd complain but they seem to appreciate me. Look, every evening they crowd around me. I'm the center of attention.

6. Share each scene with the class. Follow up with a question and answer session from the audience.

Tips and Variations:

1. If you want to perform the skits for someone outside the classroom, consider adding a song between each group, which everyone will perform while the scenes are changing. Have each group announce their section before they begin.

2. Have each group write three questions which the audience must answer after seeing their skit. They need to make sure the answers are clearly given within their scenes.

5-8
S
O
C.

S
T
U.

Cultural/Historical Fashion Show

Is there a logical explanation for fashion in colonial times? How much did available materials and technology affect what people wore? How much of fashion was just rather strange? Are there legends behind the native or traditional dress of a given culture?

Ask your students to find out and present their results in a fashion show.

Ages: Grades 5-8

Directions:

1. Read the directions to Fashion Show in the Ingredient Games.

2. Have students do research on a given culture and present it in a fashion show.

3. Each participant will create a mock costume out of available materials, and provide the Master of Ceremonies with a card of at least five facts about the outfit, and its historical origin.

4. Does all the information have to be true? It depends on your goals for your unit. Perhaps there is no logical explanation for the outfit. Can your classmates tell if your explanation is true or a brand-new legend? If you want these to be legendary explanations of unexplainable fashion trends, then so be it.

The following activities can be found in Social Studies 3-4:

Immigration

Look for the following activity in Social Studies K-2:

Look for the following activity in Social Studies 3-4:

Mythology Scenes

Ages: Grades 5-8

Directions:

1. Re-create an ancient story in an ancient setting. The story should show gods/goddesses' personalities and symbols.

2. Re-create an ancient mythology story in a contemporary setting.

Example: A favorite Poseidon story with a modern-day fish shop setting.

3. Create an original mythology story, showing characteristics of gods/goddesses' personalities in either an ancient setting, a contemporary setting (your school), or a historical setting (Athena during World War II).

4. Create a commercial featuring one of the following:

   A. A real or original product that will solve problems many god/goddesses face every day.
   "Snakefree Shampoo, rids your head of ugly snakes forever." Brought to you by Perseus products. It's less expensive than Suave!

   B. A real or original product endorsed by a god or goddess.
   "Hi, I'm Hera, and even though we're immortal, goddesses as beautiful as I am must do what they can to keep our skin nice through the centuries. So, I recommend...

   C. An original product in a mythological setting.
   * Hermes Messenger and Delivery Services!
   * Spell protector! Don't risk having a god turn you into a cow! Protect yourself against the petty jealousies of gods and goddesses.

5. Create a fashion show of gods and goddesses, complete with a description of how the clothing complements their personalities. Read the directions to Fashion Shows in the Ingredient Games.

6. Try reconstructing an evening news/entertainment program with a feature about current escapades of a specific god or goddess.

Example: "Mythology Tonight." Consider a story about the current political causes your chosen god/goddesses would support. Would they be a modern-day actor or political activist? What current movies would they be starring in?

7. Demonstrate excerpts from a fictional TV show, "Lifestyles of the Gods and Goddesses." Show a modern-day announcer interviewing a god/goddess in their ancient or contemporary home.

8. Show excerpts from a game show.

Examples:

   A. Create an original show called "Name That God." As a prize, contestants could win a trip to Mount Olympus, appear on the current Myth TV show, or meet their favorite goddess.
   B. Play To Tell the Truth, or What's My Line?, The Dating Game, or Who Wants to Be a Millionaire? For further instructions, see Game Shows in the Ingredient Games.
   C. Re-create a talk show. (Tip: In years past, students were interested in re-creating Phil Donohue or Oprah interviewing Gods and Goddesses and questioning them about a specific story and their choices at the time. The last three times I've taught this workshop, I've encountered a group of boys who want to re-

create Jerry Springer, because it has a violent and sexual flair. My suggestion to them each time is a reminder that Jerry Springer is, supposedly, marketed to an adult audience and the students' talk show will be marketed to other students and hence will need to be appropriate for that audience. This disclaimer applies to the borderline appropriate topics within mythology as well.)

9. Present an episode of the current fictional soap opera "Mount Olympus" or "All My Goddesses" or "As the Universe Turns."
In our last episode Aphrodite was...Let's see what happens next.

Tips for Mythology Scenes:

1. In all scenes make sure there is a clear beginning, middle, and end.

2. Make sure the audience knows who the characters are. Warn the students about the all too common trap of assuming the audience knows the character's identity because the actors do. Include lines in the script or improvised skit that reveal the characteristics and even the name of the character. It wouldn't be against a goddess's nature to introduce herself saying, "I, Hera, will not stand for such disloyalty. You'll pay for your mistakes!"

3. Encourage the students to seize every opportunity to include as much information about mythology as possible in the skit. Doing so will make the skits more interesting and educational.

3. Remember that there is nothing low-key about mythological gods and goddesses. They are all passionate about their causes and ideas. Think of the skit idea as a framework in which to pack high drama and education, and you will succeed in educating and entertaining.

Medieval Times

Knights and Castles: 50 Hands-On Activites to Experience the Middle Ages, a Kaleidoscope Kids Book by Avery Hart and Paul Mantell, has been very helpful in introducing me to a basic overview of the Middle Ages. It also includes many visual arts activities and more stationary, though no less exciting, games for kids ages 6-12. If you are doing an in-depth unit on the Middle Ages, you will truly find value in this book.

Plan A Modern-Day Quest

Ages: Grades 5-8

Directions:

1. Divide your class into groups of six.

2. Have each group choose a quest, or special mission, where knights search for something elusive, powerful, and mysterious. Perhaps the missing chalkboard eraser, with magical erasing power, or the teacher's missing grade book, or the secret to getting along with an older brother or sister. Perhaps the knights solve a riddle that has baffled the king or teacher for years? The mission could be an individual's plan or a group decision.

3. Each quest should involve obstacles requiring brain power to solve them. If a battle is involved, as was sometimes the case in medieval times, it should only be posed in frozen picture statues.

4. Each group should choose a director to guide the class presentation.

5. Students should become all the scenery as they tell the tale. Remember, students can be dragons, castle gates, a princess whose long hair had a life of its own, especially because it's being played by another student.

Tips:

1. For tips on becoming the scenery, see directions to Statues and Machines in the Ingredient Games.
2. If your class needs the structure into which to pack their ideas, I suggest the following general plan.

General Plan:

Scene 1: Set the setting. Discover the challenge. Begin on the quest.

Scenes 2-4: Encounter two or three obstacles. These could be natural, such as a cliff, manmade, such as a human giving the wrong directions, or an evil character who is bound to throw them off, or fantasy, such as Biff, the three-headed dragon, who won't let them into the castle unless they provide him with peanut butter and fluff sandwiches.

Scene 5: The main event includes finding the source of the mission, and escaping the scene with it. You may want to encounter some obstacles on the way home, in which case you may want to run into fewer of them in the beginning. (This was never intended to be a three-hour Kevin Costner picture.)

Scene 6: Closure. Learn something. (Hint!!! Perhaps you could gain more by doing the quest than by having the object.)

Example:

The children's story "The Paper Bag Princess," by Robert Munsch, is a great comical example of a quest. In this quest, Elizabeth, the princess's, castle is burned down, and her prince to be is kidnapped by a dragon. Elizabeth, donning the only appropriate outfit she could find, a paper bag, tracks down the dragon and outwits him in a series of three encounters, saving Donald, a shallow, unworthy fellow. Donald ignores all that she has done for him, and insults Elizabeth's appearance. She realizes her own power, and sends Donald on his way. This is an excellent story, for all ages. I've dramatized it with high school students and second graders.

3. Keep the costuming simple. Draped cloths can be gowns. Paper towel tubes can be swords, paper bag bottoms with face holes can be helmets. Please encourage the students to complete the dramatized project first before they concentrate on decorating it. This will help you avoid the glamorously dressed quest without out a plot.

Vows of Silence

This week, during her school vacation, I went against my best judgment and told my six-year-old daughter that she could stay home for the morning to play with our new kitten, instead of other arrangements I had made for her, while I buckled down on a writing deadline of three colonial plays which was looming. The deal was she had to play by herself and not talk to me. (Are you laughing yet?) This idea had sounded logical to both of us the night before. The only problems were that new kittens sleep more than we remembered, and that Marisa had no idea how to leave me alone, much less stop talking. While she concentrated on not interrupting, I focused on not leaping out of my skin and strangling her. I think I included the colonial phrase, "Children should be seen and not heard" about eight times in the plays. To make matters worse, every time I tried to remind her to leave me alone, I felt like the scummy mommy of the universe. The longest span of silence she demonstrated was fifteen minutes, and during that time she drew pictures to me instead of talking. As someone who is usually interested in what she has to say, I noted just how great a gift of gab she truly has. (Wonder where she got that?)

What would taking a true vow of silence be like? Could your students benefit from a little silence? Could you? You may enjoy this activity more than you want to admit, but don't worry, I already won the scummy award.

Ages: Grades 5-8

Directions:

1. Choose a classroom activity that involves independent work, with some quiet discussion among class-

mates.

2. Introduce the idea of taking a vow of silence.

3. Declare a designated length of time during which no one will talk. Simple sign language, gestures, or written notes are acceptable.

4. Design a harsh consequence for breaking the vow. (The Middle Ages were harsh times.) Write something fifty times. Add a two-page report on feudalism. If these seem too mean, give a number of silent warnings, first.

5. Consider playing quiet classical music in the background, or simply enjoy the quiet.

6. If you only have the students for forty-five minutes at a time, consider doing it for several days in a row.

Medieval vs. Modern Tools: Pass the Object

This game, itself, is a great tool for any age. I've played it with kindergartners, adults, and every age in between. This game provides an enjoyable structure for people to learn kinesthetically, visually, interpersonally, intrapersonally, and logically.

Tools: A chalkboard eraser, or a scarf (see other options in the Ingredient Games).

Directions:

1. Using the directions to Pass the Object in the Ingredient Games p. 62, pass a nondescript object, such as a chalkboard eraser, around in a circle, having students pretend it is an everyday tool for contemporary times.

2. Pass the object around a second time, re-creating tools from the Middle Ages.

3. Usually this game has the strict no-weapons rule, but you may choose to waive this rule to understand the harsh realities of the Middle Ages and the weapons of the day.

Medieval Commercials

The ranking system in the Middle Ages was strict and impenetrable. The boundaries on one's behavior and opportunities were decided well before you were born. A democracy, where everyone has the chance to work hard and earn their lifestyle, provides many more options for economic growth for individuals and communities. Look at contemporary advertising. Commercials don't say "For Kings Only," or "Only the Nobles Need Inquire." Our economy would rather try to sell us something we don't even need based on the idea that the product will make us feel like a king. How would the medieval ranking of peasants, knights, priests, monks, nobles, and kings affect modern-day commercials?

Ages: Grades 5-8

Directions:

1. For more information read Commercials p. 37, in the Ingredient Games.

2. Compare and contrast medieval life with contemporary life by suspending reality long enough to create and perform original commercials on any of the following topics.

   A. Sell life as a noble, a peasant, a priest, a monk, a lady of the court, or a king and queen. Point out all the great aspects. Shine up the not-so-great elements with great salesmanship. Pretend for a moment that the listeners would be able to choose a position in life.

   B. Perhaps you're selling travel to the Middle Ages, with a variety of accommodations. How about a cold night with a peasant family where everyone slept on straw on the floor? If it was truly cold, the farm animals joined them *(p. 63, Knights and Castles)*. There's nothing like playing footsie with the family cow!

C. Try selling some of the advantages across the classes. "Imagine, you could smell like a lady of the court. With this one little product, your whole life could change. Try soap!"

D. Advertise modern conveniences, but divide them among the classes, and sell them to the appropriate group. "I'm telling you, Mr. and Mrs. Peasant, one flick of this little product, and you can start a fire from scratch. Imagine! Send your hard-earned coins to Matches, the year 2000.

Medieval People: Monologues

Ages: Grades 5-8

Directions:

1. Examine and reflect the inner thoughts of a peasant, a knight, a priest, a monk, a king, a noble, or a peasant child through monologues.

* What are your daily obligations? At work? At home?
* What do you do for recreation?
* What is your attitude toward others?
* How and when, if ever, do you find joy?
* What are your hopes and dreams?
* Is happiness related to class?
* Is survival related to class?
* What secrets would your character want to share with us in confidence that he or she would never say out loud to his or her families, or peers?

A Medieval Feast

Some schools have full-scale medieval feasts, complete with authentic food, elaborate costumes, music, original plays, jesters, jugglers, etc. If that is your interest, by all means, do so. It sounds fabulous. I'll be looking for my invitation in the mail. The following ideas are a simpler skeletal version of a feast, where students can create and comprehend the ideas in a short amount of time, without all the calories.

Grades 5-8

Directions:

1. Choose several volunteers for jesters and acrobats. Send them to a corner of the room to practice short routines, or work on their jokes. If you have any students with juggling talent, they could pantomime juggling, or juggle small scarves, which move more slowly and are easier to catch, or tennis balls or fruit.

2. Choose one student to be in charge of the entertainment order. This wasn't strictly a medieval role. It will simply allow you to eat your lunch, while someone else is in charge.

3. Ask for volunteer troubadours (singers) to sing a real song. These were generally ballads, but you may have a few more volunteers if you open the musical selection.

4. Choose a King and a Queen to approve or disapprove.

5. Choose several nobles to sit at a table and forget all their manners.

6. Choose a few servants.

7. Have a few dogs, or a squirrel or two, to catch the scraps.

8. Arrange the desks in your room into long tables, with the head table only having people seated on one

side, as it is often arranged for weddings.

9. Extend these ideas by using one of the following variations.

Tips and Variations:

1. Set up the entire scene as a Statue or Pop-up Statue (see p. 66 & 68 in the Ingredient Games for directions). Each entertainer would need only a sound bite of material. Follow up with a written account of a feast from a specific point of view. Pantomime all the food being served and eaten. (It's easier to clean up this way.)

2. Have students research their roles, enough to understand their expected behavior, and plan out routines and songs. Each student could wear a simple costume of scarves, etc. Have a feast during the real lunch, where students eat without utensils, or manners. (Just make sure the school isn't serving sloppy joes that day.)

3. Have a few students bring in bread or dessert on a volunteer basis to share among the rest of you. Keep in mind, this does not need to be elaborate.

4. Look through "Knights and Castles," by Avery Hart and Paul Mantell, for a script to St. George and the Dragon, and a few tips on simple, pain-free stage fighting.

Movement Westward

Writing Songs

Ages: Grades 5-8

What would "Home on the Range" be like in a contemporary version? Rewrite one with your class, to an existing tune, and explore life as it was, by comparing it with life today. Could you stake out your land via the Internet?

Traditional version:
Home, home on the range,
Where the deer and the antelope play,
Where seldom is heard a discouraging word
And the sky is not cloudy all day.

Contemporary Version:
Home, at Range Condominiums
Where there's traffic on Route 56,
Where seldom is heard a bee or a bird,
And the sky doesn't get in your way.

Look for the following activity in Social Studies 3-4
Conflict Resolution: Historical and Contemporary (Grades 4-7) p. 205

What if the Other Side Won?

Ages: Grades 5-8

Think for a moment what our daily life would be like if we hadn't won the American Revolution. Would we still be a part of England, or would England have been overthrown, and we would be part of some other government? Would we be a democracy complaining about the misuse of freedom, or would most of us not be here, because the standing government would have decided that we can have only one child?

What would have happened if the Native Americans had been able to stand their ground and we never did expand westward? What would have happened if the Civil War, or World Wars I and II had ended differently?

Explore the possibilities of how different our lives would be through written essays, short scenes, and statues with narration.

Government

Abstract Layers: Lean and Leave

Ages: Grades 5-8

Directions:

1. Read the directions to Lean and Leave in the Ingredient Games p. 52.

2. Discuss the relationship between the layers of the game and the layers of command. How does Lean and Leave relate to democracy? Every level leans on and supports another level, while each maintains its own independence. A dictatorship, for example, would lean on and crush the little guy. I usually don't tell them there is any specific right answer, but rather want to know what they think. More often than not, they surprise me with intriguing insight.

Look for the following activity in Social Studies 3-4

American Revolution Stamp Tax Game

This game gives students that passionate, desperate feeling the colonists had just before the American Revolution. It gets to the heart of Taxation Without Representation p. 206.

The Three Branches of Government: A Play

After playing the Stamp Tax Game, I wrote a play for Mr. Desrocher's fifth-grade class in Colchester, Connecticut. You may find reading through it, or even presenting it, a tool for understanding the three branches of government.

I have divided this play into twenty-five parts to accommodate special circumstances in Mr. D's class. If your class would like to read it/act it out, feel free to change the parts around as needed.

Assign parts by numbers 1-25.

5. We're supposed to fire up this whole time machine, and fill it with years and years of hard-earned knowledge, so that we can travel to a concept.

1. How do you travel to a concept?

2. It's not like it's a place.

9. What kind of concept?

8. I was thinking about the Stamp Tax.

9. The Stamp Tax?

10.   Oh, yeah, the Stamp Tax.

1.   Now, there's a bad concept.

11.   That's where we were taxed in school for anything the king wanted to tax us for.

10.   like being tall,

7.   or wearing green,

12.   or having letters on our shirts.

8.   I hated that tax!

6.   Remember being taxed because we didn't eat any breakfast?

8.   Yeah, and because we were boys,

7.   or because we were girls.

8.   I really, really hated that tax!

9.   I thought it was fun.

10,11,12. Fun!

10.   We couldn't argue about it, or we'd be taxed.

11.   We couldn't point out that the tax collector was cheating.

8,10. Or we'd be taxed.

11.   We didn't have any control at all.

9.   Wasn't that the idea?

12.   What?

9.   Wasn't it supposed to make us mad?

8.   It wasn't fair!

9.   Wasn't it supposed to make us feel out of control?

8. How was I supposed to know not to wear stripes? Why should I have to pay money because I like stripes? In fact, I don't even like stripes. It just so happened that the stripes were clean!

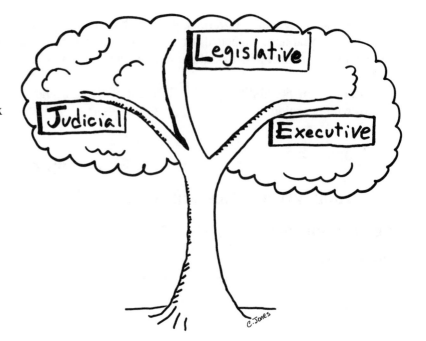

10. So, I wore blue, but no, I had to be taxed for it. I hated it. I hated every minute of it. I wanted more control. I should be able to wear what I want ...or even what I don't want without any old king telling me what to do.

12. You hate taxes!

8. Yeah, I hate taxes, but I know they're needed to pay for some pretty important things.

10. What I hate is that we didn't have any control.

11. We didn't even know what King George really was using them for.

13. My definition of tax is something that makes my parents grumpy.

14. But at least our parents are represented in government.

8. I really hated that tax.

13. How did we get on this in the first place?

1. Because it's a concept. We were learning about a concept.

16. Oh yeah, and we're supposed to be firing up our engines and traveling to a concept right now.

14. But look, how bad can it be, we're supposed to be traveling to a tree.

15. A tree?

13. The liberty tree?

16. That's a bell.

13. How do you know it's a tree?

14. It says something about branches.

15. A concept of government with branches? (looks confused)

16. Let's get going.

17. This better be good.

(Time Machine fires up, makes noises, etc., and lands in the same place, rather quickly)

3,4,5. Was that the whole trip?

16,17. That was it?

13. I guess it doesn't take very long to travel to a concept.

14. We've definitely been gypped. This just isn't fair.

15. Wait, what's this?

16. It's a note from Mr. Desrocher.

15. What does it say?

16. I don't know, it's hard to read his invisible writing.

17. What do you think it says?

16. I think it says that after we're done with our visit to a concept we can cruise around in the ship awhile and check out some of those American Revolutionary battles.

11. But those are farther back in time.

12. Before the Bill of Rights!

13. Before the Constitution!

14. This is a time machine, isn't it?

10. Relax, it'll be all right, we'll leave the time line on so the audience won't be confused.

17. Look, there are three branches!

14. Told you.

18. The legislative,

19. The executive,

20. and judicial branches.

(At each branch there are people in a statue picture, almost like an exhibit)

2. That one has two branches all by itself.

3. Which one is that?

4. It says legislative.

5. Push the button and find out what's going on.

(Robotlike voices)

18. Legislative branch, a lawmaking body,

21. made up of two houses

22. The Senate

23. And the House of Representatives.

22. Before any idea becomes a law, it must first be passed by us,

23. and by us!

19. And signed by me.

6.   Which branch are you?

19. The executive.

(Presses the button)

19. I'm a leader, like a king or a president.

8. You're a president, we've had enough of kings, thank you very much.

19. That's pretty much what the framers of the Constitution felt.

7. What does the Constitution have to do with this?

20. The Constitution is the trunk and the roots of this tree. The Constitution is the document that puts this concept in writing.

9. What branch is this?

20. The Judiciary.

10. Go ahead, push it.

20, 24,25. We're the courts. There are courts from towns all the way up to the Supreme Court.

24. We uphold the law.

11. Which one of you is the biggest, most powerful branch?

(All three raise their hands.)

25. That's misleading. We all have equal power.

12. If you all have equal power, then why are there three of you?

18. We have equal power, but we don't have the same job.

20. It's a matter of

2. checks

3. and balances.

13. I know about those. My mom is always trying to get her checks to balance.

18. It's a little different from that.

22. We keep each other in check.

19. President: I'm commander in chief of the army and the navy,

21. Legislative: But only Congress can declare war.

23. That would be us.

18, 21,22,23. Congress: We can pass a bill

19. President: And I sign it into law.

20. Judicial: Unless it's unconstitutional,

20, 24. Then we'll invalidate it.

25. But that doesn't happen too often.

19. President: I appoint the presidential cabinet members,

22. Congress: And we approve them.

25. Judicial: It's all give and take, so no one gets too much power.

12. Sounds pretty simple.

(all three branches laugh too loud)

24. Well, sure it sounds simple.

25. Every good concept does.

21. It's the simplicity that has helped make the Constitution work for so many years. It has lasted over 200 years already.

2. But make no mistake, there are complications and things can get pretty heated up around here.

8. That's still better than one king making decisions all by himself.

All 3 branches: We're glad you think so.

13. Thanks a lot, we have to go.

14. Can I, or we, come back if we want to?

19. Sure, sure. Stop by whenever you want, it's your government too, you know.

13. I think there's more here than meets the eye.

20,24,25. Well, you've got that right.

4. We have some battles to check out, from the American Revolution.

18. You know, kids today are entirely too interested in violence.

21. I think it's the media.

22. I think it's the breakdown of the family.

23. I think we better do something about that, right now.

20. You'd better take off, now that you've got them started, they'll be at this all day.

All Kids. Thanks.

20. Take a good look at the Battle of Bunker Hill, it's my favorite.

24. I prefer Lexington and Concord.

18. You're encouraging them.

20. We're not encouraging them to like war. No one likes war, but these battles are ones where the Colonies stood up for themselves at great risk, because they believed in something greater.

21. What could possibly be great enough to put themselves and their families at risk?

All 3 branches, except 21: Us.

19. The three branches of government.

21,22,23. Legislative,

19. Executive,

20,24, 25. and Judicial.

15. Thanks again. Bye

Judicial: Bye.

Executive: Bye,

Legislative: Bye.

2. That wasn't so bad after all.

4. No, it wasn't, but let's get on with the battles, okay? Can we drop right down into the middle of them?

2. Nope, way too dangerous, but we can watch them through our battle viewfinder.

3. Battle viewfinder? What's that?

2. How do I know? I just made it up.

5. Look, there's the Battle of Bunker Hill.

6. There's the battle of Lexington.

7. And there's Concord.

8. The shot heard round the world.

9. There's Paul Revere, he's getting captured.

10. Captured?

11. I know. I know. It's a big myth.

.

15. We better get going.

16. Where shall we go now?

15. To a place where people stand up for their rights.

All: Engage Machine.

(Machine lifts off but lands in the same place)

6. Where are we?

7. Back at school.

8. Did I push the wrong button?

9. No. Where people stand up for their rights. We do it here every day. It's called democracy.

10. Some schools aren't really a democracy. They're more like a dictatorship.

6. I know. We're pretty lucky.

9. We were pretty lucky to go on that trip.

10. Democracy, it's quite a concept.

6. It better be. It's lasted for more than 200 years.

Passing a Bill Game

Originally created for an eighth-grade class, this game could be played in grades 5-8. The basic structure of the game is the same as the three branches of government. We introduced the three branches and all the players, electing and appointing enough of them to understand the process. Next we initiated a bill, using a soft playground ball to symbolize it, and passed it through all the phases of approval, amendments, etc. Every possible complication came to pass. The students had a great time, and it solidified the process for all of us. The key to its success was allowing the students to decide what the bill would be about. We had a better cafeteria food bill which ended up with a Ferrari for all eighth graders in it. The bills were ridiculous but effective. As in the Stamp Tax Game, the students quickly understood the loopholes and the frustrations in a system where the final bill to be passed often barely resembled the original one. Some students became passionate about the ideas, while others were only interested in their one point. Some deliberately added on outrageous conditions in order to force the bill to be voted down, or vetoed. Angered at having to veto a good bill because of a few outrageous additions, the eighth-grade president complained about not having a line-item veto.

Directions to Prepare: (Remember students can do this for you.)

Tools: Construction paper, scissors, markers, three large sticks (5-6').

Make signs to label the three branches of government, and all the characters involved. As students are playing, having a label to remind them who these people are in government will help reinforce the role of each player. The size of the leaf doesn't matter, as long as people can read them. The measurements below are only an idea. Do what works for you.

A. Cut out three large construction paper leaves. (Nothing fancy. Mine looked more like footballs than leaves. They were 8" 11" and green.) Write a branch of government on each leaf. Legislative, Judicial, and Executive.

B. Cut out five medium-size leaves. Label them House and Senate, in one color (I chose orange) and President and Vice President in another color (I chose green). The fifth leaf will be Speaker of the House, in a third color.

C. Cut out six to ten small leaves (2" x 3") in an entirely new color and write Senator on them.

D. Cut out six to ten small leaves (2" x 3") in an entirely new color and write Representative on them.

E. I brought in three large sticks from my yard, 5 to 6 feet tall, and as the people were elected or appointed, I had three students, the Speaker of the House, the Vice President, and a Supreme Court justice, to hold them in front of the room. These branches have deep roots which go back more than 225 years to the words of the Constitution. (Obviously, the branches are optional, but they reinforce the visual, and add the theatrical element of play which helped to loosen any lids clamped on the creativity.) I taped the three largest leaves, Judicial, Executive, and Legislative, to the three branches.

Directions to Play:

1. *Elect a president.* Choose two students who would like to run. Give them a whole sixty seconds to talk about the issues they think are important to their class. Take a moment to talk about the electoral vote. (I think I told them that when this nation began, the people did not have the advantages of media to help them know more about the actual candidates. The electoral vote was established to help protect the country, by adding that additional level of first-row scrutiny. I did not take the time to appoint or elect an electoral college. We explained it, told the students that they were the electoral college for the rest of the school, and each one of their votes represented many voices.) Take a moment to point out that anyone running for president knows that voters are fickle, and has a thick enough skin to know that it's not personal. Vote.

This structure of this game is designed to provide ample opportunities for plugging in specific information that you want them to know. If you want to spread out the game over two days, you could talk about all the responsibilities of being president. Or you may want to use the game as an introduction before stu-

5-8
S
O
C.
S
T
U.

dents do personal research to find out their own facts. For information on responsibilities by job, look at the end of Passing a Bill Instructions.

2. *The Vice President:* Discuss running mates, and how it works in government. You could have the president choose a running mate, either before the election or after the fact. Again, in the interest of time, I allowed the presidential runner-up to be the VP. Have the President and the VP hold their leaves, and sit center stage in front of the class, in chairs.

3. *Presidential Cabinet:* Talk about how the president appoints a Cabinet of leaders for fourteen departments which are subject to confirmation by the Senate: Agriculture, Commerce, Defense, Education, Energy, Health and Human Services, Housing and Urban Development, Interior, Justice, Labor, State, Transportation, Treasury, and Veterans Affairs. (I didn't go into the specifics on them, in my fifty-minute limit. It's up to you how in-depth you want to go here.)

4. *Appoint a Supreme Court Justice:* Explain that the justices are appointed for life, and a president only has the opportunity to appoint one if there is a vacancy, due to rare retirement, or death. The president's choice is subject to approval by two-thirds of the Senate.

Have the president select a justice for the Supreme Court. Have the Senate ask questions. I usually asked a few questions to frame the boundaries or lack thereof, for the kinds of questions the Senate tends to probe into. Remember Lani Guinere, who was rejected because she didn't pay social security for her child's nanny? Some questions we asked the appointees were real and some fantasy. I reminded them that we were acting and they did not need to share any of their own private information, but that the appointees do.

Do you always do your homework? Do you ever lie? Were you ever arrested? Do you have nice handwriting? Have you ever stolen anything? Do you owe any back taxes to the government? Is your room clean at home right now? Did you eat a healthy breakfast? The students added a few about what music they liked, whether or not they believed in school uniforms, etc.

In each of the classes the appointee became flustered at the questions, and was either elected or rejected by the Senate. In some cases I rushed it along because this process could have taken the entire time. In each case I pointed out that decisions and choices they make today will come back to haunt them if they ever wanted to become a Supreme Court justice, or run for political office.

The Legislative Branch: The Lawmaking Body

5. Elect a Senate. I passed out Senate leaves to roughly half of the remaining students. As I did so, I told them I was sure they all were thirty years old, had been a U.S. citizen for at least nine years, and a resident of the state they represented. They all agreed. They would be in office for six years. A third of them would have to be reelected every two years, in order to stay in office. Every state has two senators.

6. Elect a House of Representatives: Roughly a third of the class would need to be Representatives. Everyone must be twenty-five years old, citizens of the United States for at least seven years, and must live in the state they represent. The number of representatives for each state is proportional to the population of that state. Each state will have at least one.

7. Elect a Speaker of the House: From the majority party.

8. Choose one or two students to be constituents.

Directions for Passing a Bill:

Tools: A soft ball to toss in discussion.

9. Have a constituent think about a change they want in their town or school and tell their congressperson. Have the student toss the ball to their congressperson.

10. Create a bill in a small committee in either the House or the Senate. For purposes of explanation, we'll say House. Take the student suggestion, and build it into a bill. Toss the ball around in the committee, each time adding or adapting to make the bill something that is important to them. If the ball is tossed to you, you need to respond in some way—an idea, a nod, a grunt. The committee will decide to pass it, amend it, or defeat it.

11. The bill is then sent to the floor of the House for debate, where it is either passed, amended, or defeated. Toss the ball idea from member to member, adding opinions and possible amendments before they vote.

12. The ball, as the bill, is then sent to the Senate, and discussed. (In the Senate, there is more freedom to debate than in the House. A vote must wait until all members who want to have spoken.) Toss the ball from member to member.

13. Introduce a filibuster, where a member deliberately postpones a vote, by talking so long there isn't time to vote. Invite a student to stand up front, hold the ball, and talk as long as possible about a subject. Remind them, this discussion does not need to be logical or coherent. (I've heard of members of government reading names out of the phone book in a filibuster.) In my class, our bill was about cafeteria food. The senator who discussed it went on a rampage about how parents like nutrition, but how horrible nutritional food tastes.

14. You could end the filibuster by a two-thirds vote to stop it, or just explain that's how to do it, and move on.

15. The Senate must pass, amend, or defeat the bill. The Vice President calls for the vote.

16. If the bill is amended, and most of our classroom model bills were, it must be sent back to the first group, in this case the House of Representatives, where a conference committee passes it or defeats it. (Students who were passionate about this bill resented that a few members had the opportunity to make a decision without them.)

17. If it passes, the Speaker of the House signs it. (Signing the ball with an imaginary pen.)

18. The Vice President signs it.

19. The bill is passed on to the President.

20. The President either signs it or vetoes the bill. (He might want it, but can't pass a small part of it. He does not have a line-item veto.)

21. If it is vetoed, a two-thirds vote from both houses can override his veto. If they can't override it, the bill is killed.

22. If the President doesn't sign or veto the bill in ten days, it becomes law, unless Congress is not in session, in which case it dies (a "pocket veto"). Give all these options to each decision maker as the bill is tossed along. Let them make the decisions.

23. Just when you thought you were finished, I added in the Supreme Court justice to determine if the new law was constitutional. If it is not, they have the opportunity to declare it invalid.

24. Phew! No wonder it takes so long to get a bill passed. Even though the bill may be ridiculous—about rainbow napkins or hour-long recesses—the passion behind it is very real. Occasionally, during this process, I would look back to the constituent who wrote his congressman or -woman to begin the bill in the first place to see how he felt about the process. These students understood the value of checks and balances, but were horrified at how much their ideas had changed.

Job Responsibilities:

Presidential Responsibilities Include:

Enforcing all federal laws

Supervising all federal agencies

Granting reprieves or pardons

Negotiating treaties (with 2/3 Senate approval)

Nominates ambassadors, ministers, consuls to represent the United States abroad

Be the Commander in Chief of the armed forces

Submit the budget

Head the Cabinet

Appoint justices

Vice Presidential Responsibilities Include:

To preside over the Senate. He or she does not participate in the deliberations, but casts a deciding vote if there is a tie.

Role of Congress:

1. Collect tax money.

2. Spend money.

3. Have legal control over government employees.

4. Approve presidential nominations.

Responsibilities of the Senate Include:

1. Approving presidential nominations

2. Approving treaties, with a two-thirds majority vote

3. Serve as the court for impeachment trials

Responsibilities of the House Include:

1. Originating revenue bills

2. Beginning impeachment proceedings

Democracy/Communism/Dictatorship: Compare and Contrast Commercials: Our Government Is What You Need!

Ages: Grades 5-8

Directions:

1. See Commercials in the Ingredient Games p. 37.

2. Divide your class into small groups of three or four.

3. Have them research a form of government and sell it to the class.

4. Companies do not pay advertisers to create commercials that waver in opinion. Each commercial must be 100 percent convinced that this government is the way to go.

Three Scenes: Home Life, Work Life, Community Life

Ages: Grades 5-8

Directions:

1. Divide your class into three groups.

2. Give each group a category: home life, work life, or community life.

3. Have each group devise a similar scene from each form of government you want to examine. You could compare two, three, or four forms.

Example: Group 1 would do

> A A home life scene in a democracy.
> B: A home life scene in a communist government.
> C: A home life scene in a dictatorship.

4. Each scene should be relatively similar in general structure, so that the different governmental influences could be easily compared.

Example: All of them should be about the dinner hour, talking about the day, or getting off to work and school in the morning and talking about their plans for the weekend. Each scene would demonstrate how these common activities are affected by the reigning government.

Geography

Vocabulary Ball Toss

Tools: A basketball-size earth ball or earth beach ball.

Ages: Grades 5-8

Directions:

1. Read directions to Ball Toss in the Ingredient Games p. 34.

2. Toss a ball that looks like the earth from student to student.

3. As their thumbs land on a part of the earth, they should say what it is.

4. Be as general or specific as your age group/curriculum requires.

Examples:

A. Lower grades: land, water, equator, north pole, south pole, northern hemisphere, southern hemisphere.
B. Middle grades: Add in which continent, which body of water, etc.
C. Higher grades: Add in which continent, exports, imports, political regimes.

Look for directions to these activities for grades 4-7 under Geography in Social Studies 3-4:

Group Up (Grades 3-8) p. 212

Chant Dancing (Grades 3-6) p. 213

CHAPTER EIGHTEEN

Language Arts: K-2

Table of Contents

Letters

Be a Shape: Group Letters

Ages: Grades K-2

1. Look for directions to Be a Shape in the Ingredient Games p. 35, for a game that helps reinforce letter shapes as well as building teamwork skills.

2. Instead of having the group stand in a circle or triangle shape, have them be a letter E or F, etc.

Individual Letters:

Write the letter. Be the letter.

Tools: A board with the letters written on it.

Directions:

1. Have each child independently trace a designated letter with their finger on their hand while whispering the letter to themselves.

2. Have them trace it a little larger on the floor in front of them while saying the letter.

3. Have them paint it with a giant imaginary paintbrush in the air.

4. Have them write it with their elbow, their head, and their nose.

5. Next have them try to be the letter with their body.

6. If the letter is hard to make with one body, discuss how many people they think you would need, and have them become the letter together. They may do it standing or sitting, or lying on the floor, whichever the space allows.

7. Go around the room tapping the human letters. As you do, have them say "My name is letter _____ and I sound like this _____."

8. If an entire class of human letters is too much, have three to five of them demonstrate their letters in front of the class.

9. Ask students to think of something that starts with that letter and act it out in front of the class.

Letter Ball

(See Ball Toss in the Ingredient Games p.34.) You can play this game sitting and rolling the ball, or standing and tossing the ball. Decide if you need the game to rev them up or calm them down. Perhaps you need to rev them up in order to calm them down!

Ages: Grades K-2

Tools: A soft ball with letters written on it in a grid. (Use permanent marker or the letters will smear all over your kids.)

Directions:

Identifying letters

1. Sit in a circle on the floor and roll the ball to a student.

2. The student should identify the letters in the squares on which their thumbs land when they catch the ball.

3. They can also tell you which one is their favorite letter.

4. Make sure each student has a turn.

Variations:

Letter Sounds: Have them tell you the sounds of the letters under their thumbs.

Words: Have them tell you a word that begins with that letter.

Alphabetical Order: Which letter comes first in alphabetical order?

Match Up

Ages: Grades 1-2

Tools: Open space. Letters, words, and/or pictures on small pieces of paper.

Directions: Letters to Words

1.   Read the directions to Match Up in the Ingredient Games p. 58.

2. Divide your class into two groups.

3. Give each student in Group One a letter on a piece of paper.

4. Give each student in Group Two a word that corresponds to a letter for Group One.

5. Play Match Up.

6. Take a moment to show each pair, correct any mistakes, celebrate their matching ability, and reinforce the match for the whole class.

7. To play again without having to collect and pass out the cards again, have each child trade his or her card with other students two or three times. Then play again.

Directions: Pictures to Words

Play as you would for letters and words, but this time give Group One pictures, and give Group Two matching words. (These can be magazine pictures, old calendar pictures, student drawings, if it's clear what they are.)

Directions: Sight Words

1. Play as you would for letters and words, but this time hand out matching sets of the same sight words. Each child will receive one card, as usual.

2. When the individual students have found each other, give them a chance to announce their own sight words.

Movement for Short Vowels

This game stamps a visual and kinesthetic imprint of short vowel sounds onto the minds of your students. For those kids who have a tendency to fade out when you're teaching, this game is invaluable. Take it from a kinesthetic learner.

Dr. Susan Snyder, president of Inventive Designs of Education and the Arts, is certified as an Orff Master Teacher, and has a book called *Total Literacy: Music and Movement in the Literacy Classroom* that teaches reading through music. If you like the next activity, which was inspired by one of her workshops, you'll enjoy her book.

Ages: Grades K-2

Tools: Space.

Directions:

1. Decide on a movement for each vowel. It could be a small inconspicuous movement, or a grand movement that involves standing up and using your whole body. Perhaps you have a designated set of each, to accommodate the broad spectrum of personalities in your class. The movements within each set should be consistent every time.

2. Put some words with short vowels in a goofy hat. The first time it may help to compare two vowels. Change those two vowels as you learn new ones. When your class is up to it, add a third, a fourth, and a fifth vowel into the hat.

3. Pull out a word and show it to the class.

4. Have someone read the word. Can they tell you the short vowel sound? Would they rather show you instead? Have the student show the movement for the designated short vowel.

Go Foot: Sight Words (2-5 players)

Go Foot is not a drama game, but rather a game I made up as a mom to play with my daughter to reinforce sight words. I'm including it, because we had so much fun playing it that it's worth passing on. It started when I tried to reinforce Marisa's sight word knowledge by playing with flash cards at home. I'm not good at rote practice of anything, and I was sure my impatience with it would rub off on her, so by the second night we were playing Go Foot. It's a riot to hear your child saying, "Mommy, do you have a 'this'?"

Ages: Grades K-2

Tools: Cards. These could be 3 x 5 cards. We went to the local educational supply store and bought card shapes as a special treat for our new game. They're a little thicker than paper, and you can't see through them. A good game needs around 100 cards. Now we have several decks, of ducks, rabbits, and fish, but the feet were the easiest to hold. (There's a reason playing cards aren't shaped like doughnuts!) We tried to change the name with each kind of card, but finally gave up and called them all Go Foot.

Directions:

1. Make two cards for each word you want to learn. If you make a very large deck, then you can break it down and only play with parts of it.

2. Play as you would Go Fish.

3. Ask another player for a word, saying "Do you have 'with'?"

4. If the child doesn't know how to spell it, she can ask. Either ask her what she thinks it is, or spell it for her and reinforce the word.

5. Make as many decks as you like. We added a short vowel deck and plan to play to make a word blend and word ending deck.

Acting Parts of a Story

Setting and Character Statues

For younger grades, setting statues usually bring up an immediate discussion about what is setting versus what are characters. I often do statues of each to help differentiate the two. For older grades this works well to provide a visual aid for adding detail into students' writing. After setting up haunted house settings with several groups of fifth graders, I found that the written descriptions were dramatically more creative and vibrant than in workshops where I simply explained the writing task.

Ages: K-8

Directions:

1. Read the directions to Statues in the Ingredient Games p. 66.

2. Read a story, pointing out all the elements in the setting.

3. Have each student become part of the setting, by posing as frozen inanimate objects. I never worry about how many want to be the fence, or the rock wall, as long as we're not leaving any other important elements out.

4. For Character Statues in the younger grades, using a big family photo pose of all the characters involved works well. If your statue has many of the same character, try having them pose doing different activities that character does within the story.

Characters

Whole Body Voices

If your students are performing, even for their classmates, the presentations will be much more interesting if you can get them past the quiet "fear of success when put on the spot" voices. Encourage them to use their whole bodies to make a sound. Babies can scream all night without losing their voices, because they loosen up their bodies and let the sound out. Tightening up voices only makes them smaller, thinner, and boring.

Students have no idea how loud they need to be to project to others. (The ones who do can be heard.) I know they don't understand because I tell students that no one can hear them past the first row, and they look at me as if they truly don't believe me! How can this not be loud enough if it feels loud to them? Often they'll choose a point of compromise, which is entirely too quiet, and hot-glue themselves in that spot.

Fear of projecting voices is different from the ability to be loud. Kids who can bellow their guts out on the playground will tighten up and be thin-voiced onstage, because they have chosen a comfortable boundary, and fenced it in with the belief that while it may not be as big as they can go, it's as big as they're willing to give.

The fun part of whole body voices is that in order to form them your body automatically takes on the character's movements as well. Faces will change to express age, or surprise. Characters will spring to life right off the page into your students.

Ages: K-8

Directions:

1. Warm up their bodies with a simple warm-up. Look for Shake, Shake, Shake in the Warm-ups chapter.

2. Practice deep voices for villains and kind old bears, by imagining your bodies are big and heavy and low. Take the time to create the character posture with your body. Breathe in a great deal of air and let the deep, heavy voice out.

3. Practice high, squeaky voices by imagining you are ten feet tall. Draw your voice up from your toes, and say something squeaky to your students. Have them repeat or respond in their high, squeaky voices. Don't

just say it from your throat. If you do you're cutting off the air and the energy.

4. Play with some other voices. Go around in a circle and give each student a chance to experiment with a new character, or demonstrate their version of one already touched upon.

5. Try adding anger, or a snotty attitude. Try adding body posture to support the voice. It will feel funny to do, so you'll get some uncomfortable laughter, but if you keep it light and experimentally free of criticism, you may get some unusual characters.

6. Encourage your students to pay attention to voices on cartoons and movies. Then next time you need some character voices for reading out loud or acting short skits, your class will have a vast vocabulary to choose from.

Whole Body Movements

If your students were TV or movie stars, the cameras would zoom in to make each blink of their eyes look enormous. Acting onstage or in front of the class is just the opposite. No one would even notice a blink of the eye. Each movement must be large enough for a person at the other end of a football field to see it. (That's the extreme I push for in order to get something a moderate range.)

Expanding yourself beyond your comfortable everyday range of movement or projected energy will do more than help the back row audience see you onstage. It becomes a physical manifestation of stretching your growth potential, helping you step out just beyond the halting restrictions you place on yourself. It fills you with self-esteem, relaxes you, and gives you presence. When you're finished, even a tiny mouse character will shine with the energy that makes him the steal the scene. So will the student beneath the mouse.

If you're worried that the expanding energy of more than twenty small beings will destroy your classroom, don't. If a student has presence beyond his or her small body, the actual body becomes a control center of sorts. The center doesn't have to act out to feel powerful, because it already is.

Ages: K-8

Directions:

1. Stand in a circle and have one student lead at a time doing large movements. The other students should follow. If you prefer, have a student stand in front of the class and lead, as in an innovative version of "in place" follow-the-leader. It's important that you either lead them, or follow with them. Everyone will feel much more self-conscious if there is someone present who is not participating.

2. Have them imagine that their bodies are actually bigger than they are. Have them picture ten-foot arms, and fingers that extend inches beyond their hands. Imagine that they are princes and princesses of the theater or classroom, and a beam of light expands to several feet around them. Sometimes it helps to have them pick a color for the light. The brighter the better. Examples:

    A. If their character has wings, picture that they're ten feet wide, even if your actual student is only using his elbows to fly. How would their entire body react to huge flapping wings? Does their back hunch over? Do their knees bend? Do they need to hold their heads up very proudly?

    B. What if their body is a big balloon that has been blown up to be huge? How would they move around the room?

    C. Show excitement with more than a raised eyebrow. Build up a big, giant, silent hooray from their extended toes to their arms waving above their heads.

    D. I would try joyous emotions first, because anger tends to pull you in tighter. If they want to try anger, have them do it in very slow motion, like a giant who is stuck on slow speed.

    E. Imagine that you are ten feet tall and your arms stretch ten feet wide.

    F. Imagine that you are made of precious shining gold. Walk around the room without bumping into one another and pretend your shine takes up the entire room.

Whole Body Emotions

Chances are that if you've tried Whole Body Voices and Movements, you've already touched upon Whole Body Emotions. If you have time it can also be a worthy exercise in itself.

For the younger grades, try beginning the activity by reading *Today I Feel Silly and Other Moods That Make my Day*, by Jamie Lee Curtis, and following up with a discussion about how to handle feelings appropriately.

What does angry look like? Does it make you grit your teeth, flatten your eyelids, and tense your kneecaps? When your fists are clenched, do you wiggle your fingers just a touch, as if you're a cat waiting to pounce? Does sad look the same on every person? What does angry or sad look like to you? What does it feel like on the inside?

Ages: K-6

Directions:

1. Read the instructions to Emotional Statues in the Ingredient Games p. 66.

2. Create statues with several students at a time, allowing the others to observe.

3. Point out the many ways one feeling can look.

4. Compliment the detailed emotional expression, from curling toes to flared nostrils. As you point out the glory in articulating emotion with your whole body, the statues will ease into a deeper level of expression.

5. Try melting one feeling into another with a slow count of five. At one, they're as angry as they can be, and gradually, as you count, they shed the anger and absorb sheer joy.

There are many acting methods that delve into portraying a specific emotion by pulling the emotion from deep within you, or remembering a past experience where you felt that way. Hence the cliché student actor line, "I must remember this feeling so I can use it in my acting."

Gestures can express the shell of emotions held deep within, but they can also initiate them. Standing in an angry pose for even a few moments can make you feel angry inside. Try not to leave students in an angry posture for too long without giving them a chance to shake it out, or share a happier one before they switch to another activity—or it may ruin their whole day, not to mention yours.

Character Rounds

As actors in the Penny Ante Theater, we were forever doing Character Rounds. Before any one of us could put a limited stamp on a character's movements and attributes, we would explore each character as a group, to open up the range of acting choices. It's an extremely helpful tool for actors which transfers beautifully into the classroom. I do have a distinctively painful memory of being a leaping frog over and over for an entire afternoon, and then working all evening as a waitress without any feeling in my legs, but the final characters in *The Frog Prince* won accolades. And people think acting is glamorous!

Ages: Grades 1-8

Directions:

1. Read a story and choose a character to act out.

2. Stand in a circle.

3. Take turns stepping forward into the circle and re-creating a moment, a physical detail, or a quality of that character.

4. It is perfectly acceptable to repeat an idea, because each student may consciously or unconsciously add extra details while portraying the character.

5. It is also acceptable to combine a few ideas in one turn.

6. Each student only has a moment to express the essence of the character. The character may be moving or still. Imagine them listening, sleeping, and eating, too.

7. Take a second to point out and give positive feedback on the many remarkable details you will see.

8. Follow up, if you wish, with a momentary chance for all the students to become the whole character. For younger grades I recommend doing this five or six students at a time. You may want to explore the composite characters through drawing and writing.

Character Snapshots

Barry Lane designed the concept of a snapshot. In his book *After the End,* he encourages writers to describe a photograph using physical sensations as well as visual images. In this way the writer describes a character or scene using all of his senses.

Acting out Character Snapshots helps point out limited or nonexistent character development in writing.

Ages: Grades 1-8

Directions:

1. Choose three to five students at a time to stand in front of the class. I always choose more than one or two to dilute the performance pressure, yet I don't want too many because the entire activity is about noticing small details. In some cases choosing three students will do it. In others you'll need more. Use your best judgment.

2. Ask the students to be blank slates. As they listen to the class adding character suggestions, they should try to act it out. They should not show any character qualities unless they are described.

3. Begin with bland ideas and build from there. Show a man, or a guy, or a boy, etc. The actors won't have anything to do.

4. Suggest an old man or woman. You'll get a variety of acting ideas, usually stooped over with a cane.

5. If the actors assumed anything, suggest the opposite. What if this old person is in great physical condition, jogging and lifting weights every day? What would that look like?

6. What makes this person old? Is it a wise attitude, a little stiffness in the elbow joints, or a bright look in her eye? Perhaps she has no teeth? Explore the ideas. What does one detail do to change the picture of the characters?

7. Follow up with students writing their own character descriptions, and having groups of students act them out.

The Reaction Game: Acting out Thoughtshots

Ages: Grades 1-6

Directions:

Look for directions to Group Reaction Game in the Ingredient Games p. 64.

My daughter has an artist's soul. I've known it since she was about fifteen months old when she did nothing but color with a red crayon for three solid days. No one around her could color in another color either. I was so sick of red I could have thrown up. I was relieved to move on to "ornage" until I discovered that it would last for two weeks.

When she was four and five she often communicated her feelings in pictures. We would have entire discussions through her drawings. An angry face would be placed on a table nearby and I would talk about feeling angry to the air, in case anyone was listening. I would be supportive, but always get in my point of view.

(My communication tool has always been my mouth.) Soon the angry picture would be replaced with a happy one, or spend a short transitional period as a sad one. Each picture was a brief gesture of many thoughts and feelings, which were often too big to share out loud.

In first grade, Marisa brings home a myriad of pictures showing the setting, problem, and reaction of/to a story. I find her reaction pictures to be quite sophisticated, as I'm sure all first graders' mothers do. In Marisa's case, emotional reaction pictures are old hat.

Acting out character thoughtshots for younger grades is a theatrical extension of the reaction drawing. By acting it out, students will also have practice in verbalizing their thoughts and feelings.

In *After The End* Barry Lane describes thoughtshots as a thinking report of a writer or character. A thoughtshot will allow a character to express his deepest feelings, those little secrets that only a best friend, trusted dog, or stuffed rabbit might know. Thinking about a character's innermost thoughts, feelings, and reactions to an event can bring them to life for the writer, the reader, and the audience.

Ages: Grades 1-6

Directions:

1. Look for directions to Group Reaction Game in the Ingredient Games p. 64.

2. Either begin with a warm-up from the Warm-ups chapter, or Emotional Statues from the Ingredient Games p. 66, to flex the drama muscle a little. I wouldn't jump right into acting out thoughts and emotions—you may not get any.

3. Either act out or discuss the problem immediately before asking for a reaction.

4. Personalize the reaction by asking the students to imagine either that they were the characters, or that this problem had happened to them personally. How would they feel? What were they thinking when the main event happened?

5. Invite some characters up to the front of the room for an interview. Three to five at a time will do. Repeat the problem and ask for a reaction or comment. Try asking them to show the face they made when they reacted to the problem. Ask them to tell what they were thinking at the time. Refer to each person as their character. You may have several of the same character. If they choose to be themselves, consider interviewing them as an eyewitness to the problem.

6. It's fine if the reactions are not the same as the story you read. Giving them a chance to express different reactions will increase their reaction vocabulary. Interview characters who may have different points of view.

Solution Attempts For Stories

Is there only one way to solve a problem?

Ages: Grade 1-Adult.

Directions:

1. Divide your class into groups of four. Have each group brainstorm a variety of solution attempts for a story problem. This problem can be an actual story, a story in progress, or an original story using the same characters from a familiar story.

2. Have each group visualize the possible solutions, and the result of their solution attempts.

3. Share them with the class.

4. Discuss the solutions, their similarities, and their differences. Talk about how small details can change the entire outcome of a story.

Bringing Reading to Life

Acting Story Sequences

Ages: Grades K-5

Directions:

See Story Acting in a Sequence in the Ingredient Games p. 72.

Acting Out Stories with Moving Statues

Start with frozen poses and make them come to life. This way you have control. You can stop the story, and switch the lead character actor after applauding the first one. You can have a "wild rumpus," if it's dictated, using only the top half of their bodies, or only their noses.

Ages: K-Adult.

Directions:

1. Read the story.

2. Have the children provide the sequence of what happens next.

3. Show brief picture statues using a few students at a time. At your will, decide what can and cannot temporarily come to life. (For more directions, see Moving Statues in the Ingredient Games p. 68.)

   Example: Where the Wild Things Are, by Maurice Sendak

   Picture 1: Show a frozen Max in an imaginary wolf suit, with a fork in the air. Add the dog, looking back frightened. Now, unfreeze what your class can handle. Let the dog run off. Let Max chase him. Or simply let them each make a facial expression and a sound. It's up to you.

   Picture 2: Replace Max. Add in a Mom with a mad face. Let Max tell her he'll eat her up. Have her come to life and tell him that he's going to bed without any supper.

   Picture 3: Replace Max again. Create Max's room. Have several children become the bed. (Four posts with connected arms work well.) Have another one be the table, the carpet, and a lamp. One by one, let the room become a forest. The bed posts slowly grow fingery leaves. The carpet becomes grass. The table grows into a bush. Four students are invited in to become water. Three new ones are a boat that floats up, opening arms long enough for Max to jump in.

4. Take the story to the end, introducing a few monsters at a time. Set the movement limits for the monsters, and the students will have a great time expressing within the limits. When you reach the end, have the same students re-create the room. They'll fall right into place, adding dinner and a glass of milk on the table. (My daughter was the glass of milk in kindergarten. She still talks about it.)

Tips:

1. When you read the story the first time, take advantage of any group participation areas. In *Where the Wild Things Are,* the monsters roll their terrible eyes, gnash their terrible teeth, and show their terrible claws. Give the students a chance to act it out together while you're reading. Then when you act out the story, this part will already be worked out.

2. If there are potential danger zones for acting out a story, prepare the students in advance. In this example, the wild rumpus is a big party, where monsters go crazy, singing and dancing. In older grades I may take the time to have each monster be worked out creatively. I may have two and three students work together to create three-headed, winged, spiky-tailed creatures. In kindergarten and first grade, I like to prepare them for the wild rumpus in advance.

Example: Preparing a seated wild rumpus.

A. Ask the children to find their own space on the floor, where they have plenty of elbow room, and sit down.

B. When I say "Let the wild rumpus begin," I'll ask them to wiggle everything they have while leaving their bottoms glued to the floor.

C. I'll prepare them with a signal to stop.

D. We practice the whole thing, starting, wiggling, stopping. Can they do it? It's pretty tricky. I compliment them like crazy. Amazing! Fabulous! Unbelievable!

Exaggeration Stories: Personal Tall Tales

What are you good at? A simple question, but even the tiniest children are reluctant to admit it. Often when I ask them, they stare blankly back at me with no idea. I think this is tragic. Our society seems to dictate that we focus on what we can't do, and what we don't have. We have few skills to appreciate what we already have, which includes talents.

I like this game. It teaches exaggeration. It covers tall tales, and it provides a safe forum for children to brag a little. Protected by the fantasy aspects of the task, no one can be put down for thinking too much of themselves. Usually when I leave the students are following me out the door, boldly announcing what they're good at. I'm proud to have provided the structure for them to express and appreciate themselves. It's something I'm good at!

Ages: Grades 2-3

Directions:

1. Read *The Five Chinese Brothers* by Claire Hughet Bishop and Kurt Wiese

2. Talk about exaggeration. Could any real person hold the entire sea in his mouth, hold his breath all night, or stretch his legs to be so tall that he can stand at the bottom of the ocean?

3. Ask students to think of their special talents. If this is hard, ask them to think about what they like to do, because we usually are good at what we like to do. (Watching TV doesn't count.)

4. Model taking one idea and stretching it three times to become huge.

Examples:

A. Nathan is good at playing games on the computer.

1. Nathan is so good at working on the computer that when the computer broke, he fixed it all by himself.

2. Did you hear about Nathan? At the age of five, he's making computers in his basement, out of old tin cans, for all the kids in the neighborhood.

3. I read in the paper yesterday that IBM, the big computer company, has hired Nathan to fly all over the world and teach grown-ups how to make his world-famous computers. He's so nice he takes his mom and dad with him.

B. Maria is good at soccer.

1. Maria is so good at soccer that she can kick the ball from one end of the field to the other.

2. When Maria kicks the soccer ball, it weaves around the players so fast, they can't even see it.

3. Last week, Maria kicked the soccer ball all the way around the world. It came back and landed right on the very same field and scored the winning goal.

Variations:

1. Talk about tall tale characters, and how their stories were created, with people sitting around the campfires after working hard all day, entertaining each other in the sport of competitive exaggeration.

    A. Invite a few students up to sit in chairs with you around an imaginary campfire.
    B. Choose one student to talk about at a time. He or she need not be one of the students in the front of the room. Find out his special talent, and top it.
    C. Add to the flavor of the campfire competition with suggested introductions and eyewitness comments such as:

* Oh, that's nothing, why I saw her ...

* Of course I know it's true, because I was there!

* If you think that's amazing, wait until you hear about this.

    D. Usually two or three rounds of each presenting student trying to top the others will give the class the idea. Go as many times as you like, switching in new campfire students and talented subjects.

2. Follow up in their seats. Have students think of their own special talents, exaggerate them and draw a picture of the most exaggerated idea. If they're old enough, have them write about it.

3. I have often collected the individual talents and written one story in which all the special talented students help solve a problem and become heroes. Each time there is one giant problem, which several students discover, others help prepare the solution and the rest save the day. The students are always celebrated by their entire school, and often the President of the United States. These stories would not win one literary award, but the students love them. Consider breaking your class into small groups and having visiting book buddies help them create short stories about how three or four of their special talents were helpful and appreciated by many. This could be an ongoing project for a book buddy visit. Either read them to the class or act them out.

Acting Out Fables

Ages: Grades 2-8.

Directions:

1. Read two or three fables.

2. Divide the class into groups of four or five.

3. Ask each group to choose one of the fables.

4. Tell each group to act out their chosen fable in one of the following ways.

    A. Act out the fable as is.
    Example: The Boy Who Cried Wolf, by Aesop. A boy who is in charge of tending the sheep for the village becomes bored and seeks attention by shouting that a wolf is eating the sheep. He does this several times, earning the anger and disrespect of the sheep owners. The last time a real wolf comes. No one believes him, and the sheep are eaten.

    B. Fractured fables.
    Example: Take the existing story and change it in an interesting way.

* The wolf is watching the sheep and he shouts "boy."
* The sheep become bored and trick the boy to go fetch a variety of items for them, for example, a sheep comb, gourmet sheep food, sheep Monopoly. While the boy is gone, they have wild dancing contests, until they are caught.

C. Take the moral and/or the structure of the story and write a new similar story in a contemporary setting.
Examples:
* Two kids call the police, claiming to have a burglar, two or three times.
* A student in class claims another student hit her, again and again.
* Someone pretends to lose an important item, such as a contact lens, a wallet, or a favorite stuffed animal. Then after everyone stops what they are doing to help search, she laughs. Finally she loses something very valuable, and no one helps her.

Grammar

Acting Out Punctuation

Ages: Grades 1-2.

Directions:

1. Write a small sentence with your class, but instead of putting it on the board, use live student bodies. Have them stand in a row, facing the class, to represent the words.

   Example:
   Amy skipped to her grandma's house to deliver some apples, bananas, and birthday cake.

2. Have a child do an action or pose to represent each word. Choose children to become the commas and apostrophes.

   Example:
   Amy: (Choose the name of a child in your class, or a famous figure like the president or the principal. Have the student pose as that person.)

   Skipped: *Skipped* is the action word, so have the child skip in place.

   To: Point to Grandma.

   Grandma: Have someone pose as Grandma.

   's: Have two people pose as Grandma's apostrophe and her s, showing possession.

   House: Have one or two children pose as a house.

   To deliver: Have a child hand over invisible items, again and again.

   Apples: Choose someone to be apples.

   Comma: Choose someone to curl on the floor as a comma.

   Bananas: Choose someone to be bananas.

   And: Consider having them show a plus sign with their fingers. They may think of something they like better.

   Birthday Cake: Have someone be a birthday cake. The cake could pantomime a flaming candle while humming "Happy Birthday."

3. Read along with the class each time you add a new word. Each child should only do his action when his word is being read. Point and refer to all the punctuation as you go.

4. When you reach the end of the sentence, try out a variety of ending punctuation. Example:

   A. Have a child be a period, by squatting in a ball on the floor. Read the sentence with the class as a statement.

B. Select someone to be a question mark. You may need two students, one to be the curvy top, and one to be the bottom dot. Read the sentence as a question.

C. Finally, have two students become an exclamation point. Read the sentence several times as an exclamatory remark!

Acting Out Opposites

Ages: Grades 1-3.

Directions:

1. Model acting out opposites in front of the class. Encourage using the whole body as much as possible. Tiny demonstrations of opposites will not hold the attention of the class as well.

   Example: Sad vs. Happy—Show how the entire body looks when it is sad. The head droops, the eyes tear up. The face winces, etc. Happy is bursting with energy and enthusiasm, a bright, open, smiling face, etc.

   Example: Over and Under—Hold out an arm and have a student crawl under it. Have the arm lower very close to the ground and have a student jump or step over it.

2. Divide your class into groups of three students.

3. Give each group a pair of opposites to act out for the class.

Tips:

1. If acting the opposite requires only two students, ask the third to be the announcer. If acting the opposite requires more than three, ask the students to plan the part of the fourth student, and either help them yourself, or ask another student to step in from their group at the last moment.

2. At this age it may be best to start out by announcing the opposites rather than having students guess what they are, because sometimes it is hard to figure out what the student actors are doing. If a group announces an opposite, and the acting is difficult to decipher, take a moment to compliment them on their work, and then ask the class for additional choices the actors could have made to make their opposites clear to the audience.

3. When other students are guessing, some students feel that they have failed if the students guess their idea right away. Remind them that acting is a form of communication. You're not trying to trick the audience. Actors are telling a story. You don't want the audience to waste time trying to guess something because it will detract from the story.

Compound Words: Swoosh!

Ages: Grades 1-4.

Directions:

1. Look for the directions to Swoosh! in the Ingredient Games p. 76.

2. Use compound words as the daily subject.

Public Speaking Spelling

Ages: Grades 1-6

Projecting Voices/Characterizations:

If you'd like to dramatize spelling, but dancing it is akin to sticking needles in your eyes, consider trying public speaking spelling.

Directions:

1. Warm up with a loud call and response. You spell the word as if you are a motivational speaker for your class. They spell it back to you in the same volume and vocal range.

2. Model spelling the words in a variety of character voices.

Examples:

* As the president giving a speech

* As a shrieking hysterical person

* As a doctor giving very bad news

* As a whining sister or brother

* As a radio broadcaster

* As a rap artist, a country singer, a rock musician, an opera singer

* As a person doing an info-mercial

* As an angry mom, a sad dad, a teasing brother or sister

3. Model spelling the words using a variety of adverbs.

Examples: sadly, happily, nervously, selfishly, slowly, quickly, etc.

4. In each case, have the class try to repeat the letters back to the leader, mimicking their presentation voice.

Go Foot Spelling Card Game (2-4 players)

Ages: Grades 2-4

For a sit-down, hands-on game, see the directions to Go Foot in Language Arts K-2, p. 277. Go Foot, which I created to review sight words with my daughter, would work for tricky spelling words too. Add the game requirement of saying and spelling the word with each request.

CHAPTER NINETEEN

Language Arts: 3-4

Table of Contents

Using Drama and Writing to Bring Literature to Life

Within the giant web of activities that relate to one other, each one has a special task to achieve. The following related activities can be found in a variety of places within this book:

Look in The Ingredient Games, for:
Story Acting in a Sequencep. 72
Story Acting with Student-Written Dialogue p. 73
Storytelling with Statues p. 74
Moving Statues p. 68

Look in Social Studies 3-4 for:
Nobody Speaks My Language p. 211
Acting Out an Immigration Story p. 198
State History p. 209

Look in Social Studies 5-8 for:
Cultural Storytelling p. 217
Presentation Techniques: Characters, Voices, Fluency, Eye Contact, and Volume - 8 Strategies p. 217
Commercials: Writing and Acting Them Out (The Ingredient Games) p. 37
Historical Commercials p. 224
    Mythological Commercials p. 243
    Medieval Commercials p. 246

Look for the Following Story Structures:
Fables: (Language Arts K-2) p. 274
Exaggeration: Tall Tales: (Language Arts K-2) p. 273
Myths: (Social Studies 5-8) p. 243
Improvisation: Who, What, Where (Ingredient Games) p. 45

Look for Directions to Acting Out Parts of a Story in:
Language Arts K-2:
Whole Body Voices (For Grades K-8) p. 267

Grammar

Parts of a Sentence

How many times have you told your students to add more details? Do they sigh and moan each time? The following activities may help bring the spark back into their view of descriptive words.

Swoosh!: Adjective, Adverb, Noun and Verb

Give your students a chance to identify the terms, practice thinking of new words, and play a lively game at the same time. Each student is challenged at his or her own level.

Ages: Grades 3-8

Directions:

1. Look for instructions to the basic Swoosh game in The Ingredient Games p. 76.

2. Play a round of adjectives, or adverbs, nouns, or verbs.

3. Play a round of prepositions or pronouns.

4. Whenever possible the words should be colored by meaning.

   Example: If passing the adverbs loudly, softly, and angrily, say them loudly, softly, and angrily. If passing the verbs dashed, landed, and squatted, then do those actions, in place, as you say them. Say the adjectives creaky, wispy, and terrifying with the appropriate voices, etc.

Swoosh!: Compound Words

Ages: Grades 1-4

Look for directions in Language Arts K-2 p. 276.

Transitional Words and Phrases

"Then twenty-four hungry orphans appeared needing to be saved, and then we saved them and rode camels across the desert, and then all of that led to the half-hour exotic wrestling match with people from all over the world. Then our hero won the competition, and then saved the orphans."

This is the synopsis to a Jean Claude Van Damme movie I saw with my husband when my daughter was two. We escaped for a weekend without a plan of action, because we were too tired to make one, and found ourselves seated in a movie theater not knowing what *The Quest* was about. Neither one of us is particularly a martial arts fan, but this perfectly poorly written movie has caused me moments of uncontrollable laughter and tears ever since. My husband doesn't remember the movie, because he was watching me crumple under the seat, trying not to disturb the other moviegoers with my seemingly inappropriate cackling.

No snub intended to Jean Claude. I'm assuming English is his second language, and the martial arts sequence, his primary concern, was jam-packed with action and suspense. It may well be that most martial arts films prepare the martial arts sequences and tack the story around them. I wouldn't know. Watching this movie was like walking into a piece of problematic fourth grade writing—a series of disjointed actions without connection. Jean Claude could have benefited from a few transitional phrases. The movie would have benefited from a few transitional anything. My brother refers to this movie as my favorite movie of all time. I did enjoy myself. Perhaps I should rent it. I could use a good tear-streaking, breath-stopping, cleansing laugh.

Transitional Phrase Ball: And Then...You're Out!

Tools: One ball, of any kind. A list of transitional phrases on the board.

Ages: Grades 4-8

Directions:

1. Have students stand at their desks.

2. One student will begin to tell a story. They may say a few sentences, until a transition is required. (If you have some particularly verbose students who want to dominate the ball, limit everyone to one or two sentences.)

3. When the first student has finished his turn, he will pass the ball to another student who will continue the story from there.

4. Students may use any transitional phrase except the word then. If they use any phrase with then in it, including and then, so then, until then, they're out. They have to sit down.

5. As much as possible, try to have the story make sense.

6. Be as particular as you wish about requiring entertaining beginnings, suspense, snapshots and thought-shots, as long as no one says then.

7. Play as long as you wish.

The fun part is watching the students realize how easy it is to lapse into and then, and then, and then. The light dawns abruptly as they anxiously await their turn to add to the story, only to lose it immediately, because they blurted out the dreaded then word.

Variations:

1. Do you have other overused words that are driving you crazy? I've had students raise their right hands and swear off using "weird" and "stuff" because I thought I would gag if I read them one more time. Selectively add rules to this game as students become adept at following them.

2. See the Storytelling Cloth activity in the Ingredient Games p. 70. Instead of playing with a ball, offer students the visual stimuli of playing with a variety of objects.

Swoosh!: Transitional Phrases

Ages: Grades 4-6

Directions:

Look for directions to Swoosh! in the Ingredient Games p. 76.

Prepositions

Prepositional Swoosh!

Reinforce all levels of prepositional knowledge without being bored or losing face! As an added bonus, it's great fun.

Ages: Grades 3-4

Directions:

1. Look for directions to Swoosh! in the Ingredient Games p. 76.

Changing a Setting in a Familiar Story

Examine how changing a setting would affect an entire story.

Kathy Mariolis's fourth-grade class at Roger's Magnet School chose to adapt the famous folktale "Stone Soup" by setting it on Venus. We called it "Meteorite Soup." The children used the last of their spaceship fuel to travel to Venus in search of something other than moon dust. Using the same plot as the original version, the children tricked the town into contributing the best of their unearthly fare. The story was a hit. The slimy green helmets created in Art helped.

Ages: Grades 3-6.

Directions:

1. Take a familiar story, and have students change the setting to a radically different one. The more extreme the choice, the less confusion involved in adapting the details.

2. Have students brainstorm the necessary changes involved in switching to a new setting.

3. Divide into groups of three to five students. Have students act out a scene from the story, including as many setting-affected details as possible.

Details, Details, Details

Mrs. Addmoredetail

My friend Susan Kadin, who is now in charge of Quest, the gifted and talented program in the New London Public Schools in Connecticut, used to teach visual arts workshops, tying her ideas into the curriculum. Famous for her junk art workshops, she had students create spaceships, environmentally conservative modes of transportation, and fantasy inventions, all out of yesterday's trash. She made a habit of insisting that the students add more detail to their projects so many times, they began to call her Mrs. Addmoredetail. I stole the name outright, and created a character called Mrs. Addmoredetail.

She looks a great deal like me, but she embodies my most flighty personality traits. She constantly insists on the importance of detail, but never remembers to put it in herself. The students consistently correct her, but seem to like her anyway. She's always grateful for their kind help.

So, do I expect you to dress up, speak in a silly voice, and become a flaky personality in front of your students? I wouldn't consider it—except one year Greta Watson, from Lyme Consolidated School in Connecticut, told her students she had a surprise waiting for them after lunch. She dressed in a motorcycle jacket, and created a tough alter ego character for them to interview. I cannot remember the curriculum tie-in, but I know there was one. The students loved it, and so did she. So, come one, come all, let your students teach you about details. Help them realize the basic value of details. Help them not assume that everyone already knows the information before it is presented. Mrs. Addmoredetail could also become a nighttime visitor, much like the Tooth Fairy, only she leaves directions to parties, recipes—all lacking vital information— for students to try to follow.

The following activities were created during a period when Mrs. Addmoredetail taught many of my workshops. Now, I often teach them as part of a series, and by then the students already know me as flaky Mrs. Glynn.

The Recipe

Ages: Grades 4-6.

Directions:

1. Tell the students you'd like to share a special treat with them. Your sister-in-law gave you this recipe over the weekend and it's so incredible, you just have to pass it on. Encourage them to write it on scrap paper as a gift to a family member. This recipe for cookies (candy?) is sure to be memorable.

2. One very important point to remember about this recipe is that it must be followed to the letter or it will make everyone truly sick. If it is made correctly it will be absolutely fabulous.

3. Write a recipe on the board. The following are sample ingredients from my recipes. Feel free to add some of your own favorite, painfully unclear ingredients. You'll know just the ones to add.

Recipe
crunchy things
weird round bits
fun stuff
cool thingamajiggers
bite-sized fluffy junk
wild stuff
cook
cool
eat

4. Count to four in your head. Wipe the chalk dust off your hands, and whatever you do, look as innocent as possible. Without a doubt you'll hear, "Uh, um, wait a minute." Sometimes I may babble about how great it really is and repeat the cautionary statement about preparing it correctly.

5. I always act completely baffled that they don't understand. Sometimes I go through the entire recipe having them tell me which words aren't clear. Crunchy is clear. Things could be anything. Old tires, a grandmother's shoes. We go through to the end, where they boldly admonish me for not including the time and temperature for cooking. When I tell them they don't need to cool the food, but that I was just saying, "Cool!", they decide that I'm hopeless.

6. Sooner or later, I confess, but only partially. When I read students' writing and it is jam-packed with "things" and "stuff" (My favorite line of all time is "We did really cool fun things and stuff"), I always ask the students what they meant, and they always look back at me and say, "Well, you know what I mean." So I assumed that all students knew what these words meant even though I didn't.

7. As the light begins to dawn on the students, the classroom teacher begins to cry. The students agree not to use the "chosen, meaningless, space-wasting words" anymore. Sometimes, we stand up, raise our right hands and swear that we won't. Is the transformation permanent? Of course not. But for a little while anyway, I know that they'll think twice before assuming that their readers know what they mean. You do have to be careful of using those "chosen" words yourself after this exercise, because they'll nail you on it every time.

The Teeny Tiny Woman: Redundant Unnecessary Details

Ages: Grades 4-6.

Marisa has an early reader called The Teeny-Tiny Woman, an old English ghost tale about a teeny tiny woman who lives in a teeny tiny house. She goes on a teeny tiny walk to a teeny tiny graveyard. Every adjective throughout is teeny tiny. It's perfect for an early reader, because it reinforces the same words a zillion times. Yet even Marisa, the early reader, was annoyed by it. Sighing heavily, she suggested, "Mommy, this book is way too teeny tiny."

Right then and there we started changing it. We decided she should be kind and wrinkly, and her house should be big and red.

A few weeks later, I introduced the idea of rescuing the teeny tiny woman from her teeny tinyness to fifth graders.

Directions:

1. Replace all the teeny tiny adjectives with new ones.

2. Do it individually, in pairs, or in groups of three. No two stories will be alike.

Teeny Tiny Variations:

1. Change the teeny tiny words as a class.

2. Divide into groups and have the students rewrite the entire story.

3. Divide into groups of three or four and have each group of students change the adjectives for one section of the story.

4. Act them out in sequence. Allow for abrupt changes in personality, setting, etc.

Teeny Tiny Resources:

The Teeny-Tiny Woman (Puffin Easy-to-Read, level 2) by Harriet Ziefert and Laura Rader (contributors)

The Teeny-Tiny Woman (A Step 1 Book: Step into Reading Books) by Jane O'Connor

Using Music to Visualize Writing

Tools: A variety of musical selections (CDs, records, or tapes) without words. Something to play them on. Paper, pencils.

Optional but Wonderful: Read I Am An Artist by Pat Lowery Collins. Talk about how artists see. Talk about how writers are also artists who paint with their words. Encourage your students to take some time to "see" what they are writing about.

Ages: Grades 3-8

Directions:

1. Have them close their eyes and watch the images in their minds as you play music. The images may not be logical, but more dreamlike. Perhaps a new instrument in the music will be a new character in their image. Perhaps not.

2. If anyone is dancing in their seats, gently encourage them to put that energy into looking inside. My experience is that those who are dancing, in this case, are dancing for the class, not themselves.

3. Allow a few moments of imagination watching.

4. Ask a few students to share what they see.

5. If a student saw several violent images, which you may not want shared with the class, tell them that in this case they should filter their images to find the ones they can share appropriately. You should be able to tell if they truly saw those images, or if they're being invented for the sake of a willing audience.

6. As they tell you their images, ask questions about the color, the size, the shape, the time of day, the setting, the mood, etc. Don't let them get away with saying it was "a guy." What kind of guy? How old? What did he look like? What was he doing? Sometimes the students visualize in cartoon characters, but they rarely tell you. If the character's sound extraordinary to a comical degree, consider asking if they're cartoons.

7. It's fine if your students don't know all the answers, but they are the writers, so they should fill in the information. Their imaginations provide the shell, and their words will help color in the details for them and their audience. The combination of their visual images and their verbal skills help them, as the writers, mold the story to reflect their vision and ideas.

8. Compare two or three student ideas and then consider the differences and the similarities. Are the alike? Talk about the value of sharing their ideas. How many times have they considered sharing an idea, but changed their mind because they were certain that everyone else had the same idea? I'm known for leaping loudly on this point. Writing is a fabulous tool to express ourselves and tell the world what we think is important. Sometimes it's hard to find a live person to listen to us when we need to talk, but our ability to write is always available, and everything we write to share with others is a gift.

9. I usually play three to four pieces of music, for a few moments each. Once they're comfortable with the plan, ask them to take notes as they go, to remind themselves of images.

10. Follow up by asking them to write about their images, making it clear enough for others to understand.

11. Consider playing the music while sharing the writing.

12. Consider allowing time for students to develop the short piece into an entire story, a poem, a drawing, or a play.

Acting Out a Snapshot

In *After the End*, Barry Lane describes his concept of a snapshot. Using a magic camera, the writer takes and records a word picture using physical sensations along with what the camera sees. In this activity the students will create a life-size snapshot, as a physical model for writing, adding in sounds and describing smells in the process.

Ages: Grades 4-7

Directions:

1. Show students a photograph.

2. Ask them to re-create the photograph as a statue. (See Statues in the Ingredient Games p. 66.)

3. Interview each section of the statue for descriptive words to describe themselves. Ask them what they smell like. Do they make any sounds?

4. Ask your students to describe the scene in general, an overview of the entire picture.

5. Next, ask them to zoom in the camera lens. (In a giant photo, I've often used a hula hoop for my zoom lens.) Have them describe the zoomed-in area in fine detail.

Swat It!: Snapshots and Thoughtshots

Ages: Grades 5-8

If your students are having trouble differentiating between a snapshot and a thoughtshot, try playing Swat It (See directions in the Ingredient Games p. 75)

Tips:

1. Arm yourself with many snapshots and thoughtshot examples to choose from. It's hard to think on your feet with fly swatters whooshing through the air.

2. Caution the students to wait until the end of the statement before making their choice. I often add the word "Go" after reading each choice.

Fantasy vs. Reality

Maria Novelly has a drama activity in her book *Theater Games for Young Performers* entitled "If I Had It My Way." In the activity, students are asked to act out a realistic scene, with realistic details and circumstances. They should then act out a follow-up scene with the same premise, only this time the lines begin with "If I Had It My Way," and the students act out a fantasy of having their every dream come true within the context of the scene.

Many times I used this activity in general drama classes without thinking of any deeper implications, until one day I was working with prison inmates, who couldn't grasp the concept of having their own way long enough to play-act at dreaming it. No one had any fantasy ideas. Not one. I assumed they had either forgotten how to think of what they wanted, or that the offer was too painful a concept. Chalking it up to prison life, I offered a few suggestions, and moved on to another activity.

A few months later, I was working with middle school students in the suburbs, in the morning, and inner city kids in the afternoon. My days often hit both ends of a spectrum. Once again, I chose to do "If I Had It My Way." The kids in the suburbs had no problem creating fantasy ideas, which were completely unrealistic, but wildly expressive, beginning with Mom refusing to drive them somewhere until they've finished their homework, to elaborate scenes involving chauffeur-driven rides to the mall, a parent who could only say yes, and all the ice cream and pizza they could consume, with the snap of their fingers.

In the afternoon, the inner city kids could not think of having anything they wanted, much less exaggerating it. The concept simply wouldn't compute. In this case I stuck it through, acting out playing basketball with Michael Jordan, winning national championships, becoming the president of the United States, being the first to rocket to Mars. Who supplied the dreams? Me. Did we play this game again? You betcha!

I'm not going to pretend to know all the reasons why these students couldn't dream. I only know it to be tragic. I truly believe that in order to achieve something, you have to dream it first. You have to believe that you have value, that your ideas are worth sharing. We can't assume that everyone just does it. It takes practice. You have to give yourself permission to be worthy of the thoughts.

If your students can't think of anything to write, it may be because they are distracted that day. It may be that their stomach hurts, that they're just making excuses, or that they're stalling for the last few minutes before lunch. It also may be that their dreaming muscle is out of practice. Perhaps their imaginations are deflated by the amount of TV they watch. Perhaps their imaginations are so used to being required to provide specific information that they can't get past the requirements to see the possibilities. In any case, a little dreaming can go a long way in jump starting their creativity.

Ages: Grades 4-Adult.

Directions:

1. Dramatize group ideas of reality versus fantasy (optional).

2. Have each student write down their dreams, describing a scene of a future life if they indeed would have it their way.

3. Follow up any way that you can, with artwork, original songs, skits, plays, school published poems, a bulletin board where dreams are listed. Perhaps they're anonymous at first. Let others sign onto it, if they would like to share the dream.

4. Offer them permission to dream out loud, and the practice to make it habit-forming.

You Tell It, I'll Act It

Ages: Grades 3-Adult.

Directions:

1. See the Ingredient Games p. 71.

2. Begin telling a story with student actors. Take the story to a crossroads, and send them back to their seats to write their own endings.

3. Do you need an interesting story beginning? Have the students write interesting beginnings for this activity, and keep them in a jar or box in your room. At any time, a story beginning could be selected. The author could choose to read it or remain anonymous. Act out the beginning, and honor the beginning idea with twenty-four endings.

Look for the following ideas in Language Arts K-2

Public Speaking Spelling (Grades 2-6) p. 276
Go Foot: Spelling Card Game (Grades 2-4) p. 277

CHAPTER TWENTY

Language Arts 5-8

Table of Contents

Using Drama and Writing to Bring Literature to Life

Acting, adapting, elaborating, and extending stories and scenes is a central part of my work in putting the curriculum on its feet. Becoming the characters we read and write about ignites them, making them come to life. As a result, you'll find activities connecting drama to literature and writing all over this book. Look in the following places to find activities that will educate and entertain your students:

Look in the Ingredient Games for:
Story Acting in a Sequence p. 72
Story Acting with Student-Written Dialogue p. 73
Storytelling with Statues p. 74
Moving Statues p. 68

Look in Social Studies 3-4 for:
Nobody Speaks My Language p. 211
Acting Out an Immigration Story p. 198
State History p. 209

Look in Social Studies 5-8 for:
Cultural Storytelling p. 217
Presentation Techniques: Characters, Voices, Fluency, Eye Contact, and Volume - 8 Strategies p. 217
Writing and Acting Out Commercials (Look in The Ingredient Games) p. 37
Historical Commercials p. 224
    Mythological Commercials p. 243
    Medieval Commercials p. 246

Look for the Following Story Structures:
Fables: (Language Arts K-2) p. 274
Tall Tales: Exaggerating (Language Arts (K-2) p. 273

Monologues: Point of View

What is a monologue? It's a chance for characters to break away from their story and discuss their innermost thoughts with the audience. They can admit mistakes, complain their hearts out, brag, whine, worry, or simply explain some points in more depth, thereby giving the audience inside information.

Ages: Grades 5-12

Directions:

1. Have your students choose a favorite character from a book, and write a monologue from that character's point of view.

2. Ask the students to perform them for the class.

3. Students may want to dress as the character.

Tip: If some of your students are too shy to perform their monologues for the class, consider assigning the written monologue to everyone, and offering extra credit to the performers.

Persuasive Writing: Focus on the Positive

Ages: Grades 5-8.

To get a little, you have to give a little. The seventh graders disagreed. Several workshops in dramatizing persuasive writing skills had brought us to this point. We had begun with improvisation activities that required listening to the other party, and moved on to conflict resolution improvisations involving persuasive skills. We played games where you could only ask questions. We played games where you were forbidden to say No, but had to agree with the other side.

While these games usually worked well as a backdrop for skills in listening and thinking, for this particular group there was a giant barrier stuck right in the middle, an unwritten ironclad rule running deep through their social structure. If you agree to anything, you give up power. If you give up power, all is lost.

What was the power about? Our improvisations were about what to have for dinner, what time could the plumber come, who had dibs on the computer. No matter what, neither side could give in. There was no convincing them that using their brains to solve a dilemma was better than arguing. A strong, forceful stance was all they would consider. No matter what, the rule was to say "No."

The social implications of an entire grade level for a town unable to cooperate long enough to negotiate depressed the hell out of me. I was stuck, depressed, and oh, yes, horrified in a deep mind-numbing sort of way. Remember, I've done conflict resolution with prison inmates and it's gone better than this. There was something I wasn't getting, I could feel it.

Deciding to forget it for the evening, I rented a movie. Laughing out loud, I snapped up the week's new release, *The Negotiator,* with Samuel L. Jackson and Kevin Spacey. Jackson plays a top negotiating detective who is being framed by his department. He holds a building hostage, while the powers that be search for a negotiator who is as talented as he is. Enter Kevin Spacey. Honestly, I don't remember many details of this movie, except for one.

THE NUMBER ONE RULE IN NEGOTIATING IS:

(Drum roll, please)

NEVER SAY NO!

If you do, you'll lose everything!

I raced back to school Monday morning and told the students about the movie. Some had seen it, but all knew about it. The movie was rated R. They liked Samuel L. Jackson, and thought he was a tough guy. He certainly wasn't one to lose.

That did it. Right away we started talking about ways to make our needs known without force, how to listen to the other side for common needs, listening for ways to help the other person meet their needs so they'd be more inclined to help us reach our goals.

The following drama activities address conflict resolution and negotiation, and work well for students as practice in using their brains to reach their goals. These activities help students practice listening, persuading and the power of a positive attitude.

Look for the following activities in the Ingredient Games.

Gestures: Positive Negative p. 44

A circle game where students examine attitude and demonstrate the use of negative gestures, followed up by positive ones. (No negative gestures that mean a word, such as "the finger" are allowed.) A reminder to be kind to fellow students, especially when trying something new. Also a good teacher tool. If you see a negative gesture after this activity, you can draw attention to it in a positive way. "Excellent example of a negative gesture. Let's add that to our list of what we don't need to do in this class."

I Need to Sit There.

An improvisational game where listening to each other is required. They love it. p. 47

Who, What, Where

Basic improvisational skills in a variety of activities. Students can create their own situations to practice being persuasive in a positive way. p. 49

Look in Social Studies 3-4 for:
Conflict Resolution: Contemporary/Historical (For Grades 4-8) p. 205

Tips for getting past "No!" :

If you're having trouble in a scene getting past the other person's no, try the following ideas:
* Agree with them. It will take them off guard. "I can appreciate that."
* While they are off guard, change the subject. "Now, that is very true, I've felt that way myself sometimes. Are you hungry?"
* Approach the conflict from another direction. Tell a story about someone with the same conflict who solved it a certain way. Take a breath, and think of a way the two sides could benefit from one solution.

After a great deal of practice trying to get my seventh-grade students to be positive instead of negative, we moved on to discussing ways to use these new persuasive skills in their writing. We decided to write letters to the superintendent of schools, to ask for permission to hold a rock concert on school grounds. Even as we said it, we all knew it would never happen, but we decided to go for the big dream. We tabled a possibly lengthy discussion about who would actually perform, and decided that each student could make their own choice in their letter.

Starting out the letter with a brief complimentary statement stymied many of them, but I just kept repeating my "Negotiator" mantra, which was evolving. "Negativity gets you nothing, while being positive opens the door." Many still began with the following statements:
* "It's about time we did something good around here."
* "I know you'll never even read this."
* "My mom says you're worthless, so I'm giving you your last chance."
  Still, this was progress.

Grammar

My friend Jean Weeks is a fifth-grade teacher. Every year she teaches her students to say "I love grammar!" with buoyant enthusiasm. Each time they say it, she chuckles, with amusement and a faint touch of the absurd. (Is it possible that Jean hates grammar? Is it possible that she grew weary of hearing the opposite?) They love to make her laugh so they say it all the time. By the end of September when I visit her class each year, the students have begun to sit up and focus every time the word grammar is mentioned. It is almost uncanny.

This form of obvious brainwashing is intriguing to me. Would it work at home? "I love vegetables!" "I love to do my own laundry!" "I love to do the dishes!"

Astounding, Amazing, Alliterations

I must have an ear for these, because I'm always writing them unconsciously, only to discover them later. In the early touring days of my mythology show, "Magical Mystical Mythology," my brother, who played all the male characters, used to have me doubled over choking with laughter over the myriad of alliterations he would find. "Hephaestus, her husband, was madly looking for her, searching from town to town, while working as a welder." He would repeat the title itself over and over until tears streamed from my cheeks. I hope you enjoy your alliterations nearly as much.

Alliteration Ball

For Grades 5-6

Tool: A ball with a grid drawn on it. Each square holds a letter. (Use permanent marker.)

1. See directions to Ball Toss in the Ingredient Games p. 34.

2. A student creates an alliteration on the spot.

Acting Out Similes/Analogies

Grades: 5-8

Directions:

1. Divide your class into groups of four.

2. Ask them to write a simile or an analogy and act it out.

3. Give them points for most accurate, most creative, most dramatically presented.

Look in Language Arts 3-4 for:

Swoosh!: Adjective, Adverb, Noun, and Verb (Grades 3-8) p. 281
Transitional Phrase Ball (Grades 4-6) p. 282
Swoosh!: Transitional Phrases (Grades 3-8) p. 283

Personification Poems and Journal Entries

Delve into the possibility of being someone or something other than who you are: the king, your teacher, a chair in your classroom, a decimal point, a muscle, a cell, or a banana. For complete instructions, see the Ingredient Games p. 63.

Dr. Vocabulary

Dr. Vocabulary is famous for discovering the meanings of words, and sharing them through humor, song, and a high level of eccentricity. For more information on Dr. Vocabulary and his friends Ms. Definition, Dr. Discovery, and Grammar Man, see the Ingredient Games p. 39.

The following play was written with Mrs. Tedford's class as a means of dramatizing writing techniques.

Follow the Yellow Lead Pencil
By Carol Glynn
With Mrs. Tedford's Fifth Grade Class 2000

Ghost of Bad Excuses: (checking off a list) My pencil broke. Check. I don't have any ideas. Check. I don't feel well. Check. Oh. I've been collecting the best bad excuses. It's time to set some free, and see what trouble I can cause. I'll just fly around a little, and find a happy victim or two.

Teacher: Don't forget your stories are due on Friday. I look forward to reading your descriptive writing.

Ghost of Bad Excuses: Fabulous. Descriptive story homework, just the perfect assignment to set loose some truly bad excuses. Before I'm finished, this town will be full of lazy, ignorant people who use bad excuses as a way of life. Ha, ha, ha, ha, ha, ha!

Student 1: I have the best idea. I already have a draft. I can't wait to get home and get started revising it.

Student 2: You start your homework right away? I always take a break, get some food, and hang out awhile first.

Student 3: I never start my homework, especially writing homework, right away unless I have played a few rounds of _____(latest video game) first.

Student 1: I know, me too, but I can't wait to start revising this story.

Student 2: Maybe I should start revising mine, too. My mom always gets mad when I leave it to the last minute.

Student 3: I'm still going to eat first, then I should probably get started myself.
Once you get into it, it's not so bad, once I start picturing the details in my mind.

Ghost of Bad Excuses: Look at those kids. Enthusiastic, excited about writing and revising a story for homework. I may be a ghost, but this is a nightmare! I'll just toss out a few. Oooo, that's a good one. Ooooooooo, a personal favorite. Ooooooooo, I'm good.

Student 3: You know, my stomach is starting to feel a little queasy. On second thought, I may have to lie down for a while.

Student 2: Now that I think about it, my pencil is so heavy, it hurts my hand. The last time I tried to write a long, long story, I broke the tip right off. I better eat first and have a big snack.

Student 1: Didn't I read somewhere that doctors think writing is bad for your health? I better put this off. I'm probably in a weakened state from all the writing I did today at school.

Student 2: I thought you had a good idea you wanted to work on?

Student 1: I thought I did, but now that I'm about to actually include it in my story, it sounds kind of dumb.

Ghost of Bad Excuses: Success! I'm definitely doing my personal best. Once you start using bad excuses, they multiply on their own.

Student 3: Do you think I could rest at your house for a while? I don't think I can make it home.

Student 2: Yeah, I'm so hungry. Do you have a snack I could munch on?

Student 1: Sure, come on over. I don't have anything else to do.

Ghost of Revision: Ahhhhhhhhhhhh! I see the Ghost of Bad Excuses has been here. I can see the thick fog of laziness starting to settle on these students. I'd best get started, before they snuff out all of their creativity. (Throws spell) Whoosh!

Student 1: Wait. Where did my house go?

Student 2: I don't know, but who are those people?

Student 3: It's students from our class. They're reading something. It has your name on it.

Student 1: My name?

Ghost of Revision: Yes, your name. They're reading the story you have now, with good seed ideas, but without any snapshots or thoughtshots, or dialogue to show them the story setting, set up suspense, and explode the moment for the main event...well, you can just see how they feel about it.

Student 4: Ahhh. This stinks.

Student 5: It's so boring.

Student 6: I know. "He went to a chair and sat down." The suspense is killing me.

Student 7: Snore.

Student 8: This story would put a cup of coffee to sleep, even if it's caffeinated.

Student 9: This lead stinks.

Student 10: Yuck. Yuck. No. (shaking head)

Student 1: That can't be my story. My story is exciting.

Ghost of Revision: Sure, it's exciting in your head, but you haven't given the readers any of the juicy details yet. "Went to a chair"—I mean, please!

Student 2: Wow! I didn't know details made such a difference.

Student 3: I always kind of thought they just knew what I meant. I thought that detail stuff was just something my teachers said to pass the time.

Ghost of Revision: Look at the people now. They're reading a story with a little revision. A few dead verbs have been exchanged for more dramatic ones. A few adjectives have been tossed in .

Student 1: Is it still my story?

Ghost of Revision: How could it be? You haven't begun revising yet! No, this time it's his story.

Student 2: Mine?

Student 3: I thought you hadn't spent much time on it.

Ghost of Revision: Look at them.

Student 4: This one is a little better than the last one.

Student 5: Do you have page three? I don't have a page three.

Student 6: Do you really want page three?

Student 7: Well, I was kind of interested. I wanted to know what happened.

Student 8: No, you don't. I read it and it's a flat ending.

Student 2: A flat ending!

Ghost of Revision: They're talking about page three. You stopped revising on page two.

Student 3: Ha! They were interested in reading to the end, until you stopped revising.

Ghost of Revision: Look at this story.

Student 3: Who wrote this one?

Ghost of Revision: No one yet, but it's the one you could write if you'd stop making excuses and get started.

Student 1: You haven't even started?

Student 3: I told you, my stomach was hurting; besides, we're all out of number two pencils at my house.

Ghost of Revision: Shhhh.

Student 4: I love this.

Student 5: (smiling) Good. Mmmm. Good.

Student 6: Come on, who has the last page? I've got to have it.

Student 7: Now, this is good. I have goose bumps!

Student 8: Look at this part. I would never have guessed that that would happen. Wow!

Student 9: I've never heard a better story.

Student 3: I wish I had written that story.

Student 1: I wish I had read that story!

Ghost of Bad Excuses: (tossing excuses) Ooooooo, a thick heavy excuse for you. Oooooooo, a ripe, juicy one for you. Ooooooo, and a sharp, stinging excuse for you.

Student 1: But I can't write on that paper. It's too white.

Student 2: Isn't revising just copying over the old stuff?

Student 3: Yawn. All this talk of hard work is making me sleepy. Besides, my hair hurts.

Student 1: I'd love to have people read my writing, but it's just too much work to write it all down.

Ghost of Revision: Uhhh! All this negativity is starting to weigh me down. Writing is an exhilarating process, but it isn't instant. I'll leave you here, at the beginning of your journey.

Students: Wait.

Student 1: How do we get home?

Ghost of Revision: Come find me when you're done.

Student 2: Done with what?

Adverbeanie: The journey, of course.

Student 3: Who are you? Wait! Who are all of you? (Other adverbeanies appear. They all enter in a different way, cautiously, quickly, angrily, happily, etc.)

Student 1: Where are we?

Adverbeanie 2: You heard the ghost. You're at the beginning.

Student 2: Is there any way to skip the middle and get right to the end? My head hurts.

Adverbearnie 1: We regretfully apologize, but there'll be no leaping frantically through the writing process.

Adverbeanie 3: We'll bravely guide you down the number two pencil road.

Adverbeanie 4: And joyously hope you sucessfully complete your journey and happily learn to write and revise beautifully.

Adverbeanie 5: So that you may flawlessly demonstrate your new skills to the Ghost of Revision.

Averbeanie 6: And so the Ghost of Revision will undeniably grant your request to return home, in the blink of an eye.

Student 1: But where are we now?

Adverbeanie 1: The answer is curiously simple.

All Adverbeanies: We're in Adverb Land!

Students 1, 2, 3: What?

Student 3: Remind me never to walk home with you two again.

Adverbeanies: (singing)
We bring you adverbs so amicably,
not nervously,
or carefully,
We'll share them with you quite generously
We wish to welcome you to Adverb Land!

Student 1: What do you do here?

Adverbeanies: (singing/chanting)
We jump high and we jump low.
We run quickly, and we run slow.
We swim gracefully, and we swim fast.
We love adverbs. We have a blast!

Adverbeanie 1: Sometimes we gratefully appear as words alone.

Adverbeanie 2: Other times we astonishingly appear as clauses.

Adverbeanie 3: As in, "He plodded to the chair, as if the weight of the world were bearing down upon him."

Student 2: How did he get to the chair?

Student 3 : He plodded.

Student 1: Yes, that's the action word or verb.

Student 2 : (to Student 1): Plodded is better than went.

Student 1 : What was the rest of it?

Adverbeanie 4: "As if the weight of the world were bearing down upon him," a clause which tells how he plodded.

Adverbeanies: Or we might graciously offer a single word instead, such as wearily. "He plodded wearily to the chair."

Student 1 : I see.

Adverbeanie 5: Do you?

Student 1: Yes. When you describe it so specifically, I can visually picture it.

Adverbeanie 6: By George, I think she's got it, quite completely.

Student 2: I think we're undeniably prepared to move forward, though a bit cautiously

Student 3: Some of us are are overwhelmingly stunned.

Student :(pulling student 3) Some of us will quickly catch on, as we speedily depart.

Student 2: Where should we bravely go?

Student 3: Where good writers go passionately every time they write!

Student 2: Huh?

Students: (singing)
Follow the pencil road.
Follow the number two road.
Follow, follow, follow, follow,
happily, gracefully, sweetly

Follow the number 2 road because
The Ghost of Revision is there because,
because, because, because, because,
because of the wonderful things he does,

Adverbeanies: (waving goodbye)
Go happily, suspiciously, angrily, sadly, furiously,
curiously, frightfully, etc.

Student 3: Are you sure you won't come with us?

Adverbeanie 5: We can't. We don't take action, we just advise the action words or verbs how to do it. You'll know where to find us, when you need us. Good luck.

Students: (Singing and skipping down the road) We're off to learn revision,
a wonderful jouney with words.

Student 3: I didn't want to mention it, but I'm starving.

Student 1: Why didn't you mention it? The Adverbeanies seemed like lovely people.

Student 3: Because I was afraid they'd drown any food deliciously in adverb sauce.

Student 1: Thought you might impatiently choke on them?

Student 3: Absolutely.

Student 2: There's a tree up ahead. Maybe it has fruit on it.

Student 1: Hanging gingerly on the branches?

Student 2: Would you hurry up?

Student 3: Wait. That tree doesn't have fruit. It has nouns all over it.

Student 2: Let's gratefully grab some and get going. My mom is going to anxiously worry.

Student 3: Undoubtedly.

Student 1: Toss me one, quickly?

Student 3: Which one, be specific.

Student 1: I'll gratefully take the hot dog.

Student 2: I'll hungrily accept the popcorn.

Noun Tree: Ohhhhhh, no you won't.

Student 3: Come on. We're truly starving. No afterschool snack, remember?

Noun Tree: You children, kids, humans, who are full of excuses, reasons, roadblocks, will not know what to do with my people, places, and things, so I won't give them to you. If you steal them, you'll only be robbers, pirates, and thieves.

Student 1: I understand, Sir, or uh, Ma'am, but we're regretfully in need of your glorious nouns in order to successfully complete our journey.

Noun Tree: I know you flatter me shamelessly, but I do only have choice nouns on my tree. The plump juicy ones are at the top, where anyone would have to stretch a little to grab them.

Students : We know. We know.

Noun Tree: How will I know that you'll treat them well? How do I know if you even know what nouns are?

Student 3: But we do, we could even sing it for you.

Noun Tree: Really.

Students (singing to a whimsical original tune): For you Noun Tree, we'd love to sing, a noun is a person, a place or thing.

(Tree is swaying in the background, rather pleased)

Noun Tree: So, you do know what a noun is. I'll tell you what. Every time you use one of my choice nouns well, I'll give you another one. The more you use, the more you'll have. If my nouns are used well, I'll grow them back. But if you use the same old tired ones over and over, you'll dry up my roots and your writing.

Students: It's a deal.

Ghost of Bad Excuses: At this rate, those students are going to learn to write beautifully, and they'll never succumb to my exceptionally bad excuses. I better throw in some writer's blocks. Swoosh! Ooooooooooooo.

Students: Ahhh!

Student 1: What is this? I can't move forward. (Tries to move, the writer's block moves with them.)

Student 2: I don't know; I can't move either.

Student 3: What is this thing?

Student 1: It's big. No, large. No, humongous.

Student 2: It's black-no, dark-no, colorless.

Student 3: It's thick, and short, with an annoying bulgy shape.

Student 2: Mine too. It's frightful, harmful ... hey, it's melting.

Student 1: Keep describing it, maybe you'll take away its power.

Student 2: You try to discourage all writers, but we won't give in to you. You're dreary, foreboding, on the outside, but soft, and squishy, like wet cotton candy on the inside.

Student 3: Gross.

Student 2: Don't knock it, it's working.

Student 1: You may think you can frighten us, but we delete you. (exhale.)

Writer's blocks: (melt) Oh, I'm being erased, ahhhh, erased... erased.

Ghost of Bad Excuses: Drat. Those kids are doing their personal best to wipe me out!
I'll have to think of something, but oh—I've been coming down with a cold and I've been meaning to go to the mall.

Student 3: Phew! That was close. I wonder what would have happened if we hadn't erased the writer's blocks by free-writing some description.

Student 2: Look.

(3 writer's blocks are blocking other students. Each student is stuck, repeating the same phrases over and over.)

1st Blocked Student: And then, we did weird and cool, fun things, and stuff. And then, we did more weird and cool, fun things and stuff. And then...

2nd Blocked Student: In this paragraph, I will tell you... In the next paragraph I will tell you... In the paragraph after that, I will tell you...

3rd Blocked Student: The first reason is...The second reason is...The 999th reason is...

Student 3: Wow!

Student 2: Here we are stuck in some virtual writing dream, in search of a ghost—and I haven't been truly frightened until now.

Student 1: There's a lake or something up there, let's get a drink and collect ourselves.

(They rush to the body of water)

Student 2: Eeeeewwwww! What is that smell?

Student 3: Ahhhh! This water has dead verbs in it.

Student 1: How can you tell?

Student 3: Well, they're lying sideways on the top, just floating aimlessly.

Student 1: These action words sure aren't moving vibrantly.

Student 3: Look at the words though—go, went, see, look, came.

Student 1: These words never did move vibrantly. They always just kind of lay there floating aimlessly.

Verbs: Maaaakkkkkkee usss excitiiiinnnnng.

Student 3: Ahhhhhhh! Let's leap forward furiously before they try to come with us.

Student 2: I'm going to dash frantically.

Student 1: How about soaring wildly?

Student 3: Don't freeze solidly, they'll bog you down in dreary writing forever—catapult yourself this way!

Verbs: Help!! Help! Help! We want some action.

Student 2: They sound so lost. Shouldn't we help them?

Student 1: Help them in your writing, but not here. If they stick to you, your writing will smell as bad as they do.

Student 3: The next time you write remember to exchange all boring, dead, stagnant verbs for living, breathing action words.

Student 1: Like changing walk to slithered or lifted to heaved.

Student 3: Exactly.

Student 2: Which way are we flying dramatically?

Verbs in Sea: Went, went, go, go, said, said, got, got...

Students: AHHHHHHH!

Student 3: There are some people up ahead. Maybe they can help us.

Student 2: Hold up, slow down.

Student 3: What? Why?

Student 2: Take a closer look at them. These appear to be some pretty strange characters.

Student 3: All the more exiting.

Student 2: No. Look.

Student 1: That one is completely flat.

Student 2: So is that one.

Student 3: That one doesn't even have an arm.

Student 1: That one has no face!

Student 2: Let's find out where we are, so we can catapult out of here.

Student 3: Sir, excuse me, Sir. Mr. (looks at sign on him) old man. Would you be so kind as to tell us where we are?

Old Man: Don't ask me. I have no personality. I'm an old, man, an old, man, an old, man, an old, man, an old man, an old man.

Student 3: But old men can be interesting. My grandpa is an old man and he's lively, and full of spirit. He's always doing something, reading books, searching the Internet, walking with his dogs, playing golf.

(As the student thinks about his grandfather, he stops paying attention to the old man character, who is standing a few steps behind him adding every description to his character, and doing every activity.)

Student 3: We tease him because he always wears this old, tan fisherman's cap. Grandma claims it's hooked to his big old ears and won't come off. He shaved his beard last year. When he's laughing, his smile swallows up his whole face.

(The old man behind comes up and taps the student on the shoulder)

Student 3: Grandpa! What are you doing here?

Grandpa: You brought me to life with your clear visual description. Let's hit the road. I've been stuck in the Character Development Desert for way too long.

Student 1: How did you get here in the first place?

Grandpa: We were created by writers who didn't want to make the effort to finish us. So we've been living here, incomplete.

Girl: Young girl, young girl, young girl.

Dog: Cute pet, cute pet, cute pet, cute pet.

Student 2: But we can't leave them. I still feel guilty about abandoning the dead nouns.

Grandpa: All right then. Grab your pencils, and let's get to work. Fill them in.

Student 1: A young girl with blond, shoulder-length hair. Her vibrant pink jumper, with two pockets, matches her rosy cheeks.

Student 2: His soft brown fluffy ears framed his bright brown eyes perfectly.

Student 1: Her hair was delicately pulled back into a ponytail and tied with a pink ribbon.

Grandpa: Wow! We've needed you kids around here for quite some time.

Student 3: Bushy eyebrows, yellow teeth, and stale cigar breath.

Student 1: The girl had been one-sided before, but now, her white hair shone like fresh snow.

Girl: But we don't belong here anymore. We're not incomplete anymore.

Student 1: Why don't you come with us? People never stop growing and learning new lessons.

Girl: It's a deal.

Grandpa: Have you been to the Museum of Adjectives and Descriptive Phrases yet?

Student 3: Not yet. I forgot about adjectives.

Girl: It's not far. It has been so frustrating, being so close but not able to unlock the door to more character details.

Student 3: The door is locked. But we described you!

Grandpa: You brought those details with you. Mine were in your memory.

Girl: Mine were in your imagination.

Dog: Woof. Woof.

Grandpa: Everyone has details within them, they're just not used often. It's been tough on us characters. Opening the museum door would really help all of us.

Student 2: But why is it locked?

Girl: The adjectives did it. They refuse to come out for any old reason.

Grandpa: They refuse to come out without a good lead.

Student 1: A good lead! We just learned about a good lead in class!

Student 2: Yeah.

Grandpa: I hope it helps. We've been throwing leads at them for months. It hasn't worked.

Girl: We've been giving them well-organized, planned-out ideas. The door hasn't opened.

Student 1: What have you used?

Woman: Today I'm going to write about....

Grandpa: One day the....

Girl: The first paragraph will tell you...

Dog: (howls, rolls over and puts paws over its ears)

Student 2: I think I see the problem.

Student 1: A good lead is meant to ignite excitement in the readers, not put them to sleep.

Dog: (howls loudly)

Grandpa: Ignore him. He's just trying to get attention.

Student 1: What happens if we never get this locked door open.?

Student 2: Can we just move on with the journey, or will we be stuck here forever?

Student 3: Will the Ghost of Revision just forget all about us?

Student 1: What is our teacher's favorite lead? It doesn't have to be original. Does it have to be original?

Student 2: Don't look up. Don't even say a word!

Student 3: CRASH! The locked door was flung open wide. Our heads snapped to attention.

(The locked door does fling open wide. Their heads do snap to attention. Adjectives and phrases come flying out in all directions.)

Student 1: I want to get to my story. I have so many ideas now.

Student 3: We may need to write our stories just to get out of here. We still don't know what the Ghost of Revision will do when we reach him.

Student 2: I've been writing mine all along.

(They take turns reading it, or perhaps it is acted out in slow motion behind them, i.e., their words bring it to life.)

Every solemn word the ghost had shared kept playing over and over inside my curious, questioning mind. His evil, dark figure backed away very slowly. He outstretched his cold hand into his pocket and took out a thick, gray glowing book. The bony see-through fingers of his right hand grasped the front cover of the book and slowly opened it. Next, nodding slightly, he flipped a couple of the eerie pages with his mind.

"Come here," howled the ghost's deep, empty voice. I drifted over across the pebbles and dirt, without moving my legs, as if I were in a trance. I glared at the old, crinkled pages with my innocent, questioning eyes. "Read," murmured the mysterious ghost. My eyes fixed on the words, reading them one by one. It was so boring. A big , bright silver light crept out from the book and wrapped around my cold, terrified, shivering body. Now, I was shouting excuses, screaming why I didn't want to write. My hand hurt. My pencil was broken, my...my...my... The ghost of negativity had known I didn't care about writing. Now I would pay the price.

By Stephanie Tweedt

(The Ghost of Revision mimics the hand coming out, and taps the reader on the shoulder.)

All: AHHHHHHHHHHHHHHHHHH!

Ghost of Revision: Relax. I'm not going to hurt you. Revision can only help you.

Student 1: Please help us go home.

Ghost of Revision: You don't need my help.

Student 2: We've come all this way. We've used good nouns. We've sung to adverbs,

Student 3: Used exciting verbs to escape from the dead ones...

Student 1: We developed characters.

Student 2: We've found the key to good leads to unlock any door.

Student 3: And we've even erased the writer's blocks, and thrown off the Ghost of Bad Excuses.

Student 1: We want to go home. We need your help.

Ghost of Revision: You don't need my help. You've had the power to go home all along.

Student 3: If you tell me I can click my heels three times and say there's nothing like good writing, I'm going to barf.

Ghost of Revision: No need to be inappropriate. All I'm saying is that you're the artists. What you see in your mind and paint on your papers becomes your story. You're in charge of it. If you want to go home, then envision it.

Student 1: Suddenly, I'm scared. What if when we go home, we forget everything we've learned. What if we get lazy? If we're in charge, anything can happen!

Ghost of Revision: Well, you're the writers—what would you say?

Student: I'd say... I'd say... I'd say, BACK! I have a good sentence and I know how to use it!

Ghost of Revision: You'll be fine. Now go. Your afterschool snacks are getting cold.

(Ghost of Revision waves his hand, and the a classroom of kids forms around the three students.)

Teacher: (Reading) "And we all went home, and went to bed." Sigh! Great story, but now let's talk about lousy endings....

We followed the pencil road.
Followed the number two road.
Followed, followed, followed, followed,
happily, gracefully, sweetly.

We followed the number two road because
The art of revision is there because
Because, because, because, because, because,
because of the fabulous things it does.

We're off to be great writers,
because we know how to revise!

Great Stories to Act Out

The grades listed below are, in my experience, the optimal grades for acting out these stories. The appeal for hearing, reading, and watching these stories spans a wider audience.

The Little Old Lady Who Was Not Afraid of Anything, by Linda Williams, illustrated by Megan Lloyd (New York: Harper Collins Children's Books, 1986)

"Clomp! Clomp! Clomp!" went the boots. "Clap, Clap," went the gloves. "Boo," went the jack-o'-lantern head. The little old lady who was not afraid of anything is truly tested in this audience participation story about fear at Halloween. True to form, though, her courage wins out as this little old lady proves not only to be unafraid of anything, but also to be kindhearted and creative. Excellent for taking the scariness out of Halloween for those youngest students who may need it. Great for grades K-1.

The Rainbow Fish, by Marcus Pfister. Translated by J. Alison James (New York, North South Books, 1992)

The Rainbow Fish wants to have friends and all of his beautiful scales, too. He discovers that his own selfish behavior is causing his loneliness. Excellent for acting with a class. (Many fish parts.) I recommend using small paper fish scales for props. Tip: Several people can play the octopus. Ages K-3

The Little Rabbit Who Wanted Red Wings, by Carolyn Sherwin Bailey, illustrated by Jacqueline Rogers (New York, Platt and Munk Publishers, 1978)

"I want what Billy has. I want what Sally has. I want what everyone else has, but not because I really want it. I just don't want to be the only one without it." The Little Rabbit Who Wanted Red Wings learns the hard way that wanting what others have and being himself are two different things. Excellent for acting out the concepts of setting and characters with the youngest students. (Try a statue of the setting, and a separate one of the characters. Multiple character repetition within one statue is fine.) Grades K-2

Hiccups for Elephant, by James Preller, illustrated by Hans Wilhelm.(New York: Scholastic, 1994)

Elephant has the hiccups, waking up all the animals in the jungle. Each has a turn in trying to help him, to no avail. Finally Mouse solves the problem by scaring the elephant and dissolving his hiccups. Can the animals finally get some sleep? Who has hiccups now?
Great for acting out with K-1. Again, multiple actors playing one character part is fine. Elephant may require two or more cooperative students to play him. Grades K-2.

Today I Feel Silly and Other Moods That Make My Day, by Jamie Lee Curtis, illustrated by Laura Cornell (USA: Harper Collins, 1998)

It's okay to have big feelings, and it's okay to talk about them, or just sit with them. This story brilliantly describes the many moods in all of us in a way that young children can relate to. Great for opening discussion and drama activities on feelings. Grades K-3.

From Caterpillar To Butterfly, by Deborah Heiligman, illustrated by Bari Weissman A Let's Read and Find Out Science book, (New York: Harper Collins, 1996)

The life cycle of the butterfly, told from the students' perspective as they watch one grow in their classroom. I use it in all my butterfly workshops. Grades 1-2.

The Stone Cutter, adapted and illustrated by Gerald McDermott (USA: Puffin Books,1975)

A story about Mitako, a stone cutter, whose big dreams of power and grandeur interrupt his simple daily life. Seeking help from the spirit in the mountains, Mitako rises above his place again and again, by becoming the most powerful role in each scene. Finally, Mitako realizes, after using his newfound power to torture those around him and alienating the spirit who helped him, that everyone has power. His last, permanent, most powerful role must be to endure the daily hammering of a lowly stone cutter. Exquisite artwork. Easy to act out as a large group using revolving roles (musicians become plants, then clouds, etc.) Great for grades 1-2.

The First Forest, by John Gile, illustrated by Tom Heflin (Wisconsin: Worzalla 1978)
    Why do the trees lose their leaves in the winter? Could it be that they once had a fight and lost the privilege of keeping them? Only the evergreens stayed clear of the violence, and as a result, they can keep warm and dressed all year. Beautiful exotic illustrations. Plenty of room for creative drama about special differences in leaves (and people), plus guidance about making choices, painful consequences, and forgiveness. Great for grades 1-2.

Where the Wild Things Are, story and pictures by Maurice Sendak (USA: Harper Trophy, Harper and Row Publishers, 1963)
    Max is a true wild thing himself, but he doesn't realize it until his room transforms into a jungle, complete with an ocean and a boat with his name on it. Traveling to Where the Wild Things Are teaches Max about power, loneliness, and the true meaning of comfort. Luckily, Max returns safely to find his room intact, and his dinner waiting. Excellent for acting out. (See directions in Chapter Five.) Grades 1-2.

The Mitten, adapted and illustrated by Jan Brett (New York: Putnam Publishing Group, 1989)
    The mitten can stretch to fit a mouse, a cat, a dog, a fox, and a bear, until somebody sneezes. Great for acting with small groups, or as a demonstration for the whole class. *The Hat,* also by Jan Brett, is a slightly different version of the same brilliant plot. Grades 1-2.

Bark George, by Jules Feiffer(USA: Michael di Capua Books, Harper Collins Publishers, 1999)
    George swallows a multitude of animals who speak through him, which frustrates his mother, because she only wants him to bark. A visit to the vet resolves the problem with enough repetition and animal sounds for even the youngest children to get a kick out of it. Grades 1-3.

What Do You Say Dear?, by Sesle Joslin, illustrated by Maurice Sendak, (New York: Harper Collins, 1987)
    "You have gone downtown to do some shopping, and you are walking backwards, because sometimes, you like to, and suddenly you bump into a crocodile. What do you say dear? ... Excuse me." Outrageously silly situations with everyday etiquette answers. A great way to learn manners! I have used this with second graders who wrote their own situations and acted them out. Hilarious! Grades 1-3.

Caps for Sale, told and illustrated by Esphyr Slobodkina, (USA: Harper Trophy Book, Harper and Row Publishers, 1968)
    A peddler sells caps each day to buy his food, but one day, no one is buying, and so a very tired and hungry peddler takes a walk from town to rest by a tree. When he wakes, his caps are all gone. The peddler grows very angry as he realizes that a group of monkeys has stolen his hats and wears them in the tree behind him. "Give me back my caps!" he shouts. They mimic his angry gestures, making this a fabulous story for acting out as a class. I usually choose four peddlers, and have the others double as townspeople and monkeys. A great lesson in sequencing is involved if you take the time to have the students practice stacking the caps in proper order and walking around a circle balancing imaginary caps on their heads. Ages 1-3.

Tacky the Penguin, by Helen Lester, Illustrated by Lynn Munsinger (New York: Houghton Mifflin, 1988)
    Tacky isn't like the other penguins. He's loud, wears Hawaiian shirts, and plunges into the ocean, unlike all the other classy penguins. They put up with Tacky, but they're not sure why, until one day Tacky uses his ingenuity coupled with his unique personality to save the penguin pack from hunters. Tacky is a strange bird, but he's great to have around. Grades 1-3.

Only One, by Marc Harshman, illustrated by Barbara Garrison (New York: Scholastic Inc., 1993)
Only One is a story about mathematical concepts—without letting the kids in on the boring math aspects. They'll see subset groups, such as "five fingers," and then the larger set, which is "only one hand." Great for expanding into their own ideas of Subsets vs. Only One (larger set), and dramatizing. Great for grades 2-3.

Strega Nona, written and illustrated by Tomie dePaola (New York: Simon and Schuster 1975)
    Strega Nona has a magic pasta pot which can make pasta at her command, but only Strega Nona knows the magic behind it, including how to turn the pasta pot off. Big Anthony, Strega Nona's handy boy, only learns the first part of the spell, and makes enough pasta for the neighboring towns. Strega Nona finally stops the cooking pot and makes Anthony eat the results of his bad behavior. (Great for acting as a class. Enough parts for all, if you add narrators, a talking pasta pot, and dancing spaghetti.) Great for grades 2-3.

The Great Kapok Tree, A Tale of the Amazon Rain Forest, by Lynne Cherry, (Orlando, Florida: Gulliver Books, Harcourt Brace Jovanovich 1990)
    "Please don't cut down our tree," beg the snakes, chimpanzees, jaguars, butterflies, beetles, and sloths. The Great Kapok Tree is a home for many, and the sleeping hunter dreams his answer as to whether or not to destroy a small but vibrant section of the rain forest. The story provides a great structure for students to think and act out their own reasons not to cut down the tree. Grades 2-3.

Officer Buckle and Gloria, written and illustrated by Peggy Rathmann (New York: G. P. Putnam Son's, 1995)
    Safety is number one with Officer Buckle, and humor is Gloria's top priority. Officer Buckle gives deadly boring school speeches about safety until Gloria spices them up. The pair become famous lecturers and friends, until Officer Buckle discovers Gloria's technique. The two find out that a team cannot exist with either one of them alone, and Officer Buckle realizes that having Gloria as a friend is more important than anything. Packed full of safety tips. Excellent lead activity for students to create and act out their own safety rules. Grades 2-3

Rachel Fister's Blister, by Amy MacDonald, illustrated by Marjorie Priceman (Boston: Houghton Mifflin Company, 1990)
    Rachel Fister had a blister on her little toe, and everyone from the priest to the queen offers suggestions on how to make it better. Yet every mother knows the answer to this problem, even if Rachel's mother didn't. This is a great example of a multiple roles, with very little responsibility, story. Every student in the class will delight in doing his or her part to help Rachel Fister. Grades 2-3.

The Little House, story and pictures by Virginia Lee Burton, (Boston: Houghton Mifflin Company, 1942)
    The house was built in the country, and loved the sun, the wind, and the air. Gradually the area around the house was developed, more and more, and the house finds itself in the middle of a bustling city, boarded up and flanked by skyscrapers. As the little house is rescued by the original owner's granddaughter and returned to the country, we all learn about the importance of sun and wind and air. (Create a student statue of the house, adding and removing student-acted setting elements as someone narrates the story.) Grades 2-3.

Over the Steamy Swamp, by Paul Geraghty (London: Hutchinson Children's Books. 1988)
    The mosquito is being watched by a myriad of creatures, none of whom is looking behind themselves to see who is watching them. This hilarious food chain story provides an excellent acting structure and some sophisticated vocabulary in an easy-to-read-and-understand story. Grades 2-3.

The Paper Bag Princess, by Robert Munsch, illustrated by Martchenko, (Toronto, Annick Press Ltd.,1986)
 Who wouldn't appreciate a woman whose castle has been torched, whose clothes have been burned off, whose precious fiancé Ronald has been kidnapped by a treacherous dragon, yet she survives, dons a paper bag dress, follows a path of burnt forests and horses' bones to find and trick a dragon using her wit and ingenuity,

saving Ronald from a fate worse than death—that is, being eaten by said dragon? Who wouldn't appreciate her? Ronald, that's who. After she has saved his life, the first words out of his mouth are "Elizabeth, your hair is all messy, and you're wearing a paper bag. Come back when you look like a real princess." Does she? Of course not. A woman like that can do much better than Ronald. This story provides great twists on old themes, as well as fabulous settings for group statues. Act out the settings of the castle, the cave, and the path with bones and trees, and then follow up with three character statues. Everyone who wants to be the princess can form one large statue, expressing a part of Elizabeth's personality. Show her after her castle has burned down, as she is outsmarting the dragon, as a fancy princess at the beginning, and yelling at Ronald at the end. Follow up with similar statues for the other characters. Don't be surprised if no one wants to be the evil Ronald. Grades 2-3.

The Three Wishes, a folk tale, retold by M. Jean Craig, pictures by Yuri Salzman
   A woodcutter is blessed with three wishes to improve his wife, but he blunders his chances by snarling at her: "I wish you had sausages stuck to your nose!" In the end he needs all his wishes to return his life to its original state. (I often add three fairy kids, three sausage kids, and a cat who makes smart remarks. Using the lines directly from the book, plus a few student-created ones, this story can be presentation quality in no time. Grades 2-3.

Why the Sky Is Far Away, by Mary-Joan Gerson, illustrated by Carla Golembe (Little Brown and Company, 1995)
   There was a time when the people could reach to the sky and select the food they wanted. Apples, peaches, pears, ripe melons, everything they could ever ask for, yet the people decided to take advantage of the privilege, and now the sky is far away. Enough parts for many, with a great lesson tossed in. Grades 2-3.

Bringing the Rain to Kapete Plain, by Verna Aardema, illustrated by Beatriz Vidal, (Picture Puffins, 1999)
   Straight from the story, each child can take a part. (Build a statue of the setting, and create a pop-up statue each time their line appears.) Grades 2-3.

The Fish Who Could Wish, by John Bush and Korky Paul (New York: Kane Miller Book Publishers, 1991)
   What if you could wish for anything you wanted and have it come true? Wouldn't it be great? Would it make you so different that you would feel left out? The fish who could wish discovers what's truly important, a little too late, when he wishes to be like all the others who don't have his special talents. Great for creating statue scenes of all your class's wish ideas, with an important lesson about the power of being different. Grades 2-4.

The Relatives Came, by Cynthia Rylant, illustrated by Stephen Gammell (New York: Bradbury Press1985)
   This one reminds me of my family at weddings. The relatives come in hordes, sleeping in every available nook and cranny in the house. They dance, share tales of times past, eat until their sides ache, enjoy each other and depart. Great for statue groups of family during the process of a memorable visit. Grades 2-4.

The True Story of the Three Little Pigs, as told by Jon Scieszka, illustrated by Lane Smith (New York: Scholastic, 1989)
   This story tells the tale from the wolf's point of view, and as you would expect, it is quite different. Of course, he's been framed. He was only trying to borrow a cup of sugar to make a cake for his poor sick grandmother. So what if he sneezed, and accidentally knocked over the house which, by the way, killed the pig? Of course he ate it. Why waste a perfectly good pig? Great perspective is provided within these pages, as the wolf denies all evil. Can other fairy tales be rewritten by looking at other perspectives? This delightful story serves as a model example for writing and acting new versions of old fairy tales. Grades 2-4.

Why Mosquitoes Buzz in People's Ears, by Verna Aardema pictures by Leo and Diane Dillon (New York: Dial

Books for Young Readers, 1975)

Verna Aardema has magical language which molds this story into something wonderful. A sort of "Just So Story" with a cultural twist. This has many parts included, and room to add many more. Grades 2-4.

Too Much Noise, by Ann McGovern, illustrated by Simms Taback (Boston, Houghton Mifflin Company1995)

I've used this story so many times I'm sick of it, but that doesn't make it any less valuable. I'm sure I'll use it many times more. For a reliable story structure where students can design their own details, Too Much Noise is a winner. Grades 2-5.

Just So Stories, by Rudyard Kipling, Peter Levi (Editor) (USA: Penquin, 1990)

Why does the rhino have a horn? Find out in Just So Stories. But don't stop there. Write your own. Why do cars go when the light turns green? Why do donuts taste so good when they're so bad for you? Act these out or write your own *Just So Stories* to act and share. Rudyard Kipling won't mind. He'd be delighted Grades 2-5.

Rootabaga Stories, by Carl Sandburg,, illlustrated by Maude Fuller Petersham and Miska Petersham (Applewood Books 1998)

These stories beg to be acted out. They inspired the creation of my old stomping grounds, The Penny Ante Theater. Grades 2-5

Anything by Shel Silverstein

He's delightful, truthful, hilarious, and disgusting. Explore the unimaginable with Shel Silverstein. (Divide your class into groups and have them dramatize their favorites.) Grades 2-6.

A Light in the Attic
Where the Sidewalk Ends
Falling Up
The Giving Tree
Giraffe and a Half
The Missing Piece
The Missing Piece meets the Big O
All from Harper Collins Juvenile Books.

Ben's Trumpet, by Rachel Isadora (New York: Mulberry Books1979)

Every evening, from his fire escape, Ben listens to the music from the the Zig Zag Jazz Club. Pantomiming his own trumpet, he joins in. Each day he stops by the club to watch the musicians practice. His dreams seem ludicrous to kids on the street, who declare blatantly that Ben has no trumpet. Ben nearly gives up, until another trumpet player invites him in to learn for real. Great black and white illustrations. Fun to act out, with groups pantomiming musicians. Excellent jump starter for discussions and stories about future dreams Grades 3-4

The Dancing Man, stories and pictures by Ruth Bornstein (New York: Seabury Press, 1978)

A personal favorite. (I've been dramatizing this one in performance for years.) The dancing man dances the world's dances, with everyday details like reaping and sowing the corn. Share this story with your class and discover the joys in acting out and doing everyday activities.(I usually ask students to dance their favorite activity and their regular chores. I ask parents and teachers to dance their most important job.) Grades 3-5.

Tar Beach, by Faith Ringgold (New York: Crown Publishers,1991)

What if you lived on a roof and your only way of surviving was through your dreams? Tar Beach shows the possibility of dreams in a story for all of us. Good for acting out scene statues and opening discussions on dreaming and reaching for your goals. Grades 3-5.

Frog Prince, by Jon Scieszka, paintings by Steve Johnson (New York: Puffin Books, 1991
    Jon Scieszka does it again! What happens after the fairy tale ends? This years-later version of *Frog Prince* has a few unusual twists as it models the possibilities of looking beyond the end of the story. Grades 4-7.

The Sneetches, by Dr. Seuss (New York: Random House, 1988)
    "We're better than you are because we have stars!" (money, toys, clothes, shoes, cars, houses, etc.) Mr. McBean throws a wrench into the works when he makes a boatload of money selling trips through his Star On, and then later his Star Off machine. Before it's over, the Sneetches, with and without stars, are broke, confused, and definitely mixed up. (Create colorful cardboard machines, with student sound effects. Let them dance their way through it. Add a few narrators and take the lines straight from the book. Who wants to mess with Dr. Seuss? Great for grades 3-8. The older classes have the excuse of performing for younger students, while they learn the messages within.)

Folk Tales, from all over the world
    Often the stories from across the globe are the same, though the cultural details might be different. Whatever the version, folk tales are treasures from every culture. Mix them up, match them, or combine a few favorite characters to cook up and act out your own. Grades K-8.

Fables, by Aesop
    Act them out as is, fracture them for humor ("The Fox Who Cried Boy"), or put them into contemporary settings. Any way you cook them up, fables are great for acting out. (I recommend pre-selecting a group for your students to choose from. There are a few inappropriate ones in every volume.) Grades 1-8.

Trickster Tales, including Brer Rabbit, Iktomi, Coyote stories
    Using your brain, your humor, and your wit instead of violence is a great lesson in any culture. Trickster tales have been doing this for decades. Yet they're not all sweetness and light, either. Readers have delighted in their foibles and lessons as long as they have existed. Great for acting out. Add a few characters here and there. Don't forget that inanimate objects can talk, and you'll be fine.

Legends
    A historical base, on which time has built magical beliefs. Believe them or not, but read them and act them out. You'll learn about history and timely belief systems as you go. I've been performing and teaching Connecticut legends for years. I recommend searching out the local and state legends for your school. It's well worth it.
    Legendary Connecticut, Traditional Tales from the Nutmeg State, by David E. Phillips (Willimantic, CT, Curbstone Press, 1992)

    Folk Tales of Connecticut, collected and edited by Glenn E. White, illustrated by Rose. M. Zangari. (Meriden, CT, The Journal Press, 1977)

    Folk Tales of Connecticut, Volume II, collected and edited by Glenn E.White, illustrated by Rose M. Zangari, (Meriden, The Journal Press, 1981)

Myths
    Whether mythological, historical, or celestial, myths have been a part of every culture since man began. Learn about ourselves and others as you explore, and act out the characters who have lasted for centuries.
    D'Aulaire's Book of Greek Myths: (New York: Doubleday, 1962)

Good Books with Stories to Act Out and Tell

Spinning Tales, Weaving Hope, Edited by Ed Brody, Jay Godspinner, Katie Green, Rona Leventhal, and John Porcino of Stories for World Change Network, Illustrated by Lahri Bond. (Philadelphia: New Society Publishers, 1992

The following books are all from August House Publishers, Arkansas.
Ready to Tell Tales: Sure Fire Stories from America's Favorite Storytellers, edited by
    David Holt and Bill Mooney (1994)
How and Why Stories: World Tales Kids Can Read and Tell, by Martha Hamilton and
    Mitch Weiss (1999)
Eleven Nature Tales: A Multicultural Journey, by Pleasant DeSpain (1996)
Twenty Two Splendid Tales to Tell, by Pleasant DeSpain (1994)

Good Instructional Books for Further Exploration

Games for Math, written and illustrated by Peggy Kaye (New York, Pantheon Books 1987)

Improvisation for the Theater, by Viola Spolin (Illinois:Northwest University Press,1987)

Development Through Drama, by Brian Way (New Jersey: Atlantic Highlands Press, 1967)

On Stage: Theater Games and Activities for Kids, by Lisa Bany-Winters (Chicago Review Press 1997)

Theater Games for Young Performers, by Maria C. Novelly (Colorado Springs: Meriwhether Publishing Ltd. 1985)

The Incredible Indoor Games Book, by Bob Gregson (Torrance, CA, Fearon Teacher Aids, 1982.
The Friendly Classroom for a Small Planet, by Gretchen Bodenhamer, Leonard Burger,
Priscilla Prutzman, and Lee Stern. (Philadelphia: New Society Publishers 1988)

Integrate with Integrity: Music Across the Elementary Curriculum, by Dr. Sue Snyder
(Norwalk, CT : IDEAS Press, 1996)

Interactive Arts for Total Literacy: Volume 1: K-2, by Dr. Sue Snyder, (Norwalk, CT, : IDEAS Press, 1996
aeIDEAS.com

Frames of Mind: The Theory of Multiple Intelligences, by Howard Gardner (Basic Books, 1993)

Art Education and Human Development, by Howard Gardner, (Getty Center for Education in the Arts, 1991)

The Disciplined Mind: What All Students Should Understand, by Howard Gardner (Simon and Schuster: 1999)

Teaching with the Brain in Mind, by Eric Jensen, (Assn for Supervision and Curriculum Development: 1998)

Bibliography

Breaking Through: Drama Strategies for 10's to 15's by Barbara Goodwillie, (Rowayton, CT: New Plays Books 1986)

Biological Science, Second Edition, by William T. Keeton, (New York: W. W. Norton and Company, Inc. 1972)

The Declaration of Independence, by Thomas Jefferson

Dem Bones, by Bob Barner, (New York: Scholastic, Inc. 1996)

Everyday Mathematics: Journal by The University of Chicago, School Mathematics Project, (Chicago: Everyday Learning Corporation, 1999)

Experimenting With Illusions, by Robert Gardner, (New York: Franklin Watts, 1990)

Handy Homework Helper: Science, Study Reference Guide, by Devi Mathieu, Edee Norman Wiziecki, Consultant (Lincolnwood, Illinois: Publications International, Ltd.1999)

Improvisation for the Theater, by Viola Spolin, (Evanston, Ill: Northwestern University Press,1963)

Knights and Castles by Avery Hart and Paul Mantell, (Charlotte, VT: Williamson Publishing, 1998)

Sound, by Charles D. Neal, (Follett Publishing Company)

Volcanos and Earthquakes, by Patricia Lauber, (New York: Scholastic, 1985)

PA DCNR - Forestry, Common Tree Parts, Parts Types Positions of Leaves, P. 3. 2/5/2000, as retrieved from the World Wide Web, March 2000, at http://www.denr.state.pa.us/forestry/commontr/TableofContents/Parts3.htm

The Water Cycle, Live From Earth and Mars, *Water: A Never Ending Story,* as retrieved from the World Wide Web, March 2000, at http://www-k12.atmos.washington.edu/k12/pilot/water_cycle/grabber2.html

Pollination, California Native Plant Society, Kids Page, as retrieved from the World Wide Web, November 1999, at http: //www.cnps.org/kidstuff/pollin.htm

The Connecticut Society of the Sons of the American Revolution, *Captain Nathan Hale,* by Reverend Edward Everett Hale as retrieved from the World Wide Web, May 2000 at http://ctssar.org/patriots/nathan_hale.htm.

The Concise Columbia Encyclopedia, Third edition, Electronic Library, Enclopedia.com, "Congress of the United States, President, Cabinet, Supreme Court, Electoral College," as retrieved by the World Wide Web at http://www.encyclopedia.com/

"Home, Home on the Range", *The Usborne Children's Songbook,* Illustrated by Stephen Cartwright, Music arrangements by Caroline Hooper,(London, Usborne Publishing Ltd. 1988)

DISCOVER WRITING PRESS

To view our other titles and

to order more copies of

Learning on Their Feet

visit our website at

www.discoverwriting.com

Phone: 1-800-613-8055 • Fax: 1-802-897-2084

Or mail in the form below with your check, credit card or purchase order.

METHOD OF PAYMENT: ☐ Check or money order enclosed   ☐ Purchase order attached P.O.#_____

☐ [MasterCard] Mastercard   ☐ [VISA] Visa   ☐ [DISCOVER] Discover Card

Signature_____

Credit Card#_____ Exp.Date_____

PLEASE PRINT

NAME _____ HOME PHONE _____

HOME ADDRESS_____

CITY_____ STATE _____ ZIP CODE _____

Make check payable to: DWC, P.O. Box 264, Shoreham, VT 05770